Harry Droste

PETER R. ACKROYD

EXILE AND RESTORATION

PETER R. ACKROYD

EXILE AND RESTORATION

A Study of Hebrew Thought
of the Sixth Century B.C.

The Westminster Press
Philadelphia

Published by The Westminster Press®
Philadelphia, Pennsylvania

PRINTED IN THE UNITED STATES OF AMERICA

TO EVELYN

CONTENTS

THE HULSEAN LECTURES 1960–1962

The electors to the Hulsean Lectureship in the University of Cambridge honoured me by inviting me to deliver the lectures on the subject 'The Age of Restoration: a study of theological developments in the sixth century BC and of their significance in the understanding of post-exilic Judaism and of the New Testament', and these lectures were delivered in the Lent Term of 1962. A copy of the preliminary text was deposited in the University Library. The present work represents a complete reworking and elaboration of the text of the lectures, the title of which was subsequently somewhat modified.

It is laid down that the Hulsean Lectures shall be 'on some branch of Christian Theology', and although the Old Testament forms a normal part of a theological curriculum, there has sometimes seemed to be a doubt whether the electors viewed the Old Testament as falling within the definition. Certainly, so far as I am aware, no course of Hulsean Lectures has been delivered in this century on an Old Testament theme pure and simple. But it is clear that the original intention of John Hulse included this field. The courses of sermons for which he provided in his will and out of which the present scheme of lectures has in part evolved, included some which were to be on 'some of the more difficult texts or obscure parts of the Holy Scriptures, such, I mean, as may appear to be more generally useful or necessary to be explained, and which may best admit of such a comment or explanation without presuming to pry too far into the profound secrets or awful mysteries of the Almighty' (*Endowments of the University of Cambridge*, ed. J. W. Clark (Cambridge, 1904), p. 120).

It may be regarded therefore as proper that the claims of the Old Testament to lie within the field of Christian Theology have been given such a recognition by this course of lectures, and at a time when uncertainties about the place of the Old Testament in the Christian Church are frequently voiced, it may seem not improper that this study is devoted, if not solely to 'the more difficult texts or obscure parts' of the Old Testament, yet to an aspect of its thought which repays closer examination and may also provide a fuller measure of understanding of the New Testament and the Christian faith. Whether I have at any point presumed to 'pry too far' is no doubt best left to the judgement of the reader, or indeed of higher authority.

London, 1967   P.R.A.

ACKNOWLEDGEMENTS

The author wishes to record his indebtedness to friends and colleagues who have helped by their advice and by the loan of books and articles; to the staff of libraries in various places, both in Great Britain and in the United States; to the members of the graduate seminar at the Lutheran School of Theology at Chicago in the spring of 1967, for the stimulus of their discussion, and to other audiences who have heard parts of this book in its earlier forms. In particular, thanks are due to those who have typed the manuscript, and especially to Mr K. W. Carley for his assistance with proof-reading and indexing.

BIBLICAL QUOTATIONS

The biblical passages quoted have been translated direct from the Hebrew, but so far as possible the wording of the RSV has been followed. Chapter and verse enumeration follow the Hebrew text; except in the Psalms (where the deviation is often of a single verse only) the deviations are noted in RSV.

PREFACE

THE present study is the outcome of a number of years of teaching and thinking about the Old Testament, centring upon the questions and problems which belong to the sixth century BC. What prompted the rethinking was in the first place the necessity of studying closely the textual and exegetical problems of the book of Haggai, simply because this happened to be a set text for a particular group of students; and the recognition that this little prophetic book, so often dismissed as hardly worthy of attention because in the study of prophecy it is the great prophets of the eighth and seventh centuries to whom we turn, offers not only a number of quite difficult exegetical problems, but also certain clues to the thinking of the immediate post-exilic period. The natural sequel was a reconsideration of the companion to Haggai, Zechariah 1–8. These two collections of prophecy, often examined because of the importance of their contribution to the understanding of the historical circumstances attending the re-building of the Temple, are in reality most valuable pointers to the theological mind of a generation whose history remains at many points as obscure as ever.[1]

One line of thought which develops from this, and which can only be considered as an aside to this study, is the revaluation of Old Testament prophecy on the simple assumption that for its full understanding we must take it as a whole, and not begin as is often done from certain notions derived mainly from eighth-century prophecy and make these the criteria for the assessment of later and supposedly degenerate types.[2] Nor may the very valuable consideration of

[1] Cf. P. R. Ackroyd, 'Studies in the Book of Haggai', *JJS* 2 (1951), pp. 163–76; 3 (1952), pp. 1–13; 'The Book of Haggai and Zechariah 1–8', *JJS* 3 (1952), pp. 151–6; 'Some Interpretative Glosses in the Book of Haggai', *JJS* 7 (1956), pp. 163–7; 'Haggai', 'Zechariah', in *The New Peake's Commentary on the Bible*, ed. M. Black and H. H. Rowley (Edinburgh, 1962), pp. 643–51; 'Haggai', *HDB*, rev. ed. (1963), pp. 358–9; 'Zechariah, Book of', *HDB*, rev. ed., pp. 1053–4. Cf. below ch. X, XI.

[2] Even so excellent a work as B. Vawter, *The Conscience of Israel* (London, 1961)

extra-biblical prophetic phenomena as background to the understanding of biblical prophecy be permitted to detract from the major point of
interest which is the assessment of biblical prophecy as such, like and
unlike as it is to the other phenomena with which it may properly be
compared. Valuable as the wider background is, it must not obscure
the fact that the prophetic movement in Israel is a unique phenomenon, unique not in the Melchizedek sense of being 'without father or
mother', but in its coherence, its central place within the Old Testament (though it need not therefore be regarded as the solely interesting or important central feature), and its enormously far-reaching
influence beyond the Old Testament. Yet all too often Old Testament prophecy has been thought of in terms too narrow to include all
Old Testament prophets, and the later ones—especially Ezekiel,
Haggai and Zechariah—have been felt to be not quite respectable,
decadent examples of a movement now declining and about to peter
out into the period when there was 'no longer any prophet' (Ps. 74.9).

This reassessment can be treated only incidentally to the main
theme, but it is important that it should be in mind if only to enable
us to clear our minds of the feeling that a preoccupation with the
later stages of prophecy must inevitably be rather dull. The com-
mentator who chooses them as his field is not, in fact, to be pitied as
having to deal with what is pedestrian; he is fortunate in having so
rich a field to cultivate.[3]

It was fortunate that at the moment at which the study of Haggai
and Zechariah 1–8 imposed itself upon me I was able to derive a
great deal of help and inspiration from association with two Old
Testament scholars who had particular interest in the same general
field. Professor D. Winton Thomas, whose fields of interest are, of
course, very much wider than this, has for many years made the text
and versions of these two prophetic collections a particular matter for
study, and my first detailed reading of the Zechariah text over twenty

---

is unfortunately deliberately restricted to the examination of the earlier prophets.
Cf. the comments on the transformation of prophecy during the exile in A. Lods,
The Prophets and the Rise of Judaism (ET, London, 1937), pp. 249f., 265, 279f. Cf.
the comments of H. H. Rowley, *Worship in Ancient Israel* (London, 1967), p. 144.
T. C. Vriezen's discussion of the exilic period (*The Religion of Ancient Israel* [ET,
London, 1967], pp. 240ff.) offers a balanced statement, but perhaps also not
sufficiently doing justice to the early restoration period.

[3] Cf. the comment of G. A. Smith, *The Book of the Twelve Prophets* II (London,
1896–8, 1928), p. 210: 'No one can fail to be struck with the spirituality of the
teaching of Haggai and Zechariah.'

years ago was, in fact, done under his guidance.[4] That he has a wider interest in the sixth century BC, an interest shared by his predecessor in the Regius Chair of Hebrew in Cambridge, S. A. Cook,[5] is evident from other work which he has done, as in his Michael Fidler lecture of February 1960,[6] to which reference will be made subsequently. Professor Laurence E. Browne, whose interests have ranged over the much wider field of the comparative study of religion, had also concerned himself with the problems of this particular period in his book *Early Judaism* (Cambridge, 1920),[7] a book which covers some of the ground which falls within the scope of the present study. His interest and his kindly acceptance of the fact that my approach to the period differed at many points from his own provided a useful stimulus to the further pursuing of the questions raised by the two prophetic collections. I am glad here to acknowledge my indebtedness to these two scholars. My indebtedness to many others will be everywhere apparent.

[4] Cf. his commentaries on Haggai and Zechariah in *IB* 6 (New York, 1956), pp. 1037–88.

[5] Cf. W. A. L. Elmslie, 'Prophetic Influences in the Sixth Century BC', in *Essays and Studies presented to S. A. Cook*, ed. D. Winton Thomas (Cambridge Oriental Series 2, London, 1950), pp. 15–24: on p. 15, Elmslie quotes Cook's expression of interest from *The Cambridge Ancient History* III (Cambridge, 1925, 1929), p. 489. At the end of the section, on p. 499 Cook wrote: ' . . . the sixth century (roughly) is the point upon which all the great problems of the Old Testament ultimately turn.' Cf. also his 'Le VIe siècle, moment décisif dans l'histoire du judaïsme et dans l'évolution religieuse de l'Orient', *RHPhR* 18 (1938), pp. 321–31. Elmslie's own article contains some interesting material, but its approach is somewhat oversimplified.

[6] 'The Sixth Century BC: a Creative Epoch in the History of Israel', *JSS* 6 (1961), pp. 33–46.

[7] Cf. also his *From Babylon to Bethlehem* (Cambridge, ²1951).

I

THE EXILIC AGE

I. REVALUATION

IN A POPULAR WORK, *Everyday life in Old Testament Times* (London, 1956), which vividly presents many aspects of the life which is portrayed within the Old Testament, E. W. Heaton has chosen to present as one of his illustrations a picture of the reconstructed city of Babylon of the period of Nebuchadnezzar (605–562 BC), with its gates and hanging gardens and ziggurat, and to caption the picture: 'The Closing Scene of Old Testament Times: the Babylon of Nebuchadnezzar' (fig. 4, p. 26). A careful examination of the book makes it clear why this particular caption was chosen. Not without justification, Heaton has portrayed in this book the everyday life of the *earlier* Old Testament period. Information regarding everyday life for the later period is much scantier, and, even where we may suspect its existence, often difficult of assessment. Thus the Chronicler's evidence, important as it is, is always subject to the difficulties of interpretation which arise from his portraying in the main his own understanding of a period in the more distant past. Much contemporary information must be present, but it is not easy to disentangle it. L. Köhler in his delightful study *Hebrew Man*[1] also presents a picture drawn largely from earlier evidence, though he indicates the persistence of beliefs and practices, and at one point draws a portrait of the ideal Hebrew as he was seen at two quite different periods, namely in the figure of David and in the figure of Daniel (pp. 30ff.).

Heaton's book is in reality a study of 'Everyday Life in Pre-exilic Israel'. But the choice of the caption 'The Closing Scene of Old Testament Times', explicable though it is, produces a most misleading impression. It suggests that the Old Testament really stops at the Exile, which is absurd. Nor does Heaton really suppose that it stops

[1] London, 1956—ET of *Der Hebräische Mensch* (Tübingen, 1953).

there. Yet the caption is, in fact, reinforced in its undesirable impression by the statement that 'it is a fortunate . . . circumstance that the best documented phase of Israel's life is also the most representative and intrinsically important' (p. 29). And this is followed by the affirmation that 'most of the new developments' of the post-exilic period 'were borrowed from the great empires' of that time. 'This post-exilic period was a time of great cultural expansion and reformation in Judaism and, despite the dictates of strict chronology, the study of it belongs less to Old Testament times than to the background of the New Testament' (*ibid*). Such a statement invites one or two comments. We may ask why if six centuries of Old Testament times (or perhaps four if we limit ourselves rather narrowly to the period 587–165 BC, and regard the apocrypha and pseudepigrapha as falling entirely outside our purview) can be dismissed as 'background of the New', the preceding six centuries or so, 1250 to 587, should not be similarly regarded?[2] This is, of course, exactly what some Christians believe to be the only proper view, but it is one which introduces so constricting a tendency as to make proper Old Testament exegesis impossible.[3] Or we may ask by what right the Christian is so intolerant as to exclude the claims of Judaism also to be considered as a successor to the Old Testament? The Christian has a perfect right to claim that the revelation of God in Christ is such as to necessitate a complete revaluation of all life and experience, including the Old

---

[2] It is one of the dangers of the common division of the Old Testament at the fall of Jerusalem in 587 that an artificial break is made; yet there is a certain rightness in the instinct which sees the profound significance of this moment in the people's history. It is proper, however, that a different division should also sometimes be made, as, for example, by A. Lods, whose volume *The Prophets and the Rise of Judaism* (ET, London, 1937) spans the exile, and by R. H. Pfeiffer, *Religion in the Old Testament*, ed. C. C. Forman (London, 1961), who divides at 621 (p. xi, but also p. 200 for his further comments).

[3] Christian exegesis of the Old Testament which works from a typological viewpoint or applies a narrow 'prophecy-fulfilment' pattern, inevitably limits the areas of the Old Testament which can be reasonably taken into account. What does not provide a 'type' or cannot be seen to be 'fulfilled' must take a subordinate place or be ignored. A full Christian exegesis takes the whole Old Testament seriously as an essential element in the context of the Christian revelation. T. C. Vriezen, *An Outline of Old Testament Theology* (ET, Oxford, 1958), shows full appreciation of this variety (cf., e.g., p. 75), yet he appears at times to exclude certain parts of the material as not containing 'a revelation of the Spirit of God, but rather the revelation of the spirit of the age (Ecclesiastes) or of the spirit of the Jewish people (Esther)' (p. 89). But all revelation is tied to a particular human context, and the discerning of its nature in that context is part of the fascination of Old Testament study.

Testament. But he has no right to deny that to those who are unable to accept this claim the Old Testament may nevertheless be a meaningful and vital document which enriches faith and knowledge of God the more it is read and studied. Not infrequently one suspects that dogmatic closure of the mind precludes such rich appreciation, so that the Old Testament provides mere confirmation of convictions already held. While openness of mind is often a mask for indecision or superficiality of thinking, there is a half-way house in which the firmness of convictions accepted and held does not preclude the realization that 'the Lord has more truth yet to break forth out of his holy word',[4] in which the richness of the Old Testament thought contributes to the deepening of those convictions and their enlargement, since it is not seriously to be supposed that the acceptance of the revelation of God in Christ as final and decisive carries with it an automatic understanding of the nature and purpose of God in its totality.

Such an attitude as Heaton's to the post-exilic period is not uncommon. It is found in the often-quoted but misleading statement of A. B. Davidson, made with reference to Jeremiah: 'Prophecy had already taught its truths. Its last effort was to reveal itself in a life',[5] though admittedly this has a rather narrower reference. Many of us would at least be inclined to wonder whether the claim of Deutero-Isaiah to be perhaps the greatest of them all may not be admitted—though this is a judgement which is purely subjective and not capable of plain demonstration. To say, as Professor D. Winton Thomas does, that 'He (Deutero-Isaiah) is the last of the great Old Testament prophets'[6] is again understandable, but is not this, too, somewhat unsympathetic towards the later members of the line? Does greatness cease with Deutero-Isaiah, or is it not also to be found in such men as Haggai and Zechariah, men of the moment as well as men of insight into the divine will, not entirely unlike their great— even if greater—predecessors? Again judgement is subjective, but if it is allowed to suggest the comparative decadence of post-exilic thought, it is damaging to a right assessment unless we can find some more substantial ground for making the statement.[7] In a recent,

---

[4] John Robinson (?1576–1625), pastor of the pilgrim fathers. The words purport to be quoted from his address to the departing pilgrims. Cf. *Dictionary of National Biography*, Vol. 49 (London, 1897), p. 21. [I am indebted to Dr G. F. Nuttall for this reference.]

[5] *HDB* II (1899), pp. 569–78; 'Jeremiah the Prophet' (see p. 576).

[6] *JSS* 6 (1961), p. 39.

[7] Cf. H. H. Rowley, *The Faith of Israel* (London, 1956), p. 147: 'Nor should we

though in many respects antiquated, presentation of the history of
Old Testament religion, R. H. Pfeiffer wrote of 'the notion that
Judaism consists of the observance of the law revealed by Jehovah
[sic] to Moses—a notion quite different from the religion taught by
the prophets and by Jesus'.[8] It is clear that he regards the religion of
the prophets and of Jesus as being comparable, and utterly different
from some other notion which, in the context, can hardly imply
anything other than the religion of the post-exilic age.[9]

Recent years of Old Testament study have brought great enrich-
ment to our view of the earlier period. The revaluation of the Exodus,
the centrality of the Exodus faith in the *Heilsgeschichte*, the appreciation of prophets and psalmists in that context, have brought about a
greater sense of coherence in our thinking. The problems of the cult,
on which so little agreement has been reached, with the uncertainty
about prophetic relationship to it, and the position of the king, have
brought in another element which makes for the appreciation of
continuity.[10] But with such changes as these there has not always gone

forget, when we are inclined to think of post-exilic Judaism as hard and legal and
unspiritual, that it was in the post-exilic days that the rich treasury of the Psalter
was gathered together, and that it was employed in the worship of Judaism. . . .
It is but a distortion of the teaching of the Bible which concentrates on certain
elements of the teaching of the Prophets and ignores all else. . . .' It may indeed
be hoped that the 'inclination' itself may be corrected, since it is so much a survival from earlier trends of thought. Cf. also his *Worship in Ancient Israel* (London,
1967), pp. 1f.

Cf. also the ironical statement of K. Koch, 'Sühne und Sündenvergebung um
die Wende von der exilischen zur nachexilischen Zeit', *EvTh* 26 (1966), pp. 217–39,
see p. 218: 'It is well known that for any self-respecting Old Testament scholar,
the real Old Testament comes to an end with Deutero-Isaiah, or at the latest
with Ezra. Everything which comes after that is Judaism and is of no interest.'
It is odd, however, to find that elsewhere Koch seems to be anxious to defend
post-exilic thought from being regarded as 'Judaism', as if the latter were a derogatory term. So in 'Haggais unreines Volk', *ZAW* 79 (1967), pp. 52–66, he concludes
by remarking: 'With the prophet Haggai, everything is still thought out and
experienced in Israelite terms; nothing, absolutely nothing at all, is specifically
Jewish' (p. 66). Cf. also below, ch. X.

[8] *Religion in the Old Testament* (1961), p. 54.
[9] While New Testament scholarship has moved a long way from this oversimplification, the notion that Jesus' teaching represents a revival of the prophetic
thought, overleaping the intervening centuries of 'priestly' ideas, is one that still
persists popularly. An example of such oversimplification is cited in T. W. Manson,
The Teaching of Jesus (Cambridge, 1935), p. 14, and cf. also W. D. Davies in *Christian News from Israel* XVI, 3 (Sept. 1965), pp. 18f. This is not to deny the relevance
of prophetic categories to the discussion of the person of Christ.
[10] Cf. P. R. Ackroyd, *Continuity: A Contribution to the Study of the Old Testament
Religious Tradition* (Oxford, 1962), esp. pp. 20–25.

a sufficient realization of the consequences. The old schemes still persist: prophecy, psalmody, law as a chronological scheme—even if older elements are to be found within both the latter—with the consequence drawn that originality must always lie with the prophets. It is still affirmed that Jeremiah and Deutero-Isaiah, so far from using psalm forms, must have been creators of them. Cult and law are still thought to be lower levels of religious thinking than prophecy and piety; the rite is evaluated as less than the word.[11] Later prophecy, because it does not always seem to show a direct concern with questions of 'morality', is thought to be lower than earlier prophecy; its concern, too, with cultic matters, such as the rebuilding of the Temple and the reorganization of a pure worship, is evaluated as lower than the ideal of a religion without a Temple, a worship without cultus.[12]

In suggesting a change of emphasis, we are always in danger of going too far. The concentration on the great prophets was always in the past in danger of making too great a contrast between them and the religion of their time, with a resulting belief in the antagonism of prophet and priest, typified in the meeting of Amos and Amaziah. We can now see that this antagonism was not one of principle—in the sense that prophets and priests must be at daggers drawn—but was a matter of right emphasis;[13] not an exclusion of the cult, but a right

[11] Cf. P. Volz, *Prophetengestalten des Alten Testaments* (Stuttgart, 1938), p. 56, and 'Die radikale Ablehnung der Kultreligion durch die alttestamentlichen Propheten', *ZSTh* 14 (1937), pp. 63–85; also C. F. Whitley, *The Prophetic Achievement* (London, 1963), esp. ch. IV. Cf. N. H. Snaith, *The Jewish New Year Festival* (London, 1947), for the argument that Pss. 93, 96–98 are 'so thoroughly dependent upon Isa. 40–55 that if the Deutero-Isaianic elements are removed the residue is negligible' (p. 200); and cf. also his *Studies in the Psalter* (London, 1934), pp. 66–69. For other references, cf. H. H. Rowley, *Worship in Ancient Israel* (1967), p. 2. An opposite extreme tends to be reached in works such as those of H. Graf Reventlow, e.g. *Das Amt des Propheten bei Amos* (FRLANT 80, 1962); *Wächter über Israel* (BZAW 82, 1962); *Liturgie und prophetisches Ich bei Jeremia* (Gütersloh, 1963). For a judicious statement, examining the forms and language used, cf. E. Würthwein, 'Kultpolemik oder Kultbescheid?' in *Tradition und Situation*, ed. E. Würthwein and O. Kaiser (Göttingen, 1963), pp. 115–31.

[12] Popular assessments of the Old Testament, such as find their way into school textbooks and remain unchanged in edition after edition, do not always correspond to the developments in more scholarly study in which a much more just assessment of the cultic aspect of religious life is to be found. Yet the older ways of thinking persist, as, for example, in T. Chary, *Les prophètes et le culte à partir de l'exil* (Tournai, 1955), e.g. p. 276, arguing that Jeremiah had gone too far in criticism of the cult, and describing Ezekiel as breaking with earlier prophetic tradition on this matter.

[13] Cf. A. C. Welch, *Prophet and Priest in Old Israel* (London, 1936).

interpretation of it,[14] and in this priests, too, were intimately concerned, as may be seen in the mass of priestly legislation, and in the
occasions of priestly oracular utterances.[15] The contrast between the
prophets and the religion of their time has sometimes been stated in
such a way as to deny all continuity to religious patterns within the
life of the people.[16] But a fuller appreciation of both priestly functions
and of cultic continuity must not allow us to underestimate the protest
made against wrong practice,[17] against wrong thinking about the
nature of God; nor to discount the religious evils of the sanctuaries of
both kingdoms.

Similarly, too, appreciation of the richness of post-exilic religion
must not consist simply in picking out its best moments. We are to see
not only the great creative personalities of that period—Haggai and
Zechariah and their like; Ezra and the Chronicler and the author of
Job; and then contrast these baldly with the disasters of the second
century BC—the party strife, the apostasy, the Hellenization. The
ideals and the realities lie side by side. The handling of the law which
is so important an aspect of post-exilic religion[18]—though it originated
far back—is expressed both in the delight in the works of God which
is always an element of true worship and also in the meticulousness
of observance which is a necessary consequence of the full acceptance
of obedience, but may issue in the casuistry of the worst forms of
Pharisaism. Side by side with the concern for the existence of a holy
people, a holy and separate community, at its highest in Ezra, we see
the narrowness of Zealots and of some aspects of the life of Qumran.[19]

[14] Cf. the survey by H. H. Rowley, 'Ritual and the Hebrew Prophets', in
Myth, Ritual, and Kingship, ed. S. H. Hooke (Oxford, 1958), pp. 236–60, which ap-
peared also in *JSS* 1 (1956), pp. 338–60, and has been again reprinted in *From
Moses to Qumran* (London, 1963), pp. 111–38.

[15] Cf. below ch. VI on the 'Holiness Code' and the 'Priestly Work'.

[16] Cf. N. W. Porteous, 'The Prophets and the Problem of Continuity', in
Israel's Prophetic Heritage. Essays in honor of James Muilenburg, ed. B. W. Anderson
and W. Harrelson (Philadelphia, London, 1962), pp. 11–25.

[17] Cf. T. Chary, *Les prophètes et le culte à partir de l'exil* (1955), p. 285: 'It is a
great mistake to leave the post-exilic prophets out of account in the discussion of
the legitimacy of the cult. They help us to assess the preaching of their great predecessors.'

[18] Cf. below, pp. 254ff.

[19] This is seen in the militant spirit of the War Scroll. It is stressed, for example,
by K. Schubert, *Die Gemeinde vom Toten Meer. Ihre Entstehung und ihre Lehren* (Munich,
1958), ET by J. W. Doberstein, *The Dead Sea Community: its origin and teachings*
(London, 1959); by C. Roth, *The Historical Background of the Dead Sea Scrolls*
(Oxford, 1958); and by G. R. Driver, *The Judaean Scrolls* (Oxford, 1965), esp.
ch. IV.

It is a zeal often uncontrolled and harsh; but where should we be without our extremists? We see in the period faith and joy and worship; and also folly and apostasy and 'Sadduceeism'.[20]

The description of any period of thought must see all sides of the picture. We may neither ignore the narrowness because of our realization of the richness of thought which also exists, nor pick out the highlights—Jonah and Ruth and their like—and think of their authors as voices crying in the dark. So, too, with the exilic age. Lack of information means that there is much of the life of the time which remains obscure. The attempt must be made to assess what throws light on the period without false sentimentality, and without overemphasis on those parts of the thought which are congenial to us. The pattern of the period is a rich and complex one and deserves to be seen as a whole.

2. THE EXILIC PERIOD AS A 'CREATIVE AGE'

It has long been realized that the sixth century BC was an epoch in which a variety of important events took place, not only within the more limited field of Old Testament history, nor even within the confines of Near Eastern civilization, but throughout the world. It is the century of Confucius, of Zoroaster, of Buddha. It is also the century of the Ionian philosophers. For the biblical scholar it is the century of Jeremiah, Ezekiel, Deutero-Isaiah; but not only of these three, for they may be joined by a relatively large number of others, known by name or unknown, who contributed to the development of thought. It is with these men, known and unknown, that we shall be concerned.

But it seems important that the practical delimiting of our attention to the thought of the one people in this notable century should be considered. Professor D. Winton Thomas in his lecture 'The Sixth Century BC: a creative epoch in the History of Israel'[21] devotes almost

[20] The form is used here in its conventional negative sense. But an assessment of the Sadducees in such purely negative forms should not lead to a description of them as if they were simply the descendants of Hellenizers among the priests in the Maccabaean period (cf. M. Noth, *History of Israel* [ET, London, [2]1960], p. 374). It is difficult to believe that this is really what they were, though their political activities suggest their being in a line with politicians of even earlier periods. (A comparison might be made with the politicians as described in W. McKane, *Prophets and Wise Men* [SBT 44, 1965], e.g. pp. 65ff. For a comment on this, cf. below, p. 69 n. 27.) Their beliefs, however, suggest religious conservatives rather than anything else.

[21] *JSS* 6 (1961), pp. 33–46.

the whole of his attention to the historical situation, both internal and external, and to the literature and thought which belong in the Old Testament context. In the penultimate paragraph he notes the significance of this for Jews, Christians and Muslims. 'This sixth century was a century of hope renewed. Rebirth followed on ruin, new life on decay. The disaster of the opening years was the opportunity for a new outburst of faith in the future' (p. 46). He then mentions the wider significance of the period, by alluding to Zoroaster, Confucius, and the Buddha. 'A creative epoch in the history of Israel indeed it was . . . But this century was more than a creative epoch in Israel's history. It was a creative epoch in the history of the world' (ibid.).

Now, as a matter of historical fact, there can be no doubt that this is so. The history of a considerable part of the world was to be directly influenced by the lives of three great religious leaders of the east—Zoroaster, Confucius and the Buddha. If, following C. F. Whitley,[22] we add a reference to the Ionian philosophers, then we may claim for this century that it saw the birth—or more strictly the development—of ideas which were to be decisive in the development of later Greek philosophy as well as of scientific thinking. But it is one thing to note the chronological coincidence, and perhaps to use it, as Professor Thomas does, for his was a popular lecture, as a pointer to the kind of response which we in the twentieth century AD might make to our own situation. 'Like today it was a period of great danger, but of great opportunity also. The danger was overcome, no doubt at heavy cost, and the opportunity was not lost. Perhaps we, who live long after, in another outstandingly creative epoch of history, may, as we reflect upon the earlier situation, draw from it fresh hope and faith to adventure courageously in our own most difficult quest' (ibid.). It is a quite different matter to draw from the chronological coincidence conclusions regarding the interrelationship of thought in

[22] *The Exilic Age* (1957), p. 2. (Whitley also quotes G. F. Moore, G. Galloway, S. A. Cook, H. Butterfield, and W. F. Lofthouse.) Cf. also R. H. Pfeiffer, *Religion in the Old Testament* (1961), p. 10: '. . . 600–500 BC, the most fruitful period in the religious history of mankind, to which belong Jeremiah, Isaiah 40–55, Zoroaster, the beginnings of Greek philosophy, Confucius, Buddha, etc.' (The omissions from the list are interesting, as is the wide open 'etc.' at the end.) C. F. Pfeiffer, *Exile and Return* (Grand Rapids, 1962), makes a similar point (p. 7). His rather simplified account of the period 600–400 BC quotes much from extra-biblical sources, but its conservative viewpoint prevents the author from using much of the relevant biblical material for the discussion of the period. Daniel is used as if there were no problems: Deutero-Isaiah is not mentioned. The bibliography is somewhat misleading.

different parts of the world, and to endeavour to prove an international continuum which provides a basis for the explanation of the movements within Old Testament thought. Yet this is what Whitley and others have done, and it is a temptation which must be resisted unless we can demonstrate without doubt that there are interconnections.

It is, of course, true that the wealth of discoveries, particularly in the whole Near Eastern area during the last century or so, has demonstrated the many interconnections within the area; and indeed there are some indications of even wider links and patterns of thought. We can see the occurrence in a number of different places of similar myths and legends, the transference of images, the common inheritance of law. But precision of linkage is rarely possible; the situation is far too rich in ideas for there to be a simple explanation at every point. The recognition of common elements within the Hebrew and Babylonian creation myths does not provide us with an exact genealogy of such myths, though we may, without precision, indicate that they are related. In such a context to overstress differences and treat every phenomenon in isolation would be absurd. But to imagine that points of similarity necessarily point to direct influence or interconnection is also hazardous. Our knowledge of the rich texture of more recent times, of the uncertainties (even with all the modern facilities of communication) in tracing the exact development of the mind of a particular great person or the evolution of a particular pattern of thought, must make us cautious in detecting precise interrelationships in a world about which inevitably, with all our knowledge, we are so much in the dark.

The discovery of patterns in history, fashionable as it has sometimes been, is always in danger of being an oversimplification. To refuse to see such patterns may be to invite the accusation of insular-mindedness.[23] For the historian to restrict the scope of his studies so as to treat the history and thought of one particular group in one particular century, and for practical purposes to ignore the movements of thought contemporary with it, may seem to suggest an overconcentration on a narrow abstracted circle, of which the picture will be

[23] The criticisms of A. J. Toynbee's *Study of History* (London, 1934–61) indicate the difficulties of such discoveries of pattern. E. Voegelin's *Order and History* (Louisiana, 1956ff.) attempts such a synthesis: but to one who has some knowledge of the area under survey, the first volume, *Israel and Revelation*, reads at times very strangely.

one-sided because it is seen in isolation. Yet it has two advantages. On the one hand, the attempt may ultimately make possible a true assessment of the interrelationships just because the picture has been drawn without these being too much in mind. To deny that there were influences from outside on Israel's thought would be absurd; the pattern of Old Testament thought reveals again and again the assimilation and reinterpretation of material which was alien. Part of the fascination of Old Testament thinking derives from the realization of its capacity for transforming what we can see elsewhere in rudimentary forms or in more developed but differently developed ideas. But the understanding of any element of external influence demands a true appropriation of the internal situation, since it would appear *a priori* unlikely that a new idea from outside can make itself really effective within a new environment unless it can find some point of contact. Thus, to take only one simple example, the understanding of the development of the full range of Jewish angelology, so often depicted in terms of Persian, Zoroastrian influence, is possible only if an adequate conception can be reached of those elements within Israel's own thinking—ideas concerning the 'angel of God', the 'sons of god', the 'other gods'—on to which newer conceptions could be grafted. The more pedestrian task—as it may seem to some—of investigating those native elements (native in the sense that at a given period they have come to be fully an expression of Israel's own thought, though evidently this cannot be entirely detached from an earlier synthesis or grafting, by which the particular form was reached) may provide a firmer basis for the consideration of the nature of Babylonian or Persian or other influence on the thought of Israel in this particular century and later.

On the other hand, and this is an interrelated point, the assessment of that external influence and contact demands a wider range of knowledge, an intimacy of understanding of the other cultures, if we are not to be guilty of interpreting those cultures as if their terminology were our own or were that of sixth-century Israel. To see the relationship in general terms between Israel's wisdom and that of Egypt, and even to go further and see in the *Wisdom of Amen-em-ope* an example in which the contacts may be particularly vividly illustrated, is one thing. To choose between differing interpretations of a difficult Egyptian text—whether or not one can lay claim to knowledge of the complexities of the language—on the basis of the similarity or otherwise of possible renderings to a particular Old

Testament passage, is a more hazardous proceeding.[24] To see a golden figure from Ur as a 'ram caught in a thicket' because of Genesis 22.13,[25] in spite of the fact that it appears more probable that the figure represents a goat,[26] and that so far from being caught in a thicket, it may more probably be regarded as eating the twigs of a bush,[27] is, understandably, tempting enough, but results in not a little confusion of thought. It is more important that we should have exact studies of the thought of different communities, as far as possible from within. The comparison may then be undertaken by those who are able to master the differing types of thought and have the knowledge necessary for appreciating both. If this is a counsel of perfection, at least it serves as a warning against too hasty comparison, based on understanding of only one side and not of both. We are the more readily convinced by descriptions of things we know nothing about, because we have no criteria for judgement, than by discussions of the interrelationships of thought where we have some knowledge which enables us to check. I am reminded of a comment made by Professor David Daube in the New Testament Seminar conducted in Cambridge by Professor C. H. Dodd when the latter was Norris-Hulse

[24] Cf., for example, W. O. E. Oesterley, *The Wisdom of Egypt and the Old Testament* (London, 1927), esp. pp. 42ff. The tendency to use 'biblical language' in translating such ancient works adds to the impression of a relationship which may not exist at all. For a reliable recent appraisal cf. R. J. Williams, 'The Alleged Semitic Original of the *Wisdom of Amenemope*' *JEA* 47 (1961), pp. 100–6.

[25] Cf. C. L. Woolley, etc., *Ur Excavations* II Text (London, 1934), frontispiece and pp. 264ff. The text refers to 'goat statuettes' and subsequently states 'inevitably the subject of the sculpture, a he-goat, "a ram of the goats" . . . recalled the Old Testament story and the phrase "a ram caught in a thicket". It is obvious that the figures cannot be illustrations of an event which is claimed to have happened nearly fifteen centuries later, but the parallelism is not to be altogether overlooked.' Cf. Illustrations pl. 87. Similarly, *Excavations at Ur* (London, 1954), frontispiece 'The "ram in a thicket" ', but pp. 74f. indicate that the parallel is 'difficult to explain'. Cf. *Ur of the Chaldees* (London, 1929), pp. 67f. and pl. VI.

[26] Cf. *Adam to Daniel*, ed. G. Cornfeld (New York, 1961), p. 75: 'a goat standing upright beside a thicket'. 'It has been customary to authenticate Isaac's story by calling these objects erroneously "the ram caught in a thicket".' Is the representation perhaps in reality connected with the goats portrayed, for example, as accompanying a fertility goddess at Ugarit? Cf. *Views of the Biblical World*, ed. by M. Avi-Yonah and A. Malamat, I (Jerusalem, 1959), p. 192. Cf. J. Finegan, *Light from the Ancient Past* (Princeton, 1946), p. 35 n.: 'little likelihood of any connection'; ([2]1959), p. 42 n.: 'difficult to see any actual connection'; J. B. Pritchard, *The Ancient Near East in Pictures* (Princeton, 1954), figs. 667–8.

[27] H. Cazelles, 'David's Monarchy and the Gibeonite Claim', *PEQ* 87 (1955), pp. 165–75, in a different connection says: 'The animal which devours the spirit of the grain is elsewhere more kindly represented in the form of the ibex eating the leaves of the tree of life' (pp. 169f.).

Professor; Daube confessed to being most persuaded by the validity of Toynbee's theories in his *Study of History* when Toynbee was treating the history of obscurer parts of the world such as Ancient China. Where the survey comes nearer to our own field of study, we begin to hesitate and to criticize.

In any case, the period of exile and restoration is so rich in thought within the Old Testament itself that it does not seem unreasonable thus to narrow the field. If this study stimulates further thought about wider aspects of the sixth century BC, and also encourages a more positive appreciation of the post-exilic period which stems from it, it will have achieved its main purpose.

3. THE SCOPE OF THE PRESENT STUDY

The effect of these general considerations is to emphasize the importance of seeing the Old Testament as a whole, not in any oversimplified manner, but as a continuum within which we can trace many patterns of thought. The arrangement of such a complete survey is a problem to which different scholars have given different answers, and those Old Testament theologians who have attempted it have often been very sensitive to the difficulty of discovering precisely where each element in the pattern belongs.

Such a complete survey is not our present purpose, but the more limited study of the exilic age must inevitably stand within a larger and more comprehensive view of the Old Testament, and must therefore avoid that tying up of loose ends which would suggest that it is a period complete in itself. Both the beginning and the end of the period are open, and the decision where to begin and where to end must be made without laying ourselves open too easily to the charge of arbitrariness.

The assumption upon which the lines are here drawn depends upon the point at which my own thinking about the period began, namely with the thought of the restoration period, centred upon the rebuilding of the Temple and so conveniently limited to about 540–500 BC (with enough latitude of date to allow the inclusion of Malachi, but not so much as to include Nehemiah, who may better be seen as belonging within the 'Age of the Chronicler'). But the understanding of this period depends upon the reasonable further assumption that not a little of the inspiration of those engaged in restoration depended upon those who had preceded them in the dark years of exile. So a reasonable upper limit is set in the fall of Jerusalem, artificial as this may be in some respects, because it means that Jeremiah and the other late seventh-century prophets will lie largely outside the scope of this study, and Ezekiel, too, while he may properly be considered within the exilic age, belongs also to the preceding period and cannot be fully understood without seeing him against that background. But desirable as it is to trace the continuity across the time of Judah's collapse, lest that momentous event should be given wrong proportions and its effects seen out of perspective, it is perhaps not improper to designate that earlier period the 'Age of Josiah', and to express the hope that a detailed study of that period—less conditioned by arbitrary notions about the development of individualism than is Whitley's *The Exilic Age* (1957)—may be forthcoming to draw together the many strands of thought and indications of liveliness in the Old Testament people of that particular moment.

In another direction there will be a limiting of the field. The political world of the exile and after must be in part our concern. The understanding of the development of thought cannot be undertaken without an appreciation of the situation in which it grew. Prophets and historians, poets and legislators, do not work in a political vacuum, and the general situation must be continually in mind, imaginatively, whether or not the precise events can be described. But the exact relationship between political events and religious thinking is not easy to determine. The impulse of political crisis—as in the time of the accession of Darius I—may well stimulate the thinking of prophets such as Haggai and Zechariah. But this is far from suggesting that their prophecy is the outcome of the events, for it would be equally true to affirm that their reading of the events is itself determined by their apprehension of the nature and purpose of the God in whose name they spoke, and for that they are likely to have been much more dependent upon a continuing religious tradition than upon the impulses of a moment. Here again chronological coincidence cannot without careful investigation be regarded as determining interrelationships and the attempts which have been made at providing exact correlation between events and prophecy[28] have rarely carried conviction. We may readily see the influence of the larger

[28] Cf., e.g., on Isaiah 40–55, S. Smith, *Isaiah XL–LV. Literary Criticism and History* (Schweich Lectures, 1940, London, 1944), and M. Haran, 'The Literary Structure and Chronological Framework of the Prophecies in Is. xl–xlviii', *VTS* 9 (1963), pp.

elements in the background—the fall of Jerusalem, the end of the state and the monarchy, the destruction of the Temple, and the large-scale political changes which followed on the rise to power of Cyrus, and hence the fall of the Neo-Babylonian empire. But to trace exact relationships between the smaller incidents of political life and the detailed working of the minds of the thinkers of the age is much more hazardous. We do better to place the two side by side without attempting too precise a definition of the contact. Some brief statements must be made about the situation in the years of the exile, and some attempt must be made at assessing the process of restoration, but our concentration will be upon the thought rather than upon the events.

4. THE SOURCES

When the attempt is made at tracing exact lines of thought, processes of development, and literary interconnections, the precise dating of particular sections of Old Testament material is obviously necessary. But such dating is rarely obtainable. A history of Old Testament literature, such as was conceived by Adolphe Lods in his *Histoire de la littérature hébraïque et juive depuis les origines jusqu'à la ruine de l'état juif, 135 après J.C.* (Paris, 1950), can command only limited acceptance, because inevitably there are elements of subjective judgement, and where dating depends upon a scheme of the development of thought, the scheme itself, whether following older or newer patterns, is subject to modification.

Ideally, it is true, we must have such dating, for the discussion of theological development; the consideration of the relationship between one part of the material and another cannot be fully undertaken without it. The discussion of the teaching of a particular prophet cannot be fully undertaken unless we can distinguish between *ipsissima verba* and the elaborations and glosses of a later date. But such discrimination, often undertaken with considerable confidence, as, for

127–55. Cf. also the latter's *Between RI'SHONÔT (Former Prophecies) and HADA-SHÔT (New Prophecies)—A Literary-Historical Study in the Group of Prophecies Isaiah XL–XLVIII* (Hebrew) (Jerusalem, 1963). On Haggai and Zech. 1–8, cf., e.g., L. Waterman, 'The Camouflaged Purge of Three Messianic Conspirators', *JNES* 13 (1954), pp. 73–78. On this latter and for other similar references, cf. P. R. Ackroyd, 'Two Old Testament Historical Problems of the Early Persian Period. A. The First Years of Darius I and the Chronology of Haggai, Zechariah 1–8', *JNES* 17 (1958), pp. 13–22.

example, by R. H. Pfeiffer,[29] does not always or even generally command assent. Nor is it satisfactory to treat the later elaborations as so much intrusive material to be set on one side. For in so far as we are here concerned with reactions to the exile and to the exilic situation in general, the later comment may well provide us with a further insight into what these experiences meant. So the glossing of Ezekiel's Temple descriptions reveals to us that this presentation of the hope for the future remained an inspiration even after events had overtaken it; and eventually such idealistic patterns were to project themselves into an eschatological event. Distinguishing is obviously desirable; but where we cannot be sure we may nevertheless see the effect of the prophet's basic message in the reinterpretation which was subsequently placed on it by himself and by others. And what is true of prophecy is true also of other varieties of Old Testament material.

To use Jeremiah, Ezekiel and Deutero-Isaiah is obvious—and I do not propose here to argue in favour of what are now generally accepted views of their period of origin.[30] It will also be desirable to take account of the earlier prophetic material as reapplied particularly to the exilic situation, though this will be touched on only very briefly.[31] Alongside these, it will be proper to mention such other passages as clearly reflect reaction to the events of 587, for example, Lamentations. The two major historical works—D and P—will be our concern in chapters V and VI and some brief words of explanation and justification will be in place there.

For the period of restoration the sources are clearer. Haggai and Zechariah 1–8 are primary and concentration will properly, as I believe, be on these two prophets whose words so unequivocally indicate the period of the Temple rebuilding.[32] The use of other material, particularly in Trito-Isaiah and to a lesser extent in Malachi, depends upon often difficult exegetical decisions, and it is not always easy to avoid the danger of writing a study of the period based upon the assignment to it of passages which are placed there for want of a better dating. In so far as this other material is subordinated to the

---

[29] *Introduction to the Old Testament* (London, 1941, 1948); cf., e.g., pp. 431f., 582f.

[30] Reference may be made to the literature in O. Eissfeldt, *The Old Testament: an Introduction* (ET, Oxford, New York, 1965), *ad loc.*

[31] Cf. below, pp. 44f.

[32] The space devoted to these two prophets in ch. X and XI may be justified on the grounds that relatively less attention has been devoted to them than to their exilic predecessors.

contemporary or largely contemporary material, it may be invoked. Ezra 1–6 has to be used, but with a full recognition of the problems of its use as a source for the historical and ideological reconstruction. This passage is of importance both because it evidently contains documentary materials of primary significance and also because it presents a coherent—though historically incomplete—picture of restoration. In this latter feature it belongs more with the study of the ideology of exile and restoration than with strict history. But this is not outside the scope of our concern.[33]

It is the whole range of thought which turns around the ideas of exile and restoration with which we are to deal. That these are primarily connected with the period of the events themselves is obvious enough. But thinking on this subject, the interpretation of exile and restoration, is not limited to that period. The whole work of the Chronicler cannot here be discussed, yet it is essential to take account of what he made of this moment in Israel's history, as it is important also to realize some of the repercussions of the thinking of the sixth century and of the thinking of those who contemplated the sixth century from a more distant perspective in the development of post-exilic Judaism. Very much in outline, these matters will concern us in the last part of this study.[34]

[33] Cf. the comments in A. C. Welch, *Post-exilic Judaism* (Edinburgh, London, 1935), ch. I.
[34] Cf. ch. XIII.

II

THE HISTORICAL SITUATION IN
THE EXILIC AGE

I. THE HISTORICAL BACKGROUND

A FULL DESCRIPTION of the historical events in the larger world of the ancient Near East would be inappropriate here. But a short review of the most important features is desirable to give a sufficient historical setting and to make subsequent reference to political conditions plain.[1]

The rapid rise to power of the Neo-Babylonian empire under Nabopolassar and Nebuchadrezzar (604–562) is attested by a variety of ancient documents, and impinges especially upon the events in which Judah was involved. After a short period of Egyptian control following the death of Josiah (609), Syria and Palestine came under Babylonian rule soon after 605. The breaking of allegiance led in turn to the first capture of Jerusalem in 597, and subsequent rebellion led to its destruction after a long siege in 587.[2] The wider position of Babylonian power has to be seen in relation to that of the Medes, whose help in the overthrow of Assyria marked them out as chief allies or rivals of the Babylonians. Eventually this was to be an important factor in the downfall of the Neo-Babylonian empire, but for the time being an agreed partition of territories appears to have

---

[1] For fuller discussions, cf. M. Noth, *History of Israel* (London, ²1960), pp. 280ff.; J. Bright, *A History of Israel* (Philadelphia, 1959; London, 1960), pp. 302ff., 332ff.; *Cambridge Ancient History* Vols III, IV (Cambridge, 1925, 1926). References to sources are given in these works. Cf. also K. Galling, *Studien zur Geschichte Israels im persischen Zeitalter* (Tübingen, 1964), pp. 1–20.

[2] Cf. also below, pp. 20ff. For some comments on the archaeological evidence for this period, cf. D. Winton Thomas, 'The Age of Jeremiah in the Light of Recent Archaeological Discovery', *PEQ* 82 (1950), pp. 1–15. G. Brunet, 'La prise de Jérusalem sous Sédécias. Les sens militaires de l'hébreu bâqa'', *RHR* 167 (1965), pp. 156–76, maintains that II Kings 25.4 means that the wall was opened up by the defenders, not breached by the enemy.

been achieved, perhaps by Nebuchadrezzar soon after his accession.[3]
There are indications of an attempted rebellion in Babylon in
595/4 BC,[4] and it is possible that this was the occasion for the activities
of prophets both in Babylonia and in Jerusalem, anticipating the
overthrow of the ruling power and looking for restoration for the
king, Jehoiachin, still evidently regarded as the legitimate ruler, at
least in some circles.[5] The sending of envoys to Babylon by Zedekiah
(Jer. 29.3), perhaps even an actual visit by him to indicate his submission (Jer. 51.59),[6] may be associated with the same general situation. Subsequently a new move to rebellion came in the west, insti-
gated perhaps by Egypt or at least with promise of Egyptian support,
at the end of the reign of Psammeticus II (593–588) or at the beginning of that of Hophra (588–569). Indications of Egyptian contacts
may be seen both in Jeremiah (34.8–11—if it is assumed that the re-
enslaving of liberated slaves occurred when a lull in the siege was
brought about by the approach of an Egyptian army; and clearly
37.5ff.) and in the Lachish letters, where the reference to Konyahu's
visit to Egypt may indicate an appeal for help.[7] Judah was not alone
in the rebellion, for certainly Ammon was involved,[8] and the fact
that Nebuchadrezzar subsequently subjected Tyre to a thirteen-year
siege, beginning in 585, may suggest that other areas, too, were im-
plicated, though there may be other reasons for the intervention in
Tyre. The repulsion of Egypt during the siege of Jerusalem was

[3] So K. Galling, *Studien* (1964), pp. 1ff., where he discusses the problem of
determining the exact border.
[4] Cf. D. J. Wiseman, *Chronicles of Chaldaean Kings (626–556 BC) in the British
Museum* (London, 1956).
[5] Cf. Jer. 27–29 for these prophetic activities. The legitimacy of Jehoiachin
would appear to be indicated by the datings from the years of his reign in Ezekiel
(cf. 1.2; 8.1, etc.), and perhaps also from the Weidner tablets (cf. below, p. 31).
On this general point, cf. K. Baltzer, 'Das Ende des Staates Juda und die Messias-
Frage', in *Studien zur Theologie der alttestamentlichen Überlieferungen*, ed. R. Rendtorff
and K. Koch (Neukirchen, 1961), pp. 33–44, see p. 38.
[6] MT '*et* 'with' indicates that Zedekiah went, too, but it is odd that the king
should be mentioned last. LXX παρά suggests *me'et* 'from'. Cf. BH³, etc.
[7] Lachish Ostracon III. Cf. *DOTT*, pp. 214f., for the translation of the text
and for cautious remarks on its interpretation by D. Winton Thomas.
[8] Cf. Ezek. 21.23–37. The involvement of Ammon may perhaps also be inferred
from Jer. 40–41, where Ammonite support for the assassins of Gedaliah could
indicate the aftermath of rebellious activity. This, however, belongs to a rather
later date. The flight of Judaeans to Moab, Ammon and Edom (Jer. 40.11) may
suggest that these areas were not, in fact, affected by the disaster (cf. M. Noth,
History, p. 293), though the fact that Ammon was involved in rebellion indicates
that we cannot prove that the others were not. Cf. below for Josephus on the events
of 582.

apparently not followed by any immediate action against her in the years after the fall of Judah, but later, after a successful mutiny by the Egyptian army led by Amasis in 570,[9] Nebuchadrezzar led a campaign there in 569/568. Josephus refers to an earlier campaign in 582, when Ammon and Moab were also subdued during a campaign against Coele-Syria,[10] but there is no confirmation of this. Later, when Cyrus threatened Babylon, Nabonidus was able to form an alliance with Amasis and with Croesus of Lydia; this suggests that the relationship between the two powers of Babylon and Egypt remained neutral or friendly after Nebuchadrezzar's campaign in 569/568.

The Babylonian power weakened after the death of Nebuchadrezzar in 562. His successor Amel-marduk (Evil-merodach, 562–560) is of significance for the Jewish community because of his release of Jehoiachin from prison (II Kings 25.27ff.).[11] Nergal-shar-uṣur (Neriglissar), who succeeded him, perhaps as a result of rebellion, reigned only four years, leaving a young son, Labashi-marduk, in 556. A group of rebels removed him and placed one of their number Nabu-na'id (Nabonidus), on the throne in 556, a man already at least of middle age and perhaps even older.[12] His policy is by no means fully intelligible; its possible effects on the Jewish exiles in Babylonia will be mentioned subsequently. Yet it is clear that he must have been a man of very considerable ability, who maintained himself on the throne during a very difficult period both politically and economically, in spite of the hostility of important groups, both in Babylon itself and elsewhere.[13] If, as seems possible, he was partly at least of Aramaean stock, and particularly linked through his remarkable mother,[14] Adda-Guppi, with Harran,[15] we may see here a

[9] Cf. Jer. 44.30.
[10] Ant. X, 9.7. Cf. the discussions in M. Noth, History, pp. 293f., J. Bright, History, p. 333.
[11] On the interpretation of this event, cf. below, pp. 78–81.
[12] On this question and generally on the policy of Nabonidus, cf. K. Galling, Studien (1964), pp. 5ff.; also his 'Isa. xxi im Lichte der neuen Nabonidtexte', in Tradition und Situation, ed. E. Würthwein and O. Kaiser (Göttingen, 1963), pp. 49–62, see pp. 49–55. Cf. also H. Lewy, 'Nitokris-Naqî'a', JNES II (1952), pp. 264–86, see p. 286.
[13] Cf. K. Galling, Studien (1964), p. 6. Also H. W. F. Saggs, The Greatness that was Babylon (London, 1962), pp. 145ff.; 'Babylon', in Archaeology and Old Testament Study, ed. D. W. Thomas (Oxford, 1967), pp. 39–56, see pp. 46f.
[14] Cf. E. Dhorme, 'La mère de Nabonide', RA 41 (1947), pp. 1–21.
[15] Cf. the comments of S. Smith, Isaiah Chapters XL–LV: Literary Criticism and History (1944), pp. 24f., who thinks the idea of Aramaean ancestry cannot be legitimately inferred. For the texts, cf. S. Smith, Babylonian Historical Texts relating to the Capture and Downfall of Babylon (London, 1924), pp. 27–123.

reason for his fostering of the cult of Sin, the moon-god, and perhaps in relation to his building programme in Harran and elsewhere a reason for his occupation of the desert area of Tema', vital as a trading centre and no doubt bringing an access of produce and income from trading dues.[16]

In the end, however, Nabonidus could not maintain himself against the attacks of the developing power of Cyrus, who took over the Median empire and proceeded to take control of Asia Minor. The discontent within Babylonia made the advent of Cyrus acceptable to the older influential groups, and for the Jewish exiles it appeared to offer a hope of a renewed and better future. To these aspirations we shall return at a later stage.

2. THE SITUATION IN JUDAH

That Jerusalem was captured by the Babylonians in March 597 BC[17] is now established on the basis of the biblical evidence and of the Wiseman tablets which provide us with a precise sequence of events.[18] The same type of evidence is not available as yet—though we may perhaps hope for a similar fortunate discovery—for the second capture of the city and its consequences in 587 or 586.[19] That the events took

[16] Cf. K. Galling, *Studien* (1964), pp. 17f. On the presence of Jews in Tema', cf. p. 19 and also C. J. Gadd, 'The Harran Inscriptions of Nabonidus', *Anat. Stud.* 8 (1958), pp. 35–92, see pp. 79–89: 'The Kingdom of Nabonidus in Arabia'; I. Ben-Zvi, 'The Origins of the Settlement of Jewish Tribes in Arabia', *Eretz–Israel* 6 (1960), pp. 130–48, 35*–37*; H. W. F. Saggs, in *Archaeology and Old Testament Study*, ed. D. W. Thomas (1967), p. 47.

[17] A survey appears in J. Finegan, *Handbook of Biblical Chronology* (Princeton, 1964), pp. 198–209, with some bibliographical references.

[18] D. J. Wiseman, *Chronicles of Chaldaean Kings (626–556 BC) in the British Museum* (1956).

[19] Here the decision between 587 and 586 is less firm. Cf. D. N. Freedman, 'The Babylonian Chronicle', *BA* 19 (1956), pp. 50–60, see p. 55 and n. 20 (=*BA Reader* [1961], pp. 113–27, see p. 119 and n. 20), firmly rejecting 586. Cf. also, e.g., E. Kutsch, 'Zur Chronologie der letzten judäischen Könige (Josia bis Zedekia)', *ZAW* 71 (1959), pp. 270–4; M. Noth, 'Die Einnahme von Jerusalem im Jahre 597 v. Chr.', *ZDPV* 74 (1958), pp. 133–57, see p. 150. But cf. E. Vogt, 'Die neubabylonische Chronik über die Schlacht bei Karkemisch und die Einnahme von Jerusalem', *VTS* 4 (1957), pp. 67–96, who favours 586 (see pp. 95f.); so, too, H. Tadmor, 'Chronology of the Last Kings of Judah', *JNES* 15 (1956), pp. 226–30; S. H. Horn, 'The Babylonian Chronicle and the Ancient Calendar of the Kingdom of Judah', *Andrews University Seminary Studies* 5 (1967), pp. 12–27; E. Auerbach, 'Wann eroberte Nebukadnezar Jerusalem?', *VT* 11 (1961), pp. 128–36; C. Schedl, 'Nochmals das Jahr der Zerstörung Jerusalems, 587 oder 586 v. Chr.', *ZAW* 74 (1962), pp. 209–13.

place is quite certain; but the precise nature of the destruction which followed the capture of the city and the extent of the general devastation in Judah and of the deportations of population remain a matter of debate. A discussion of the biblical evidence[20] shows how difficult it is to be certain about the relative value of the statements which are made. On the one hand, the impression is given of large-scale devastation and deliberate destruction (cf. II Kings 25); the depopulation is indicated as wholesale (25.11), in addition to executions and the probability of numerous casualties during the campaigns and sieges of Jerusalem and the other centres (notably Azekah and Lachish). On the other hand, an attempted assessment of the probable total population of Judah at this time, together with a consideration of the more modest figures provided by the parallel text to II Kings 25 in Jer. 52, has suggested that the depopulation cannot have been so extensive. The view held in extreme form by Torrey[21] that the exile

[20] Cf. E. Janssen, *Juda in der Exilszeit: Ein Beitrag zur Frage der Entstehung des Judentums* (FRLANT 69, 1956), pp. 24–56; A. C. Welch, *Post-exilic Judaism* (1935), ch. IV; S. Herrmann, *Prophetie und Wirklichkeit in der Epoche des babylonischen Exils* (Arbeiten zur Theologie I, 32, Stuttgart, 1967), pp. 9–17. Also G. Buccellati, 'Gli Israeliti di Palestina al tempo dell'esilio', *Bibbia e Oriente* 2 (1960), pp. 199–209, who finds in the book of Lamentations indications of the situation in Jerusalem, noting the concentration of the poems on that city, and suggesting that this might be in direct opposition to Gedaliah, whose centre was at Mizpah (p. 206). This interpretation would appear to be related to that which sees Mizpah as the religious centre, though the evidence for this is doubtful (cf. p. 25).

Buccellati bases his argument on the allusions in Lam. 5.2 to alien rule, 5.4 to enemy occupation (the population having to pay for water and wood), 5.11–13 to ill-treatment and forced labour, 5.5 having a general reference to the yoke of conquest. In Lam. 3.34–36 he finds other evidence of hostility to the occupation, and in particular wonders if the reference here to the Most High may not indicate the Jerusalem viewpoint, the sense that Yahweh's presence is still known there. Although he admits that the hostility could be later than Gedaliah's governorship, this he thinks less likely, and indeed we may agree that there are likely to have been various groups in Judah and certainly some hostile to Babylon in an active manner and hostile to Gedaliah as a Babylonian nominee. (A. Fenna, 'Godolia', *Enc. Catt.* 6 (1951), p. 890, is cited by Buccellati as suggesting, on the basis of Jer. 38.19 that Gedaliah may have been a deserter. The inference is doubtful, but Gedaliah's motives, like those of Jeremiah, are likely to have been questioned. Cf. p. 57.)

Such interpretation of the Lam. material as Buccellati offers is possible, but hazardous, since there is here so much stereotyped phraseology. How far can we really deduce actual political and social conditions from poetic language? The problems are very much the same as those involved in the historical interpretations of the psalms. (On Lam., cf. also below, pp. 29, 45ff.)

(I am indebted to the editor of *Bibbia e Oriente* for kindly sending me a copy of this issue.)

[21] Cf. C. C. Torrey, *The Composition and Historical Value of Ezra -Nehemiah* (BZAW 2, 1896), esp. pp. 51–65; *Ezra Studies* (Chicago, 1910), pp. 285ff.; 'The Chronicler's

hardly happened at all may readily be dismissed on the grounds of archaeological evidence for destruction in Judaean sites[22] and also of the very existence of the later view of the exile in the Chronicler; for it is impossible to believe that the later ideas grew out of little or nothing at all.[23] But there is no doubt that due attention must be given to the indications of continuity of existence which are to be found in the biblical material, and to the general probabilities of the situation, which point to some measure of immediate revival.

The assessment of numbers is inevitably hazardous. Yet comparison with the Assyrian statements from the eighth century and consideration of the biblical estimates at the time of the loss of Galilee and of Samaria in 732 and 722 respectively, make it probable that the deportations affected only a small proportion of the population.[24]

History of the Return under Cyrus', *AJSL* 37 (1920/1), pp. 81–100; *The Second Isaiah* (Edinburgh, 1928), pp. viii, 94ff.; *Pseudo-Ezekiel and the Original Prophecy* (Yale Oriental Series 18, New Haven, 1930), pp. 5, 102ff.; *The Chronicler's History of Israel* (New Haven, 1954), esp. pp. xxivff.

Torrey was himself dependent upon W. H. Kosters, *Het Herstel van Israel in het Persische Tijdvak* (Leiden, 1893), German translation *Die Wiederherstellung Israels im persischen Zeitalter* (Heidelberg, 1895). On this, cf. also G. A. Smith, *The Book of the Twelve Prophets* II (1898, 1928), p. 209 n.

The significance of Torrey's work on this problem lies not in his attempted rewriting of the history and his redating of the literature, but in his repeated stress on the importance of the Palestinian community—which has had repercussions in many more moderate studies—and in his recognition of the growth of the *idea* of the exile (cf. ch. XIII, pp. 237ff.).

[22] Cf. W. F. Albright, *The Archaeology of Palestine* (Penguin Books, rev. ed. 1960) pp. 141f.; *Archaeology of Palestine and the Bible* (New York, 1932), p. 171. Cf. also the evidence for the destruction of Engedi in the excavator's reports in *IEJ* 11 (1961), pp. 76–77; 12 (1962), pp. 145–6; and in B. Mazar and I. Dunayevsky, 'En-Gedi, Third Season of Excavations. Preliminary Report', *ibid.* 14 (1964), pp. 121–30. Cf. B. Mazar, T. Dothan, I. Dunayevsky, *Engedi excavations in 1961–62* ('*atiqot* 5, Jerusalem, 1966); B. Mazar, 'En-gedi', in *Archaeology and Old Testament Study*, ed. D. W. Thomas (1967), pp. 223–30, esp. pp. 225f. The cities are primarily in the Negeb area of Judah and in the Shephelah. These areas, according to A. Alt, 'Judas Gaue unter Josia' *PJB* 21 (1925), pp. 100–16, see p. 108=*Kl. Schr.* 2 (Munich, 1953), pp. 276–88, see p. 280, lie in the area which was separated from Judah in 598 and came into Edomite hands. Cf. E. Janssen, *op. cit.*, p. 42. D. J. Wiseman, *Illustrations from Biblical Archaeology* (London, 1958), p. 73, notes that 'towns in the south (Negeb) and to the north of the border (Bethel), and in the Babylonian province of Samaria, have been found undestroyed at this critical time'. But cf. also Y. Aharoni, 'The Negeb', in *Archaeology and Old Testament Study*, pp. 385–403, see pp. 392ff., and *BA* 31 (1968), pp. 2–52, on Arad.

[23] Cf. the comments of E. Hammershaimb, *Some Aspects of Old Testament Prophecy* (Copenhagen, 1966), pp. 97f., on the 'spiritual initiative' being with the deported. Cf. also A. Causse, *Les Dispersés d'Israël* (Paris, 1929), p. 54.

[24] On the problems of such figures, cf. H. H. Rowley, 'Hezekiah's Reform and

The removal of the landed citizens, officials and priests was probably partial, though it seems clear that a considerable social revolution was effected by the raising to positions of greater influence of those who could be described as the 'poor of the land' (*dallat hā'āreṣ*),[25] the presumably propertyless members of the community who now came to be landholders or tenants under the Babylonian authority,

---

Rebellion', *BJRL* 44 (1961/2), pp. 395–431 = *Men of God* (1963), pp. 98–132. See p. 403=p. 105: the figure of 200,000 claimed by Sennacherib may be interpreted as meaning that 'all the population of the occupied regions, generously estimated, were counted as "captives" '. Cf. bibliographical data added.

The figures for 597 and 587 are also difficult to assess. II Kings 24.14 records 10,000 captives in 597 (the eighth year of Nebuchadrezzar), but II Kings 25.11f. gives no numbers for 587, simply recording that 'the rest of the people' (*yeter hā'ām*) were taken, except for 'some of the poor of the land' (*middallat hā'āreṣ*). This latter point is covered also by Jer. 52.15f., where the text is less satisfactory. Here it is said that there were taken 'some of the poor of the people' (*middallat hā'ām*) and 'the rest of the people' (*yeter hā'ām*), where it seems likely that the first phrase is due to erroneous anticipation of the 'poor of the land' (*middallōt* [plural] *hā'āreṣ*) in v. 16. The scribe responsible may have been endeavouring to give a more complete statement by indicating that if some of the poor were left, some must have been exiled. The real point of the reference to the poor of the land may, however, be to the changed social situation.

Jer. 52.28–30 adds to the information, but not in a very illuminating manner. Here three stages of captivity are listed: in the 7th year, 3,023 *yehūdīm*; in the 18th year 832 'from Jerusalem'; in the 23rd year 745 *yehūdīm*, making a total of 4,600. E. Vogt in his account of the Wiseman volume (cf. n. 18), 'Nova Chronica Babylonica de Pugna apud Karkemiš et Expugnatione Ierusalem', *Biblica* 37 (1956), pp. 389–97, notes that Jer. 52.28 correctly attributes the fall of the city to Nebuchadrezzar's 7th year (p. 397), though in his study of the chronology in *VTS* 4 (1957), pp. 67–96, he suggests that perhaps we should read '17th year' (p. 94, n.1). A. Malamat, 'A New Record of Nebuchadrezzar's Palestinian Campaigns', *IEJ* 6 (1956), pp. 246–56 (originally published in Hebrew in *BIES* 20 [1956], pp. 179–87, IV) suggests (pp. 253ff.=pp. 185f.) that the term *yehūdīm* in Jer. 52.28 'apparently implies that the deportees were inhabitants of the provincial cities of Judah, who might have been carried away while Jerusalem was still under siege' and compares for this Jer. 13.18f. (discussed by him in 'The Last Wars of the Kingdom of Judah' *JNES* 9 [1950], pp. 218–27, cf. p. 223). He finds an analogy for this in the events of Sennacherib's campaign in 701. Both Malamat and Wiseman (*op. cit.*, pp. 34f.), appear to be attempting a harmonizing of the evidence on the basis of Josephus's statements (*Ant.* X, 6.3–7.1) that there were two deportations, of 3,000, and more than 10,000. It seems inherently more probable that Josephus has here conflated the two figures taken from the two accounts in II Kings 24–25 and Jer. 52. Malamat admits (*JNES* 9 [1950], p. 223 n. 22) that the 'various statistics for the exile of Jehoiachin contradict one another'. He reckons the total as about 10,000 men, which with their families, would mean about 30,000 actual deportees. K. Galling, *Studien* (1964), pp. 51f., estimates not more than 20,000 including wives and children.

25 While this view of the *dallat hā'āreṣ* is here accepted, some further comments are made subsequently (cf. pp. 29f., 66 n. 17) in view of the possibility that the term might carry a theological rather than a social overtone.

perhaps occupying royal lands, perhaps also taking over lands which had been expropriated from other property-owners.[26] It is reasonable also to assume, too, that there were many refugees from the Babylonian attacks who hid themselves in caves as their forefathers had done before them (cf. Judg. 6.1 ff.) and as their descendants were to do in later years.[27] At any rate, Jer. 40.7ff. describes how the 'captains of the forces in the open country' reappeared when they heard that Gedaliah had been established under the Babylonian authority, together with some of the *dallat hā'āreṣ* who were occupying property and tending it (cf. II Kings 25), and they were reassured in such a way as to suggest that, however much of destruction had taken place, the Babylonians had by no means carried out a complete devastation of the land. Gedaliah told them to 'gather wine and summer fruits and oil, and store them in your vessels, and dwell in your cities that you have taken' (40.10).[28] The narrative continues: 'Then all the Judaeans returned from all the places to which they had been driven (there is reference in the previous verse to Moab and Ammon and Edom and other lands) and came into the land of Judah, to Gedaliah to Mizpah; and they gathered wine and summer fruits in great abundance' (40.12). Mizpah, identified as Tell en-Nasbeh, is only about six miles from Jerusalem, and thus certainly not remote from the campaign area.[29] If, as appears clear, many or most of the cities of Judah were destroyed by the Babylonians, then even this did not prevent a certain measure of reoccupation.[30] A comparison with the

[26] Cf. Malamat's comments on the short-sightedness of Babylonian policy in *JNES* 9 (1950), p. 224.

[27] Cf. I Macc. 1.53; 2.31, etc., and the evidence from the Qumran region and the Judaean caves further south; e.g. J. Aviram and others, 'The Expedition to the Judean Desert, 1960', *IEJ* 11 (1961), pp. 3–72; 'The Expedition to the Judean Desert, 1961', *IEJ* 12 (1962), pp. 167–262. Such evidence could easily be multiplied.

[28] *tāpas* normally means 'capture' in such a context: perhaps here it should be understood to have the extended meaning of 'reoccupy'. Cf. *bānā*='build' or 'rebuild'.

[29] The line of advance indicated in Isa. 10.28–32 follows the other, more easterly road, via Migron, Michmash and Geba to Ramah. This may be the Assyrian route, and if the Babylonians followed the same route, Mizpah might well have been the nearest town which escaped their depredations. But it is possible that the route in Isaiah is that of the Syro-Ephraimite invaders (cf. R. B. Y. Scott in *IB* 5 [1956], p. 246), since the road is not the one to be expected: more probably the Assyrians and Babylonians would advance up the valleys from the coastal road, attacking Jerusalem and other centres (cf. Sennacherib at Lachish, II Kings 18.13, and the evidence of the Lachish letters for the period of the campaign of Nebuchadrezzar), the Babylonians having their headquarters in the north at Riblah.

[30] Cf. E. Janssen, *op. cit.* pp. 41ff.

position in Jerusalem at the time of what we may suppose to have been at least as terrible a period of devastation at the hands of Titus suggests that if people could continue then to live in caves in the hillsides of Jerusalem they could certainly re-establish themselves, even if on such a scale that little archaeological evidence remains.[31]

The condition of the Temple site also remains uncertain. Jer. 41[32] shows that some continued or revived worship was to be found there in the period of Gedaliah.[33] The Temple was burnt (II Kings 25.9);[34] the bronze pillars, furniture and 'sea' were smashed (v. 13) and the bronze itself removed; vessels remaining from the previous capture of the city were removed (vv. 14–15). The narrator speaks impressively of the vast quantity of bronze involved (vv. 16–17: cf. Jer. 52.13, 17–23). It has often been assumed that the ark, too, was destroyed.[35] Nothing is said of the altar, and it is sometimes simply assumed that it remained in position.[36] D. R. Jones[37] comments that 'It would have required a deliberate act of demolition, for it was as solid as the walls of the city.' The walls of the city were, in fact, pulled down.[38] Was

[31] Cf. K. M. Kenyon: 'Excavations in Jerusalem, 1961', *PEQ* 94 (1962), pp. 72–89, see pp. 85f., where the possibility is suggested that cave-dwellers of the first century AD (in the grounds of the church of St Peter in Gallicantu) could have been refugees at this time. Dr Kenyon, in a private communication of 5 March 1965, said that the evidence had not then been further investigated.

[32] Josephus, *Ant.* X, 9.4 reinterprets the passage by omitting any reference to worship.

[33] Not at Mizpah as proposed by F. Giesebrecht, *Das Buch Jeremia* (Göttingen, 1907), *ad loc.*; H. W. Hertzberg, 'Mizpa', *ZAW* 47 (1929), pp. 161–96, see pp. 165f.; J. N. Schofield, *The Religious Background of the Old Testament* (London, 1944), pp. 130f.; E. Hammershaimb, *Some Aspects of Old Testament Prophecy from Isaiah to Malachi* (Copenhagen, 1966), pp. 99f. Cf. the comments of D. R. Jones, *JTS* 14 (1963), p. 14 n. 2; M. Noth, 'La catastrophe de Jérusalem en l'an 587 avant Jésus-Christ et sa signification pour Israël', *RHPhR* 33 (1953), pp. 81–102, see pp. 85f.=*Ges. Stud.* (²1960), pp. 346–71, see pp. 351f., ET in *The Laws in the Pentateuch and Other Essays* (Edinburgh, 1966), pp. 260–80, see p. 264; W. Rudolph, *Jeremia* (HAT 12, 1947), p. 215 (³1968), p. 252; E. Janssen, *op. cit.*, pp. 101f., 117 and n. 7.

[34] Cf. K. Galling, *Studien*, p. 129; cf. *Verbannung und Heimkehr*, ed. A. Kuschke (Tübingen, 1961), p. 68.

[35] M. Haran, 'The Disappearance of the Ark', *IEJ* 13 (1963), pp. 46–58, argues that it had probably been removed already by Manasseh. Cf. below, p. 54.

[36] Cf. W. O. E. Oesterley, *History of Israel* II (Oxford, 1932), p. 92; A. Lods, *The Prophets and the Rise of Judaism* (ET, 1937), p. 208.

[37] 'The Cessation of Sacrifice after the Destruction of the Temple in 586 BC', *JTS* 14 (1963), pp. 12–31, see p. 12.

[38] Cf. II Kings 25.10 and the excavation reports by K. M. Kenyon, *PEQ* 94 (1962), pp. 81f.; 95 (1963), pp. 14ff.; 98 (1966), pp. 81f., and D. R. Ap-Thomas, 'Jerusalem' in *Archaeology and Old Testament Study*, ed. D. W. Thomas (1967), pp. 277–95, esp. pp. 291f.

the altar deliberately defiled? Such an action was performed by Josiah at Bethel, where, in addition to having the altar pulled down, he had human bones from near-by tombs burned on it to ensure its defilement (II Kings 23.15–16). Such a defilement certainly took place in the time of Antiochus IV Epiphanes, when the altar, having been used for alien religious practice (I Macc. 1.54; 4.38), had subsequently to be demolished and replaced (4.42–51). No such precise evidence is available for the exilic period. That it was technically defiled is likely enough, but such defilement could be brought about by many causes, and it is reasonable to suppose that regular provision was made for re-consecration.[39]

The stress in I Kings 8 on the Temple as a place of prayer, rather than as a place of sacrifice, has been thought to point to continued observances of a rather more limited kind.[40] Thus D. R. Jones has further pointed to the actual terminology used in Jer. 41.5—$minḥā$ and $lᵉbōnā$, but not $ʿōlā$. Whereas the term $minḥā$ may be used more broadly of all sacrificial offerings,[41] it is used more naturally, especially in the post-exilic period, of non-animal sacrifices.[42] He also relates to the prayer of Solomon in I Kings 8 passages in the book of Isaiah

---

[39] Cf. the interpretation of Ps. 74 by F. Willesen, 'The Cultic Situation of Psalm 74', *VT* 2 (1952), pp. 289–306. Poetry of this kind uses a variety of analogies for the idea of defilement, but the interpretation of these poetic phrases as literal description leads to dangerously uncertain ascription of such poems to precise historical moments. This is evident in the narratives in I Macc., where psalm quotations make vivid the events of the period. The phrase in Lam. 2.7:

> Yahweh has rejected his altar,
> he has despised his sanctuary

cited by D. R. Jones (*op. cit.*, p. 12 n.) as 'suggesting' the defilement is not very satisfactory evidence. The parallel between 'altar' and 'sanctuary' indicates that the phrases should not be pressed too literally.
[40] Cf. E. Janssen, *op. cit.*, p. 105. E. Hammershaimb, *op. cit.*, pp. 98f., comments on the use of this as evidence, indicating how uncertain such a conclusion is.
[41] E.g. Gen. 4.3–5. Cf. *KBL*, p. 538.
[42] R. de Vaux, *Ancient Israel* (ET, London, 1961), pp. 421ff. D. R. Jones, *op. cit.*, p. 95, appropriately adduces the evidence of the Elephantine papyri. The other passages cited are less persuasive, particularly the dubious interpretation of Mal. 1.11 as 'in every place that is censed, a pure offering is made unto my name', cf. *Haggai, Zechariah and Malachi* (TBC, 1962) pp. 186f. The rendering of $muqṭār$ as 'censed' is without parallel; elsewhere the hophʿal of the root means 'to be made to smoke as sacrifice', i.e. to be burnt, cf. Lev. 6.15, where it is used of the $minḥā$. The suggestion (cf. *BDB*, RV, RSV) that it means 'incense' here is possible, but not certain. Equally possibly it could mean 'what is burnt (sacrificed) is offered to my name, even as a pure (i.e. acceptable) offering'; or it could be interpreted impersonally 'there is a being burnt' to which $muggāš$ could be a gloss or an alternative reading, i.e. 'worship is offered'.

(Trito-Isaiah) which are quite probably, though not certainly, to be dated in the period between the advent of Cyrus and the rebuilding under Zerubbabel and Joshua. Some reference must be made to this material later (cf. pp. 227–30), but it is useful here to note that it contains denunciation of religious practices (cf. 57.3–13; 65.3–7; 66.17) in terms strongly reminiscent of the condemnation of 'Canaanite' practices in earlier denunciations.[43] This, of course, proves nothing about the Temple and its state, since wrong practice can be seen alongside legitimate religious observance at many periods in the Old Testament. The people involved are said to be 'you who are forsaking Yahweh and forgetting my holy mountain' (65.11). This latter phrase gives no indication whether or not there was a temple in Jerusalem, though one must admit that for such forsaking to be possible it might be supposed most reasonably either that a temple existed to which recourse could be had or that if a temple did not exist those condemned ought to have been concerned to re-establish it. Of the two the former appears to be more natural.[44]

The emphasis on the Temple as a place of prayer in I Kings 8[45] may indeed reflect the needs of the exilic period. But this is not all that the prayer contains. Verses 31–32 envisage the taking of an oath as a declaration of innocence, 'and the oath comes before your altar[46] in this shrine (house)': we may have here an element which belongs to the period of the Temple's actual existence—as indeed do other

---

[43] E.g. Jer. 3.6ff., 13; 7.9, 18; Deut. 16.21f.; Isa. 1.29. On one such 'stereotyped' phrase, cf. W. L. Holladay, ' "On every high hill and under every green tree" ', *VT* 11 (1961), pp. 170–6.

[44] D. R. Jones (*op. cit.*, p. 20) appears at this point to be arguing in a circle, though his conclusions are not necessarily wrong. He says that it 'is significant that the only references to sacrifice in III Isaiah (i.e. in passages which may be dated before 520 BC) are to this illicit sacrifice . . . and have nothing to do with the Jerusalem Temple'. The argument is from negative evidence; it is less dependable than one would like. But more significantly it is based on the dating of the relevant passages so as to put before 520 all those which do not reflect the existence of the Temple; passages which reflect its existence are dated later. But if a sanctuary existed between 586 and 539 or between 539 and 520, is there anything here which really comments on its actual condition and use? Cf. also H. H. Rowley, *Worship in Ancient Israel* (1967), p. 227.

[45] Cf. D. R. Jones, *op. cit.*, pp. 22–23; E. Janssen, *op. cit.*, p. 104.

[46] The use of the term *mizbah* clearly implies sacrifice, so that it is improper to maintain, as D. R. Jones and others have done, that the prayer 'contains not a single word about the Temple as a place of sacrifice'. If the prayer reflects the exilic age, the reference to the existence of the altar in the shrine is highly significant: but it is more proper to see here a use in the later form of the prayer of material reflecting an earlier situation.

passages in the prayer, where invocation is made in time of war, of famine, of drought. But it is significant that in all these cases, even where the actual existence of a fully utilized temple is presupposed, the prayer is directed to Yahweh as the one who 'will hear in heaven'. This is, of course, closely linked with the 'name-theology' so characteristic of Deuteronomy: God is in his heaven: he has caused his name to be in the shrine.[47] Such a statement may well have become even more meaningful to those exiled from their homeland,[48] but it is a commonplace of ancient thought that heavenly dwelling and shrine are in some mysterious way intimately related.[49] For the people of the exilic age to be invited—as the prayer in I Kings 8 indicates—to turn towards the Temple so that their prayers might be heard by Yahweh in his heavenly dwelling, does not involve the artificial conclusion that Yahweh was thought to be absent from his shrine. It is to recognize—as I Kings 8.27 and Isa. 66.1 recognize, and as is also indicated in the mysterious poetic fragment of I Kings 8.12–13—that Yahweh is the God of the heavens who condescends to dwell or to set his name in the shrine, but is not tied to it in any artificial manner. When Ezekiel stresses the withdrawal of Yahweh from the shrine (10.18–19; 11.22–23) and sees the prospect of his return (43.2ff.) he is not indicating a physical presence or absence,[50] but rather a denial of that protective presence which maintained the people's life and well-being through the Temple, and indicating—as we shall see subsequently and as is clear in Haggai and Zechariah 1–8 (cf. pp. 155ff., 171ff.)—that the 'real' presence of Yahweh is not be be confused with that idea of a 'tied presence' which had been frequently condemned by the earlier prophets (cf., e.g., Micah 3.11).

Rebuilding after the exile—in spite of the Chronicler's emphasis on the part played by the exiles—does not appear to have been from a totally disused site, and this would also suggest an earlier revival,

---

[47] Cf. R. E. Clements, *God and Temple* (Oxford, 1965), pp. 90ff.; W. Eichrodt, *Theology* I, p. 106.

[48] Cf. D. R. Jones, *op. cit.*, p. 23 and n. 3.

[49] Cf. R. E. Clements, *op. cit.*, pp. 68f.; 90ff.

[50] D. R. Jones, *op. cit.*, p. 21 n. 3, would seem here to confuse the issue by assuming that Ezekiel (and Second Isaiah) believed in an actual physical presence of Yahweh in his Temple. In view of the nature of their theological thinking this seems highly improbable, and indeed it may even be that it was the level of their thought which made possible the use of language and metaphor which if taken literally would seem to be markedly anthropomorphic (cf. Isa. 51.9–11 and also the use of such mythological material in Job). Cf. R. E. Clements, *op. cit.*, pp. 102ff.

a clearance of the site, an improvised or temporary altar. Janssen indeed finds evidence for the existence of such an altar in the opening of Ezra 3 in the implication that re-establishment of the altar in its original place provoked the opposition of those who had been accustomed to using a different altar.[51] The evidence for such an interpretation is far from clear. The general probability is that so sacred a site as that of the Jerusalem Temple could not have been thought to have lost its sanctity entirely and that some attempts must have been made at re-use.[52]

Janssen's study is devoted entirely to a consideration of the situation in Judah during the exilic period. He is therefore concerned to demonstrate what parts of the Old Testament material are likely to have originated there and so to utilize them for depicting the situation and thought.[53] If his judgement of the Palestinian origin of the Deuteronomic History and of Lamentations and of various prophetic passages is correct,[54] then we have impressive evidence for the existence in Judah of a community which was able to produce very substantial and profound assessments of the meaning of the events and their significance for the development of thought. To some extent we may then be compelled to see that where II Kings speaks of the leaving of only some of the *dallat hā'āreṣ* it is likely to be stressing the impression which the situation made rather than giving a precise description of it. According to Jer. 5.4 the 'poor' (*dallīm*) 'have no sense for they do not know the religion of Yahweh, the proper

---

[51] *Op. cit.*, pp. 102f. Cf. D. R. Jones, *op .cit.*, pp. 13, 16f.

[52] Cf. the comment of F. I. Andersen, 'Who built the Second Temple?' *ABR* 6 (1958), pp. 1–35, see p. 8. In reference to the uncertainties of the exilic period, Andersen concludes: 'All we need notice among the several reconstructions of the period is a common feeling, judicious enough, among historians of this time that there must have been some kind of religious life in Jerusalem during the exile.'
A. C. Welch's view that Neh. 10.2–28 (with which he relates various other passages) provides a list of clergy and laity representing a Judaean remnant and northern loyal Yahwists concerned in reviving Temple worship after 586 is highly speculative (*Post-exilic Judaism* [1935], pp. 67–86). It is odd to read his comment a few pages later on a theory concerning the Sheshbazzar-Shenazzar problem (cf. below, p. 143): 'Now it may be that I have an undue dose of Scottish caution. But this glittering fabric of conjecture piled on hypothesis leaves the impression of great ingenuity rather than of discovering the sober basis of history' (*op. cit.*, p. 106). As not infrequently, one man's sober statement is another's wild conjecture.

[53] Cf. *op. cit.*, pp. 9–23, on the sources available.

[54] Janssen lists: Lamentations, Isa. 21, the Deuteronomic History, Obadiah, Pss. 44, 74, 79, 89, 102. Cf. further below, pp. 65ff. Some scholars, e.g. J. D. Smart, would place Deutero-Isaiah in Palestine (*History and Theology in Second Isaiah* [Philadelphia, 1965], pp. 10–39; cf. below, p. 120).

requirements (*mišpāṭ*) of their God'.[55] To take this as a general judgement may well be wrong, for Jeremiah is here using poetic hyperbole
in stressing the total failure of his people. Yet it would appear that
to those among whom the Deuteronomic movement was found, the
dallat hā'āreṣ were not impressive—in general—for their piety and
religious understanding. If there were pious among them—and the
Old Testament narrative not infrequently suggests that this is likely
to have been so—the general impression will not have been so very
unlike that of almost any community, in which the proportion of
those who make a serious effort to understand and to face the problems of life is small compared with those who—no doubt partly for
reasons of necessity and the pressure of conditions—live from hand to
mouth with little time to concern themselves with the broader issues.
Existence for the Judaean peasant can hardly have been more con-
ducive to constructive thinking then than it is for such people now.
If there was much production of literature in Judah itself during the
exilic period, then either there must have been present a larger proportion of those who were educated and used to positions of responsibility or the changed social conditions must have made it possible
for the abilities of some of the less favoured groups to be revealed as
they took on new responsibility and became full citizens. Probably
both of these happened.[56] Later judgements on the *'am hā'āreṣ* equate
the term in some instances with the religiously illiterate; the term
cannot in all contexts be regarded as a complimentary one.[57] Both
this term and the term *dallat hā'āreṣ* can only be interpreted precisely
in the contexts in which they occur. It is probable that at this point,
while there were some—perhaps many—of those who took on new
responsibilities and became influential whose religious ideas were
undesirable and who could therefore rightly be accused later of fostering alien religious practice,[58] there must have been others, particularly in the entourage of Gedaliah, of whom no word of criticism is
ever spoken in the Old Testament material,[59] who responded to the

---

[55] For *derek*=religion, cf. Jer. 10.1–16; P. R. Ackroyd, 'Jeremiah X. 1–16',
JTS 14 (1963), pp. 385–90, see p. 388 notes 1, 3, 8. For *mišpāṭ* in this sense, cf. II
Kings 17.27.
[56] Cf. also below, p. 66 n. 17.
[57] For some comments on the use of *'am hā'āreṣ*, cf. below, p. 150 n. 50.
[58] Cf., e.g., Isa. 57.1–10.
[59] E. Janssen, *op. cit.*, pp. 47f.; K. Baltzer, 'Das Ende des Staates Juda und die
Messias-Frage', *Studien zur Theologie der alttestl. Überlieferungen*, ed. R. Rendtorff
and K. Koch (Neukirchen, 1961), pp. 33–43, see pp. 34ff.

new situation. The contrast, as always, is not between one social class and another—though this may often appear in the nomenclature used; it is between those who were sensitive to the demands of God and those who were not, and these differences of reaction no doubt showed themselves in the differing attitudes towards the events which had taken place and to the interpretations which were to be put upon them.

3. THE SITUATION IN BABYLONIA

The situation in Babylonia is equally difficult to describe with precision.[60] A tantalizingly allusive piece of information about food allocations made to Jehoiachin and his family as well as to various craftsmen, possibly foreign craftsmen from Jerusalem,[61] leaves us in doubt as to whether the exiles were treated as captives in the strictest sense, kept on small rations, or whether they were given reasonably generous allocations.[62] The subsequent reference to the release of Jehoiachin indicates imprisonment, but we have no means of knowing whether the imprisonment was constrictive or reasonably humane, except that it is clear that Jehoiachin's royal status was acknowledged.[63] Of the other exiles we have little knowledge apart from the

[60] For a general statement, cf. K. Galling, *Studien* (1964), pp. 52f. Cf. also the older study of E. Klamroth, *Die jüdischen Exulanten in Babylonien* (BWAT 10, 1912), for a detailed examination of relevant texts, somewhat outmoded in its approach, but containing much useful information on the more material aspects; A. Causse, *Les Dispersés d'Israël* (1929), pp. 24–31. The study by E. Ebeling, *Aus dem Leben der jüdischen Exulanten in Babylonien* (Wissenschaftliche Beilage zum Jahresbericht des Humboldt-Gymnasium, Berlin, No. 71, 1914) contains only an account of the *Murašu* documents, translation of them, and a list of Jewish names occurring in them. (Cf. below, p. 32 n. 65.)

[61] Cf. II Kings 24.14, 16, and compare Weidner's comment on p. 935 of the article cited in the next note.

[62] Cf. E. F. Weidner, 'Jojachin, König von Judae in babylonischen Keischrifttexten', *Mélanges Syriens offerts à M. René Dussaud* II (Paris, 1939), pp. 923–35. The tablets are to be dated between 595/594 and 570/569. One of the relevant texts is dated in the thirteenth year of Nebuchadrezzar. Cf. *DOTT*, pp. 84–86; *ANET*, p. 308. The tablets indicate quantities, but not the period for which these quantities were allocated, though Weidner (p. 924) states that allocations were made monthly. Cf. F. M. T. de Liagre Böhl, 'Nebukadnezar en Jojachin', *NTS* 25 (1942), pp. 121–5 = *Opera Minora* (Groningen, 1953), pp. 423–9. W. F. Albright, 'King Joiachin in Exile', *BA* 5 (1942), pp. 49–55, (=*BA Reader* [1961], pp. 106–12), suggests later imprisonment as a result of suspicious activities. Cf. also D. Winton Thomas, *PEQ* 82 (1950), pp. 5–8.

[63] This fact has very great importance for understanding both the situation in Judah (cf. A. Malamat, *JNES* 9 [1950], p. 224, and 'Jeremiah and the Last Two

indirect information in Ezekiel and Jeremiah for the early years of the exile. Here the indications are of reasonable freedom, of settlement in communities—perhaps engaged in work for the Babylonians, but possibly simply engaged in normal agricultural life—of the possibility of marriage, of the ordering of their own affairs, of relative prosperity.[64] That subsequently we find Jewish individuals engaged in trade proves nothing for the conditions in the early sixth century BC, since the Murashu evidence belongs to the Persian period and is at least a century later.[65] The uncongenial nature of the situation should not, however, be understated.[66] The heartfelt cry of Psalm 137 suggests real sensitivity to its oppressiveness; so, too, does the distress of Ezekiel (e.g. in 4.14) and that of his compatriots who feel themselves to be as 'dry bones', crushed under the weight of disaster, and either complaining of the injustice of what has befallen them (Ezek. 18) or of the impossibility of escape from the consequences of divine judgement (Ezek. 37).

There is little on which any conclusion can be based regarding worship in the exilic situation.[67] The frequently voiced supposition that this is when synagogues emerged is without clear foundation.[68] If the school of thought is right[69] which places their origin in the

---

Kings of Judah', *PEQ* 83 [1951], pp. 81–87) and that in Babylonia. (Cf. below on Ezek. and Deutero-Isaiah, pp. 114, 125ff.) Cf. also the article by K. Baltzer quoted in p. 30 n. 59 above, and M. Noth, *RHPhR* 33 (1953), pp. 87, 99ff.=*Ges. Stud.* (²1960), pp. 353f., 369f.; ET *The Laws in the Pentateuch and other Essays* (Edinburgh, 1966), pp. 266f., 278f.

[64] Cf. S. Daiches, *The Jews in Babylonia in the Time of Ezra and Nehemiah according to Babylonian Inscriptions* (Jews' College Publication 2, London, 1910), p. 6. But compare also E. Klamroth, *op. cit.*, for a less favourable assessment.

[65] Cf. *DOTT*, pp. 95f., where T. Fish emphasizes that the firm was not a Jewish firm, though a small proportion of their clients bear Jewish names. G. Cardascia, *Les Archives des Murašû. Une famille d'hommes d'affaires babyloniens à l'époque perse (455–403 av. J.—C.)* (Paris, 1951).

[66] Cf. E. Klamroth, *op. cit.*, pp. 31ff.

[67] Cf. the very brief review in H.-J. Kraus, *Worship in Israel* (ET, 1966), pp. 229–31.

[68] For a review, with ample bibliographical reference, cf. H. H. Rowley, *Worship in Ancient Israel* (1967), pp. 213ff. It is unnecessary here to cover the same ground or to give references to all the discussions of the question.

[69] Cf., e.g., A. Menes, 'Tempel und Synagoge', *ZAW* 50 (1932), pp. 268–76, who, from an examination of a variety of biblical passages, presents the view that much of the literature of the exilic age is concerned with providing a substitute for the Temple. 'The substitute for the ancient cultus had to correspond as closely as possible to its original. In response to this need there arose a fairly extensive literature concerning the nature of the building of the Jerusalem Temple (Ezek.

exile, then the subject should be treated in this discussion. But no concrete evidence exists to confirm this. Ps. 137 has been thought to provide an indication of assemblies by water,[70] and is linked by Kraus to the vision of Ezekiel by the Chebar;[71] but Ps. 137.4 has also been thought to provide a counterweight to such conjecture by implying that worship was totally impossible in such a situation, though we may doubt whether a poetic utterance of distress such as this should be generalized into proof of anything.[72] The fact that a group of elders comes together seeking the advice of Ezekiel[73] may or may not indicate an act of worship. Kraus again makes an assumption: 'It is here that new ways of cultic expression were no doubt explored'; but as so often the lack of evidence is covered by the 'no doubt', and Kraus goes on to admit that 'all the presuppositions were lacking, for the exiles had neither cultic objects nor insignia'.[74] It has been argued that the elders were wishing to develop some new kind of worship. Thus M. Schmidt states: 'We are not told what the elders had in mind when they came to him (Ezekiel), but it is very probable that it was a plan to build a new Temple for Yahweh in Babylonia.'[75] They may have been engaging in some act of worship; they may have had such a plan in mind. The passage which follows provides no satisfactory clue, for its attack on the faithlessness and idolatry of the whole people throughout its history[76] could be

---

40–48) or of the Tabernacle (cf. the relevant Pentateuchal passages) to the pattern of which synagogues were to be built' (p. 275). Similarly the sacrificial laws had to be set out so that they could be used for public reading. This argument depends upon an interpretation of P as anti-Jerusalem and anti-Temple. It also seems to overlook the fact that Temple and synagogue were not alternatives, but existed, at some periods, even in Jerusalem, side by side, and had different functions. (Cf. K. Galling, 'Synagoge' *RGG* 6 [³1962], col. 557; H. H. Rowley, *op. cit.*, pp. 229f.)

[70] Cf. Acts 16.13.
[71] *Op. cit.*, p. 229. Kraus states that 'it is reasonable to assume that the cultic assemblies of the exiles were held in the same place'. But have we any right to make any such assumption? It would appear at least equally possible either that later religious practice—such as Acts 16.13 suggests—in part evolved from the interpretation of such a passage as Ps. 137, or that those who were familiar with such places of prayer 'searched the scriptures' in order to discover a sound basis for an existing practice which could have had other origins.
[72] On this psalm, cf. also p. 225.
[73] Ezek. 8.1; 14.1; 20.1.
[74] *Loc. cit.*
[75] *Prophet und Tempel* (Zurich, 1948), p. 154. Again the 'very probable' covers the lack of evidence.
[76] Cf. below, p. 110.

regarded as a sermon preached in some kind of assembly. It could be directed against a specific proposal. But it more probably represents a further development of the homiletic tradition already clearly known in the Deuteronomic expositions of law and history and to be found also in the book of Jeremiah and frequently elsewhere in Ezekiel. The elders here are not very clearly real figures, performing some regular duty, but rather stylized representatives of the people to whom the prophetic message is addressed.

Ezek. 11.16 states that God will be for the exiles a *miqdāš mᵉʿaṭ*; this may mean a 'temporary sanctuary'[77] or 'a sanctuary in small measure';[78] it could denote an actual building, for the absolute prohibition of other sanctuaries according to the Deuteronomic law does not automatically mean that the injunction was universally accepted or obeyed, nor is it certain that it was applied outside Palestine.[79]

Real evidence of synagogues belongs to a later period, though we may be permitted to see in Ezra's reading of the law in Neh. 8 a picture of the kind of practice familiar at the beginning of the fourth century BC. It may be justifiable to read back from this to earlier practice—even pre-exilic practice[80]—as is indicated by the presuppositions of Deut. 31.11 or by the possible *Sitz im Leben* of the sermon-speeches of Deuteronomy and other books.[81] The conclusions

---

[77] So RSV.

[78] Cf. W. Zimmerli, *Ezechiel* (BK 13, 1956ff.), pp. 29f., who indicates (cf. Lev. 19.30; 26.2) that *miqdāš* may denote the presence of the person of God: i.e. it could as it were represent a 'token' presence of God. G. Fohrer, *Ezechiel* (HAT 13, 1955), p. 61, treats it as a later gloss, and therefore irrelevant to the exilic situation.

[79] Cf. the later existence of shrines at Leontopolis and elsewhere, as discussed by F. M. Cross, 'Aspects of Samaritan and Jewish History in Late Persian and Hellenistic Times', *HTR* 59 (1966), pp. 201–11, see p. 207. He instances also 'Arâq el-Emîr (cf. P. Lapp, *BASOR* 171 [Oct. 1963], pp. 8–39, see pp. 29ff., and M. J. B. Brett, *ibid.* pp. 39–45), Gerizim, and tentatively Qumran. On this subject, cf. R. de Vaux, *Ancient Israel* (ET, 1961), pp. 339ff. Also C. C. Torrey, *Ezra Studies* (1910), pp. 316f. (Note Deut. 12.1: 'all the days that you live on the ground' i.e. of Palestine.)

[80] The period of religious centralization—that of Josiah or still earlier that of Hezekiah—raises questions to which the answers are unknown. Could all worship be centred in one place? What did the ordinary Israelite do by way of formal observance other than at the great festivals? Could this be the point at which the much older observance of the sabbath came to be emphasized (cf. below)? If so, what kind of observance would be likely? Cf. also H. H. Rowley, *op. cit.*, pp. 222ff. The possible earlier origin of the institution is argued by J. Weingreen, 'The origin of the synagogue', *Hermathena* 98 (1964), pp. 68–84; the arguments are suggestive rather than precise.

[81] Cf. E. Janssen, *op cit.*, pp. 105–15, and cf. the comment above on Ezek. 20.

can, however, be nothing but tentative, like so many which are drawn on the basis of form-critical analysis of Old Testament material, and it is essential to recognize the complete uncertainty of the matter.[82] For this reason, no assumptions have been made here about the exilic situation and the subject is not further discussed.

We may, however, note one other aspect of this problem. This is the further assumption that, in default of other religious observances, institutions such as that of the sabbath and rites such as circumcision came into prominence.[83] Not that it is doubted that the sabbath was of much earlier origin, but it is claimed that 'with the loss of the holy place the "holy time" became more important'.[84] It is further suggested that this can be traced particularly in Ezekiel[85] and the Priestly writings. There is no doubt of the importance of the emphasis, both in relation to the observance of the sabbath and to the warning against desecration. It is also clear that the Priestly writings offer a particular interpretation of the sabbath in relation to creation.[86] Yet we may hesitate to pronounce on this interpretation as having originated in the exilic period, since there is no good reason for supposing that the creation narrative of Gen. 1 was a completely new composition of the sixth century, or that the interpretation of the sabbath in Ex. 20.8-11 in relation to creation was thought up at that time. The fact that in Deut. 5.12-15 a quite different interpretation is offered points to the diversity of religious tradition within the community which could develop the understanding of the one basic law of the sabbath in such sharply divergent ways. The most that we can say is that, like other aspects of Israel's religious life, it was re-examined and re-presented in the exilic age, and to this there testify the various

[82] Cf. R. de Vaux, *Ancient Israel* (ET, 1961), pp. 343f. H. H. Rowley, *op. cit.*, pp. 224-7, accepts the exilic date as 'more likely' than other proposals: it can 'claim much probability'.

[83] Cf., for example, the discussion by H.-J. Kraus, *op. cit.*, pp. 87ff., 230.

[84] H.-J. Kraus, *op. cit.*, p. 87. Cf. also G. von Rad, *Genesis* (ET, OTL, 1961), p. 60.

[85] But on the interpretation of the Ezekiel material, cf. W. Eichrodt, 'Der Sabbat bei Hesekiel: Ein Beitrag zur Nachgeschichte des Prophetentextes', in *Lex Tua Veritas* (*Festschrift H. Junker*), ed. H. Gross and F. Messner (Trier, 1961), pp. 65-74. Eichrodt points out that there is no special emphasis on the sabbath in Ezek. 44-46; the references in ch. 20, 22, 23 are, he considers, linked to the P tradition; this material has been used in the later elaboration of the Ezekiel tradition. This view, which perhaps oversimplifies literary relationships, indicates the uncertainty of the evidence adduced for associating the sabbath particularly with the exilic period.

[86] Cf. below, pp. 94f.

works which we shall subsequently be examining in more detail.[87] The same point is to be made in regard to circumcision, also an ancient rite, described in various narratives of different periods, and subject therefore to reinterpretation; but whether it became specially prominent in the exilic period is unknown. Its greater prominence in the Priestly Work[88] provides some indication of a further development in its interpretation, but already in Jeremiah[89] a spiritualized interpretation is evident, which may suggest that there were earlier stages in the evolution of the thought concerning the rite than those precisely known to us. Here again the general statement that it is not hard to find an explanation for it becoming 'the distinctive mark of a man who belonged to Israel and to Yahweh',[90] is of a kind which is made without any real reference to evidence. Some ancient peoples appear to have dropped the custom; Israel maintained and reinterpreted it. But precisely when this happened is not clear.[91] The whole theme is one of great obscurity, and the evidence insufficiently secure for it to be proper merely to repeat here the assertions that the exilic age was the special moment for its reinterpretation and emphasis.[92]

There are some indications to suggest that the relatively congenial situation of the early part of the exile did not last.[93] The policy of the

---

[87] Cf. below ch. v–viii. On the sabbath theme, cf. also J. J. Stamm and M. E. Andrew, *The Ten Commandments in Recent Research* (SBT II, 2, 1967), pp. 90–95; and A. R. Hulst, 'Bemerkungen zum Sabbatgebot' in *Studia Biblica et Semitica T. C. Vriezen dedicata* (Wageningen, 1966), pp. 152–64.

[88] Cf. R. E. Clements, *Abraham and David* (SBT II, 5, 1967), pp. 73f.

[89] Cf., e.g., 9.24. Cf. Deut. 10.16.

[90] So R. de Vaux, *op. cit.*, p. 48; cf. H.-J. Kraus, *op. cit.*, p. 230.

[91] R. de Vaux, *op. cit.*, pp. 47f., reminds us that the term 'uncircumcised' was early used for the Philistines; by implication, Semites practised the rite. Ezek. 32.30 describes the Sidonians as uncircumcised; Judith 14.10 the Ammonites. But between the period of the Philistines or even that of the narratives concerning them and the time of Ezekiel there is a fair lapse of years. We cannot know how far the rite had developed or how far elsewhere it had lapsed during this period. We also need to consider the nature of the reference in each case; thus it may be that Ezek. 32.30 simply witnesses to the alien nature of the Sidonians, and does not necessarily bear the weight given to it by de Vaux.

[92] A different theme is developed by V. Maag, 'Erwägungen zur deuteronomischen Kultzentralisation', *VT* 6 (1956), pp. 10–18. He suggests that centralization, involving also the de-sacralizing of animal slaughter for food, alleviated the conditions of the exile; for without this change of practice the exiles would have been in very considerable difficulty. This may be so, but we may wonder whether, then as now, expedients would not readily have been found to meet the case; we may compare the incident described in I Sam. 14.31–35.

[93] Cf. J. M. Wilkie, 'Nabonidus and the Later Jewish Exiles', *JTS* 2 (1951), pp. 34–44.

later neo-Babylonian ruler Nabonidus, is, as we have seen, not altogether simple to follow. Information about it derives partly from hostile sources, and although there are some indications of the positive aspects of his policy, it is not clear just what he was hoping to achieve. It is probable that a combination of political, economic and religious motives led to an attempt at achieving greater coherence and unity, and that this involved him in religious actions which to the Babylonian population itself appeared undesirable—or at least to the priesthood whose position was threatened by him.[94] The survival in Jewish circles of stories concerning the exilic period, perhaps originally concerning Nabonidus and later transferred to Nebuchadrezzar as the destroyer of Jerusalem is suggested by the Qumran fragment parallel to Dan. 4.[95] The view that Nabonidus was mad[96] and possibly also that he attempted to impose religious uniformity—on the assumption that the story in Dan. 3 might also originally have been a Nabonidus tradition[97]—was in circulation in the Babylonian Jewish community. Perhaps it originated in a combination of genuine reminiscences of hardships in the later exilic period—with possible repercussions in the words of Deutero-Isaiah—and of Babylonian popular tales about the rulers of the previous dynasty, circulating under the Persians, like that which in I Esdras 3–4 is associated with Darius I, and those which survive in Esther and possibly in Judith and Tobit and the Additions to Daniel. Yet with all this it must be admitted that there is relatively little of violent hostility to Babylon in either Ezekiel or Deutero-Isaiah (ch. 47), though something also (ch. 46) of ridiculing of the Babylonian gods. Hostility is to be found in Isa. 13–14 and 21;[98] in Jer. 50 and 51; and in Zechariah. The last may with greater probability reflect the situation in the time of

[94] Cf. above, pp. 19f. T. Fish in *DOTT*, pp. 89–91; A. L. Oppenheim in *ANET*, pp. 308–15, esp. pp. 314f.

[95] Cf. Millar Burrows, *More Light on the Dead Sea Scrolls* (London, 1958), pp. 169, 173, 247, 400, including references to discussions of this point; N. W. Porteous, *Daniel* (OTL, 1965), p. 70; O. Plöger, *Das Buch Daniel* (KAT 18, 1965), p. 76; A. Bentzen, *Daniel* (HAT 19, 1952), p. 45. Cf. also O. Eissfeldt, *Introduction*, p. 663.

[96] Cf. 'The Verse Account of Nabonidus', *ANET*, pp. 312ff. (A. L. Oppenheim), see p. 314.

[97] Cf. earlier W. von Soden, 'Eine babylonische Volksüberlieferung von Nabonid in den Danielerzählungen', *ZAW* 53 (1935), pp. 81–89; S. Smith, *op. cit.*, p. 132.

[98] Cf. K. Galling, *Studien* (1964), p. 20, on Isa. 21, 45 and 47, and pp. 53f. on Isa. 13–14, Jer. 50.8–10; 51.6, 45; and 'Jesaia 21 im Lichte der neuen Nabonidtexte', in *Tradition und Situation*, ed. E. Würthwein and O. Kaiser (Göttingen, 1963), pp. 49–62. On some of these passages, cf. below, pp. 219ff.

Darius I, when there is a possibility that the Jews had less sympathy with the Babylonian rebels than with the Persians in whom they had hope of restoration.[99] The other oracles might also belong to this later situation, though perhaps rather more probably reflect the viewpoint of some members of the community at the very outset of the exile. There is no need to look for a uniformity of view at any one period, since diversity in reaction is to be expected. The reactions to the disaster were presumably almost as many as those who expressed them in speech and writing.

[99] On this, cf. below, pp. 179f.

III

THE RESPONSE TO THE EVENTS

A. GENERAL CONSIDERATIONS

SOMETHING IS TO BE said subsequently about the major reactions to the exilic period—those of Jeremiah, Ezekiel and
Deutero-Isaiah, the Deuteronomic History and the Priestly
Work, and about the developments from these in the post-exilic
period. It is possible also to make some general comments about the
reactions of the members of the community, both in Judah and in
Babylonia,[1] reactions which cannot necessarily be fully documented,
but which are sufficiently to be seen in the material at our disposal.
Uncertainty about the dating of individual passages makes it virtually
impossible to say how far we can detect immediate reactions and how
far we are looking at reflections on the events from some distance. In
the nature of the case, however, both those who actually experienced
the disaster and those who for one reason or another were not directly
involved in the fall of the city and kingdom, are hardly likely to have
recorded their feelings immediately: an element of reflection and
interpretation is surely present. Thus there are indications of the
numbing effect of the calamity;[2] but the use of conventional language
does not enable us easily to detect precisely what is involved.

[1] Some mention is made in what follows of the reactions of those who took
refuge in Egypt as described in Jer. 41.11–44.30. The negative comment of Jeremiah (44.24–30) is not altogether clear or consistent, since it appears to envisage
total rejection (vv. 26–27, 29) and a small remnant which will return to Judah
(v. 28). It is clear that Jeremiah saw no future for them in Egypt: it is altogether
unknown to us what became of them. But at the same time it must be evident that
some members of that group (? including Baruch) did return to Judah, since the
preservation of the description and oracle presupposes some continuity. (Cf. also
below, pp. 55f., 67.) For the Egyptian diaspora, cf. A. Causse, *Les Dispersés d'Israël*
(1929), pp. 17–23.
[2] Cf. J. Bright, *A History of Israel* (1960), p. 329, citing Isa. 63.19; Ezek. 33.10;
37.11.

The main types of reaction may be conveniently arranged under four headings. Two of these are, as it were, negative and two positive.

I. RETURN TO OLDER CULTS

The evidence of Ezek. 8, of Jer. 44, of certain passages in Zechariah and Trito-Isaiah, and that of Deuteronomy and its History, shows that there were not a few members of the community whose reaction to the disaster was to turn to the worship of other deities, and particularly of the old, familiar deities of Canaan. Ezek. 8 presumably reflects the religious situation in the interim period between the two falls of Jerusalem, and to some extent may represent the infiltration of Babylonian cults into Jerusalem. The precise nature of the cults here described is not clear, apart from the direct mention of Tammuz (v. 14). No doubt the allusions were clear enough originally, though it is possible that the chapter has been overlaid partly with later interpretation and partly with an intentional vagueness to avoid offence in public reading.[3] The stress (in 8.12 and 9.9) is upon 'Yahweh has forsaken his land, he does not see'. Jer. 44 provides a completely clear example of reversion to an older cult, and in view of the close relationship between the books of Jeremiah and Deuteronomy we may reasonably assume that this is intended as

---

[3] The suggestion, e.g. by J. Smith, *The Book of the Prophet Ezekiel: A New Interpretation* (London, 1931), pp. 18ff., that this passage cannot be dated in this period because we have no other knowledge of the practice of such cults at this time appears to beg the question. If it can be established on other grounds that parts of the book of Ezekiel are of earlier origin, this could be regarded as reflecting a different time. But even such a conclusion is not necessarily correct. Similarly the contrast between Ezekiel's visionary experience here described and the Jeremiah material in which no such precise indications are given has led Kaufmann to see here reflections of an earlier age, the earlier practices, though no longer in vogue, having not yet received their true retribution (Y. Kaufmann, *The Religion of Israel* [ET, London, 1961], p. 430). But while this may in part be true, it is reasonable to accept that there was sufficient such practice for Ezekiel's condemnations to be relevant, even if his descriptions are poetic. Kaufmann appears to overdo his unwillingness to take Ezekiel's allusions seriously: but other scholars have certainly built too much on obscure passages. (Cf. H. H. Rowley, 'The Book of Ezekiel in Modern Study', *BJRL* 36 (1953/4), pp. 146–90 = *Men of God* (London, 1963), pp. 169–210.) G. Fohrer, *Ezechiel* (HAT 13, 1955), pp. 50ff., comments on the various rituals mentioned, and notes particularly the possibility of allusions to Egyptian cult practices here, presumably introduced under pressure of Egyptian rule (608–605) or by those who favoured an Egyptian alliance. Cf. also W. Zimmerli, *Ezechiel* (BK 13, 1956ff.), pp. 209ff.

a typical case. The disaster is attributed to the neglect of the worship of the Queen of Heaven. It provides indirect evidence for the carrying through of Josiah's Reform—though here again we have to recognize the possibility that the affinity with the Deuteronomic work has been responsible for the form of the material. But more important for our present purpose is the nature of the reaction. There are some members of the community for whom the disaster finds its explanation in the neglect not of Yahweh but of another deity, evidently familiar over a long period of time.[4] The other indications in the earlier Old Testament material of the existence of this cult are hereby confirmed, and so, too, is the recognition of Israel's syncretistic tendencies. The stress in the Deuteronomic material (and to a lesser degree in the Holiness Code) on the destruction of Canaan and its gods is simply the obverse of this.[5] This is what ought to have happened; it is a necessary preliminary to any future. It is directed, not in theory to a distant past, nor to a present generation for whom such worship of alien deities is unreal, but to a community for whom this is a contemporary problem which must be resolved drastically.[6]

2. ACCEPTANCE OF THE RELIGION OF THE CONQUERORS

If the Ezekiel description does indicate in part the infiltration of Babylonian religious ideas, then we have already evidence of the second type of reaction, related to the first. The difference is simply that the first represents a regression to older practice; the second represents the acceptance of the obvious consequences of Babylonian conquest, namely that the Babylonian gods have been victorious.[7] The successes of the Assyrians in the period of Tiglath-pileser and his successors led to the willingness of Ahaz to accept not only Assyrian suzerainty but also at least a token observance of Assyrian religion.[8] The same is evidently true in the harshly condemned period of Manasseh, when subservience to Assyria inevitably carried with it a

---

[4] Cf. D. N. Freedman, 'The Biblical Idea of History', *Interpretation* 21 (1967), pp. 32–49, see pp. 33ff.

[5] Cf., e.g., Deut. 7.23ff.; 9.2f.; 12.2f.; Lev. 18.3, 24f.

[6] Cf. below, pp. 73ff.

[7] Y. Kaufmann, *op. cit.*, p. 441, affirms that there was no idea of the superiority of Babylonia's gods over Yahweh. He bases this on the lack of attacks on such a view, and on a rather twisted interpretation of Ezek. 20.32–44.

[8] II Kings 16.10ff.

42   THE RESPONSE TO THE EVENTS

religious acceptance. We should expect the same to be true of the
Babylonian period. But the probability is that we should recognize a
rather fuller acceptance than this relatively formal one.[9] For in
Deutero-Isaiah we find protests against alien religion and polemical
statements about the oneness and absoluteness of Yahweh which are
to be understood not as the first statements of real monotheism but
as directed against on the one hand the Babylonian claims for their
own deities and on the other hand the acceptance of those deities by
Jews. It is true that the polemic of Isa. 44.9ff. does not indicate the
nature of the deities worshipped, but is directed against the absurdity
of images. But it is clear that this is directed to Jews and it seems
reasonable enough to suppose that it is concerned in part at least
with the acceptance of Babylonian gods.[10] Elsewhere in Deutero-
Isaiah the Babylonian gods are directly ridiculed (46.1f.). The thought
of worshipping other gods—equally ridiculed as being nothing but
wood and stone—is to be found in Ezek. 20.32. It seems right to
see here the despairing outlook of those who see no hope for the
future, and look only to an assimilation to the ways of the nations.[11]
The prophet's forceful repudiation of such an idea is only too vivid a
testimony to the reality of its experience. Similarly, though less
directly, we may see in the kind of story preserved in the book of
Daniel[12] a reflection of the reaction of Babylonian Jewry, now made
to serve as a warning to those who face the similar situation of the
Maccabaean period. The setting up of a great image—whether or
not it has a historical basis in the period of Nabonidus[13]—represents
the kind of domination which Babylonian religion is likely to have

[9] When N. W. Porteous, 'Jerusalem-Zion: The Growth of a Symbol', in
Verbannung und Heimkehr, ed. A. Kuschke (1961), pp. 235–52, see p. 237, says that
the view that Yahweh was impotent 'was decisively rejected' . . . 'not to be
entertained by responsible men', it is clear that this is true so far as the continuing
Old Testament religious tradition is concerned. We cannot, however, measure
just how much loss of faith there was, any more than we can assess the degree of
apostasy in such another period as that of Antiochus IV Epiphanes.
[10] J. D. Smart, *History and Theology in Second Isaiah* (1965), p. 114, interprets
more generally, but comments on the pressure of the temptation to idolatry in
this seemingly hopeless situation. Cf. also Ezek. 20 and the comments of G.
Fohrer, *Ezechiel* (HAT 13, 1955), pp. 107ff.
[11] So W. Zimmerli, *Ezechiel* (BK 13, 1956ff.), pp. 453f.; cf. also 'Le nouvel
"Exode" dans le message des deux grands prophètes de l'Exil', in *Maqqél shâqédh*,
Hommage à W. Vischer (Montpellier, 1960), pp. 216–27, see pp. 217f. = *Gottes
Offenbarung*, pp. 193f.
[12] E.g. Dan. 3 and 6. Cf. also Additions to Daniel.
[13] Cf. above, p. 37.

exerted over those whose faith was not large enough to compass disaster as a direct outcome of the will of Yahweh himself.

3. THE RECOGNITION OF DIVINE JUDGEMENT

The idea of a deity judging and bringing disaster upon his own people is a very ancient one.[14] It is therefore not altogether without precedent to find the reaction of acceptance and penitence, though we may not unreasonably recognize that in the case of the Jewish community this acceptance issued in much more positive results than we may suppose to have been the case, with, for example, the Moabites. For the reaction expressed on the Moabite stone— recognition of the wrath of Chemosh—appears, so far as we know, not to have led to any ultimate realization of the total purpose of that deity for Moab, whereas the Old Testament depicts a deeper understanding and acceptance.[15] The assessment of 'might have beens' is never very satisfactory; we can only observe the significance of what appears to have happened. The deportees of 732 and 722— perhaps only a relatively limited number—do not, so far as we know, reappear again in history.[16] Guesses that contact was made with

[14] Cf. the interesting discussion by H. Gese, 'Geschichtliches Denken im Alten Orient und im Alten Testament', *ZThK* 55 (1958), pp. 127–45, esp. pp. 140–5; ET, 'The Idea of History in the Ancient Near East and the Old Testament' in *The Bultmann School of Biblical Interpretation: New Directions = JThC* 1 (1965), pp. 49–64, esp. pp. 61–64; A. Gamper, *Gott als Richter in Mesopotamien und im AT* (Innsbruck, 1966), pp. 212–16. On the tension between history and faith, cf. also B. Albrektson, *Studies in the Text and Theology of the Book of Lamentations* (Lund, 1963), pp. 218f., 237ff.

This question is more fully discussed in B. Albrektson's more recent monograph, *History and the Gods* (Coniectanea Biblica, Old Testament Series 1, Lund, 1967), esp. pp. 112ff. Albrektson raises in this monograph the whole question of the nature of the Old Testament understanding of history in the light of a careful examination of the extra-biblical parallels. This study only became available to me after the completion of this book, but I have been able to indicate its relevance to the discussion at certain points. It is a very significant contribution to the study of Old Testament theology, and particularly relevant to such a survey as this, in which an attempt is made to understand a certain period.

[15] Cf. T. C. Vriezen, *The Religion of Ancient Israel* (ET, 1967), p. 240. B. Albrektson, *History and the Gods* (1967), pp. 100f.

[16] On these earlier exiles, cf. A. Causse, *Les dispersés d'Israël* (1929), pp. 12–16. We may note the suggestions of L. Gry, 'Israélites en Assyrie, Juifs en Babylonie', *Le Muséon* 35 (1922), pp. 153–85; 36 (1923), pp. 1–26, that Hebrew names appearing in the Assyrian Kannu' contracts from about a century after 722 reflect northern exiles. He connects this with *kannēh* (Ezek. 27.23), and notes that this is in the

them during the exilic period by the Babylonian exiles are without any real foundation. The deportees of 597 and 587, however, came to form one of the most important and influential parts of the Jewish community, and the impulse to new life from Babylonia is marked at several stages in the post-exilic period. Estimates differ as to how much of the Old Testament material was produced in Babylonia, but it is difficult not to conclude that Deutero-Isaiah, Ezekiel, and the Priestly Work came from there. Nor is it impossible that the Deuteronomic work belongs there, too, in spite of the arguments for Palestinian origin.[17] How far is this radical difference due to a greater absorption by the later generation of the teaching of the great prophets, as well as to the influence of the Josianic Reform in which some at least of the values of the prophetic movement were enshrined for a limited period in the public religious and social life? It is at any rate possible that the difference is in part due to this, even if other unknown factors also contributed to it. It would, of course, be proper to add that the later situation was also influenced by knowledge of the earlier, and that not a little of the thought of the northern kingdom contributed to the development of the thought of Judah during the succeeding century or so.

Whatever the truth about the situation, it remains clear that the acceptance of the prophetic verdict was an important factor in determining the attitude to the disaster. What the prophets had said would happen was now seen to be reality. If the disaster of 722 gave an impulse to the gathering of the prophetic words of Amos and Hosea, as we may well believe to be the case,[18] then the disaster of 587 gave a new impulse to the understanding both of the eighth-century prophets and of their successors. In the case of Jeremiah and Ezekiel their prophecies bridge the event, and we shall be looking at their contribution more fully.

The reapplication of older prophetic words to the new situation

---

region of Haran, ʿEden (cf. Ezek. 27.23), Halakhu and Guzana. Cf. II Kings 17.6, which mentions ḥᵉlaḥ ḥābōr nᵉhar gōzān wᵉʿārē māday. (On these place names cf. G. R. Driver, *Eretz Israel* 5 (Jerusalem, 1958), pp. 18*–20*.) Cf. also D. Sidersky, 'L'onomastique hébraïque des Tablettes de Nippur', *REJ* 87 (1929), pp. 177–99.

[17] Cf. below, pp. 65ff.

[18] The disaster could be seen to validate the prophetic word and thereby to establish its lasting truth. Cf. I. Engnell, *Gamla Testamentet. En traditionshistorisk inledning.* i (Stockholm, 1945), p. 159: the disaster was 'almost a triumph for the prophetic condemnations'. Cf. pp. 158–61 for Engnell's comments on the exile.

can be detected in all the older books. The more detailed references to Judah in Hosea,[19] the final words of Amos,[20] the hopeful passages in Micah,[21] the detail of the opening chapters of Isaiah,[22] all suggest that in the disaster there were some who carried on the prophetic tradition—whether we think of them as 'prophetic circles' or as 'prophetic preachers'—who saw in the fulfilment of the words of judgement a manifestation of the genuineness of prophecy and of the validity of the divine word which had come through its agency.[23]

With this we may associate the poems of the book of Lamentations and, with less assurance, some of the psalms. The linking of the poems of Lamentations with the events of 587 is well established, though some attempts have also been made at slightly later datings.[24] Whether it is right to be so confident in regard to the actual origin of the poems might well be questioned, since their affinities with the types of the psalm of lamentation and the funeral dirge make it difficult to give precise historical reference to the allusions they contain. They might well be earlier poems now applied to a particular situation. That they are now so applied seems, however, clear, and this is sufficient for our present purpose. The same may be said of such psalms as 44, 74, 79, though here even the application to 587 remains in some measure in doubt. At no point can we with complete confidence affirm that specific statements could only refer to the exilic situation. The once commonly held Maccabaean dating for these psalms has gone out of fashion, though it may well be that some phrases are, in fact, due to interpretation in reference to events of the second century BC.[25] These and other psalms are likely to have been understood in reference to many historical occasions, and the exilic situation is likely to have contributed something to their

[19] E.g., esp. in ch. 3.
[20] 9.11–15.
[21] 2.12–13; 4.1–5; 4.6–7 (8–14); 5.1–14; 7.8–20. An analysis of these passages and their detailed interpretation is not necessary to the general point here under discussion.
[22] On this, cf., e.g., D. R. Jones: 'The Traditio of the Prophecies of Isaiah of Jerusalem' $\mathcal{Z}AW$ 67 (1955), pp. 226–46, see pp. 238ff.; J. Becker, *Israel deutet seine Psalmen* (Stuttgart, [2]1967), pp. 26ff. on Isa. 12.
[23] Cf. N. W. Porteous, *op. cit.* (p. 42 n. 9), p. 237.
[24] Cf. O. Eissfeldt, *Introduction*, pp. 503f. Cf. also N. K. Gottwald, *Studies in the Book of Lamentations* (SBT 14, 1954); H.-J. Kraus, *Klagelieder* (BK 20, 1956), p. 11; ([2]1960), pp. 13ff.; W. Rudolph, *Klagelieder* in KAT 17, 1–3 (1962), pp. 193ff.
[25] For a full discussion and references, cf. P. R. Ackroyd, *The Problem of Maccabaean Psalms* (Diss., Cambridge, 1945). Cf. more briefly 'Criteria for the Maccabaean Dating of Old Testament Literature', *VT* 3 (1953), pp. 113–32.

present form.[26] The allusiveness of the language of psalmody, however, makes it hazardous to pinpoint definite modifications.[27] The significance of such poetry as an expression of the mood of the time lies in the designation of the poems of the book of Lamentations as 'dirges' or 'laments'. For in either case, the acceptance of judgement is inherent in the material. The disaster is the result of divine wrath;[28] it is the consequence of his people's failure.[29] Distress at the present situation is mingled with appeals to God for renewed action.

The basis of the theology of Lamentations is shown by Albrektson to lie in the close links which the author(s) reveal with the Zion traditions,[30] traditions of the inviolability of Zion which he traces also in Isaiah, Ezekiel and Deutero-Isaiah.[31] The disaster of 587 produced a 'tension between history and faith'.[32] The relationships between the poems of Lamentations and psalms of Zion[33] indicate the position occupied by the poet or poets. Albrektson shows also a relationship between Lamentations and Deut. 28 and other passages in that book[34] and suggests that the dilemma of the disaster finds its solution 'in the Deuteronomic view of the catastrophe as a divine judgement'.[35]

In general, this delineation of the position of Lamentations is valuable. That there were traditions of the inviolability of Zion seems clear from Jer. 7.4 and from Ezekiel's concept of the withdrawal of the glory of God before the Temple's destruction.[36] Albrektson suggests that the Deuteronomic concentration on a

---

[26] Cf. O. Eissfeldt, *Introduction*, pp. 113f.

[27] Cf. B. Albrektson, *Studies in the Text and Theology of the Book of Lamentations* (1963), p. 221, and the references in n. 1; the comment here is on Ps. 48 in particular, but the point is relevant to other psalms.

[28] E.g. Lam. 1.12; 2.1ff.; 3.1; 4.11; 5.22, i.e. the theme is found in all the poems.

[29] E.g. 1.14; 2.14; 3.40–42; 4.6; 5.7, 16.

[30] B. Albrektson, *Studies in the Text and Theology of the Book of Lamentations* (1963), pp. 214–39. Albrektson builds here on the earlier study of N. K. Gottwald, *op. cit.*, esp. pp. 47–62, but traces more exactly the background to the theology. For references to the literature on the theme of Zion, cf. Albrektson, p. 219 n. 2, and also R. E. Clements, *God and Temple* (1965), e.g. pp. 71 n. 1; 81 n. 3, and the bibliography. On this theme, cf. also N. W. Porteous, *op. cit.* (p. 42 n. 9), pp. 237ff.

[31] *Op. cit.*, p. 223.

[32] The phrase is Gottwald's: *op. cit.*, pp. 52f., quoted with this deeper interpretation by Albrektson, *op. cit.*, p. 223.

[33] For detailed comparison with Pss. 48, 50, 76, cf. B. Albrektson, *op. cit.*, pp. 224ff.

[34] *Op. cit.*, pp. 231–7.

[35] *Op. cit.*, p. 239. On this theme, cf. below, pp. 77f.

[36] Ezek. 10.

centralized cult brought it close to the Zion traditions.[37] This suggests that the Deuteronomic thinking itself enshrined elements of both acceptance and rejection of the shrine and city as it contained elements of acceptance and rejection of the idea of kingship. We should add that the Zion tradition, too, in the forms in which we meet it, also contained positive and negative elements: for whereas it is possible to trace in the Isaiah tradition, especially in ch. 36–39 = II Kings 18.13–20.11, clear reflections of the inviolability idea, it is less certain that we should regard such an idea as accepted by Isaiah without qualification.[38] Albrektson makes use of the present form of ch. 29 to point to such a theme;[39] but the opening verses, with their anticipation of disaster, taken alongside parts of ch. 28 and of ch. 1–6 suggest that Isaiah was prepared to envisage total disaster for Judah, and that deliverance in 701 was to him an act of unexpected grace,[40] not a vindication of the concept of inviolability.

To the faithful adherents of the old traditions—what Janssen calls the 'faithful in the land',[41] but not to be restricted to the community in Palestine—there would be particular appropriateness in expressing their distress in the language of older psalms of lamentation, and possibly also in newly formulated utterances of the same kind. They could thus express their loyalty to the past, their penitence at failure and resolve to amend their ways,[42] and their recognition of dependence upon divine grace, themes so frequently voiced in psalmody of this kind.[43] How such material was used we have no means of knowing: the indications of Jer. 41 and later references to fasts,[44] as well as the very existence of such a collection as Lamentations, traditionally associated with Jeremiah and certainly linked with this period,[45] suggest that there were public occasions of mourning for which they would be appropriate.[46] The poems of Lamentations also offer a further comment in that they look beyond disaster to a hope grounded

[37] Op. cit., p. 238.
[38] Cf. B. S. Childs, Isaiah and the Assyrian Crisis (SBT II, 3, 1967).
[39] Op. cit., p. 223.
[40] Cf. Isa. 1.9.
[41] Op. cit., pp. 68ff.
[42] So, e.g., Lam. 3.40.
[43] Cf. O. Eissfeldt, Introduction, pp. 113f.
[44] Cf. Zech. 7.3, 5; 8.19.
[45] Perhaps cf. also Isa. 63.7–64.11.
[46] For this, cf. the discussion by H.-E. von Waldow, Anlass und Hintergrund der Verkündigung des Deuterojesaja (Diss., Bonn, 1953), pp. 104ff., who argues both from quotations of words of lament in the oracles of Deutero-Isaiah and from other lament material that such celebrations were held both in Palestine and in Babylonia.

in the action of God. Like other such laments, they see in the supremacy of Yahweh the ultimate basis of assurance.[47]

4. THE DISASTER AND THE 'DAY OF YAHWEH'

Closely related to this, and indeed a variant on it, is the understanding, in the light of the events of 587, of the concept of the 'Day of Yahweh' in terms of contemporary actuality. This may be seen in the poems of Lamentations,[48] in the reinterpretation of earlier prophetic passages on this theme,[49] as well as in some contemporary utterances.[50]

This does not mean that the Day of Yahweh is thereby understood to be in the past, a single event over and done with. It means that there has been an embodiment in history of an event which is by nature suprahistorical, and if the cultic interpretation of psalm material concerned with a day of disaster is correct which sees in it not originally a description of a particular historical moment but of a cultic situation—the defilement of a sanctuary which arises from a variety of causes, whether real or fictitious—then there is a sense in which the repeated experience of the Day of Yahweh as a moment of judgement is now historified into the day of the disaster of 587. The cultic interpretation of psalmody and the historical expectation of judgement in the prophets—not unrelated to it—are drawn together into an appreciation of the reality of the divine intervention in history. In a new and fuller sense, Yahweh has come in judgement.

[47] Cf. G. Buccellati, *Bibbia e Oriente* 2 (1960), p. 209.

[48] Cf. L. Černý, *The Day of Yahweh and some Relevant Problems* (Prague, 1948), pp. 20, 105, with particular reference to Lam. 2.22; N. K. Gottwald, *op. cit.*, pp. 84–85; D. R. Jones, *ZAW* 67 (1955), p. 244.

[49] On Isaiah, cf. D. R. Jones, *op. cit.*, pp. 244f.

[50] Ezek. 13.5 which understands the disaster in terms of divine visitation, the Day of Yahweh. Cf. also Ezek. 34.12. Cf. G. von Rad, 'The Origin of the Concept of the Day of Yahweh', *JSS* 4 (1959), pp. 97–108; and the comments on von Rad's approach in F. M. Cross, Jr., 'The Divine Warrior in Israel's Early Cult', in *Biblical Motifs*, ed. A. Altmann (Philip W. Lown Institute of Advanced Jewish Studies, Studies and Texts 3, Cambridge, Mass., 1966), pp. 11–30, see pp. 19ff. Von Rad's approach is also criticized in M. Weiss, 'The Origin of the "Day of the Lord"—Reconsidered', *HUCA* 37 (1966), pp. 29–60 (with three tables), who traces the phrase to Amos, but the ideas to ancient theophany motifs; and in F. C. Fensham, 'A Possible Origin of the Concept of the Day of the Lord', in *Biblical Essays* (Proc. of Die Ou-Testamentiese Werkgemeenskap in Suid-Afrika 9, 1966, Potchefstroom, 1967), pp. 90–97, who sees it rather as a day of visitation than merely as an idea derived from the concept of the holy war.

Just as experiences of deliverance subsequent to the Exodus tend to take on elements of that particular event,[51] with the result that in the exilic period itself the prospect of a new Exodus is frequently envisaged,[52] so the experiences of judgement prior to the exile are drawn together in that moment, and subsequent experiences of judgement—and in due course the anticipation of final judgement—tend to gather to themselves elements which belong to that moment.[53]

These two latter appreciations of the exilic disaster are more fully developed in the more positive treatments of the period which we shall be concerned to examine in succeeding chapters. In differing ways and with differing emphasis, the great prophets and historians of the period see this moment as a decisive one. But they all have in common their acceptance of disaster as representing a necessary moment in the divine economy, resulting from the human failure which has so marked Israel's history. They go on from that to a fuller appreciation of what is to be the outcome of this nadir of Israel's experience.

[51] Cf. e.g., A. Bentzen, 'The Cultic Use of the Story of the Ark in Samuel', *JBL* 67 (1948), pp. 37–53, see pp. 52f.

[52] Cf. below on Jeremiah, the Deuteronomic History, Deutero-Isaiah and Ezekiel.

[53] Cf. the discussions of apocalyptic imagery in, e.g., D. S. Russell, *The Method and Message of Jewish Apocalyptic* (OTL, 1964), pp. 92ff. etc.

IV

THE RESPONSE TO THE EVENTS (*continued*)

B. THE BOOK OF JEREMIAH

JEREMIAH IS THE FIRST of the known prophets who actually experienced the disaster of 587. Yet although this is true, it is clear that by far the greater part of the Jeremiah material is directed primarily towards the years leading up to this moment, and the discovery of the prophet's mind in regard to the event itself is not easy. We may, in fact, detect various lines of approach, and recognize that in the form in which we now have the material, this diversity has in some measure been overlaid by particular kinds of presentation. Thus in the primarily oracular collections of ch. 1–25 the same kind of reapplication of the earlier message meets us as in the collections associated with the prophets of the preceding century. If we are not to make arbitrary distinctions between words of doom and words of promise, we have to recognize the problem of deciding just what part of the material belongs to the years before the disaster—and thus how far the prophet himself may be considered to have looked beyond the disaster to hope; what part belongs to the activity of the prophet after 587, in which period we might hope to detect his re-action to the events and the measure of his rethinking of his position; and what part belongs to the subsequent development of the Jeremiah tradition. In the more narrative sections of ch. 26–45, similar problems appear, though the presentation is very different; we have here to detect not merely what the narratives may tell us about the prophet and his activity, but also what understanding of the prophet and of the events is presented by the series of passages now collected into these chapters.[1]

[1] The whole problem of the Jeremiah tradition is far too complex to discuss here, though I am persuaded that it is right to make this broad division of the book and to discuss the evolution of the material in the two sections separately.

But although these problems are real, and their solution is not easy and indeed can never be more than speculative, we may nevertheless attempt an indication of the attitude of the 'Jeremiah tradition' to the period with which we are concerned.[2] The same type of problem is present when we deal with Ezekiel and Deutero-Isaiah; but as we are concerned less with portraying individuals and their thought, and more with understanding the mind of a period and its significance, we need only to avoid using any material which is virtually certainly of much later origin—though even this, in so far as it reflects on the situation in the sixth century from a greater distance, is not without its relevance in the development of thought.[3]

In this limited presentation of the Jeremiah material, as again in the chapters on Ezekiel and Deutero-Isaiah, it seems appropriate to distinguish between the attitude towards the disaster itself, and the outlook towards the future, though these are not completely separable either logically or in the present form of the material.

I. THE DOOM OF THE STATE

The consequences of Judah's failure are presented with considerable frequency in the opening chapters of the book, particularly in terms of the onslaught of an enemy from the north[4] whose identity is not made plain and which has been variously interpreted. The interpretations are not here our concern; we may note that there are indications that precise identification with Babylon as the instrument of divine judgement is made within the material, though it is very unlikely that this was the original identification. In the second half of the book we have a narrative (ch. 36) which suggests a background to the reinterpretation of the prophet's earlier message and points to the

---

(The 'foreign nation' oracles of 46–51 present a different series of problems; some mention of this material will be made in ch. XII.) Within 26–45, it seems most appropriate to subdivide into 26–36 and 37–44 with 45 as an appendix. These questions are taken up in an unpublished paper entitled 'The Nature of the Jeremiah Tradition', which I propose to develop into a fuller study of the structure and purpose of the material.

[2] Cf., e.g., J. W. Miller, *Das Verhältnis Jeremias und Hesekiels sprachlich und theologisch untersucht* (Assen, 1955), pp. 7–66, which presents a rather oversimplified picture.

[3] Cf. also ch. XIII.

[4] E.g. 1.13–15; 4.5–8; 6.1–8, 22–26.

reapplication of such judgement oracles with precise reference to Babylon.[5]

The theme of judgement is also vividly portrayed in the symbolic actions of the loincloth (13.1–11) and of the broken jar (19.1–13), as also in the visit to the potter's house (18.1–11). In these, the absoluteness of divine judgement is made explicit,[6] though the last passage is concluded with an exhortation to repentance. In fact, the linking of absolute judgement with warning and exhortation to repentance is a common characteristic of much of the first part of the book: apparently absolute statements, such as 18.1–11a, are alleviated by the warning and hortatory words of 18.11b, and the possibility of repentance is both affirmed (so, e.g., 3.12–14; 4.1–4) and apparently denied (3.1–5).[7] The unfaithfulness of Judah to the covenant, the failure to heed the warning contained in the fate of her sister Israel (3.6–11), the religious and social evils which make relationship with God impossible (cf. 7.1–8.3), all point to the impossibility of a renewed relationship and to the inevitability of doom. The elements of promise for the future in these chapters may be in large measure due to later elaboration of the material, perhaps by the prophet himself, perhaps by his immediate followers in the years after 587; yet they attach intelligibly to words of exhortation, and the recognition of the closeness of the relationship which exists between God and his people.

The narratives of 26–29, 32–36, 37–44 and the epilogue of 45 show a comparable pattern of thought, though the presentation is so different. That the prophet's pronouncements of doom are set in a context of warning and of summons to repentance is indicated, for example, by the provisos of 26.3 and 36.3. Similarly, the various narratives which depict his relationship with Zedekiah show him pointing to submission to the Babylonians as the only possible way by which deliverance from disaster may be found.[8] Alongside this are the various examples of those who by their loyalty will be delivered in the day of disaster. Thus, Ebed-melech will be spared even when

---

[5] Cf. 36.29. This application may also be seen in the material of ch. 25, though this passage has been subjected to a further state of reinterpretation so that the judgement is now pronounced on Babylon. (Cf. C. Rietzschel, *Das Problem der Urrolle* [Gütersloh, 1966], pp. 27ff. and endpapers. I find it difficult to accept the argument here offered, but it shows the complexity of the redactional problems.) 25.1–11 (14) may not inappropriately be regarded as in some sense parallel to ch. 36.

[6] Cf. 13.10; 18.11a; 19.11.

[7] Cf. W. Rudolph, *Jeremia* (HAT 12, 1947), p. XI; ([3]1968), p. XII.

[8] So 38.2, 17ff.; cf. also 21.8–10.

the city falls, because of his trust in Yahweh (39.15–18); so, too, the faithfulness of the Rechabites to their covenant (ch. 35), which contrasts so markedly with the unfaithfulness of the community at large, will be rewarded by their being maintained as a family (35.19)—the promise here is of a much more conventional kind, and does not precisely link with the disaster to city and kingdom, but it contrasts sharply with the absolute doom pronounced on Judah and all its inhabitants (35.17). The epilogue to the main book in ch. 45 also pronounces blessing and deliverance to an individual, Baruch, to whom his life is promised in the insecurities of the time.[9]

Just as in Ezekiel,[10] there is thus in the moment of absolute doom a deliverance for those who are responsive, though neither prophet makes clear precisely how such deliverance is possible. Since the hazards of war and siege would be less discriminating, it is perhaps more important to note that both prophets are also concerned to make clear that those who escaped the fate of exile in the disaster of 597 could not regard themselves as thereby marked out for divine blessing.[11] No logical consequences are drawn: the prophet more appropriately sets out a variety of reactions to the situation, judged in the light of his own insight into the divine will within the tradition in which he stands. The divine judgement upon the people is proclaimed; their disloyalty to the covenant inevitably brings disaster. The faithful are to be delivered—in this Jeremiah stands close to the protest against retributive justice in the corporate sense as that protest is made in Deut. 24.16.[12] The resolving of the inconsistencies of experience is not made, but nevertheless in what is said about the actual situation of those who stand beyond the disaster there are indications both of the way the judgement is to be accepted and of the meaning that this judgement has for the future. The people, seeing the situation in which they find themselves, are depicted as asking the reason for it; they are told that it is their apostasy which

[9] On the promises to Ebed-melech and Baruch, cf. O. Eissfeldt, 'Unheils-und Heilsweissagungen Jeremias als Vergeltung für ihm erwiesene Weh-und Wohltaten', *WZ Halle* 14 (1965), pp. 181–6. Eissfeldt adds a comment on the rewarding of Nebuzaradan (39.11–40.6), which he argues is now omitted from the text. Some rearrangement of the material is necessary to prove this, and it cannot be regarded as certain, but there are parallels to the other two examples which are of interest.

[10] Cf. Ezek. 9.4.

[11] Cf. Jer. 24; Ezek. 11.1–13.

[12] Cf. also Ezek. 18 and the discussion by B. Lindars, 'Ezekiel and Individual Responsibility', *VT* 15 (1965), pp. 452–67.

has brought them to this fate, of servitude in an alien land (so 5.19; and the variant on this theme in 16.10–13 which condemns them to service of alien deities; both these passages may probably best be understood as justification after the disaster of the judgement which has overtaken the people). Yet even here the context, in 5.18, is that of a judgement which is not absolute.

In certain passages the doom to come is specifically concentrated upon the fate of the Temple. This is clear in the two versions of the comparison of the impending destruction of Jerusalem's shrine with that of Shiloh,[13] though this theme of the destruction of the shrine is not elaborated as it is in Ezekiel.[14] The exposition of doom in ch. 7 is developed into a promise of restoration if there is a rejection of all that offends; though such a promise is absent from the corresponding narrative of ch. 26, this narrative presents the threat in a conditional form (cf. 26.3–5). Elsewhere a similar point is made in relation to the re-establishment of Jerusalem, a centre for both north and south, and for all the nations.[15] This is linked with the point that the ark, presumably lost at the time of the disaster or perhaps even earlier,[16] will not be replaced, and its absence will not be significant, because Jerusalem itself is to be God's throne.[17] As so often, doom and hope are interwoven.[18]

[13] 7.12–14; 26.6.
[14] E.g. in Ezek. 8–11.
[15] 3.15–18. Cf. Isa. 2.2–4; Micah 4.1–4.
[16] Cf. M. Haran, 'The Disappearance of the Ark', *IEJ* 13 (1963), pp. 46–58, who argues for its removal under Manasseh. (W. Rudolph [*op. cit.* (³1968), p. 26 n.] notes that he had no access to C. C. Dobson, *The Mystery of the Fate of the Ark of the Covenant* [London, 1939]. This is no loss, since this book, in addition to trying to prove the accuracy of all parts of the biblical record, including the traditions of the rescue of the ark by Jeremiah, goes further to suggest that the story is linked, via Jeremiah and Irish legend, with the coronation stone in Westminster Abbey. The etymological evidence [Tara connected with Torah, for example!] is on the 'British Israel' level.)
[17] The fact that the ark is not to be replaced is interpreted by W. Rudolph, *op. cit.*, p. 25, as being 'completely in accord with the way of thinking of a prophet to whom everything external in religion is repellent'. But it may be doubted if such a construction should be put on the passage—quite apart from the doubtfulness of this understanding of Jeremiah. The ark will not be missed, because its function, here indicated as that of throne, is replaced by Jerusalem itself. The passage indicates an enlarging of conception commensurate with the centrality of the throne of God for all nations. Cf. A. Weiser, *Das Buch Jeremia* (ATD 20/21, ⁵1966), p. 31. On the nature of the ark, cf. R. de Vaux, *Ancient Israel* (ET 1961), pp. 297ff.; and M. Haran, 'The Ark and the Cherubim', *IEJ* 9 (1959), pp. 30–38, 89–94, esp. pp. 90f.
[18] On the ambiguity of Jeremiah's attitude to the Temple, cf. also M. Schmidt, *Prophet und Tempel* (1948), pp. 97–108, see esp. p. 107.

2. JEREMIAH AND THE FUTURE

(i) *The exiles of 597*

Two passages in the book direct particular attention to those who had been exiled from the city in 597. Jer. 24, in the vision of the two baskets of figs, portrays the exiles as likened to the good figs, and promises of restoration and blessing and renewed relationship to God are declared to them. By contrast, those who are in Judah and Jerusalem, and those in Egypt, are condemned to utter destruction. Two points must be made in relation to this material. In the first place, it must be seen as arising out of an *ad hoc* message, directed to a particular situation in which it was necessary to indicate that the exiles were not automatically to be regarded as condemned and the community in Jerusalem and Judah as vindicated. In this, as already noted, the passage is comparable with Ezek. 11.1–13.[19] In a situation in which an immediate release from the burden of Babylonian rule was envisaged,[20] a simplified theological understanding of the fate of both parts of the community might well be expected. The prophet's message counters such an understanding. A similar countering of false hopes is seen in 22.24–30, the oracle on Jehoiachin, who epitomizes the fate of the exiles, which is that they should not return to the land in which they were born. In the second place, it seems clear that this passage in ch. 24 has been given a measure of redirection by the inclusion of a reference to those who are in Egypt (v. 8); this reference in itself suggests later reinterpretation, for though it may well be that there were refugees in Egypt at an earlier date,[21] the passage becomes fully intelligible only in the light of the narrative of ch. 44, which gives a basis for the extreme words of denunciation here. The view that the future lay with the exiles in Babylon alone eventually takes up a substantial place in the thought of the Chronicler, and no doubt was characteristic of a whole trend in the post-exilic period.[22] But here it is only obtained by an extension and a generalizing of the original *ad hoc* message. Such a representation of the position of Jeremiah is to be found also in the whole narrative section of 26–36 and 37–44, which, in effect by a process of

---

[19] Cf. also Ezek. 33.24 for a comparable *ad hoc* oracular utterance.
[20] Cf. Jer. 27–28, and 29.8, 21ff.
[21] The fact that Uriah took refuge in Egypt should probably be understood to mean that there were settlers there at an earlier date still (cf. 26.21).
[22] Cf. below, ch. XIII.

elimination, presents the view that it is the exiles in Babylon who hold the future; but, as we shall see, this is not the only viewpoint which may be discerned in these chapters. The epilogue to the book in ch. 52, a variant form of the last part of II Kings, also points to the exiles.[23]

In the material of ch. 29, partly parallel to 24, a similar viewpoint and presentation may be detected. Indeed, the theme of good and bad figs is here utilized, though in a different manner, with only the negative element taken up by way of providing a counter to the message of prophets in Babylon who have been proclaiming speedy release. So 29.15–23 introduces a variety of other elements, along with the bad fig theme, to indicate the absoluteness of judgement against the population and leadership in Jerusalem and against those in Babylon who look for immediate restoration. A shift in emphasis is detectable here. This judgement passage also stands in contrast to 29.1–14, which presents the message to the exiles in Babylon—a message clearly comparable to that of 24.4–7, but reinforcing the point that the well-being promised to the exiles is bound up with the well-being of Babylon. Again we may detect something of the process by which an original message to the exiled community has been given a different context and direction by being linked with a more precise definition of return, which contrasts sharply with the exhortation to settle firmly in Babylon, and further by being set in contrast with judgement upon those who predict return soon and those in Jerusalem who are under sentence of death. The theme of 'only in the exile' is here again brought out.

The meaning of the exilic experience is also indicated in such a passage as 5.18f. Hope here is seen as resting with those who are doomed for their apostasy to serve aliens in a land not their own.

(ii) Submission to Babylon

There is no direct indication in the book of Jeremiah of his attitude to the exiles after the destruction of the city in 587. But an indirect light is shed on this question by the narrative of his refusal to accept the offer of protection in Babylon, made to him by Nebuzaradan, and his choice of remaining in Judah with the newly appointed governor Gedaliah (40.1–6). This may be linked with his advocacy of a policy of submission to Babylon as offering the only hope for the

---

[23] Cf. below, n. 27.

future,[24] for Gedaliah as governor, supervised by the Babylonian soldiers who were sent to be with him,[25] represents that part of the community which was willing to accept Babylonian overlordship. To his nationalistic contemporaries, represented by Ishmael ben Nethaniah of the royal house, Gedaliah was a traitor, to be struck down when opportunity offered; in this he has as his counterpart certain modern personalities who have adopted a similar line of co-operation with conquerors, though there may be various motives for such co-operation. And though Jeremiah is reported as having denied a charge of desertion to the Babylonians when he was in an obviously compromising position,[26] it is easy to see that he laid himself open to a charge of being what in modern terminology is described as a 'fellow traveller'. It is significant that neither in the narrative in its brief form in II Kings 25.22–26, nor in the longer form which appears in Jer. 40.7–41.18,[27] is there any word of condemnation of Gedaliah.[28] It is natural to believe that, underlying the narratives as they are now presented, there is a clear tradition that Jeremiah, at the point at which Judah collapsed, saw the real hope for the future not particularly with the exiles in Babylon, but with the community gathered round Gedaliah. His adherence to that community when the choice was offered suggests this,[29] and his subsequent advice to the avengers of Gedaliah's death to stay in Judah and not to go to Egypt confirms the point.[30] Again Jeremiah's policy is open to simple misunderstanding; he, and even more so Baruch, are virtually seen as undercover agents for the Babylonian overlords.[31]

A hope for the renewal of life in Judah itself is also presented by the symbolic action of 32.6–15, in which Jeremiah redeems a piece of family land at Anathoth. The action is interpreted in the elaborate series of sermonic passages which follow in 32.16–25, 26–44, in which the theme of total judgement[32] is developed and countered by a reversal of the message of doom in vv. 37ff., and by a declaration of

[24] 38.2, 17–20; cf. also 27.12f.
[25] 41.3; cf. 40.10.
[26] 37.11–14.
[27] The Gedaliah material is significantly absent from Jer. 52, which thus, even more clearly than the narratives of 26–36, 37–44, implies that the future lies only with the exiles.
[28] Cf. p. 30.
[29] 40.1–6.
[30] 42.7–22.
[31] 43.1–3.
[32] Cf. 32.1–5.

the future occupation of the land in vv. 42–44, again in terms of a reversal of the words of judgement. The whole passage is of great interest for the understanding of the development of the Jeremiah tradition. But for our immediate purpose its significance lies in its emphasis on the recovery of life in its normal forms within the land of Judah itself, described with its technical geographical terms as including the land of Benjamin, the places about Jerusalem, and the cities of Judah, the hill country, the Shephelah and the Negeb. All Judah is to be returned to normality. This elaboration of the message of the symbol, which is more simply stated in 32.15, may reflect a later attitude to the words of the prophet, but the whole passage is significant in that it brings out clearly that aspect of Jeremiah's teaching which is to be found also in relation to Gedaliah.

(iii) *Restoration themes*

The restoration of an obedient community to its land—a theme to be compared with some aspects of Hosea's message[33]—is found in other passages in the book of Jeremiah, and not simply in the elaborated form which is presented in ch. 32. Thus the exposition in 7.1–8.3 of Jeremiah's judgement upon the community for its false trust in the Temple, bound up with the condemnation of idolatrous practices and social evils,[34] pictures the possibility of a resettlement in the land if there is obedience to the requirements both of justice and of absolute loyalty to Yahweh:

'then I will settle you in this place,[35] in the land which I gave to your fathers in perpetuity' (7.7).

The main point is a complete re-establishment of relationship. How far this element in this sermonic exposition is to be regarded as Jeremiah's is not certain; but it is clear that the Jeremiah tradition envisaged such a re-entry.

With such a passage as this, we may link the exploration of the new Exodus theme, particularly as this is expressed in the restatement of the Exodus credo in 16.14–15 and 23.7–8.[36] The promise here is of a new redemptive act which will bring about the restora-

33 Cf., e.g., Hos. 2.16f.
34 7.5–20.
35 *māqom* here (cf. p. 156 n. 11) may be simply a synonym for 'land', but could also indicate the city, or perhaps most naturally the shrine. But the extension from shrine to holy land is a natural one (cf. pp. 156, 249f.).
36 On these passages, cf. the further discussion on pp. 238ff.

tion[37] of the scattered members of the community from the many lands in which they are now to be found. The thought is difficult to dovetail with the expressions of doom already noted, and although such statements as this may mark a late stage in the prophet's thought, it is again much more probable that this represents a further and fuller elaboration of the Jeremiah tradition. It finds close linkage to the reiterated statement of the basic covenant relationship:

'I will be your God and you shall be my people.'[38]

This is to be found in passages which by reason of their sermonic style are often described as Deuteronomic;[39] it occurs in relation to more hopeful sayings and in the context (in ch. 30–31) of oracles of hope. The Jeremianic insistence on the nature of the covenant relationship makes it an appropriate epitome of his demand and hope for his people. The mode of its understanding may well be reckoned to be deepened and made more inward than in some earlier statements.

Such a hope of restoration and re-establishment of the community is particularly elaborated in the oracular collection of ch. 30–31, the so-called 'booklet of consolation'. The detailed analysis of this section and the problems of its origin and its unity have been much under discussion.[40] But again, with the recognition that in its present form it belongs after 587—31.38–40 clearly points beyond the fall of the city to the prospect of rebuilding—it is possible to look at its present import, and see it as a collection directed towards the nature of restoration. One might describe it as a collection of Jeremianic prophecies which, in the exilic age—in the situation which was eventually to produce the oracular utterances of a Deutero-Isaiah —has been shaped to show the fuller meaning of words which may originally have been in some way related to the religious and political movements of the time of Josiah. If at times its style and language are closely akin to Deutero-Isaiah, this is perhaps better to be attributed to the use of psalm style and language than to the supposition of any

[37] On the theme of 'return from exile', cf. W. L. Holladay, *The Root Šûbh in the Old Testament* (Leiden, 1958), esp. pp. 146f., pointing out how the idea of repentance (return to God) is extended to refer to return from exile.
[38] So, e.g., 7.23; 11.4; 24.7; 30.22.
[39] On this cf. W. L. Holladay's analyses in *JBL* 79 (1960), pp. 351–67. The relationship between poetry and prose in Jeremiah and between Deuteronomic and Jeremianic style certainly needs further investigation. The kinship of these latter two does not seem really to be in doubt; it is the nature of the relationship which is less easy to define precisely. Cf. J. W. Miller, *op. cit.* (p. 51 n. 2), pp. 23–28.
[40] O. Eissfeldt, *Introduction*, pp. 361f.

direct relationship. The period of distress is one for lament (30.5–7; 31.15), and for a recognition of failure and of divine discipline (30.12–15; 31.18–19); it is also one for recognition of the supreme creative and restoring power of God, whose works in the past are tokens of the reality of his activity to come (30.8–9, 10–11, 16–24; 31.2–6, 7–14, 16–22). The assurance of this action is as the enduring order of creation (31.35–37). In what may be regarded as a prose exposition of the theme, the element of covenant relationship is drawn out as a counter, in part, to those who are unable to see the working of the divine purpose (31.27–34). It is noteworthy that these chapters provide the same kind of interweaving of themes as is so commonly characteristic of Deutero-Isaiah.[41]

Included among the themes is that of the restoration of the Davidic house (30.9). This also finds a place in the exposition of disaster and restoration in ch. 33, utilizing in vv. 14–16 the same theme of the 'righteous branch' which is found also in 23.5–6.[42] Again we find two types of presentation of the same material. In ch. 23 the oracle promising a new Davidic ruler comes as the culminating statement to a series of royal oracles, linked to the warning to Zedekiah in 21.1–10.[43] This warning is followed by a series of more general oracles on the doom of the house of David (21.11ff.), and a general exhortation to obedience addressed to the royal house in the context of a foretelling of the disaster to the city of Jerusalem (22.1–9). Such material is reminiscent of the conditional promises to the house of David to be found in the books of Kings,[44] and shows the same

---

[41] Cf. pp. 119f.

[42] The absence of 33.14–26 from the Greek text is clearly a point of importance in the study of the textual transmission of the book. The affinities between the LXX and Qumran texts suggest further clues to the complexity of the problems. Nevertheless the longer MT in ch. 33 presents us with one form of the Jeremiah tradition, and the evidence of overlap with other material in the book shows that we are not merely dealing with very late additions. Even if it be judged that the original form of the text in ch. 33 did not contain these verses, a consideration of their content is still relevant and a study of their placing in the book is important. On the David/Messiah theme, cf. J. Coppens, 'L'espérance messianique royale à la veille et au lendemain de l'exil', in Studia Biblica et Semitica T. C. Vriezen Dedicata (Wageningen, 1966), pp. 46–61, see pp. 47–54. The discussion by M. Sekine, 'Davidsbund und Sinaibund bei Jeremia', VT 9 (1959), pp. 47–57, attempts too precise a chronological attachment of the material.

[43] A. Malamat, 'Jeremiah and the Last Two Kings of Judah', PEQ 83 (1951), pp. 83–87, has a rather fanciful interpretation of the relationship between Jeremiah and Zedekiah.

[44] Cf., e.g., I Kings 2.2–4; 9.4–9, and cf. also the more absolute statement of II Sam. 7.12ff. Jer. 22.8–9 closely resembles I Kings 9.7–9.

appreciation of the relationship between the unfaithful royal house and the judgement on the community which is characteristic of the framework passages of the narratives there. The series of oracles on particular rulers in 22.10–30 is similarly resumed in 23.1–4 by a general promise of the removal of evil rulers and the substitution for them of good ones,[45] which provides the occasion for the Davidic promise of 23.5–6.

In ch. 33 the theme of absolute doom for the city (33.4–5) is countered by a promise of restoration (33.6–9),[46] and similar reversals of the doom message follow in vv. 10–13.[47] In this context, the promise of a righteous Davidic ruler (vv. 14–16) is elaborated with an unconditional promise to both royal and priestly lines (vv. 17–18), and the point is underlined (in vv. 19–26) by the same kind of allusions to the natural order and its dependability as a witness to the actions of God as is to be seen in the 'new covenant' passage of 31.27–37. The restoration of the whole community is thus assured.

The book of Jeremiah thus presents a variety of insights—some of which are to be closely associated with the prophet himself, even where they are not necessarily consistent with one another.[48] In depicting the disaster, the primary emphasis is on the rightness of God's judgement and its consistency with the earlier understanding of his will for and his requirements from his people. In looking beyond disaster, the tradition in the book shows how various elements within the community's experience may be seen to link with hope—a hope which lies beyond the disaster and which is ultimately rooted in the enduring nature of divine promise, and expressed in terms of a reversal of the words of doom on the basis of the bond with his people which God is willing to maintain.[49]

[45] Cf. also 3.15.
[46] Cf. the similar promise to the city in 3.15–18.
[47] So 33.12–13; cf. 32.44.
[48] Thus the stress on the exiles in 24 and 29 and the stress on Judah in 32 and 40–43.
[49] Reference should also be made to S. Herrmann, *Die prophetischen Heilserwartungen im Alten Testament* (BWANT) 85, 1965), pp. 155–241. This study came to my notice too late to be fully examined here.

V

THE HISTORIANS AND THEOLOGIANS
OF THE EXILIC AGE

A. THE DEUTERONOMIC HISTORY

I. THE NATURE OF THE DEUTERONOMIC PRESENTATION

THE FIRST of the great compilations, a theological history of Israel, is the Deuteronomic History.[1] Behind it lies a mass of earlier tradition, both legal and historical; it is evident that its compilers have made use of already existing corpora of law, and probably also of skilfully constructed 'literary' works, such as the 'Succession History of David' in II Sam. 9–20, I Kings 1–2.[2] Among this material is to be found prophetic legend (I Kings 17–II Kings 13—which also now includes other material; II Kings 18–20), as well as extracts from annalistic works, temple archives and the like. Our concern is not with these earlier compilations and pieces of material, since they are expressions of various aspects of pre-exilic life. It is therefore possible for us to leave on one side the very important but difficult questions which arise concerning the nature and method of the compilation, as well as the problem of editorial stages. If there was a first edition produced just before the exile and a second edition produced during the exile, this will not fundamentally affect the question of what the exilic compiler or editor was doing.[3] Nor do we need to decide absolutely between the possibility

---

[1] Cf. M. Noth, *Überlieferungsgeschichtliche Studien I. Die Sammelnden und bearbeitenden Geschichtswerke im A.T.* (Schriften der Königsberger Gelehrten Gesellschaft, 18/2, Halle, 1943; Tübingen, ²1957), pp. 3–110; H. W. Wolff, 'Das Kerygma des deuteronomistischen Geschichtswerks', *ZAW* 73 (1961), pp. 171–86 = *Ges. Stud.* (ThB 22, 1964), pp. 308–24.

[2] Cf. R. N. Whybray, *The Succession Narrative* (SBT II, 9, 1968).

[3] Cf. the discussion of the different approaches in O. Eissfeldt, *Introduction*, pp. 241–8, for references to the relevant works. In my own view, there is no simple

that the whole work is the product of one great individual, an interpreter of the exilic situation,[4] and the alternative that it belongs in a tradition, whose primary emphasis is one of an edifying, didactic character.[5] Indeed, it is difficult not to feel that both possibilities can be held together. While Janssen[6] is right to criticize the too modern, individualizing tendency of Noth's description of the work as that of a man 'who undertook on his own initiative to interpret the catastrophe which he had experienced',[7] he does so on the grounds that this misses the Deuteronomist's tendency to instruction and edification. But such a tendency can certainly belong to an individual

---

alternative between the Tetrateuch/Deuteronomic History view here accepted as the basis of discussion—though I do not accept many of the points of detail—and the Pentateuch/Hexateuch/Heptateuch/Octateuch/Enneateuch view variously expounded by O. Eissfeldt, C. A. Simpson and others. What is commonly called JE (including L or whatever other term is used to indicate that J is not a unity) can be traced both in the Tetrateuch and in the underlying materials of the Deuteronomic History. It may be that the allocation of the land in Josh. 13–19 belongs in its final form to what is conveniently if not entirely accurately described as the 'P work'. The last chapters of Deuteronomy certainly contain a complex mass of material. But this is to suggest that the earlier historico-theological surveys—J and E—traced a period which overlapped those eventually covered by P and D: the Chronicler, on this assumption, was the first to cover the whole, from creation to his own time, but it is noteworthy that he did so by a process involving both genealogical summarizing and substantial omission. In each and every case, the task of the exegete is to discover, so far as is possible, what belongs to a survey, and to expound on the basis of this material what aim the historian/theologian had in view. For a broad review of the problems, cf. E. Jenni, 'Zwei Jahrzehnte Forschung an den Büchern Josia bis Könige', *ThR* 27 (1961), pp. 1–32, 97–146, esp. pp. 97–118.

[4] M. Noth, *op. cit.*, pp. 87–95, 109f. Cf. his further comments in 'Zur deuteronomistischen Geschichtsauffassung', *Proc. XXII Congress of Orientalists, Istanbul, 1951* II (Leiden, 1957), pp. 558–66, see pp. 564–6.

[5] B. Maisler (Mazar), 'Ancient Israelite Historiography', *IEJ* 2 (1952), pp. 82–88, compares contemporary concern with antiquity and its interpretation in Neo-Babylonian activity, and points to the similarly synchronistic method in Assyrian and Neo-Babylonian works. The main source is in the '*debārīm* of prophets and other great men' (p. 84); it represents a mingling of 'records and folk legends, prose and poetry, fact and fancy' (p. 86). Cf. also C. R. North, *The Old Testament Interpretation of History* (London, 1946), pp. 92–106. For Hittite historiography, cf. H.-G. Güterbock, 'Die historische Tradition und ihre literarische Gestaltung bei Babyloniern und Hethitern bis 1200' (I), *ZA* 42 (1934), pp. 1–91; (II), on Hittites, *ZA* 44 (1938), pp. 45–145.

[6] *Op. cit.*, p. 65 n. 2.

[7] *Op. cit.*, pp. 109f. Cf. the comments of E. W. Nicholson, *Deuteronomy and Tradition* (Oxford, 1967), pp. 25ff., and references there, and also his discussion of 'Deuteronomy and the Deuteronomist' on pp. 107–18.

author, and we need not suppose that Noth is unaware of the place which his author occupies within a larger tradition.[8] The interconnections of Deuteronomic language and thought with other Old Testament strands (e.g. with prophecy and psalmody as well as with older law) make it impossible to think of an original author independent of anyone else. The wholeness of the Deuteronomic work suggests that it is one who stands within a tradition who has given to it the final form which it has, and that his originality, the newness of what he is doing, should not be ignored. With all the diversity of the material which the work contains, and with all the variation in handling of this material which makes Judges, for example, so different from Joshua or Samuel, and different again from Kings, there is an overall impression of unity, a moving appeal which is more effectively appreciated when the whole work is seen together than appears in the consideration of individual parts of it, impressive as these are. The pressure of the sources which results in the retention of often conflicting elements has meant that the final compiler has produced a work in which the total message is given more by means of punctuating comments, occasional sermons and addresses and summaries, than by a complete rewriting. Such a punctuating tendency, visible also in the Tetrateuch, reveals an appreciation of the unity of the events of the whole period described.

The date of origin of the complete work is not difficult to discover. The final verses concerning the release of Jehoiachin from prison in 561 BC mark a *terminus a quo*. If it be argued that this piece of narrative was added to an already effectively complete work, the consideration of the whole will not be greatly altered: the addition may be seen to be in the spirit of the whole. The significance of this passage must be our concern subsequently. Again the *terminus ad quem* is reasonably fixed by the lack of any indication that the Temple had been rebuilt, so that 520 or thereabouts must be the latest date. Perhaps more decisive still is the lack of reference to the taking over of the empire by the Persians. Whatever the compiler's view of what went on in Judah, it is reasonable to suppose that so momentous a political change as the Persian conquest could hardly have passed entirely unmentioned. Though the Babylonian provincial governor in Samaria probably remained in office, and though Persian control

---

[8] Cf. also the comments and references given by H. W. Wolff, *op. cit.*, p. 183 = p. 320.

of Palestine only became really effective with Cambyses (529–522), the change could hardly be ignored.[9]

Place of origin is more difficult to establish. Noth and others have argued for a Palestinian origin. To Noth's three main arguments, Janssen has added some further points. Noth stresses (1) that the sources for the work were most readily available in Palestine. On the assumption that it would not be easy to imagine the exiled officials carrying the archives with them, we may suppose that these archives were taken over by the 'provisional government' under Gedaliah and so were available.[10] Alternative possibilities are that we should suppose the Babylonians to have seized them—but would they then permit their use? Or that we should suppose the use of oral traditions rather than written works, following the 'Scandinavian' tendency; but the compiler's frequent reference to written sources and the indications of his use of archival material make this very improbable.[11] (2) Noth draws attention to local traditions of the Bethel-Mizpah area.[12] These could, of course, have been equally well incorporated already in the source material. (3) Noth considers that the lack of a hope of the restoration of Israel in the work argues also in favour of Palestinian origin. But this depends particularly on the negative view which Noth takes of the work.[13] None of these points seems conclusive.

Janssen adds four further points. (1) He notes that the speeches, both in the Deuteronomic history and in Jeremiah, are concerned with departure from the law and the tendency to idolatrous practice. This latter refers to Canaanite cults, and is therefore relevant to the situation in Palestine, rather than to the temptation to worship Babylonian gods, treated differently in Deutero-Isaiah. (2) Solomon's

---

[9] Cf. below (pp. 141ff.) for a consideration of the possible historical effects of this political situation. On the situation itself, cf. A. Alt, 'Die Rolle Samarias bei der Entstehung des Judentums', *Festschrift O. Procksch* (Leipzig, 1934), pp. 5–28 = *Kl. Schr.* 2 (Munich, 1964), pp. 316–37.

[10] Cf. E. Hammershaimb's comment on this problem: *Some Aspects of Old Testament Prophecy* (Copenhagen, 1966), pp. 95ff. Discussion of this involves, of course, the whole question of the kind of situation in which such large works were written, as well as the question of what audience was envisaged by the author(s).

[11] Cf. the comments on this problem by S. Mowinckel, 'Israelite Historiography' *ASTI* 2 (1963), pp. 4–26, see pp. 22ff.

[12] Cf. the connections of Deuteronomy with Bethel suggested by F. Dumermuth, 'Zur deuteronomischen Kulttheologie', *ZAW* 70 (1958), pp. 59–98. No clear evidence exists for regarding Bethel as the leading sanctuary of the exilic period as he assumes (p. 97).

[13] For Noth's discussion, cf. *op. cit.*, pp. 96f., 107ff.

dedication prayer (I Kings 8) depicts the Temple as a place of prayer rather than as a place of sacrifice.[14] This, as Noth believes,[15] points to the exilic situation, and Janssen believes it also points to a Palestinian locality, where the ruined Temple may be considered to offer just this. The weakness of this argument has in effect already been examined. (3) The stress in the later narratives in II Kings is on Judah's destruction rather than on exile. This envisages the situation of those in Judah rather than those in Babylonia. (4) The work hardly refers to the ideas of $g\bar{a}l\bar{a}$ and $\bar{s}\bar{a}b\bar{a}$, and the only reference to exiles in I Kings 8 (vv. 46ff.) is from the standpoint of a compiler in Palestine. Janssen explains away the impression given by the work that there is nothing left in Judah as due to the theological interpretation of the disaster. It must also be linked with his stress upon the rise in status of the $dallat\ h\bar{a}'\bar{a}re\d{s}$,[16] which he believes was viewed by the Deuteronomic compiler as disastrous, since the latter's viewpoint is that of the established land-owning population, the $'am\ h\bar{a}'\bar{a}re\d{s}$.[17]

Of these latter arguments, none is conclusive, but they are on the whole stronger than those of Noth, and the sole reference to the release of Jehoiachin[18]—an event which we may well believe had

[14] Cf. also above, pp. 26ff.
[15] Op. cit., p. 105.
[16] E. Janssen, op. cit., pp. 49ff.
[17] On the nature of the $'am\ h\bar{a}'\bar{a}res$, cf. also p. 150 n. 50. Doubt about the view that the term points in these contexts to a definite 'establishment' also raises questions regarding Janssen's view of the $dallat\ h\bar{a}'\bar{a}re\d{s}$. Is it possible to see in the use of this expression—no doubt historically determined by the fact that changes in occupation of land took place after the collapse of Judah—a theological statement linked to the stress on the maintenance of the rights of the unprotected in Israel? Cf., however, the very cautious review of the whole problem of the poor, with reference to the literature, by J. van der Ploeg, 'Les pauvres d'Israël et leur piété', OTS 7 (1950), pp. 236–70. A. S. Kapelrud 'New Ideas in Amos', VTS 15 (1966), pp. 193–206, stresses the importance of the place of the poor in the teaching of Amos. At a much later date we may trace the expression of ideals in terms of 'the poor' as the true heirs of ancient Israel. (Cf. Matt. 5.3; Luke 6.20, 24, and the various uses of the term Ebionite. Cf. A. Causse, Les "pauvres" d'Israël [Strasbourg, Paris, 1922], pp. 81–136, on the reflection of these ideas in the psalms, and pp. 137–72, on messianic hopes.) Is it possible that the Deuteronomic historian is expressing an intermediate stage in this development of thought? Judah has been condemned; its leaders have failed and are in exile. Hope lies in a new community. This thought also appears to be present in Jeremiah's acceptance of Gedaliah and apparent view of this as containing a seed of hope: as the narratives are now presented in Jer. 37–44, however, this hope is shown to be illusory (cf. pp. 55ff).
[18] On this matter, cf. also pp. 78ff. The recognition of the legitimacy of Jehoiachin's kingship would make a reference to this an appropriate conclusion to the work. The true king of Judah is now freed: what may not follow from this in the providence of God?

repercussions in the exile and in Palestine—does also suggest that the author's interest does not really lie in the exile. On the more negative side, however, we can only register some surprise that there is no real indication of the conditions in Palestine and the reference to the assassination of Gedaliah in II Kings 25 ends simply with the statement that 'all the people, both small and great . . . went to Egypt' (v. 26), which does not much suggest an author who is concerned with the maintaining of the religious tradition in a Palestinian locality. One further possibility does, however, remain open here. It is that of a return to Palestine after a period in Egypt, for the same problem arises in regard to the prophecies of Jeremiah. Since the tradition in Jer. 44 places Jeremiah in Egypt—along with those leaders of the community who seem to be specifically indicated in II Kings 25—the eventual compilation of the book of Jeremiah, with its markedly Deuteronomic speeches, usually assumed to have undergone considerable expansion,[19] presumably took place in circles closely connected with those which produced the Deuteronomic History; and unless we are to assume—which seems unlikely—that these works were only subsequently brought from Egypt, it seems more probable that they and their circle came to Palestine during or shortly after the exilic period.[20]

[19] Cf. Janssen on this, *op. cit.*, pp. 105ff. It must be acknowledged that the point is not so secure as appears at first sight. The so-called Deuteronomic sermons in Jeremiah owe not a little to the poetic prophetic passages (cf. on this W. L. Holladay, 'Prototype and Copies: A New Approach to the Poetry-Prose Problem in the Book of Jeremiah', *JBL* 79 [1960], pp. 351–67; *idem*, 'Style, Irony, and Authenticity in Jeremiah', *JBL* 81 [1962], pp. 44–54.) The real closeness of relationship is to be found in Jer. 26–45, where the narrative sections concerning the fall of the city and after are evidently dependent on the same kind of traditions as are utilized in II Kings. It is difficult to avoid the conclusion that parts of the Jeremiah material represent a fuller form of the II Kings narrative, and since there is evidence to suggest that the Chronicler made use of a different and expanded form of the Samuel/Kings narratives (cf. W. Rudolph, 'Problems of the Books of Chronicles', *VT* 4 [1954], pp. 401–9, see pp. 402f. and *Chronikbücher* [HAT 21, 1955], pp. XIf.; O. Eissfeldt, *Introduction*, pp. 532–5), it seems most natural to suppose that several variant forms of this material existed—as indeed might be expected, since at this stage it is more reasonable to speak of each copy of a work being in a sense a new work, rather than regarding them as 'published in an edition'. The investigation of the relationship between the prophetic oracles in Jer. 1–25 and the corresponding oracular material in 26–45 suggests that in reality we possess two books of Jeremiah. Cf. p. 50 n. 1.

[20] Jer. 44.13f. appears to exclude any return from Egypt, though the last phrase admits the possibility that some survivors, or fugitives, will return. The same point appears in 44.28. It seems likely that an original negative pronouncement of Jeremiah has been qualified to explain that there was a very limited return. Cf.

No definite statement can therefore be made about place of origin.[21] We must consider what this work indicates about the outlook for the people as one aspect of the religious thinking of the period.

If we attempt to assess the reasons for which the work came into being, we are inevitably in some measure drawn back into the earlier period. Without necessarily subscribing to the identification or near-identification of the Deuteronomic Law with that found at the time of Josiah's religious reform,[22] we may recognize the kinship between the two movements. The account of the reform in II Kings is quite evidently intended to point to Deuteronomy as the law which became normative at that point, and even if this were a misreading of the events by the historians, it would still be significant because of its claim that a reordering of the people's life on the basis of this law had been undertaken, that it met with divine approval, and that though it came too late to avert the final disaster, this was at least delayed. What had so nearly succeeded once could be seen to be a potential source of restoration subsequently.[23]

Such an association with the period of Josiah—probably historical though written up and seen in a new light—would suggest that underlying the Deuteronomic movement there is a strongly nationalistic element,[24] and indeed this point is amply substantiated by the work of such scholars as G. von Rad and G. E. Wright.[25] Israel is in this recalled to her ancient life, her older patterns of thought; and this,

---

W. Rudolph, *Jeremia* (HAT 12, 1947), pp. 222, 225; (³1968), pp. 260, 262, who attributes the last phrase of v. 14 to the influence of v. 28. A. Weiser, *Das Buch Jeremia* (ATD 20–21, ⁵1960), pp. 368, 373f., sees in v. 28 a genuine hope for the future, but agrees that 14b is a later addition. Josephus, *Ant.* X, 9.7 interprets the narrative in such a way as to state that the refugee group in Egypt was later taken to Babylon, after Nebuchadrezzar had conquered Egypt. (Cf. also p. 17.)

[21] H. W. Wolff, *op. cit.*, p. 172 = p. 309 favours Palestinian origin, and specific-ally in the Judah-Benjamin area.

[22] Cf. the critical comments of N. Lohfink, 'Die Bundesurkunde des Königs Josias. Eine Frage an die Deuteronomiumsforschung', *Biblica* 44 (1963), pp. 261–88, 461–98.

[23] G. Östborn, *Yahweh's Words and Deeds* (UUÅ, 1951. 7, 1951), p. 27, describes the Deuteronomic History as written 'from the viewpoint of man's relation to the law given through Moses'. Cf. the whole section, pp. 26–35.

[24] Cf. O. Eissfeldt, *Geschichtliches und Übergeschichtliches im Alten Testament* (ThStKr 109/2, 1947), pp. 15f.

[25] Cf. G. von Rad, *Theology* I, pp. 219–31; *Der Heilige Krieg im alten Israel* (ATANT 20, 1951), pp. 68ff.; *Studies in Deuteronomy* (ET, SBT 9, 1953), pp. 45ff. G. E. Wright, 'Deuteronomy', *IB* 2 (1953), pp. 325ff.; also brought out by E. Voegelin, *Israel and Revelation* (1956), pp. 374ff.

in the historical narrative, is seen against the background of what is now described as the period of apostasy under Manasseh, but which we may more appropriately describe as the period of low national fortunes under the pressure of Assyria—the two are not contradictory statements but complementary. With the lessening of Assyria's power in the decade 630–620—indicated clearly by both Babylonian independence under Nabopolassar and Judaean upsurge under Josiah —there comes the real possibility of establishing again the older values, and repudiating all those religious and political elements which are associated with the life of a subject people. The emphasis of a Jeremiah on the totality of failure which leads him to the full expectation of disaster suggests at first sight a contrast with the optimism of a nationalistic movement. In fact, as the Josiah narrative shows, the immediate effect of the reading of the law-book was the realization of doom —confirmed by the prophecy of Huldah; this is as the historian sees it in the light of the events. Those who put the reform into effect were probably more optimistic about its outcome, but their position was not that of the prophet, any more than the position of Isaiah and that of Ahaz could be equated a century earlier.[26] The politician's attempt at organizing a society on a religious basis is not likely to be identical with the prophet's judgement upon the condition of that society seen in the light of the nature and will of God. The tension between political programme and religious judgement is not necessarily absolute. Both sides may—as here—be seeking to assess the position on the basis of the same fundamental beliefs.[27]

But the upsurge which stressed the possibility of the recovery of the past, a recovery which appeared to find ample justification in the extension of Judah's domain under Josiah so as to reach into the old northern territory[28]—as witness the biblical account—and even to the sea coast—as witness the recent discovery of a letter, probably from

[26] Cf. A. C. Welch, *Kings and Prophets of Israel* (London, 1952), p. 215.
[27] I find it difficult to share the absoluteness of the distinction made by W. McKane, *Prophets and Wise Men* (1965), where he tends to equate wisdom and secular politics (cf. pp. 48–54) in a way which does less than justice to the religious convictions of both the wise and the politicians. The status of wise (= elders) in Jer. 18.18, Ezek. 7.26 alongside priests and prophets suggests that such simple distinctions cannot be made.
[28] As far as Megiddo, if Josiah met his death there protesting against Necho's unlawful passage through what was claimed as Josiah's own territory. Herodotus in his account of Necho (*Hist.* II, 159) mentions Magdolus as a place of battle with the Syrians (?Migdol)—this might be a corruption of Megiddo, but could be a reference to a locality in the coastal plain, militarily perhaps a better place to

the period of Josiah and possibly reflecting this extension,[29] was then shattered by the destruction of kingdom and religious centre in the years 597 and 587. It says much for the vitality of the religious faith which moved the Deuteronomic school that it was not so tied to national emblems—kingship, temple, land—that it could not accept the obvious consequences of this failure, though the shattering nature of the experience may well account for the apparently negative and pessimistic tone of the work.[30]

That Jer. 44, as we have seen (pp. 40f.), records the attitude of some —even among those in the entourage of Gedaliah and of Jeremiah himself—who blamed the forsaking of the Queen of Heaven for these untoward events, only serves to underline the reality of that faith which could say as firmly as does the Deuteronomic History that the events confirmed the reality of the judgement which belonged in the law and was exemplified in the history.

It is here that we may see the relationship and perhaps also the interaction of the prophetic contribution with that of the whole Deuteronomic movement. It has been maintained, particularly strongly by G. von Rad and E. Janssen against Köhler, that the Deuteronomists 'assimilated the message of the prophets to the theology of Deuteronomy'.[31] The relationship appears to be much closer than this.[32] Janssen argues that the prophets had found little hearing and could only come into their own when the disaster had

---

halt the Egyptian march, possibly Meṣad Ḥashavyahu. Cf. J. Naveh, 'The Excavations at Meṣad Ḥashavyahu—Preliminary Report', *IEJ* 12 (1962), pp. 89–113; see pp. 98f. for a note to the effect that Judaean control of this fortress appears to have ended with Josiah's death in 609 BC.

[29] Cf. J. Naveh, 'A Hebrew Letter from the Seventh Century', *IEJ* 10 (1960), pp. 129–39—from Meṣad Ḥashavyahu; S. Talmon, 'The New Hebrew Letter from the Seventh Century BC in Historical Perspective', *BASOR* 176 (Dec. 1964), pp. 29–38.
[30] Cf. G. Östborn, *op. cit.*, p. 35.
[31] Janssen, *op. cit.*, p. 74. Cf. G. von Rad, *Studies in Deuteronomy* (ET, 1953), pp. 69, 81f. For comments cf. E. W. Nicholson, *Deuteronomy and Tradition* (1967), pp. 107ff.
[32] Cf. L. Köhler, *Hebrew Man* (ET, 1956), pp. 165ff.; E. W. Nicholson, *op. cit.*, pp. 65ff., 76ff., 117f. Cf. also R. A. Henshaw, 'Prophetic Elements in the Book of Deuteronomy', a paper read to the Mid-West Section of the Society of Biblical Literature, April 1967, probably to be published in *JBL*. The views of H. W. Wolff, 'Hoseas geistige Heimat', *TLZ* 81 (1956), cols. 83–94 = *Ges. Stud.*, pp. 232–50, are also relevant in that he attempts to trace a relationship between Hosea and levitical circles, so closely associated with Deuteronomy by G. von Rad. See the comments of E. W. Nicholson, *op. cit.*, pp. 73ff.

confirmed the truth of their message.[33] This seems an oversimplification, linked with the idea that a clear distinction can be made between prophets of doom and prophets of weal (*Heilspropheten*), with the implication that the more optimistic views of the Deuteronomists belong more with the latter than with the former. Yet here again—as with the relationship between Jeremiah and the Deuteronomic movement—there is a community of thought which should not be missed. The distinction between two types of prophecy as such is understandable in view of the violent attacks of certain of the great named prophets upon their contemporaries. But we should not necessarily generalize from particular situations (such as Amos 7.10ff.), in which the problem of the prophet's authority is very much in debate. The recognition that we cannot just excise hopeful words from prophecies of doom is a recognition that, in fact, doom and hope belong together. As the closing words of the book of Hosea recognize (14.10), the effect of the divine word—which is one—is determined by what it meets, whether wisdom and uprightness, or sin and failure. Judgement is the obverse of salvation.[34]

So the appreciation of judgement is no new thing in Israel, but goes back—as may be seen in the psalmody of lamentation—to earlier concerns with the problem of divine displeasure. Jeremiah had a realism which saw that disaster was inevitable, yet could record his prophecies because 'perhaps the house of Judah may heed all the disaster which I am planning to do to them in order that they may turn back each man from his evil way of life and I may forgive their guilt and sin' (36.3). The Deuteronomic school could build on the

---

[33] *Op. cit.*, pp. 84f. Janssen utilizes too simply the indications of opposition to the great pre-exilic prophets without taking account of the preservation and re-application of their message. Cf. N. W. Porteous, 'The Prophets and the Problem of Continuity', in *Israel's Prophetic Heritage*, ed. B. W. Anderson and W. Harrelson (1962), pp. 11–25; P. R. Ackroyd, *Continuity* (1962), pp. 12ff. and *ASTI* 1 (1962), pp. 7–23. We may discount the attitude expressed by R. H. Pfeiffer, *Religion in the Old Testament* (London, 1961), p. 55, that the author of the Deuteronomic Code combines 'the unpopular religion taught by the prophets with the attractive worship of the God of Israel', while recognizing that the full values of prophetic teaching were not necessarily assimilated (cf. L. Köhler, *op. cit.*, p. 168).

[34] There is clearly contact here with the ideas of 'wisdom'; cf., e.g., M. Weinfeld, 'The Origin of the Humanism in Deuteronomy', *JBL* 80 (1961), pp. 241–7; 'Deuteronomy: The Present State of Inquiry', *JBL* 86 (1967), pp. 249–62, see pp. 256–7 on wisdom; W. McKane, *Prophets and Wise Men* (1965), pp. 102–13; J. Malfroy, 'Sagesse et Loi dans le Deutéronome', *VT* 15 (1965), pp. 49–65; C. M. Carmichael, 'Deuteronomic Laws, Wisdom, and Historical Traditions', *JSS* 12 (1967), pp. 198–206.

hope that an acceptable people of God would receive divine blessing, but yet could comprehend the disaster of loss of kingship, temple and national entity without abandoning their faith in the overruling will of God. Prophetic judgement served to reinforce this. Prophetic homiletic—so closely akin to Deuteronomic homiletic[35]—could point to what might be learnt from the experience of judgement and the discovery of divine mercy in judgement.

The disaster when it came produced a shattering effect on those who experienced it. Ezekiel shows us plainly the reaction of one who could only with time adjust himself to the new situation.[36] It is interesting to note that the Jeremiah tradition—though it is not clear how far this can be associated at this point directly with the prophet himself—contains a judgement upon the Babylonians who were the instruments of that disaster,[37] just as we find in Isaiah the twofold estimate of the Assyrians, as the instrument of God and as the recipient of divine condemnation.[38] Is there perhaps here a reflection of the fact that the genuine prophet, sensitive as he is to a failure which merits condemnation and to a divine holiness which sears and destroys, is nevertheless also deeply moved by the experience of what he believes with his mind to be divine judgement, but knows in his heart to be anything but an adequate expression of the divine will. The sight of Judah devastated, its cities in ruins, its capital systematically destroyed, its leadership for the most part taken into exile or dead, is not an occasion for glib statements about the relentlessness of divine retribution or the rightness of divine judgement, or at least not for these alone, but for the deep distress of one who sees the people of God so brought low as to leave the final issue in great doubt.[39]

It was in this situation—not immediately but after the passage of

[35] Cf. L. Köhler, *Hebrew Man* (ET, 1956), pp. 165ff.; P. R. Ackroyd, 'The Vitality of the Word of God in the Old Testament', *ASTI* I (1962), pp. 7–23, esp. p. 12; E. W. Nicholson, *op. cit.*, pp. 108ff.

[36] Cf. below, pp. 107f., and Ezek. 24.25ff.; 33.21f.

[37] Jer. 50–51, cf. 25.12–14. Cf. below, pp. 219ff.

[38] Isa. 10.5–11, 12–19. For a full discussion of the problems here, cf. B. S. Childs, *Isaiah and the Assyrian Crisis* (SBT II, 3, 1967).

[39] Cf. Jeremiah's expressions of anguish, e.g. in 4.19; 8.22f.; 10.19f.; and in ch. 13 and 14. So, too, in the so-called 'confessional passages'. Cf. H. Graf Reventlow, *Liturgie und prophetisches Ich bei Jeremia* (Gütersloh, 1963), pp. 205ff., for a stress on the corporate aspect of these statements—a useful if exaggerated protest against merely 'personal' interpretation of prophetic sayings. The opposite extreme may be found in P. E. Bonnard, *Le Psautier selon Jérémie* (Lectio Divina 26, Paris, 1960), where an attempt is made to prove the prophet's direct influence on twenty-three psalms. Cf. also Micah 1.8, 10, and pp. 245f. below on Job.

years which both dull the memory of the immediate disaster and also serve to impress the uncertainty of any possible restoration—that the Deuteronomic history as we now have it offered a presentation of what Israel had experienced[40] and what she was to learn from that experience.

2. THE CRITERIA OF THE DEUTERONOMIC PRESENTATION

The basis of the Deuteronomic presentation of history is twofold. It is that of the ancient confessional formula, so clearly expressed in Deut. 26 and Josh. 24, and echoed so often elsewhere in the Old Testament (cf., e.g., Jer. 2.4–7). It is combined in the Deuteronomic work with an extension forwards in history, with an assessment of the significance of the great moments which are decisive within the historical period following the conquest. So the second basis is that of the experience of that history, in which the great points are seen to be King and Temple.[41]

The first part of the work—from Deuteronomy to the end of Joshua—serves to emphasize the confessional basis of Israel's experience. By historical retrospect, we are put in the position of the Israel of the wilderness, on the threshold of the promised land. The events by which the deliverance has been effected are rehearsed, most probably on the basis of some liturgical usage such as is indicated in Deut. 31.9ff. In this context the law is presented, its meaning is homiletically expanded, warning and promise accompany it. The acceptance of it is the prelude to the conquest, and the culmination of the conquest is the reaffirmation of this acceptance.[42] The second part of the work (Judges and Samuel)—a dividing point may be made after Samuel or at the end of the reign of Saul, or perhaps at the establishment of David: the stages of the work are interwoven so that although the clarity of the thought is evident, the 'chapter division' is not necessarily made as we might make it—traces in the series of judge stories the repeated pattern of failure and divine grace,[43] with its culmination

[40] Cf. S. Herrmann, *Prophetie und Wirklichkeit in der Epoche des babylonischen Exils* (1967), pp. 13–16, 20–21.
[41] Cf. E. W. Nicholson, *op. cit.*, pp. 109ff., 114ff.
[42] Josh. 22–23 (24).
[43] Cf. also H. W. Wolff, *op. cit.*, pp. 175f. = pp. 312f. Wolff makes the division at I Sam. 12, which certainly punctuates and comments on the narrative. It looks both backwards and forwards, however, and does not necessarily indicate a break.

in the recognition of the need for a more enduring form in which the maintaining of the law and so the receiving of the promises can be guaranteed, with a link back to the kingship law of Deut. 17.14–20. This ushers in the founding of the monarchy, in which the various traditions are now so interpreted as to indicate that the monarchy is both a human institution, under divine judgement, and also a divinely ordained medium of divine grace.[44] Alongside this runs the establishment of the true shrine, for as one after another of the great religious centres of the earlier period is shown to be no longer the one chosen,[45] the choosing of Jerusalem, intimately connected with the establishment of true monarchy, makes the way clear for the building of the shrine which embodies that willingness of God to make his dwelling in the midst of the people;[46] and the establishment of the priestly line which is to serve him there[47] again runs parallel with the choosing of the royal line with which covenant is to be made. The climax is reached in the place of David as king, for already with Solomon, though he was the builder of the Temple, the decline sets in. Here— and the point is to be later made even more explicitly by the Chronicler[48]—all Israel is one under a ruler who is representative of God, a man after God's own heart, the maintainer of the law—as Deut. 17 had said he should be—for whom disaster follows from his infringement of it,[49] but whose position and succession are nevertheless established by divine grace at work even in the situation which was the cause of disaster.[50] The third part of the work, covering the remainder of the story of the kingdoms, shows a recurrent pattern of failure and grace. The north has split away into apostasy and the

[44] While it is true that the kings of Israel are treated with uniform hostility and only two kings of Judah escape blame, it is a mistake to underestimate in the books of Kings the recognition of a divine purpose within the institution. The Davidic line was ultimately to be a focal point of future hope, and this, surely, not because it had failed, but because it was regarded as divinely appointed. J. A. Soggin, 'Der judäische ʿam-hāʾāreṣ und das Königtum in Juda', *VT* 13 (1963), pp. 187–95, oversimplifies the matter both in regard to criticism of the monarchy and in regard to the status of the ʿam-hāʾāreṣ, but (p. 194 n. 2) he rightly criticizes the separation of Deuteronomic and monarchical ideas. There is a similar too-negative attitude in H. W. Wolff, *op. cit.*, p. 176 = p. 313, though this is in some measure balanced by the paragraphs that follow. (On ʿam hāʾāreṣ, cf. p. 150 n. 50.)
[45] Cf. Ps. 78, esp. vv. 60ff.
[46] Cf. R. E. Clements, *God and Temple* (1965), esp. pp. 63–78.
[47] This is anticipated in I Sam. 2.35.
[48] I Chron. 11.1–3.
[49] II Sam. 11–20.
[50] II Sam. 12.24–25.

forsaking of the Davidic line with which promise has been made—though even so there is no lack of indication of the faithfulness and patience of God with them.[51] The south, too, continually fails through her kings to abide by the pattern of obedience to the law, as this is particularly expressed in relation to the worshipping of God in the one place chosen, and so the avoiding of those wrong ideas of God which inevitably follow from a plurality of sanctuaries and from contamination with Canaanite ideas. The zeal of reformers such as Hezekiah and Josiah, particularly the latter in his obedience to the law, shows that there is always the possibility of a recovery of the promise. God himself for David's sake spares to his family this small southern kingdom, and long after it has merited disaster its life is continued,[52] only in the end to meet its inevitable doom.

The whole pattern of history is seen portrayed in rebellion and forgiveness. Moses stands as mediator between God and Israel, interceding on behalf of the people because of their failure; rebelliousness and divine forbearance and care are brought out in the opening chapters of Deuteronomy,[53] and seen as a pattern for the whole course of history as it is reviewed in Deut. 30, in Josh. 22–23, in Judg. 2–3, in I Sam. 12, in II Kings 17.[54] The whole work provides a detailed demonstration of the curses and threats,[55] as well as of the efficaciousness of the promises, so that it may be seen as a justification of the rightness of divine action, an acknowledgement of Israel's position before God.

In all this it is the law which is the fundamental test of Israel's obedience and at the same time the vehicle of divine promise. At the outset the law is expounded as the pattern upon which life is to be

[51] Cf. esp. II Kings 14.23–29 and 17.13ff.
[52] Cf. II Kings 17.19f. On the Deuteronomic judgement on the Davidic kings, cf. A. H. J. Gunneweg, VT 10 (1960), p. 340.
[53] Deut. 6.10–12; 8.18; 9.4–6.
[54] Cf. Janssen, op. cit., pp. 17, 70, 84ff.; also J. Muilenburg, 'The Form and Structure of the Covenantal Formulations', VT 9 (1959), pp. 347–65. Cf. below, p. 77. D. J. McCarthy, 'II Samuel 7 and the Structure of the Deuteronomic History', JBL 84 (1965), pp. 131–8, argues for the addition of II Sam. 7 to this series. Its structure is, however, rather different, though it certainly provides a link between the earlier promise (cf. Deut. 12.10) and the subsequent fulfilment in Temple and Kingship.
[55] Cf. M. Noth, ' "Die mit des Gesetzes Werken umgehen, die sind unter dem Fluch" ', in In piam memoriam A. von Bulmerincq (Riga, 1938), pp. 127–45 = Ges. Stud., pp. 155–71; ET in The Laws in the Pentateuch and Other Essays (London, 1966), pp. 118–31, esp. on Deut. 28. On the Deuteronomic History as illustrative of the law, cf. B. Albrektson, History and the Gods (1967), pp. 82ff.

lived when once Israel has come into the promised land, for the law's demand is based on the action of God, by which Israel was made a holy people.[56] Every detail is elaborated, so that it is made clear that law covers all human conduct. The natural casuistry which is associated with law[57] is here, through the centrality of the decalogue, linked with the position which Israel is to occupy, and indeed does already occupy, through the divine choice and action in the Exodus, as the people of God. The Deuteronomic Law is concerned throughout with the right ordering of the people of God.[58]

The same concern with the fitness of the people of God is to be found in the prophets, so that we need not immediately speculate whether Deuteronomy was influenced by the prophets or the prophets by the legal principle, but simply recognize that here are two different but not unrelated ways in which the fundamental position of the people is examined and maintained. If it is to be the recipient of divine promise, to enjoy that $m^enūḥā$ (rest) which God wills to give, it must be in the position of offering the right response,[59] so that the law may become the vehicle of divine blessing.[60] This point is amply clarified by the stress in Deuteronomy itself upon the conditions of divine blessing. When Israel has come into the land which it is God's pleasure to give to it, then obedience must follow as the proper response. Before the people at that time will be the choice between life and death,[61] and the outcome unavoidably depends upon Israel's acceptance of the exhortation to choose life. Warnings are there in plenty, but the stress is much more upon the appeal to choose the way of life and so to receive the divine blessing. This is the more impressive when it is remembered that the final setting of these appeals is not a moment of success, not even a moment in which a

[56] Cf. νόμος, *TWNT* 4, pp. 1033–5, ET, *Law* (London, 1962), pp. 33–37, and *TDNT* 4, pp. 1040–2; G. von Rad, *Theology* I, pp. 228f.

[57] Cf. below, p. 255.

[58] On Deuteronomy and the history as based on the *rîb* (lawsuit) theme—its only covenant a broken covenant—its exposition of covenant theology in terms of obedience—cf. G. E. Wright, 'The Lawsuit of God: A Form-Critical Study of Deuteronomy 32', in *Israel's Prophetic Heritage*, ed. B. W. Anderson and W. Harrelson (1962), pp. 26–67, see esp. pp. 59ff. Cf. also B. Lindars, 'Torah in Deuteronomy', in *Words and Meanings*, ed. P. R. Ackroyd and B. Lindars (Cambridge, 1968), pp. 117–36.

[59] This is the essential point made in Ps. 95.

[60] Cf. the discussion of this whole subject, and the cautions entered by W. Zimmerli, 'Das Gesetz im Alten Testament', *TLZ* 85 (1960), cols. 481–98 = *Gottes Offenbarung* (1963), pp. 249–76.

[61] Cf. Deut. 30.15ff.

prosperous outcome to the present situation seemed probable, but the moment when the people has suffered almost total loss and destruction, and when little or nothing points to a new life ahead.

In the event, Israel is portrayed as choosing the way of death, and so is brought to disaster. At the point at which the northern kingdom falls, a long reflective passage[62] indicates how Judah might have been expected to learn wisdom from this disaster. This is a theme in the prophets, too, for both Micah and Isaiah in the eighth-century situation point to what has befallen the northern kingdom in order to make plain to Judah just what are the inevitable consequences of her present condition.[63] Again in the later prophets both Jeremiah and Ezekiel[64] point to this, both using the same picture to show how Judah, who ought to have learnt from the disaster to Israel, showed herself to be even more unfaithful, to have surpassed her elder sister. The situation is typified in the reign of Manasseh; but again for Jehoiakim and Zedekiah the same point is made; and, without comment, simply with a factual relating of the events, the downfall of Judah is portrayed.[65]

All through it is made clear that the control lies with God. At every point it is God himself who acts, and however much the nations are described as bringing about the disasters which overtake the people, it is always God who is sovereign.[66] But the affirming of this, in statements which appear to be directed to those on whom earlier disasters fell, is directed really to the present audience. 'In the continuous falling away from Yahweh which is to be seen in the history of the people, the present generation sees its own guilt. The second person of the address in these speeches (i.e. the reviews which punctuate the narrative) does not simply refer to the hearers in the time of Joshua, or Samuel, or Solomon; for these are sermons. Everyone who hears them aright knows himself touched by them.[67] The same point is made by the fact that in the introduction to these speeches every different social group is enumerated (as similarly in the book of Jeremiah "all Judah" is named).[68] Law and history preached touch

[62] II Kings 17, esp. 19ff.
[63] Cf. Micah 1.5–9; Isa. 28.1–4, 7ff. (cf. P. R. Ackroyd, *ASTI* 1 (1962), pp. 7–23, see pp. 14f.); 9.7–20; 5.25–30.
[64] Cf. Jer. 3.6ff.; Ezek. 23, cf. 16.
[65] II Kings 24.20–25.21.
[66] Cf. Josh. 23.15; I Sam. 12.22, 24; I Kings 9.8f.; II Kings 17.10ff.; 21.14ff.; 23.26; 24.3, 20.
[67] Cf. E. J. Tinsley, *The Imitation of God in Christ* (London, 1960), pp. 53ff.
[68] E. Janssen, *op. cit.*, p. 70.

the hearts of the exilic community, and so the whole work, in so far as that community accepts it as a true interpretation of its history, comes as a confessional statement. It is the acknowledgement of Israel's faith before God, an acknowledgement of his justice. Von Rad calls it a *'Gerichtsdoxologie'*—an act of praise at the justice of the judgement of God;[69] and in that paradoxical term the two aspects of it are brought out, for it is both a recording and an acceptance. The type of the psalm of lamentation, with its apparent complaints at the silence and inactivity of the deity, is turned into its obverse—though this is in reality part of that psalm form—in which the acceptance of the rightness of divine judgement is in itself an anticipation of what may follow.[70]

3. THE OUTLOOK OF THE DEUTERONOMIC HISTORY

The acceptance of the judgement, the acknowledgement that it is the right outcome of the events which have now come upon Judah (and indeed upon all Israel), is the preliminary to whatever may follow. Only in this moment of acceptance can the people be in a right condition,[71] because only thus are they brought back to the realization of their complete dependence upon God. Just as the historical retrospect in psalms and histories demonstrates the prerogative of God, and binds the people to him afresh, so this statement with its apparent lack of hope for the future lays the only possible foundation for the future. The recalling and acceptance make possible—if it is God's will to show mercy and to begin the scheme again—a renewed life of Israel as his people. It is contingent, but it depends upon the one thing which Israel has reason to believe is sure, namely the absolute rightness and justice and assuredness of divine action.

Noth considers that the interpretation offered stops short of the moment of promise.[72] It is true that there is no explicit statement in

---

[69] *Theologie des AT* I (Munich, [2]1958), p. 340, cf. pp. 354ff.; ET, p. 343, cf. pp. 357ff., 'doxology of judgement'.

[70] Cf. also the comments below (p. 82) on H. W. Wolff's stress on the theme as one of a 'call to repentance'.

[71] O. Eissfeldt, *Introduction*, p. 225, describes the 'law of warfare' in Deut. 23.10–15 as applied to the purification of Israel. Cf. G. von Rad, *Der heilige Krieg im alten Israel* (ATANT 20, 1951), pp. 69f.

[72] M. Noth, *Überlieferungsgeschichtliche Studien* (1943, [2]1957), pp. 107ff.; *History of Israel*, p. 290. Cf. also the negative comments in ' "Die mit des Gesetzes Werken Umgehen, die sind unter dem Fluch" ', in *In piam memoriam A. von Bulmerincq* (Riga, 1938), pp. 127–45, see esp. pp. 141ff. = *Ges. Stud.*, pp. 155–71, see esp. pp. 168ff.; ET (cf. p. 75 n. 55), see pp. 126ff.

the last part of the work to suggest that there will be a happy outcome. We may recall that the writer was looking at the situation in a moment when years had already passed since the disaster, and still no sign appeared which augured hope. The same type of concern is seen in Lam. 5. The poet raises the question 'Why do you, Yahweh, forget us for ever' (v. 20).[73] It is a familiar motif of the psalms of lamentation. That Yahweh is in control, the poet is firmly convinced (v. 19). That God will help his people is his hope and that an assured hope; for why else should he pray? But his distress is that Yahweh's saving hand is not yet taking hold of the situation.[74] What is said of this passage may equally well be said of the Deuteronomic History. It is true that the latest event recorded there, the release of Jehoiachin, does not explicitly indicate hope. It is possible—with Noth—to interpret it as being the denial of a forlorn hope, an answer to those who pinned their faith to a renewed Davidic kingship through Jehoiachin. That it raised speculation among both the exiles and those in Palestine is to be supposed, for why else should it be recorded, and may it not be supposed too that it lies in the background of Deutero-Isaiah's thought?[75] But Noth thinks that 'all the days of his life' II Kings 25.30) is an indication that Jehoiachin is now dead.[76] The hopes raised are dying. The flame had flickered once and gone out. No alternative appears.

It may be doubted whether this gloomy interpretation is the right one,[77] for it must be recalled that there is a link, implicit not explicit, with the promises of eternal covenant with David.[78] Here at the end of the narrative the legitimate descendant of David, the recognized

---

[73] Or 'utterly'—if lāneṣaḥ is taken to be superlative rather than temporal in sense. Cf. D. Winton Thomas, 'The Use of nēṣaḥ as a Superlative in Hebrew', *JSS* 1 (1956), pp. 106–9. Here, however, lāneṣaḥ is paralleled by leʾōrek yāmīm so that the temporal meaning is not absent.

[74] So E. Janssen, *op. cit.*, p. 71.

[75] Cf. below, pp. 124ff.

[76] Cf. his more detailed discussion, 'Zur Geschichtsauffassung des Deuteronomisten', *Proc. XXII. Congress of Orientalists Istanbul, 1951* II (Leiden, 1957), pp. 558–66. Cf. below n. 79.

[77] Cf. H. W. Wolff's criticisms of Noth, *op. cit.*, pp. 172f. = pp. 309f.

[78] Cf. G. von Rad, *Theology* I, pp. 343ff. Wolff's criticism that there is no direct allusion to the Nathan promise may be accepted (*op. cit.*, p. 174 = p. 311), and yet it be recognized that the hope though hesitant is none the less a real one. The historian does not develop all his themes fully. Cf. also the review of Noth, von Rad and Wolff in H. Timm, 'Die Ladeerzählung (I Sam. 4–6; II Sam. 6) und das Kerygma des deuteronomistischen Geschichtswerkes', *EvTh* 26 (1966), pp. 509–26; Timm points to the parallel between Israel's situation at the loss of the ark and

king, is restored to favour 'all the days of his life', i.e. in perpetuity, for the phrase need not be so narrowly construed as to mean that this was already at an end.[79] Throughout the whole work, the overtones of promise are present.[80] It is when Israel is an obedient people, responsive to the law, that it becomes the recipient of divine promise. The apparently hopeless situation of the exile has raised questions about the future, for it might well appear that the conditions for obedience no longer exist. Certain of the obvious necessities under the previous system are no longer present; there is no Temple in the full sense, though the possibility that some kind of practice at the Temple was still being observed must not be forgotten.[81] The land is in a sense lost. The king was in prison, but still acknowledged as king, as we may see both from the Babylonian records and from the book of Ezekiel, as well as from the statement in II Kings 25.27.[82] Now he is

---

in the exile. Hope then rested in Yahweh alone; so, too, for the period of the exile. A comparison might also be made with the exposition in II Kings 17, esp. vv. 19ff., giving the reasons for a delay in the execution of judgement on Judah.

[79] A comparison of the text of II Kings 25.30 with its parallel in Jer. 52.34 reveals what must clearly be regarded as a duplicate reading (cf. S. Talmon, 'Double Readings in the Massoretic Text', *Textus* 1 [1960], pp. 144–84, see p. 165). Of the two phrases, 'all the days of his life' (*kōl yᵉmē ḥayyāw*), and 'to the day of his death' (*'ad yōm mōtō*), II Kings 25.30 (MT, LXX and Targ.) has the former alone; Jer. 52.34 (MT, Targ.) has both; Jer. 52.34 (LXX) has the latter alone. Talmon, surely rightly, describes them as 'synonymous expressions'; in that case, the more obvious sense of the positive form is not excluded in the negative 'to the day of his death'—i.e. both phrases mean primarily 'in perpetuity, continuously, without further interruption'. Can we detect which is the more original? M. Noth (*op. cit.*, in n. 76 above, p. 561) thinks no proof is possible, but prefers the form in II Kings 25.30. It could be argued that the negative form belongs to a later stage when Jehoiachin must have been dead, whereas the positive form could be stated while he was still alive. On the other hand, we might need to take account of the fact that II Kings 25.30 forms the end of that section of the Hebrew Canon which is known as the 'Former Prophets', and a positive note might therefore be more important here than at the end of Jer. (so Jer. LXX). But Jer. (MT) has also been given the positive ending because it completes a book. The positive form could, on that basis be, as some commentators think, a 'euphemistic substitute' (cf. J. A. Montgomery, *Kings*, ed. H. S. Gehman [ICC, 1951], p. 569, for references).

[80] Cf., e.g., Deut. 4.30f.; I Kings 8.46–50.

[81] Cf. above, pp. 25ff.

[82] Cf. above p. 32. Cf. K. Baltzer; 'Das Ende des Staates Juda und die Messias-Frage' (cf. p. 30, n. 59), pp. 37f. Hesitation in regard to the monarchy may be seen in the sharply diverging narratives concerning its foundation in I Sam. and perhaps also in the royal law of Deut. 17.14–20; though the latter may reflect a period earlier than the exilic situation (cf. K. Galling, 'Das Königsgesetz im Deuteronomium', *TLZ* 76 [1950], cols. 133–8), it may be seen as meaningful for that period.

released. In the desperate situation of the years of depression, God has acted. Jehoiachin has 'put off his prison garments'—an expressive way of indicating the change of situation, just as in Zech. 3 the change of raiment shows a change of divine favour.[83] A change of raiment means a change of fortune, and so the indication of divine blessing is here.

It is this which indicates the promise to a generation which has, by implication, been depicted as the generation of the wilderness. Transported in imagination—as well as in cultic celebration—into the wilderness situation, Israel is metaphorically once again in the plains of Moab, able to look back and forward.[84] The experience of the Exodus, the knowledge of disobedience even in that,[85] is now reinforced by the experience of the whole history. The 'now' of the cult, the 'this day' of Deuteronomy is actualized for them in the present realities.[86] The hope for the future[87] lies in the assurance of the mercy of God, and of the supremacy of the one who cannot be allowed to have been defeated any more than he has been defeated in his former contests. As in his contest with Baal in the Gideon story (as it is now told),[88] in his contest with Dagon in the land of the Philistines,[89] in his contest with the Baal at Carmel,[90] as against the claims of the Assyrian Rabshakeh,[91] so here, too, in the contest—for such it is—with the alien powers which have for the moment overrun his people at his behest, he is still supreme, and in his willingness to show favour there is hope.[92]

[83] Cf. below, pp. 184f., on Zech. 3. The provision of changes of clothing as a mark of favour appears, for example, in the Joseph story, Gen. 45.22.

[84] Cf. G. von Rad, 'Ancient Word and Living Word', *Interpretation* 15 (1961), pp. 3–13, see p. 7; J. M. Myers, 'The Requisites for Response: On the Theology of Deuteronomy', *ibid.*, pp. 14–31.

[85] Cf. Ps. 95.8–11.

[86] Cf. E. J. Tinsley, *op. cit.*, p. 54; G. von Rad, *Das Gottesvolk im Deuteronomium* (BWANT 47, 1929), pp. 59ff.; *Theology* I, pp. 334ff.; E. Voegelin, *Israel and Revelation* (1956), p. 374; E. P. Blair, 'An Appeal to Remembrance: The Memory Motif in Deuteronomy', *Interpretation* 15 (1961), pp. 41–47. G. M. Tucker, 'Witnesses and "Dates" in Israelite Contracts', *CBQ* 28 (1966), pp. 42–45, points to a significant legal usage which enlarges our understanding of the phrase 'this day'. He shows how it is equivalent to 'from today and in perpetuity': the people's acceptance of divine action thereby pledges it to perpetual obedience.

[87] Cf. R. A. F. MacKenzie, 'The Messianism of Deuteronomy', *CBQ* 19 (1957), pp. 299–305; and cf. H. Timm, *op. cit.*

[88] Judg. 6.25–32. E. Janssen, *op. cit.*, p. 63.

[89] I Sam. 5–6. Cf. A. Bentzen, *JBL* 67 (1948), pp. 37–53.

[90] I Kings 18.17–40. E. Janssen, *op. cit.*, p. 63.

[91] II Kings 18.13–19.37; Isa. 36–37. On these passages, cf. further B. S. Childs, *Isaiah and the Assyrian Crisis* (1967), pp. 69–103.

[92] O. Bächli, *Israel und die Völker* (ATANT 41, 1962) makes interesting comments

The whole purpose of such an exhortation as this great work contains is to bring the people back to him, back to obedience, and to that maintenance of law and faithfulness which makes them in such a way the people of God that they may receive what he offers.[93] Even now they can hear the invitation to choose life, 'that you may live, you and your descendants' and dwell in the land, at present only partially occupied and controlled by alien authority, but once again to be theirs. This is presented not just as a law to be obeyed—though this is exhorted—but as a confrontation with the living God to whom response is to be made.[94] A similar stress is offered by H. W. Wolff[95] in his tracing of the use of the root *šūb* (return, repent) in a series of crucial passages,[96] and in particular in his recognition that what must come about is the result not so much of human action as of a divinely willed promise in judgement.

Here is an interpretation of the whole range of the events, an understanding of the disaster in terms of divine judgement on Israel's sin, an appreciation that restoration—adumbrated[97] but not yet realized —rests in the purpose of God to choose his people again, and for David's sake not to abandon them for ever. The new community is to be created on the pattern of the old,[98] a community which is to be a religious entity, totally in relationship to Yahweh.[99] 'The old traditions must be collected . . . and applied constructively so far as is possible for the reconstitution of life.'[100] This reconstitution is depen-

on the problem of Israel's position and the safeguarding of it from alien influence. But his treatment is too much subordinated to this one idea of averting alien influence to do justice to the much richer texture of Deuteronomic material.

[93] Cf. G. von Rad, *Das Gottesvolk im Deuteronomium* (1929); E. W. Nicholson, *op. cit.*, pp. 123f.

[94] '*νόμος*', *TWNT* 4, pp. 1033–5; ET, *Law* (1962), pp. 33ff., and *TDNT* 4, pp. 1040ff. Cf. also H. H. Schmid, 'Das Verständnis der Geschichte im Deuteronomium', *ZThK* 64 (1967), pp. 1–15, see p. 8.

[95] *Op. cit.*, esp. the summary on pp. 183–6 = pp. 321–4.

[96] For this root, cf. the full study by W. L. Holladay, *The Root Šûbh in the Old Testament* (Leiden, 1958), and see pp. 127f. on Deuteronomic usage.

[97] Cf. Wolff, *op. cit.*, pp. 185f. = 323f.; J. Hempel, *Geschichten und Geschichte im Alten Testament bis zur persischen Zeit* (Gütersloh, 1964), pp. 212–19.

[98] Cf. W. Harrington, 'A Biblical View of History', *IrishThQ* 29 (1962), pp. 207–22.

[99] Cf. O. Eissfeldt, *Geschichtliches und Übergeschichtliches im Alten Testament* (ThStKr 109/2, 1947), pp. 15f.; A. R. Hulst, 'Der Name "Israel" im Deuteronomium', *OTS* 9 (1951), pp. 65–106, see pp. 102ff.

[100] E. Janssen, *op. cit.*, p. 63, and pp. 73ff., with a stress on *menūḥā* (rest). Cf. also H. H. Schmid, *op. cit.*, pp. 10f.; A. Causse, *Du groupe ethnique à la communanté religieuse* (Strasbourg, Paris, 1937), pp. 114–79, 196.

dent on the action of God.[101] It is also directed outwards from Israel, as a witness to the nations; her obedience will evoke their response.[102]

[101] Cf. N. Lohfink, 'Darstellungskunst und Theologie in Dtn. 1, 6–3, 29', *Biblica* 41 (1960), pp. 105–34, see pp. 132–4.
[102] Cf. Deut. 4.6 and see H. Graf Reventlow, 'Die Völker als Jahwes Zeugen bei Ezechiel', *ZAW* 71 (1959), pp. 33–43, see p. 36. Ct. below pp. 115ff. A short survey of the significance of Deuteronomy—which leads on naturally into the wider questions here discussed—is to be found in R. E. Clements, *God's Chosen People. A Theological Interpretation of Deuteronomy* (London, 1968).

VI

THE HISTORIANS AND THEOLOGIANS
OF THE EXILIC AGE
(continued)

B. THE PRIESTLY WORK

THE SECOND of the great compilations is the Priestly Work, in its final form more or less coincident with the Tetrateuch, the first four books of the Old Testament, but probably including also some part of the material now to be found at the end of Deuteronomy and in the second half of the book of Joshua.[1] But here the whole discussion is much more complex because the stages in its evolution are not easily to be defined either chronologically or in precise extent;[2] and, unlike the Deuteronomic History, they provide us with no clear fixed point to which they can be attached.

Nevertheless, without any insistence on precise chronology, we may examine two aspects of the material, each of which is related in some measure to the other; and even if it is not possible to say dogmatically that one or both of these belongs precisely to the exilic age, they nevertheless belong to the general situation. They are both concerned, in one way or another, with that dilemma in which the people of Israel found themselves at the moment at which the whole structure of their life seemed to have collapsed. In some respects this great work may perhaps be seen as an alternative to—even a replacement for—the Deuteronomic structure.[3]

We may look first at the Holiness Code and second at the completed

---

[1] Cf. above, p. 62 n. 3.

[2] On problems of literary structure and editorial process, cf. K. Elliger, *Leviticus* (HAT 4, 1966), pp. 7ff., and his discussion of the traditio-historical approaches, e.g. in K. Koch, *Die Priesterschrift von Exodus 25 bis Leviticus 16* (FRLANT 71, 1959); H. Graf Reventlow, *Das Heiligkeitsgesetz formgeschichtlich untersucht* (WMANT 6, 1957 [1961]).

[3] Cf. Janssen, *op. cit.*, pp. 81f.

Priestly Work (incorporating the Holiness Code), by which is denoted the whole structure in which the material of the older sources is elaborated into a coherent and unified work. It is very generally agreed that the material in its present form belongs to the exilic period and later;[4] it is also very generally agreed that its final form is due to Babylonian rather than Palestinian groups.[5] So far as dating is concerned, it must immediately be noted that this is only a dating of the ultimate presentation,[6] since there is very evident in all this a great mass of early legal and narrative material, deriving in all probability from various centres. As in the case of the Deuteronomic History, we are not here concerned to discuss the provenance of the material, in so far as it is earlier. It may derive in some part from sanctuaries other than Jerusalem;[7] it may derive in part from the north rather than the south; it may in some respects preserve even more ancient material than do the other great sources of the Pentateuch. Our concern is the shape into which it was put in the later stages, and for this the period of the sixth and fifth centuries is the most probable. With the Holiness Code, such a date is suggested very strongly both by the intimate relationship between it and the book of Ezekiel,[8] and by the concluding hortatory message of Lev. 26,

---

[4] So for example, M. Noth, *Exodus* (ET, OTL, 1962), pp. 16ff., placing P between 587 (571) and 515. A. S. Kapelrud, 'The Date of the Priestly Code (P)', *ASTI* 3 (1964), pp. 58–64, argues for a date between 585 and 550 BC, though his argument depends rather too much on the definition of precise literary affinities. O. Eissfeldt, *Introduction*, pp. 207f.

[5] Cf. O. Eissfeldt, *loc. cit.*; G. Fohrer, *Einleitung*, pp. 201f.

[6] A. Hurvitz, 'The usage of *šeš* and *būṣ* in the Bible and its implication for the date of P', *HTR* 60 (1967), pp. 117–21, finds evidence here of a particular early linguistic use in P. Even if, as he thinks possible, more such examples may be found on a close examination of the material, the indications are simply of an early date for sections, perhaps even large sections, of the material. The date of the final presentation can still only be determined by an examination of the whole work.

[7] So J. Hempel, 'Priesterkodex', *PW* 22, 2 (1954), cols. 1943–67, who thinks of Hebron. (See references also in G. von Rad, *Studies in Deuteronomy* [ET, 1953], pp. 42f.) Cf. R. E. Clements, *Abraham and David* (1967), pp. 24ff., 35, on Hebron-connections of the Abrahamic covenant. Cf. below, p. 94. M. Haran, 'Shiloh and Jerusalem: The Origin of the Priestly Tradition in the Pentateuch', *JBL* 81 (1962), pp. 14–24, argues for Shiloh.

[8] On Ezekiel, cf. below, pp. 103ff. On H and Ezekiel, cf. O. Eissfeldt, *Introduction*, p. 238; G. Fohrer, *Die Hauptprobleme des Buches Ezechiel* (BZAW 72, 1952), pp. 144–8. On the relationships of H and P, and H and Ezekiel, cf. also L. E. Elliott-Binns, 'Some problems of the Holiness code', *ZAW* 67 (1955), pp. 26–40. Cf. also W. Zimmerli, 'Ich bin Jahwe' in *Geschichte und Altes Testament (Festschrift A. Alt*, BHT 16, 1953), pp. 179–209, see pp. 181ff. = *Gottes Offenbarung*, pp. 11–40, see pp. 12ff.; C. Feucht, *op. cit.* (p. 88 n. 17), pp. 184ff. Cf. also H. Graf Reventlow *Das,*

which evidently envisages an exilic situation.[9] Arguments from style
and language make it not unreasonable to place the main part of the
Jeremiah, Ezekiel, Deuteronomy, and Holiness Code material all
very close together in about the sixth century, not too far removed
from the style of the Lachish Letters;[10] but, of course, such an argument cannot be very precise because of the possibilities of influence of
one part of the material upon another. So far as the P material is
concerned, and also the completed work of which it provides the
basic structure and which is therefore hardly to be separated from it,
the exilic situation of the sixth century appears not unreasonable in
view of the rather reserved attitude which this material takes towards
the idea of restoration. But it is clear that such an attitude may well
have continued into the following century when, although the rebuilding of the Temple and the reordering of the life of the Jewish community were visible indications of the re-establishment of the people,
there are likely to have been some idealists who cherished the hope of a
more thoroughgoing reform, a more radical handling of the underlying needs of a community whose life had been so deeply shattered.[11]
It is difficult, as we shall see, to avoid the conclusion that the Priestly
stratum is itself a product of the exilic period in the narrower sense.[12]
The combination of this with earlier material to form the Tetrateuch[13]

Heiligkeitsgesetz formgeschichtlich untersucht (WMANT 6, 1957 [1961]) and criticisms
of this in K. Elliger, *Leviticus* (HAT 4, 1966), pp. 14ff.

[9] Cf. esp. vv. 33–39. That threats of exile as punishment could have been made
earlier is clear; but this passage depicts the exilic situation, and offers an interpretation of it (cf. below, pp. 89f.), in such a clear manner as to make the sixth-century
dating for its final form quite evident.

[10] The points of contact with these Letters (cf. *DOTT*, pp. 212f., and bibliography, p. 217) are, of course, limited by the small amount of material which they
offer. The evidence is not in itself enough to prove a sixth-century date for these
parts of the Old Testament. But it does nevertheless seem significant that it is with
these books that the closest affinities are to be found. On Jeremiah and Ezekiel, cf.
J. W. Miller, *Das Verhältnis Jeremias und Hesekiels sprachlich und theologisch untersucht*
(Assen, 1955), pp. 67–185. On H and Ezekiel, cf. p. 85 n. 8; on Jeremiah and
Deuteronomy, cf. p. 59 n. 39.

[11] Another more radical treatment of the problems of the exilic age is to be
found in the work of the Chronicler, cf. below, pp. 263ff.

[12] Cf. K. Elliger 'Sinn und Ursprung der priesterlichen Geschichtserzählung',
ZThK 49 (1952), pp. 121–43, see p. 143 = *Kl. Schr.* (ThB 32, 1966), pp. 174–98,
see pp. 197f.

[13] It is difficult if not impossible to be sure whether this is the right description
of the relationship, or whether we should more properly speak (as does I. Engnell, for
example, cf. *Gamla Testamentet. En traditionshistorisk inledning*, i [Stockholm, 1945],
pp. 209–59, where he expounds the division 'Tetrateuch-Deuteronomistic Work')

—subsequently no doubt to be elaborated at many points—could have taken place not so very long after, and the continued idealism would suggest that the background is a period in which uncertainty about the establishment of the Jewish community still existed. A *terminus ad quem* of a not very satisfactory kind is provided by the existence of the Pentateuch in the hands of the Samaritan community,[13a] together with the probability that it belongs already to the period of Ezra (for whom a date of 398 seems most probable); in which case it may be possible to see the work of Ezra as an attempt at ordering and unifying the life of a community which had two main strands of thought, the Deuteronomic and the Priestly, which are drawn together in the reconciliation of the two works, and expressed in the writings of the Chronicler who owes so much to the Deuteronomists and much also to the Priestly school. But these are speculations which go considerably beyond the scope of the present discussion, and they cannot here be dealt with in detail.

I. THE HOLINESS CODE (LEV. 17–26)

The recognition that in its present form Lev. 17–26 forms a unit goes back to the work of Klostermann in 1877.[14] The name 'Holiness Code' (H) derives from his recognition that the emphasis laid upon: 'You are to be holy, for I Yahweh your God am holy' and the use of this and similar expressions mark out the section as having special characteristics. Indeed, much of the material of the section is concerned with the problem of the holiness, the fitness in both cultic and ethical ways, of the people before their God.[15] Such a concern is also very much in the mind of the author(s) of the Priestly stratum, so that the inclusion of this independent section within the larger work is not

---

of P as the 'last tradent' ('helt enkelt är den siste tradenten och utgivaren av P-verket'), i.e. the final formulator of the already existing traditions (cf. also the account in C. R. North, *OTMS*, pp. 67f.). But perhaps, on balance, it may be wisest to distinguish two stages in view of the presence in the Tetrateuch of some quite substantial P narratives—e.g. in the rebellion complex of Num. 15–16—which though now closely combined with earlier material presuppose an earlier independent existence (cf. O. Eissfeldt, *Introduction*, pp. 205ff.).

[13a] Cf. also p. 236 n. 12.
[14] A. Klostermann, 'Beiträge zur Entstehungsgeschichte des Pentateuchs' *ZLThK* 38 (1877), pp. 401–45 = *Der Pentateuch* (Leipzig, 1893), pp. 368–418: 'Ezechiel und das Heiligkeitsgesetz'.
[15] Cf. R. H. Pfeiffer, *Religion in the Old Testament* (1961), pp. 178f.

difficult to understand. Furthermore, the stress on holiness marks one of the main points of relationship between this section and the book of Ezekiel, with which the affinities are both linguistic and theological.[16]

The whole section is by no means unified.[17] It contains within itself a whole series of smaller units, some of which may have existed as independent groups of laws, collections concerned with particular subjects. Thus the laws concerning sabbath and feasts in 23–24.9 and the laws of the sabbath and jubilee years in 25–26.2 (culminating in a demand for avoidance of idolatry) stand separate from the other material, and do not have any introductory or concluding formulae of exhortation. Included with them is the one quite odd piece of narrative in 24.10–23 which is much more like the pieces of illustrative narrative which appear in P, as, for example, in Num. 25.6–18. Such narratives serve to make precise the application of the particular law under discussion, a law which is in this particular passage incorporated into the narrative (Lev. 24.15f.) and is then elaborated with a group of other laws for which the penalty is also death.

After ch. 17, which contains regulations concerning sacrificial practice and the reason for the blood being untouched, the first main section (18) has both an introductory exhortation, warning against Egyptian and Canaanite practices (vv. 1–5), and a concluding admonition which refers back to the primarily sexual laws of the intervening passage, and warns of the consequences of following these things which are an abomination to Yahweh.[18] A similar introduction (vv. 1–4) and conclusion (v. 37) are provided for ch. 19. Here the introduction stresses the basic laws, and indeed summarizes the first half of the decalogue; the laws which follow are of various kinds, but in part they elaborate the decalogue material. The section stresses the Exodus events as basic. The concluding injunction is a very general one. Chapter 20 has vv. 22–24, 26 as a conclusion (vv. 25 and 27 appear to be additions); this section is closely similar to ch. 18,

---

[16] Cf. p. 85 n. 8.

[17] Cf., for example, the discussion in O. Eissfeldt, *Introduction*, pp. 233–7; M. Noth, *Leviticus* (ET, OTL, 1965), pp. 127f.; C. Feucht, *Untersuchungen zum Heiligkeitsgesetz* (TA 20, 1964), pp. 13–73, who identifies two main collections H1 (18–23a) and H2 (25–26).

[18] Cf. the discussion of the parenetic elements here by K. Elliger, 'Das Gesetz Leviticus 18', *ZAW* 67 (1955), pp. 1–25 = *Kl. Schr.* (1966), pp. 232–59; *idem*, 'Ich bin der Herr—euer Gott' in *Theologie als Glaubenswagnis* (*Festschrift K. Heim*, Hamburg, 1954), pp. 9–34, see pp. 10ff. = *Kl. Schr.*, pp. 211–31, see pp. 212ff.

but includes some emphasis on idolatrous practice as well as on sexual impurity.[19] Chapters 21–22 concern the priesthood and its purity, and are concluded with 22.32f., with a rather greater emphasis on profaning the holy name of God.

These various shorter exhortations to obedience punctuate the present arrangement of the legal material, though there is nothing very coherent about them. The fullest of them, in ch. 18, stresses the avoidance of the practices of Canaan (and Egypt), and this is to some extent repeated in ch. 20. But the main hortatory emphasis of the whole section is to be found in 26.3–45 (v. 46 provides the colophon to the whole passage). Here the theme is of obedience and disobedience, and in many respects it resembles the hortatory passage in Deut. 27.9–10; 28 (as also the material of Deut. 30).[20] The arrangement of the chapter clearly follows a familiar pattern. Verses 3–13 stress obedience and its effects in victory and life; vv. 14–20, 21–22, 23–26, provide a threefold warning of the consequences of disobedience: each stage of disobedience leads to a sevenfold punishment, the previous warning ignored leads on into a further disaster—the disasters are lack of fertility; famine; wild beasts; pestilence and enemy, with an obvious picture of siege conditions.[21] The final consequence is in vv. 27–33, when no warning has been heeded and the disaster is in terms which are clearly reminiscent of the horrors of the siege and warfare and devastation of 587. With such a climactic passage we may compare the poem on the northern kingdom to be found in Isa. 9.7–20 (10.1–4) + 5.25–30, where a similar climax is reached, and also the indications of warning and refusal in Amos 4. The verses which follow describe the exile (vv. 34–39),[22] the people weakened by the faintness which God sends into their hearts, while the land recovers from the wrong treatment it has had, by now being able to

---

[19] For a fresh discussion of the significance of Lev. 18 and 20 as concerned with the nature of the family and the obligations of its members, cf. J. R. Porter, *The Extended Family in the Old Testament* (Occasional Papers in Social and Economic Administration, No. 6, London, 1967).

[20] Cf. M. Noth, ' "Die mit des Gesetzes Werken umgehen, die sind unter dem Fluch" ', in *In piam memoriam A. von Bulmerincq* (1938), pp. 127–45 = *Ges. Stud.* (²1960), pp. 155–71; ET in *The Laws in the Pentateuch and Other Essays* (1966), pp. 118–31; *idem, Leviticus* (ET, OTL, 1965), pp. 195ff.; O. Eissfeldt, *Introduction*, pp. 234, 237f.; L. E. Elliott-Binns, *op. cit.*, pp. 34f.

[21] Cf. Ezek. 5.10–17; Jer. 15.3.

[22] H. Graf Reventlow, *ZAW* 71 (1959), p. 40, regards Lev. 26 not as historical retrospect but as a conditional prophetic proclamation. But it may surely legitimately be seen as both.

keep sabbaths.[23] The conclusion points to the possibility of repentance.[24] If they repent, God will remember his covenant with their forefathers (v. 42) and will remember the land. Verses 43–45 offer a second statement, perhaps a duplicate of 34–42, in which stress is again laid upon the land keeping sabbath; but God will not utterly forsake his people, nor break his covenant; he is Yahweh their God. For their sake he will remember the covenant with their forefathers, namely the generation of the Exodus. These two conclusions stress two different ways of thinking about the relationship between God and Israel, one in terms of the covenant with Abraham, Isaac and Jacob, the other in terms of the Exodus. This would seem to suggest a combining of two motifs, one more characteristic of the P material, the other belonging more definitely with the Deuteronomic line of thought.[25]

It is this final section which must really reveal the eventual purpose of the Holiness Code. The earlier groups of laws, and even some formulation of them, may antedate the exile. But here we have the indication that the compilation was seen as providing a basis for the building up of the new community.[26] The possibility of return is not clearly stated. Like P, as we shall see,[27] and like D, as we have already noted,[28] the future is not to be thought of in glowing terms as if restoration were to be a comparatively simple matter. It is only after many warnings that God has brought the disaster; so though repentance is possible, the precise outcome is not made explicit. Only the statement 'I will remember the land' (26.42) indicates the prospect of a return and a rebuilding of life in Palestine. But in such a context, even with so slight an indication, the laws governing obedience and purity and right sacrificial and cultic practice, all make sense. They are the laws for a community which has the chance of repudiating those evils of Canaan and elsewhere that in the past have

[23] It may be observed that this idea is taken up and elaborated first by the Chronicler (II Chron. 36.21) with the interpretation of the exile as a 'sabbath' period, and later by the author of Daniel (Dan. 9.1f., 24–27), both with the combining of this theme with the seventy-year prophecy of Jer. 25.11f., 29.10. (Cf. also pp. 241ff. for a fuller discussion of this point, with references.)

[24] W. Zimmerli, 'Sinaibund und Abrahambund: Ein Beitrag zum Verständnis der Priesterschrift', *TZ* 16 (1960), pp. 268–80, esp. pp. 276ff. = *Gottes Offenbarung*, pp. 205–16, esp. pp. 213f.

[25] Cf. W. Zimmerli, *op. cit.*, p. 278 = p. 215. Cf. also the combining of motifs in the Chronicler.

[26] Cf. O. Eissfeldt, *Introduction*, p. 238; C. Feucht, *op. cit.*, pp. 181ff.

[27] Cf. below, pp. 101f.

[28] Cf. above, pp. 78ff.

spoiled her life.[29] This community can now, because of God's faithfulness to his covenant, become the real people of God, and as such to testify to the nations of Yahweh's action.[30]

2. THE PRIESTLY WORK

It is an impression received by many that the Priestly work is a rather dull and repetitive collection of laws and genealogies, descriptions of the ordering of cultic matters and the like. But, in fact, it is a narrative work,[31] and in this sense may be seen as a parallel to the other Pentateuchal narrative strands, tracing the history of Israel from the very beginnings which are linked into the primeval history (as in J) to the time of the Exodus and wilderness. The precise point at which it ends is not so clear, and this is a point which has to be considered in the light of what may be traced of its purpose. Of particular interest is the chronological scheme which underlies the narrative, for although there is some inevitable uncertainty about the figures involved—in view of considerable deviations in the Septuagint and Samaritan—yet it would appear most probable that the linking of the Exodus to the Creation is deliberate and that the total of years (MT 2666) is designed to indicate two-thirds of a period of 4,000 years, at the end of which it may be presumed some terminus was to be reached. In view of the uncertainty of the figures, however, and the probability that the terminus of this period would bring us somewhere into the last two or at most three centuries BC, we may suppose that the dating has been elaborated not only in Samaritan (2,967 years) and Septuagint (3,446 years) but also in the Hebrew text to fit in with speculations concerning the end of the age which are likely to have developed markedly in the period of the emergence of apocalyptic.[32] Nevertheless, it is likely that such a later development

---

[29] Cf. A. Causse, *Les dispersés d'Israël* (1929), pp. 47–49, on the stress on purity and exclusiveness.

[30] Cf. Lev. 26.45; H. Graf Reventlow, *ZAW* 71 (1959), pp. 39f.

[31] Cf. M. Noth, *Überlieferungsgeschichtliche Studien* (1943; ²1957), pp. 7–19; K. Elliger, 'Sinn und Ursprung der priesterlichen Geschichtserzählung', *ZThK* 49 (1952), pp. 121–43 = *Kl. Schr.*, pp. 174–98; O. Eissfeldt, *Introduction*, pp. 205ff.

[32] J. Hempel, 'Priesterkodex', *PW* 22, 2 (1954), cols. 1943–67, see col. 1947. L. Köhler, *Hebrew Man* (ET, 1956), p. 41 n. G. Östborn *Yahweh's Words and Deeds* (UUÅ, 1951.7, 1951), pp. 61ff., comparing also M. Éliade, *Le mythe de l'éternel retour* (Paris, 1949); ET, *The Myth of the Eternal Return* (New York, 1954), in which pp. 87ff., 106f., 112ff., are especially relevant. Yet another chronological scheme is to be found in Josephus, *Ant.* X, 8. 5.

was not arbitrary, but represents an extension of an already existing scheme comparable with that which may perhaps be detected in the Deuteronomic work, by which the period of 480 years from the Exodus to Solomon's Temple may be thought to suggest that a further identical period should elapse from Solomon's Temple to the rebuilt Temple.[33] The hesitancy about the date of the future hope in the Deuteronomic Work would not unreasonably suggest leaving this implicit rather than making it explicit. Similarly, as we shall see, the hesitancy of P with regard to the future would suggest that no precise estimate need have been given, while those who appreciated the significance of the figures would see in them a meaningful portrayal of the past and of confidence for the future.

The dating scheme also serves to mark off the work into sections,[34] and this corresponds, too, with a recognition of stages in the development.[35] The stages may be described in various ways. There is evident a progressive narrowing of divine election—from creation, through Noah, through Abraham, Isaac and Jacob, to the tribes and through them to the special position occupied by the priests and by Judah.[36] Or again there is evident a progression through the self-revelation of God, and through the establishment of covenant relationship at varying levels.[37] But these indications of schematic arrangement cover only the main introductory sections, leading through to the Exodus events. At that point the type of material changes, and it is clear that a crucial point in the work has been reached. Now the main purpose becomes plain in the setting out of what is to be the basis of the people's life in the legal material and descriptive instructions of Ex. 25 to Lev. 16 followed by a further

[33] If the date of Solomon's temple is fixed in about 960 BC, this provides a date for the hope of the rebuilt temple not so far ahead of the actual date of the Deuteronomic compilation. The exact calculation depends on the interpretation of the lengths of the reigns of the kings of Judah, and many chronological problems are here still unresolved. On this point, cf. G. R. Driver, 'Sacred Numbers and Round Figures', in *Promise and Fulfilment*, ed. F. F. Bruce (Edinburgh, 1963), pp. 62–90, see p. 69. For the general chronological questions, cf. E. R. Thiele, *The Mysterious Numbers of the Hebrew Kings* (Grand Rapids, ²1965; Exeter, 1966), and see his bibliography; J. Finegan, *Handbook of Biblical Chronology* (Princeton, 1964).

[34] Cf. O. Eissfeldt, *Introduction*, pp. 205f. Cf. also the comments of C. Westermann, *The Genesis Accounts of Creation* (ET, Philadelphia, 1964), pp. 10f., on the epochal structure in Gen. 1.

[35] G. von Rad, *Die Priesterschrift im Hexateuch: literarisch untersucht und theologisch gewertet* (BWANT 65, 1934), pp. 167–89, esp. p. 188.

[36] Cf. also the application of this method in the Chronicler in part by means of genealogies.

[37] Cf. below, p. 95, on the relationship between the Abraham and Sinai covenants.

section in Lev. 27, Num. 1–10.10.[38] The final section of the work—
leaving for the moment the question whether the ending is now misplaced—covers the movement from Sinai to the preparation for the
entry into the promised land, with the frustrations which come upon
the people and the allocations of the tribal territories.

Each of these three main sections contributes towards our understanding of the whole work. Not that they are in any way independent
of one another, for there is a logical linkage and they are all concerned with certain basic needs. But the division is convenient for the
purpose of seeing more clearly what the whole work is about.

In the initial narrative sections the fundamental note has been
described as that of promise, a looking forward to the fulfilment of
God's elective purpose in the ultimate establishment of Israel as his
people within his chosen place. It is not necessary here to enter into
the discussion as to whether this element of promise is due to a later
imposition of the thought on the patriarchal narratives or an original
element which once referred to the occupation of particular areas and
had in view the immediacy of fulfilment, but is now applied to a
remoter event.[39] This theme of promise and fulfilment represents a
view of history which is already present in the J and E strands. It is
an element which hardly finds expression in Deuteronomic thought
where there is little real concern with the patriarchal situation; for
here we begin with the rescue from Egypt and hope based on the
covenant.[40] It is evident from a consideration of the Psalms[41] that

---

[38] On the place of the Sinai pericope and its relation to the surrounding material,
cf. W. Beyerlin, *Origins and History of the Oldest Sinaitic Traditions* (ET, Oxford,
1965). Cf. also C. Westermann, *op. cit.*, p. 7, on the link between the structure of
command and consequence in Gen. 1 and in Ex. 25–Num. 10.

[39] Cf. the discussion and references in R. E. Clements, *Abraham and David* (1967),
pp. 15ff., 23ff.; M. Haran, 'The Religion of the Patriarchs: An Attempt at a
Synthesis', *ASTI* 4 (1965), pp. 30–55, see p. 46.

[40] Cf. the rather negative attitude in Deut. 26 and Josh. 24—'beyond the river
. . . your fathers worshipped other gods' (Josh. 24.2). To a limited extent
Deuteronomy recognizes the idea of a promise to Abraham, Isaac and Jacob
(Deut. 1.8; 6.10; 9.5, 27; 29.12; 30.20; 34.4; and only thereafter in Josh. 24.3
and II Kings 13.23). In every case, with the exception of Josh. 24, which appears
to be a Deuteronomic reshaping of E material, the reference is formal; the expressions are stereotyped. They could in most cases have been introduced at a late stage
into the Deuteronomic material, or we may suppose that, like the Chronicler, the
Deuteronomist is making reference to events which he has not seen fit to include in his
narrative, e.g. the golden calf story in Deut. 9.8ff. and the Dathan-Abiram story in
Deut. 11.6. On this problem, cf. R. E. Clements, *Abraham and David* (1967), pp. 61ff.

[41] Cf. A. Lauha, *Die Geschichtsmotive in den alttestamentlichen Psalmen* (AASF 56,
1945), pp. 34–45.

the patriarchal themes take a very subordinate place. In view of their presence in the J and E traditions (as well as occasional allusions in the prophets)[42] they are quite evidently not of late origin—this is quite apart from considerations of probability and comparison with evidence from the period to which the patriarchs are likely to have belonged. But the strand of thought which makes much of them only became dominant at a somewhat late date.

In the P material—as already in J—the patriarchal theme is set in the context of primeval history. It is here possible to see that, important as is the moment at which relationship is established by God with Abraham, it is anticipated by the ordering of the world in creation. For P's creation account in Gen. 1–2.4, which in so many respects has points of contact with the Babylonian *Enūma eliš*, culminates in the ordering of the sabbath. In this it preserves an appreciation of the ultimate moment of creation as is also true in the Babylonian Marduk myth. The latter reaches its climax in the building of a temple for Marduk[43]—a motif undoubtedly familiar also in the Baal material of Ras Shamra,[44] so that we may with reasonable certainty associate the P form of the material with Canaan and only indirectly with Babylonia.[45] Similarly the P narrative reaches a first climax in the sabbath, but this is only an anticipation of the final climax which is reached in the picture of a tabernacle as the centre

[42] Cf. H. F. D. Sparks, 'The Witness of the Prophets to Hebrew Tradition', *JTS* 50 (1949), pp. 129–41; P. R. Ackroyd, 'Hosea and Jacob', *VT* 13 (1963), pp. 245–59, see p. 253; E. M. Good, 'Hosea and the Jacob Tradition', *VT* 16 (1966), pp. 137–51.

[43] Cf. *ANET*, esp. pp. 68f.; *DOTT*, pp. 4, 11–13, 16. The bibliography in *DOTT* provides references to the discussion of the question of relationship. It is difficult to agree with J. V. Kinnier Wilson that there are no points of contact (see his comments in *DOTT*, p. 14). Cf. also L. R. Fisher, *JSS* 8 (1963), pp. 40f., comparing the 'seven-year' building of the Temple (I Kings 6.38) with this 'seven-day' framework, and the 'seven-day' building of a house for Baal. (Cf. text 51, v, 113–vi, 38, and next note.)

[44] Cf. *ANET*, pp. 133f.; R. E. Clements, *God and Temple* (1965), pp. 3ff.; A. S. Kapelrud, *The Ras Shamra Discoveries and the Old Testament* (ET, Oxford, 1965), pp. 42f.; E. Jacob, *Ras Shamra et l'Ancien Testament* (Neuchâtel, 1960), pp. 44f.; J. Gray, *The Legacy of Canaan* (*VTS* 5, Leiden, ²1965), pp. 44ff.; C. H. Gordon, *Ugaritic Literature* (Rome, 1949), pp. 34f.; G. R. Driver, *Canaanite Myths and Legends* (Edinburgh, 1956), pp. 98f.

[45] Against such views as those of G. E. Wright, e.g. in *Biblical Archaeology* (London, 1957), p. 45, and earlier ideas of the exilic origin of the P form of the creation myth. It is conceivable that the exile provided a new impetus to the elaboration and interpretation of creation—cf. Deutero-Isaiah—but the mythology itself is very evidently much earlier in Israel. Cf. such psalm passages as 74.12ff.; 104 (this latter with its relationship to Egyptian hymnody; cf. *DOTT*, pp. 142ff.).

of a people which can best be thought of as a worshipping community rather than as a merely political entity.[46] Thus right across the intervening patriarchal themes there is a link to the ordering of the tabernacle in the Sinai tradition[47] and thence to the ordering of the people in anticipation of the entry into the land.

The second stage in the P stratum is the Sinai tradition itself. It has been noticed that P has little concern with the covenant at Sinai, making its appeal rather to that with Abraham.[48] Whereas H like JE and D speaks of a covenant with the generation coming out of Egypt, and lays its stress on this moment (cf. Lev. 26), P appears to eliminate the Sinai covenant,[49] and the reason is that in concentration on the idea of the fulfilment of the patriarchal promise it sees that 'Israel stands in the covenant of Abraham'.[50] Zimmerli suggests that the P material here shows a rethinking of the idea of covenant.[51] The covenant forms have been shown to have affinities with the suzerainty treaties known especially from the Hittite sources,[52] envisaging a protective relationship laying certain obligations on the partners. P shows that this covenant has now become questionable. Its legal proclamation was bound up with the pronouncing of blessings and curses.[53] With the prophets Israel came under the curse. 'The exilic period which then followed emphasized for the people standing under judgement that it was Yahweh himself who wielded the sword of judgement.'[54] The idea of a new covenant (Jer. 31.31) is one way through this dilemma.[55] For P—as also for Ezekiel, who in this represents the prophetic counterpart[56]—the only answer must be

[46] Num. 2. Cf. K. Elliger, $ZThK$ 49 (1952), pp. 135, 140f. = $Kl. Schr.$, pp. 189, 195f.
[47] Ex. 25–31; 35–40. Cf. A. Causse, $Les dispersés d'Israël$ (1929), pp. 49f.
[48] W. Zimmerli, $T\overline{Z}$ 16 (1960), pp. 266–80. = $Gottes Offenbarung$, pp. 205–16; R. E. Clements, $Abraham and David$ (1967), pp. 70ff.
[49] As the Chronicler does also. Cf. below, p. 236.
[50] W. Zimmerli, $op. cit.$, p. 276 = p. 213.
[51] Cf. J. Roth, 'La tradition sacerdotale dans le Pentateuque', $Nouv. Rev. Théol.$ 54 (1954), pp. 696–721, see pp. 710ff.
[52] But also now from a much wider area of time and space. Cf. G. E. Mendenhall, 'Covenant Forms in Israelite Tradition', BA 17 (1954), pp. 50–76; $Law and Covenant in Israel and the Ancient Near East$ (Pittsburgh, 1955). A review of more recent literature may be found in D. J. McCarthy, 'Covenant in the Old Testament: the present state of inquiry', CBQ 27 (1965), pp. 217–40; $Der Gottesbund im Alten Testament$ (Stuttgart, [2]1967).
[53] Cf. M. Noth, $op. cit.$ (p. 89 n. 20), pp. 142f. = $Ges. Stud.$, pp. 169f.; ET, p. 128.
[54] W. Zimmerli, $op. cit.$, pp. 277f. = p. 214.
[55] Cf. p. 61.
[56] Cf. below, pp. 110ff.

in an act of pure grace, and this is expressed in what happened at
Sinai not as a new event but as a 'discharging of the earlier pronouncement of grace'.[57]
Now, this ties in closely with the whole structure of the legal and
other material in the central section of P. For this section concentrates on the recognition that the 'salvation of Israel depends upon a
properly ordered cultus'.[58] R. Rendtorff[59] and K. Koch have traced
in the ordinances of the P legal material the existence of older cultic
patterns, ancient rituals for which the instructions are handed down.
These are not simply preserved because they are ancient; they have
been gathered to express the conviction that God alone—willing to
use them—can establish and preserve the life of man.[60] Their
reapplication is to be seen in the elaboration of the material and its
building into an impressive unity, covering the ordering of sanctuary,
holy garments for the rituals, and the institution of priests; together
with the taking into use of these and the formation of them into a
coherent system providing a basis for ordered and blessed life.[61] Each
section of the material is introduced by Yahweh's instruction: 'Yahweh said to Moses, "Say to the Israelites" ', and concludes with the
recognition that 'The Israelites did as Yahweh through Moses had
commanded them'.[62] Each group is prefaced with an awareness of
the glory of Yahweh—Ex. 24.15–18 (34.29–35); 40.34f.; Lev. 9.23f.
(10.2a)—thus authenticating the command, and also fixing the
revealing of these commands in history, since the divine glory is not
described as appearing before the Sinai events.[63]
The third section of the P stratum deals with the anticipations of

[57] W. Zimmerli, op. cit., p. 279 = p. 215.
[58] K. Koch, Die Priesterschrift von Exod. 25 bis Lev. 16. Eine überlieferungsgeschichtliche und literarkritische Untersuchung (FRLANT 71, 1959), p. 98.
[59] Die Gesetze in der Priesterschrift (FRLANT 62, 1954).
[60] Cf. K. Koch, Priesterschrift, pp. 103ff.; ZThK 55 (1958), p. 51; R. de Vaux,
Ancient Israel (ET, 1961), pp. 451ff.; M. Haran, Script. Hier. 8 (1961), p. 296.
[61] Cf. M. Haran, 'The Priestly Image of the Tabernacle', HUCA 36 (1965),
pp. 191–226. On the theme of cult and acceptability, cf. A. J. Wensinck, 'The
Significance of Ritual in the Religion of Israel', in Semietische Studiën uit de Nalaten-
schap van A. J. Wensinck (Leiden, 1941), pp. 51–60; and E. Würthwein, 'Kultpolemik
oder Kultbescheid?' in Tradition und Situation, ed. E. Würthwein and O. Kaiser
(Göttingen, 1963), pp. 115–31, esp. pp. 122–6.
[62] Cf. C. Westermann, op. cit., p. 7.
[63] In this, as Koch (Priesterschrift, pp. 99f.) points out, a contrast is also drawn
with Pharaoh, who made no such response to the divine word: 'Yahweh spoke to
Moses: "Say to Aaron . . . ", but he (Pharaoh) did not listen to them, just as
Yahweh had said' (Ex. 8.1, 11, etc.). Koch compares R. Borchert, Stil und Aufbau
der priesterschriftlichen Erzählung (Diss., Heidelberg, 1957).

actual conquest and the preparations for allocation of the land. There is undoubtedly much traditional material here, and, as with other sections, the point of division between what we may properly describe as the P work and what we should describe as the P presentation of the whole is not always easily determinable. But the primary emphasis is laid upon the anticipatory receiving of the land.[64] Hempel points to the conclusion, 'After Moses has allocated to the tribes the land which is later to be their own and has taken possession of it with his eyes, he dies in full power of his manhood and his successor is ready to carry out his last wishes in the power of the spirit which has been transmitted to him.'[65]

The end of P is now uncertain.[66] It is usual to suppose—and it seems very probable—that a considerable part of the presentation of the allocation of territory in Josh. 13–19 (20, 21) belongs to P.[67] The long gap is often explained by the insertion of Deuteronomy and of the narrative of the conquest,[68] but might be better explained as due to the placing after the conquest of some part of this allocation material—closely linked with the last chapters of Numbers—when once the two great works had been brought together.[69] It is sometimes objected that such a view of the Priestly work leaves it without any conquest narrative at all; whereas if Josh. 13–19 originally followed on a JE conquest narrative such a difficulty would not arise.[70] But this seems to miss the real significance of the P work. Just as in the Deuteronomic history the outcome of the exile remains in some doubt (though we are given sufficient indication of the possibilities of renewal for faith to be revived), so, too, in P there is delicacy in the

[64] Cf. G. Östborn, op. cit., p. 72; M. Noth, Das vierte Buch Mose: Numeri (ATD 7, 1966), pp. 12, 14, 130ff.

[65] PW 22, 2 (1954), cols. 1963f. This particular form of words depends upon the assumption that part of Deut. 34 is of P origin. Most often vv. 1a, 7–9, are so assigned, but not the intervening verses in which Moses is described as being shown the land by God. Nevertheless, the spirit of the statement is entirely acceptable, since Moses by allocating the land demonstrates that it is already in reality in Israel's possession.

[66] G. Östborn, op. cit., p. 20, suggests that Numbers may once have ended with Moses' death. He sees the whole complex Exodus-Numbers as a unity centred around the figure of Moses. For a parallel, cf. H.-G. Güterbock, 'Die historische Tradition bei Babyloniern und Hethitern', ZA 42 (1934), pp. 1–91, see pp. 34ff., 38.

[67] O. Eissfeldt, Introduction, p. 251.

[68] Cf., e.g., O. Eissfeldt, Introduction, p. 223.

[69] Cf. S. Mowinckel, 'Israelite Historiography', ASTI 2 (1963), pp. 4–26, see p. 5.

[70] Cf., e.g., A. Bentzen, Introduction to the OT II (Copenhagen, 1949 [²1952]), pp. 74f.

hesitant way in which the future is adumbrated.[71] The land is allo-cated; there is no doubt of the divine intention. But conquest is not to be achieved merely by military means; it is God's act.[72] It rests with him and what matters is that Israel should be a people fit for what he intends.[73] This is, like the Chronicler's ecclesiastical battles, the logical and proper outcome of a deepened understanding of the idea of the 'holy war' and also the final development of that spiritua-lization of the conquest idea from battle descriptions to divine grace.[74]

A people fit for what God intends—here in reality is the link back to the very beginning. For the observance of the sabbath, which is God's day of rest, not man's, is eventually to be expressed in the fulfilment of his promise. We may compare the stress laid in the Holi-ness Code on the judgement which falls because of the failure to keep the sabbaths, the judgement itself being a dispensation for the land to enjoy what otherwise had been lost. The ensuring of this is the primary concern of the central part of the work around which the remainder turns; and in its turn this central part is clearly a 'pro-grammatic work' (Programmschrift), anticipating what the restored community will be. 'So it was—so it is to be again.'[75] Two elements may be distinguished: the laws governing the construction of the tabernacle, which is one decisive and historic event (corresponding to the rebuilding of the Temple), and the laws governing the organiz-ing of cult and priesthood, which is a continually repeated process for the perpetuation of what has once been established. But these two are now linked together.

The central point must not be misunderstood. It is true that the book of Leviticus and the first part of Numbers, with their repetitive legal formulae, look like casuistry of the most refined kind. It is true that legal casuistry has always been a most deadly enemy of reli-gion[76]—and so it was to be again in the case of the post-exilic Jewish

[71] Cf. K. Elliger, *ZThK* 49 (1952), pp. 127f., 135 = *Kl. Schr.*, pp. 180f., 189.
[72] O. Eissfeldt, *Introduction*, p. 255.
[73] Cf. Millar Burrows, 'Ancient Israel', in *The Idea of History in the Ancient Near East*, ed. R. C. Dentan (New Haven, 1955), pp. 99–131, see pp. 123ff.
[74] Cf. K. Elliger, *ZThK* 49 (1952), pp. 140f. and 141 n. = *Kl. Schr.*, pp. 194f., on the omission of the conquest. Cf. also Ps. 44.2–4 and the Qumran War Scroll. Cf. R. de Vaux, *Ancient Israel* (ET, 1961), pp. 266f.
[75] Koch, *Priesterschrift*, p. 100. Cf. Elliger, *ZThK* 49 (1952), p. 141 = *Kl. Schr.*, p. 195.
[76] Cf. νόμος, *TWNT* 4, pp. 1036f.; ET, *Law* (London, 1962), pp. 39, 42f., and in *TDNT* 4, pp. 1041ff. Cf. also below, pp. 254ff.

community, though not so as to destroy all spontaneity of life and worship; and so in reality it had been in the period of the great prophets, for their condemnation of cult practice and wrong trust is basically related to this.[77] For the Priestly stratum it is important to recall the context; for P what happened at Sinai, as we have already noted, was the 'discharging of the earlier pronouncement of grace'.[78] No longer does Israel stand under the mere threat of blessing and curse. Here P plumbs the depths of human need more realistically than does the Deuteronomic work or than some aspects of the teaching of the prophets—with whom there is always a certain strongly appealing element of 'Israel ought to have been able to respond', and with Deuteronomy particularly a yearning exhortation to choose life.[79] The possibility of sin is not ignored; its reality is soberly appreciated.[80] P has no illusions about an original period of purity.[81] But it is God himself who not only provides the context for the re-ordering of Israel's life but also the whole process by which that life may be continually renewed and reformed. The ancient cult, seen as the life-giving contact between God and man; the ancient shrine, seen as the dwelling in which God's presence is made real and so is a

[77] Cf. H. H. Rowley: 'Ritual and the Hebrew Prophets' in *Myth, Ritual, and Kingship*, ed. S. H. Hooke (Oxford, 1958), pp. 236–60, see pp. 240ff. = *JSS* 1 (1956), pp. 338–60, see pp. 342ff. = *From Moses to Qumran* (London, 1963), pp. 111–38, see pp. 116ff.

[78] W. Zimmerli, *op. cit.*, p. 279. Even R. H. Pfeiffer, *Religion in the Old Testament* (1961), pp. 182, 190f., recognizes the positive aspects of P, while depreciating its value because of its stress on ceremonial.

[79] E.g. Isa. 1.2ff., 16; Amos 5.14f. Cf. Deut. 30.15ff. It is clear, of course, that such exhortations to obedience must be appreciated within the prophetic and Deuteronomic stress on the primacy of God's action towards Israel. Cf. J. Muilenburg, *The Way of Israel* (London, 1962), p. 67, who notes here also the radical views of Ezekiel and Jeremiah.

[80] Cf. W. Zimmerli, *op. cit.*, p. 279, on Lev. 16, the Day of Atonement, cf. below, pp. 100f. Cf. also B. D. Napier, 'Community under Law. On Hebrew Law and its Theological Presuppositions', *Interpretation* 7 (1953), pp. 404–17, see p. 416 on the pessimism of the later legal material.

[81] Cf. Koch, *ZThK* 55 (1958), p. 50. Contrast Hosea's and Jeremiah's view of the purity of relationship of the wilderness period (Hos. 2.16f.; 9.10; 12.9; Jer. 2.2f.), with Ezekiel's root and branch condemnation (Ezek. 16, 23, etc.). P by taking up into its opening section the ancient Eden and Babel traditions, and laying great stress on the Flood narrative, indicates that the origins of both failure and hope (cf. Gen. 9.1ff.) lie at the very beginnings of human experience. But the blessing (Gen. 1) anticipates the failure. (Cf. below, p. 102.) Criticism of the idea that the 'desert' period was looked to as an ideal—which is incidental to Hosea and Jeremiah—is made by S. Talmon, 'The "Desert-Motif" in the Bible and in Qumran Literature', in *Biblical Motifs*, ed. A. Altmann (1966), pp. 31–63; also by C. Barth, 'Zur Bedeutung der Wüstentradition', *VTS* 15 (1966), pp. 14–23.

source of life—these are the focus for a new interpretation of the being of an Israel which is not only sustained upon the great historic moment of God's saving act but continually renewed by the revealing of a divine indwelling power. It would be an oversimplification to describe this as the 'Catholic' element in Old Testament religion where Deuteronomy and the prophets might represent the 'Protestant' element. In fact, the two are complementary ways of approaching the same truths—the reality of the divine grace and the reality of the divine indwelling.

To this point we may attach the different aspects of the legislation: (i) the building of the tabernacle[82]—no permanent dwelling, but a tent in which God appears, but in which he does not dwell—the *miškān*, or *'ōhel mō'ēd*, the place of meeting, where the encounter between man and God takes place[83]—provides the centre and implicitly the pattern, for like Ezekiel's rebuilt Temple and like Solomon's in the Chronicler's narrative, it is built to a heavenly plan;[84] (ii) the ordering of the camp, with its concentric circles or squares within squares, reflecting both acceptance and modification of more ancient forms,[85] shows an organizing of the people not unlike that of Ezek. 47–48. It shows the people set for worship, just as the allocation of territories, more realistic because more traditional than Ezekiel, shows them set for daily life;[86] (iii) the ordering of the cult, in which the element of atonement plays the greatest part; for it is here that the possibility of dealing with the sin of the community is provided. 'In the great Day of Atonement according to Lev. 16 is concealed the possibility of so atoning for the sin of the community—

[82] Cf. W. Eichrodt, *Theolog* I, p. 106.
[83] Cf. Koch, *ZThK* 55 (1958), pp. 48ff.; νόμος, *TWNT* 4, pp. 1035f., ET, *Law* (London, 1962), p. 38, and in *TDNT* 4, p. 1042; R. E. Clements, *God and Temple* (1965), pp. 116ff.; M. Haran, 'The " 'Ohel Mô'ēdh" in Pentateuchal Sources', *JSS* 5 (1960), pp. 50–65; *idem*, *HUCA* 36 (1965), pp. 191–226.
[84] Ex. 25.9, 40; Ezek. 40.2; I Chron. 28.11f., 18f. An ancient idea (cf. Gudea's temple plan, *ANET*, pp. 268f.) is here utilized. Cf. R. E. Clements, *God and Temple* (1965), p. 129; T. Chary, *op. cit.*, pp. 24–43; M. Haran, *JBL* 81 (1962), pp. 14–24, on the Tabernacle and Temple patterns.
[85] Num. 2. Cf. A. Kuschke, 'Die Lagervorstellung der priesterlichen Erzählung', *ZAW* 63 (1951), pp. 74–105. Cf. also the comments of H.-J. Kraus, *Worship in Israel* (ET, 1966), pp. 128ff. His criticisms are mainly concerned with the antiquity of the ideas associated with the tent—a point not here under discussion. To some extent he simplifies the issues by overstressing the difference between 'semi-nomadic' and 'settled' life.
[86] Cf. M. Haran on the combining of utopian and realistic elements in P: 'Studies in the Account of the Levitical Cities', *JBL* 80 (1961), pp. 45–54, 156–65.

soberly reckoned with—that it can never again become a danger to the community.'[87]

This stress on purification, atonement, is a recognition of the community's need. The generation of the Exodus is no generation of faithful people, but one in which all but Joshua and Caleb are shown to lack faith. They alone, when the land is spied out, have faith enough to remain firm, while their contemporaries will be unable to enter the land.[88] The people's ultimate sin lies in the doubt of God's power to carry through his will to give the land to Israel for ever.[89] In the description of this lies the recognition of the uncertainty of the exilic age's position. Will the Israel of that day have faith enough in the power of her God? The inconclusiveness of the P stratum leaves us in this uncertainty. As Elliger suggests, it is perhaps to be explained as a reflection of the actual situation of the exile, when the message can be heard in which there is warning and exhortation as the older generation of the Exodus is shown dying in the wilderness and the younger generation is not yet in the land of promise.[90] Does not the situation repeat itself in the uncertainties of the sixth century?

The whole work, in which P takes up the rich mass of older traditions, is dominated by P in its present form. The older traditions, reflecting originally the achievement of conquest, and in some measure—though without any blindness to failures—reflecting the glories of the subsequent developments, are subordinated to the uncertainty of the exilic age, neutralized[91] by being set in a new context. So the salvation-history pattern is broken and, vivid and significant as it is for the understanding of the evolution of the older

---

[87] W. Zimmerli, op. cit., p. 279. Cf. K. Koch, 'Sühne und Sündenvergebung um die Wende von der exilischen zur nachexilischen Zeit', EvTh 26 (1966), pp. 217–39, esp. pp. 225–32. On the question of acceptability, and in particular the meaning of $r\bar{a}s\bar{a}$, cf. R. Rendtorff, 'Priesterliche Kulttheologie und prophetische Kultpolemik', TLZ 81 (1956), cols. 339–42; E. Würthwein, op. cit. (p. 96 n. 61).
[88] Num. 14.30.
[89] K. Elliger, ZThK 49 (1952), p. 141 = Kl. Schr., p. 196.
[90] K. Elliger, ZThK 49 (1952), pp. 142f. = Kl. Schr., pp. 196f.
[91] O. Eissfeldt, Introduction, e.g. pp. 255, 266, makes use of this convenient term to indicate the process by which the original intention of a tradition or a writing is subordinated to the interests of the larger work in which it stands. At the same time, the relationship between traditions and their subsequent re-handling is not one-sided, and the taking up of earlier material may both help in the shaping of the later work and also clarify its intention. Thus the taking up of H into P—where H, as we have seen (pp. 87ff.), reveals a clear attachment to actual historical conditions—helps to clarify the meaning of P.

traditions, it is here subjected to a critical appreciation.[92] The Deuteronomic history shows failure for what it is and warns that these are the consequences of men's refusal to accept the promises of God and to respond in the right conduct which marks the people of God. The Priestly Work shows the uncertainty. Like Ezekiel it traces failure right back into the very beginnings of life—for now it has taken into itself, too, that initial failure by which all creation was put out of joint.[93] It leaves its readers and hearers on the verge of the land, knowing that the land can be theirs—for so the familiar history would tell them. Now they are away from it, amid alien life. The question whether history can repeat itself remains open, but the issue is not really in doubt, because just as once Egypt could know that 'I am Yahweh',[94] so once again the aliens among whom they dwell will be able to know.[95] God will again bring them in, he will again meet with them.[96]

The working out of these themes—God's glory among the exiles, renewed deliverance and the presence of God amid his people—is to be found vividly in the two prophetic writings whose message must occupy us next.

[92] The value of the stress on *Heilsgeschichte*, salvation-history, must not obscure the limitations of a one-sided approach to Old Testament theological questions.
[93] Cf. above, p. 99 n. 81.
[94] Ex. 7.5; 14.4, 18. Cf. K. Elliger, *ZThK* 49 (1952), p. 138 = *Kl. Schr.*, p. 192; G. Östborn, *Yahweh's Words and Deeds* (1951), p. 17; H. Graf Reventlow, *ZAW* 71 (1959), p. 36. Cf. also p. 106 n. 17.
[95] The theme is further developed in the narratives of the book of Daniel.
[96] Cf. below on Ezekiel pp. 110ff., for a projection of this hope into the future. Although the Priestly Work appears to be describing the past, and to that extent projects its ideals into the past, it is in reality as much concerned with the future as is Ezekiel, and as is also the Deuteronomic History. This appears to be insufficiently emphasized by N. H. Snaith, *Leviticus and Numbers* (*Century Bible*, London, 1967), p. 21.

VII

PROPHECY OF THE EXILE AND THE IDEALS OF RESTORATION

A. THE BOOK OF EZEKIEL

THE COMPLEXITY of the literary and other problems attaching to the book of Ezekiel is such that any discussion ought ideally to be prefaced by a full-scale consideration of the view that is adopted.[1] But important as these problems are for a full definition of the prophet's place and function, the intention of our present discussion is rather more limited. While no underestimating of the chronological questions is proper, it is reasonable to consider the impression made by the book of Ezekiel as a whole. So K. von Rabenau writes: 'Even if we are to reckon with a considerable working over of the book at the hand of disciples, we must in view of the similarity in form and content postulate a close interconnection between prophet and redactor, perhaps direct relationship with a disciple.'[2] In so far as there are passages which are of later origin, even these, belonging within what we may term the 'Ezekiel tradition' are not without their significance for the understanding of the place which he occupies in later Old Testament thought.[3] This point is particularly relevant to the inclusion here of ch. 40–48.[4] It is the whole Ezekiel corpus with which we are concerned: its attitude to the exile and its understanding of restoration.

[1] Cf. C. Kuhl, 'Zum Stand der Hesekiel-Forschung' *ThR* 24 (1957/8), pp. 1–53.

[2] 'Das prophetische Zukunftswort im Buch Hesekiel' in *Studien zur Theologie der alttestamentlichen Überlieferungen*, ed. R. Rendtorff and K. Koch (Neukirchen, 1961), pp. 61–80, see p. 62. Cf. also his 'Die Entstehung des Buches Ezekiel in formgeschichtlicher Sicht', *WZ Halle* 5 (1955/6), pp. 659–94.

[3] Cf. also G. Fohrer, *Die Hauptprobleme des Buches Ezechiel* (BZAW 72, 1952), pp. 144–8, and cf. also pp. 155f. on the relation of Ezek. to II and III Isa. Cf. also S. Herrmann, *Die prophetischen Heilserwartungen im Alten Testament. Ursprung und Gestaltwandel* (BWANT 85, 1965).

[4] Cf. also H. Gese, *Der Verfassungsentwurf des Ezekiel (40–48). Traditionsgeschichtlich untersucht* (BHT 25, 1957); M. Schmidt, *op. cit.*(n. 6), pp. 163–6.

An increasing appreciation of Ezekiel's place in the Old Testament tradition[5] has made it less proper to think of him as remote and strange, a priestly intruder in the prophetic line.[6] A deeper understanding of the psychology of the prophets[7] makes it no longer necessary to see in his evident harshness and violence of language indications of an unsympathetic character. Violence of language may go with intensity of feeling;[8] the sensitivity of the prophet to the desperate fate of his people—with himself bound up in that fate— and above all his profound sense of the holiness of God, make his character one that is certainly never easy to understand, but one that it is rewarding to study because of his insights.[9]

What in the first place marks off Ezekiel from his predecessors is that here for the first time the actual destruction of city and temple and the experience of exile are a central reality.[10] This is, of course, also in part true for Jeremiah, who experienced it, but the understanding of the total message of Jeremiah depends much more upon the earlier stages of his activity. Some aspects of the thought of Jeremiah and of the tradition associated with him have already been examined.[11] The modifications and reinterpretations of earlier prophetic material, notably in Isaiah, also reflect the disaster. But in these there is no coherence, because the personalities to whom we owe this thinking are nebulous to us, reconstructable only on the basis of the material which we have. Something of their attitude has already been noted.[12] Ezekiel's attention is entirely concentrated upon the reality of disaster. He is concerned in this situation to justify the ways of God to man (in which 'justify' is used in its Old Testament sense [hiṣdīḳ] of 'declaring right', showing the rightness

---

[5] Cf. W. Zimmerli, 'The Special Form- and Traditio-Historical Character of Ezekiel's Prophecy', *VT* 15 (1965), pp. 515–27. A much more extreme position is taken up by H. Graf Reventlow, *Wächter über Israel, Ezechiel und seine Tradition* (BZAW 82, 1962).

[6] Cf. also M. Schmidt, *Prophet und Tempel* (1948), p. 109, describing him as 'in a particular sense marking a climax of the prophetic message'; W. Eichrodt, *Krisis der Gemeinschaft in Israel* (Basler Universitätsreden 33, Basel, 1953), pp. 4f.

[7] Cf. G. Widengren, *Literary and Psychological Aspects of the Hebrew Prophets* (UUÅ, 1948. 10, 1948).

[8] The point might be exemplified in the writings of a number of modern novelists and playwrights.

[9] Cf. G. von Rad, *Theology* II, pp. 232f.; W. Zimmerli, *Ezechiel* (BK 13, 1956ff.), e.g. p. 117, where he makes a comparison with Isa. 53.

[10] So M. Schmidt, *op. cit.*, p. 110; W. Eichrodt, *op. cit.*, p. 6.

[11] Cf. above, ch. IV.

[12] Cf. above, pp. 44f.

of what God has done).[13] Both judgement and promise turn on this. For to Ezekiel judgement is to be understood in terms of the absolute rightness of an action which has fallen upon the whole people. He is concerned to demonstrate how the disaster fits into the plan and purpose of God, and to show how the condition of the people is such that any alternative is unthinkable.[14] In this his sensitivity, in fact, makes him illogical. He declares utter corruption and also declares the intention of God that men should live, turning from their evil ways.[15] He thus combines the appreciation of what man ought to do in response to the action of God—the emphasis so characteristic of the earlier prophetic and the Deuteronomic lines of thought—with the realization of the radical nature of sin, which he traces back into the prehistory of the people, like P finding no idyllic age in the past, but a record of utter corruption punctuated only by God's concern for his 'name' which repeatedly postpones disaster.[16] The declaration of God's intention that man should live is given expression in the marking of the few who are to be spared in the disaster (9.3ff.); the realism of his recognition of corruption is found in the symbols of utter destruction, in which even that part of the people which is pictured as spared is shown as being still further subject to disciplinary action (5.1ff.). Side by side with this—and linked therefore to the recognition of the absoluteness of divine judgement—is the declaration that promise rests only upon the rightness of divine action. The exiles and any others who might think that they are the righteous because they have been spared are made aware that the saving action which they or their descendants are to experience derives not from any rightness in them but only from what God is (33.23ff.). Here we may see the drawing out of that more positive side in the thought-world of D and P in which it is recognized, though

[13] On the application of sacral law in Ezekiel, cf. G. von Rad, *Theology* II, p. 225 and W. Zimmerli, 'Die Eigenart der prophetischen Rede des Ezechiel', ζAW 66 (1954), pp. 1–26, see p. 20 = *Gottes Offenbarung* (ThB 19, 1963), pp. 148–77, see pp. 169f. On Ezekiel and the Priestly Writings, cf. Y. Kaufmann, *The Religion of Israel* (ET, 1961), pp. 433ff.

[14] Cf. W. Eichrodt, *op. cit.*, pp. 8f.; Y. Kaufmann, *op. cit.*, p. 427.

[15] A similar inconsistency may be observed in Jeremiah, e.g. in 36.3 as compared with other passages (cf. pp. 52ff.).

[16] Cf. ch. 20; also 16 and 23. On this point cf. G. von Rad, *Theology* II, pp. 225ff., and esp. p. 228. On Ezekiel's interpretation of history: G. Fohrer, *Ezechiel* (HAT 13, 1955), pp. 108f.; W. Zimmerli, *Ezechiel* (BK 13, 1956ff.), pp. 439f., emphasizing Ezekiel's dependence on older forms in his presentation of the theme, and also his article, 'Israel im Buche Ezechiel', *VT* 8 (1958), pp. 75–90, see pp. 88f. Cf. Y. Kaufmann, *op. cit.*, pp. 435f.

with only a rather hesitant statement of the consequences, that Israel's sole dependence is upon what God will do. Where their turning back is to a covenant—whether that of the Exodus or that with Abraham—to a previous declaration of the nature of God on which confidence may be rested, Ezekiel lays his stress rather upon God being what he is. The declaration 'I am Yahweh' *^{a}nî Yahweh*— characteristic of Ezekiel and H and also found in Deutero-Isaiah[17] —is the absolute ground of all events, and so the only source of hope. But Ezekiel thereby strips himself and his people of all pretensions, and in the savouring of the most bitter experience of deadness (cf. Ezek. 37) is able to acknowledge that 'thou Yahweh knowest'. Only God can determine what the outcome will be.[18] Only in the full appropriation of disaster does this radical acceptance of the action of God become possible.[19]

I. EZEKIEL AND THE DISASTER

Whether Ezekiel is understood, as the biblical tradition has it, as a prophet entirely active in Babylonia, or is considered, as some modern scholars believe, to have been active first in Palestine,[20] his concern is nevertheless in the early years primarily with Jerusalem; and this indeed remains the focal point of all his thought. The city of Jerusalem, which has its meaning in the Temple seen as the place chosen by God,[21] is about to be destroyed. And when the event does

---

[17] Cf. W. Zimmerli, 'Ich bin Jahwe', in *Geschichte und Altes Testament (Festschrift A. Alt*, 1953), pp. 179–209 = *Gottes Offenbarung*, pp. 11–40, and *Erkenntnis Gottes nach dem Buche Ezechiel—Eine theologische Studie (ATANT* 27, 1954) = *Gottes Offenbarung*, pp. 41–119. Cf. also 'Das Gotteswort des Ezechiel', *ZThK* 48 (1957), pp. 249–62, esp. p. 261 = *Gottes Offenbarung*, pp. 133–47, esp. pp. 146f., on the purpose of Yahweh's word as bringing knowledge of him, both in judgement and in restoration. M. Schmidt, *op. cit.*, p. 112.

[18] Cf. G. von Rad, *Theology* II, p. 229; H. Wheeler Robinson, *Two Hebrew Prophets* (London, 1948), pp. 106f.

[19] Cf. also G. Fohrer, *Die Hauptprobleme des Buches Ezechiel* (BZAW 72, 1952), p. 264.

[20] For a review, and bibliography, cf. H. H. Rowley, 'The Book of Ezekiel in Modern Study', *BJRL* 36 (1953/4), pp. 146–90 = *Men of God* (1963), pp. 169–210. The latter view still appears to me to be the more coherent and to make the text more fully intelligible, although it is clearly not without considerable difficulties. In view of recent trends in the study of Ezekiel, there appears to be no necessity to discuss the various theories which have placed Ezekiel anywhere but in the sixth century BC.

[21] Cf. R. E. Clements, *God and Temple*, pp. 102ff.; M. Schmidt, *op. cit.*, pp. 115–21.

take place it would seem that the collecting of Ezekiel's earlier oracular utterances centres upon the explanation of this event for the exiled community. There is relevance in this concern both to Palestinian and to Babylonian Jews. For to those in Jerusalem—as appears in ch. 11—the judgement is seen as a necessary comment upon their belief that they are secure (cf. also Jer. 29 and 24). To those in Babylonia the sole remaining hope for many would seem to have been that the worst would not happen, the final disaster of destruction would not overtake the city and Temple. So long as the worst had not happened, there could be hope. The upsurge of interest which is indicated by Jeremiah's letter to the exiles (Jer. 29), when prophetic utterances pointed to a speedy change of fortune, is answered by the relentless message of doom. Such considerations also make it clear why in the compilation of Ezekiel's prophecies there is so much detailed concern with events which are now past. Prophecies of judgement form a part of the inheritance in which the prophets belong, and so we may consider such words as usable on many occasions. But in this context they serve to do two things. They clarify the reasons for the event which has taken place—and without appropriation of this there can be no right understanding of God (cf. the popular reaction as depicted in Ezek. 18.2). They also serve—as in other prophetic collections—to validate the prophet's message, and this was, we may readily believe, particularly needful in Ezekiel's case.[22]

The great merit of that interpretation of Ezekiel, first advocated by A. Bertholet in this particular form,[23] by which he is seen as active in two distinct phases—Palestine and Babylonia—is that it suggests also a separation of visionary experiences[24] and so a fuller emphasis

[22] Cf. Deut. 18.15–22, and the refrain in Ezekiel: 'You (they) shall know that there has been a prophet . . . ' (2.5, etc.). Cf. K. von Rabenau, 'Die Entstehung des Buches Ezechiel im formgeschichtlicher Sicht', *WZ Halle* 5 (1955/6), pp. 659–94. Cf. also the article by J. Bright (p. 172 n. 4), and on the similar 'You shall know that I am Yahweh', W. Zimmerli, 'Das Wort des göttlichen Selbsterweises', in *Mélanges Bibliques . . . A. Robert* (Paris, 1957), pp. 154–64 = *Gottes Offenbarung* = pp. 120–32.
[23] *Hesekiel* (HAT 13, 1936), pp. XIIIff.
[24] I.e. of 1.1–2.7 and 2.8–3.3. The arguments for the unity of this section in W. Zimmerli, *Ezechiel* (BK 13.1, 1956), pp. 13–21, show rather the coherence and intelligibility of the final unified form of the text than prove the original unity. There are two distinct elements here, and it is noteworthy that only the first re-appears in ch. 10 and 43.1–4. Zimmerli, 'Israel im Buche Ezechiel' *VT* 8 (1958), pp. 75–90, produces arguments from linguistic usage to suggest that the prophet stands at a distance from the Palestinian political situation. But it is still necessary

on the catastrophic nature both of the disaster and of the newer experience of God which followed. Not that we should be so old-fashioned as to speak in terms of 'Ezekiel's discovery that God was present in the unclean land of Babylon', for to one who stood in the Old Testament tradition the universal sway of Yahweh was no newly discovered notion. The experience is rather to be seen in the reality of the situation, as distinct from mere theorizing about it. The reality of being in exile, in the unclean land (cf. ch. 4), produced a shattering reaction in Ezekiel—as no doubt in others who experienced it. It could not be immediately assimilated. Though the belief that Yahweh controls the destinies of all peoples carries with it the knowledge that he must therefore be accessible everywhere, the actual experience is a test of faith, just as the anticipation of disaster—as, too, in Ezekiel—can be confidently expressed, but the experience of it is such as to demand a rethinking which only the event can provoke.[25]

The divinely appointed destruction of Temple and city is most clearly set out in a whole series of visions, symbols and utterances in the first half of the book. The repeated emphasis on disaster makes its importance clear. It is Yahweh himself who decreed it. Sin and failure on the part of the people is a primary motif, and again and again the prophet emphasizes that the failure is so deep-rooted that no cure is available. The recalcitrance of the people is so deeply ingrained that no room is left for any movement of repentance (so, e.g., in ch. 2–3).

Yet incorporated in this is an element of that hortatory emphasis so characteristic of Deuteronomy, in sermon-like expansions of oracular material, and expressed particularly in the watchman passages and in the discussion of responsibility in ch. 18.[26] The marking of those who mourn for the sins of the people (ch. 9) so that they are spared in the disaster is in such a context that it cannot be seen in any way as a simple endorsement of the position of the

---

to explain how these unique characteristics came about, and what Zimmerli here notes of Ezekiel's affinities to P suggests that it is not simply the Babylonian setting which produces this characteristic way of speaking: both Ezekiel and P treat history and geography in what we might term a 'typological' manner.

[25] Cf. M. Schmidt, *op. cit.*, pp. 124ff. On other comparable reactions, cf. above, p. 39.
[26] Cf. G. von Rad, *Theology* II, pp. 230ff.

exiles as the saved,[27] nor as a merely artificial application of retributive doctrine. It is an expression of the urgency with which the prophet makes his appeal, because, whatever the outcome, the rightness of Israel's response remains a necessity. But this is in the context of the finality of judgement; and it paves the way for a future which is dependent not upon man's ability to respond but upon God's willingness to act.[28] The stress upon *responsibility* brings the judgement home to those who must accept it. The exiles in Babylonia, who are the prophet's primary audience, are the disobedient to whom it must be said that the judgement upon Jerusalem is the judgement upon themselves,[29] and not the result of some hangover of responsibility from their forefathers.

The possibility of a response from Israel—however improbable—is not wholly excluded. But at the same time it is expressed in such a way that the response is really no matter of human endeavour but entirely of divine grace. For the stress laid in these passages is upon the will of God that men should live rather than that they should die. The restoration message of the latter half of the book provides the context for this by setting out what exactly is meant by this will of God for life. In the context of the divine action, entirely self-motivated, the possibility of a rightly ordered life is indicated.

By this drawing together of what are in part divergent ideas, Ezekiel moves beyond that tendency to moral exhortation which is characteristic of D—though there it is found always in the implicit context of a new act of God—and at the same time he avoids the opposite danger of suggesting that the renewed condition of the people is an automatic result of God's establishing of the cultus, which then, as it were, operates of itself. The will of God is for life; but characteristically the second half of the book begins with a repetition of the watchman passage (33.1–9, cf. 3.16–21)—an instructive insight into the understanding of restoration. When God takes action to restore, it is the expression of his will. But the response

---

[27] The point is somewhat oversimplified by G. von Rad, *Theology* II, pp. 233f., by his introducing of the individualistic emphasis; yet it is clear in what he goes on to say that he recognizes that the future depends on a miracle, an act of God.

[28] Cf. M. Noth, 'La catastrophe de Jérusalem en l'an 587 avant Jésus-Christ et sa signification pour Israël', *RHPhR* 33 (1953), pp. 81–102, see p. 102 on the absence of human hopes = 'Die Katastrophe von Jerusalem im Jahre 587 v. Chr. und ihre Bedeutung für Israel', *Ges. Stud.* (²1960), pp. 346–71, see p. 371, ET, *The Laws in the Pentateuch and Other Essays* (Edinburgh, 1966), pp. 260–80, see p. 280.

[29] Cf. M. Schmidt, *op. cit.*, p. 115.

is never automatic, even if the precise relationship between divine action and human response is never fully defined.

2. EZEKIEL AND RESTORATION

In the present form of the book the element of hope of restoration is already written into the first part, among the oracles of judgement.[30] Those who receive the judgement—accepting its rightness and thereby acknowledging the justice of the God who has brought it upon them—are recipients of promise. A different line of approach is found in 20.32–44, where the theme of a regathering of the people from the lands where they are scattered is presented in terms of a new Exodus experience.[31] The future is described in terms reminiscent of the original Exodus events, though with modifications which are in the spirit of Ezekiel's thought.[32] The people is to meet again with God for judgement in the 'desert of the nations' (v. 35), to come not to a new entry into the land but to the Temple mountain. The main themes of the restoration, elaborated in ch. 40–48, are here made plain.

The interrelationship between judgement and promise is thus made clear in the present shape of the material. This paves the way for the larger exposition of promise and restoration in the second half of the book. After the foreign nation oracles—in which the supremacy of Yahweh over all the hostile powers is demonstrated—the various aspects of God's restoration plan for Israel are set out. As the material is at present arranged, it in part repeats the pattern of the book as a whole. The chapters from 33 to 37 are concerned more with what we might term the general principles of restoration, not without their elements of warning and judgement, with reminders of the failure of rulers and people, and indications of the present situation in which the people find themselves. Within this is set (36.16–32) the statement of the profanation of the divine name which leads to Yahweh's vindication of himself in the restoration of his people, their cleansing, and the provision of a new heart of flesh. But before the full organization of the restoration is described in detail, there intervenes the onslaught

[30] Cf., for example, 11.14–21.
[31] W. Zimmerli, 'Le nouvel "Exode" dans le message des deux grands prophètes de l'exil', in *Maqqél shâqédh. Hommage à W. Vischer* (Montpellier, 1960), pp. 216–27 = *Gottes Offenbarung*, pp. 192–204. Cf. also Y. Kaufmann, *op. cit.*, p. 440.
[32] E.g. 'the pouring out of wrath' in v. 33, which Zimmerli shows to be upon Israel, not upon the nations (*op. cit.*, p. 219 = *Gottes Offenbarung*, p. 195).

of Gog of Magog (ch. 38–39), an epitome of the overthrow of the evil powers,[33] but here serving, as we shall see, to give to the restoration a wider setting. Chapters 40–48 then describe in detail the divine action by which alone restoration is effected.[34] But although this pattern has its own logic, it may be convenient for the purposes of this survey if we take three themes which appear throughout and draw out their significance. These three are Temple, Cultus, and Land and People.

(i) Temple[35]

The action which God takes is, as we have just noted, based upon what he himself is (36.16ff.). So, too, central to the restoration is the dwelling-place of God, which marks his presence.[36] The covenant formula is renewed in the dwelling of God in their midst.

I will make a covenant of peace with them;
it shall be an everlasting covenant with them;
and I will bless them and multiply them and will set my
sanctuary in the midst of them for evermore.
My dwelling-place shall be with them;
and I will be their God and they shall be my people. (37.26–27)[37]

This is elaborated in the detailed description of the new Temple in 40.1–43.12. In vision transported to the mountains of Israel, the prophet sees something 'like a building of a city' (40.2). (The obliqueness of description is reminiscent of Ezekiel's caution in describing the appearance of God in 1.26.) The detail of the structure is set out by the process of measuring it,[38] and culminates in the appearance of the glory of God coming from the east. Just as in the judgement section (cf. ch. 1 and 10) it is made clear that the God, whose Temple and city it was and who handed it over to destruction, had then appeared in like form to the prophet in Babylonia, so here again insistence is placed upon the point that it is the same God who

[33] On the relationship of the description to ideas concerning the Day of Yahweh, cf. G. von Rad, JSS 4 (1959), pp. 502f.
[34] On the unified form of ch. 40–48, cf. H. Gese, op. cit., pp. 1ff.
[35] M. Schmidt, op. cit., pp. 129–71, surveys the whole range of Ezekiel material, emphasizing the central place occupied by the Temple in his thought; see esp. pp. 166–71 for a proper stress on the relationship of God to his Temple and to the renewed life of Israel.
[36] On the relation between Temple and heavenly dwelling, cf. also M. Haran, 'The Ark and the Cherubim', IEJ 9 (1959), pp. 30–38, 89–94, see pp. 91f.
[37] G. von Rad, Theology II, pp. 234f., compares Jer. 31.31–34. Cf. also R. E. Clements, God and Temple (1965), pp. 105f.
[38] Cf. R. de Vaux, Ancient Israel (ET, 1961), pp. 322f.

comes and is heard to speak from the Temple: 'This is the place of my throne . . . where I will dwell in the midst of the people of Israel for ever' (43.7).

It is God's own dwelling,[39] and as we see in connection with both the details of its planning and the organization of land and people, it is untouched by unclean hands, and strictly isolated, as is shown by the stress on the different boundary walls. As Zimmerli writes:[40] 'It is no accident that in the erection of the new sanctuary on a very high mountain no word is said of any human participation in the construction; what is said concerns the freely willed event of the coming of the glory of Yahweh to a dwelling in the midst of his people.'[41] Nor is it only a dwelling. The link between the presence of God and the life of land and people—an ancient motif of Temple ideology[42]—is made clear by the vision of the river which flows out from the shrine and, increasing in depth as it flows, brings life to the Dead Sea and fertility to the land through which it flows (47.1–12). The city itself, set apart from the Temple by the placing of the Levites between the two areas (48.8–20), is so sanctified by the presence of God that it is possible for it to be renamed (a theme to be found elsewhere in Zech. 8.3 and Trito-Isaiah [62.4] as well as in the probably equally late Isa. 1.26), with the emphasis upon the reality of his presence, 'Yahweh is there' (*Yahweh-šāmmā*—the pun on the name of *Yerūšālaim* marks a reinterpretation of the ancient name, 48.35).[43]

(ii) *Cultus*[44]

The mediating of the divine power is linked with the preservation of holiness, the provision of a continuous mechanism by which the life of the community is maintained and its purity preserved. The detailed description of the prescriptions here brings us into the

[39] Cf. T. Chary, *op. cit.*, p. 17, noting that Yahweh is not tied to it. There is here a spiritualizing of the relationship comparable to I Kings 8.27.

[40] *ZAW* 66 (1954), p. 26 = *Gottes Offenbarung*, p. 177. Cf. T. Chary, *op. cit.*, pp. 17f.; M. Schmidt, *op. cit.*, p. 161.

[41] On the significance of Ezekiel's conception of the Temple, cf. also R. de Vaux, *Bible et Orient* (Paris, 1967), pp. 309f. (French version of the German published in *Lexikon für Theologie und Kirche* IX [Freiburg, 1964], cols. 1350–8).

[42] Cf. R. E. Clements, 'Temple and Land', *TGUOS* 19 (1963), pp. 16–28; *God and Temple* (1965), pp. 10f.

[43] On the theme of renaming, cf. E. N. B. Burrows, 'The Name of Jerusalem' in *The Gospel of the Infancy and other biblical essays*, ed. E. F. Sutcliffe (London, 1941), pp. 118–23; O. Eissfeldt, 'Renaming in the Old Testament', in *Words and Meanings*, ed. P. R. Ackroyd and B. Lindars (Cambridge, 1968), pp. 69–79.

[44] Cf. T. Chary, *op. cit.*, pp. 22f.

atmosphere of the Priestly Code—and indeed it seems probable that at several points the Ezekiel material has been elaborated to produce conformity with that[45]—indicating that this project for the cultus continued to be influential and so was subjected to the modifications which later developments rendered necessary.[46] The details of sacrifice and of priestly organization—as in the Priestly Work—concentrate to a large extent upon the maintenance of purity. The same point is brought out in the regulations for priests and other officials, the establishment of the hierarchy and the delimitation of their spheres of action being concerned with the preservation of the holiness at the centre which is not to be contaminated by alien influence.[47] This is the obverse of the stress upon the life-giving power which flows out from the shrine. The ancient recognition of the hindrance which is introduced into the divine-human contact by man's failure to be in an acceptable condition (cf. Pss. 15, 24) is here seen in the wider context of God's intention to give life.[48] But if this is to be effectual it must not be frustrated by the people, and the organization is an expression of that propriety of approach which belongs to the true worship of God.

(iii) *Land and people*[49]

The obvious corollary of this is the purification and organization of land and people. The reorganization of government in terms of the condemnation of the evil rulers and their downfall, with its reflection of the failure of the older monarchical system, as it is set out in ch. 34, leads on to the ideal of the Davidic king.[50] This may be regarded as a conforming of Ezekiel's modified view of the prince to

---

[45] For detail, see the commentaries, e.g. G. Fohrer and K. Galling, *Ezechiel* (HAT 13, 1955), pp. X, 228, etc.

[46] This is more natural than to affirm—as does Y. Kaufmann, *op. cit.*, p. 443— that only 'those parts of 44.17–31 that agreed with P' were put into effect after the exile. Kaufmann views the whole of the material as being purely visionary. It is not easy to determine the relationship between ideals and proposals for actual reforms: but it is in any case more important to understand the motivation of Ezekiel's proposals than to determine how far he or his followers viewed his words as providing a blue-print.

[47] The priestly regulations in particular seem to have been further elaborated. On the priesthood in Ezekiel, cf. T. Chary, *op. cit.*, pp. 18ff.

[48] Cf. W. Zimmerli, ' "Leben" und "Tod" im Buche des Propheten Ezechiel', *TZ* 13 (1957), pp. 494–508 = *Gottes Offenbarung*, pp. 178–91.

[49] On the intimate linkage of land and people, cf. G. von Rad, *Theology* II, p. 224; T. Chary, *op. cit.*, pp. 21f.

[50] Cf. G. von Rad, *Theology* II, pp. 235f.

the more generally held ideas,[51] though it must also be seen in the light of the last part of ch. 37, where ideas of a new people and a new unity and covenant naturally lead to that of a new ideal Davidic Shepherd. To this may be added the point[52] that the dating of the Ezekiel material by the exile of Jehoiachin indicates a linking of restoration to the Davidic line as embodied in him. In the later chapters a due distance is kept between the prince and the cultus, though the ancient connection which the king has had is recognized in the special functions assigned to the prince. The theocratic rule here places him subordinate to the priesthood, though as representative of the people he has a special place set apart from the people for his sharing in the worship, and the land which is allocated to him—the equivalent of the old crown lands—lies in a specially close proximity to the more sacred areas surrounding the shrine.[53] The land is purified and the blessing of fruitfulness given to it, both in general terms in ch. 36 and with more specific relation to the divine power in ch. 47. In a real sense, too, it is a new land, a land reordered so that it may adequately express both the restoration of ancient splendour and the establishment of a right relationship.[54] A new and spiritualized geography[55] places the tribes in due order, according to a strict hierarchy, in a land which has become ideally regular and admits of having its population set in order, so as to place centrally Judah and Benjamin, the tribes which have made up—in theory and also in large measure in practice—the kingdom of the south to which the Temple belongs (cf. 45.1ff.; 47–48).[56] Involved in this resettlement is the unity of the

[51] On this whole question, cf. E. Hammershaimb, 'Ezekiel's View of the Monarchy', *Studia Orientalia Joanni Pedersen* (Copenhagen, 1953), pp. 130–40 = *Some Aspects of Old Testament Prophecy from Isaiah to Malachi* (Copenhagen, 1966), pp. 51–62; J. Coppens, 'L'espérance messianique royale à la veille et au lendemain de l'exil', in *Studia Biblica et Semitica T. C. Vriezen dedicata* (Wageningen, 1966), pp. 46–61, see pp. 54–59; A. Caquot, 'Le Messianisme d'Ezéchiel', *Semitica* 14 (1964), pp. 5–23.

[52] Cf. K. Baltzer, *op. cit.*, p. 39.

[53] This is here a link to the older 'amphictyonic' pattern, cf. H. Gese, *op. cit.*, p. 12; M. Noth, *Das System der zwölf Stämme Israels* (Stuttgart, 1930), pp. 151–62: Exkurs III. Cf. R. de Vaux, *Ancient Israel* (ET, 1961), pp. 124ff.

[54] Cf. A. Causse, *Du groupe ethnique à la communauté religieuse* (1937), pp. 204–7.

[55] Cf. T. Chary, *op. cit.*, p. 277.

[56] Cf. the Chronicler's appreciation of Judah and Benjamin as the true Israel, e.g. II Chron. 11.1, and note the prominence given to these two tribes in the lists in I Chron. 4 and 8, long in comparison with those of the other tribes. Benjamin as part of the southern kingdom is, however, already implied in the allocation of *one* tribe to David's house (i.e. in addition to Judah) in Ahijah's symbolic action in I Kings 11.29–36.

whole people, expressed most clearly in the symbol of the two sticks
(37.15–23).[57] The whole outline represents the expression of a desire
to reactivate the old tribal order.[58]

So organized, land and people will be fit for the position which
they occupy. Purity—expressed predominantly in cultic terms—and
justice (cf. 45.9–12) are the essential marks of a people which, having
in the past been so hardened in heart that they cannot obey, are now
renewed with a heart of flesh instead of one of stone (36.26), and
revived out of the deadness of exile into the newness of life which
comes from God (37.1–14).

All this is effected by divine action and by that alone. The new
life is divinely given (cf. ch. 36, 37); the reordered land is made what
it is by God; the new Temple is his building.[59] But it is not for Israel
alone—the concentration is upon the nature of God which motivates
his action, and it is with a wider view, too, a prospect of the knowledge of God among the nations. This broader outlook is significant
because it indicates the appropriateness of placing Ezekiel alongside
Deutero-Isaiah.

The point is brought out in the last part of ch. 39. The overthrow
of the hostile power of Gog of Magog is the preface to the restoration
visions, and the link between them is provided by a passage (39.21–
29) which stresses the new understanding among the nations of what
it is that has been done to Israel. When judgement is brought upon
the nations,

all nations shall see my judgement which I have executed . . .
The house of Israel shall know that I am Yahweh.[60] (39.21–22)

And the nations shall know that the house of Israel
went into captivity for their iniquity. (39.23)

H. Graf Reventlow in an article on 'The Nations as Yahweh's
Witnesses in Ezekiel'[61] points to the occurrence of that characteristic
declaratory phrase 'I am Yahweh' in the foreign nation oracles. With

[57] Cf. A. Causse, Les Dispersés d'Israël (1929), pp. 31–34.
[58] Cf. J. Bright, History of Israel, p. 414 n.; M. Noth, loc. cit.; T. Chary, op. cit.,
p. 22.
[59] Reorganization depends upon the presence of God and is not a prerequisite
of it. Cf. the new Temple, divinely built, in ch. 40–42, the arrival of God's glory
in 43.1–5 (against T. Chary, op. cit., p. 23). Essentially the same emphasis will be
seen in Haggai and Zechariah, cf. below, pp. 155ff., 171ff.
[60] Cf. W. Zimmerli, op. cit. (p.106 n. 17).
[61] 'Die Völker als Jahwes Zeugen bei Ezechiel', ZAW 71 (1959), pp. 33–43.

it he links the phrase 'in the sight of the nations' and others comparable with it in meaning, and shows the legal background to the expression in the context of witnessing to an action.[62] He traces further the point that witnesses in the Old Testament sense are not indifferent, but are themselves involved: 'they are to assess their own position' relative to what takes place.[63] Ezekiel stands in this tradition of usage, and the place occupied by the nations as witnesses is therefore to be understood not in the rather narrow sense of spectators, non-participants in the action of God,[64] but as witnesses who are themselves involved in what happens because they must assess their own position relative to it.[65] This is the obverse of the concern that Yahweh's name should not be profaned in the world of the nations. Just as the Egyptians were involved in the great act of divine deliverance from Egypt—and the narrative makes clear that the prolonging of the plague series was directed towards letting Pharaoh know the real nature of Yahweh (cf. Ex. 9.15f.), so now the nations, all the world, represented by Gog, are brought to the knowledge of who he is:

My holy name I will make known in the midst of my people Israel;
and I will not let my holy name be profaned any more;
and the nations shall know that I am Yahweh, the Holy One in Israel.
(39.7)

And the emphasis on the certainty of this is laid in the immediately following verse:

Behold it is coming and it will be brought about, says the Lord Yahweh. This is the day which I promised. (39.8)

'This action of God', writes Reventlow with reference to the whole event of the exile, 'is not a more or less political action, tied to history; if it were that, then the total destruction of the people would be the only possible outcome. Rather does Yahweh's action issue entirely from his own basic being and nature. But this being is such

---

[62] Cf. Gen. 23; Jer. 32.12; so also Jer. 19.10; 43.9; Deut. 31.7; Neh. 8.3; Jer. 28.1, 5, 11.
[63] Op. cit., pp. 35f. Cf. also G. M. Tucker, 'Witnesses and "Dates" in Israelite Contracts', CBQ 28 (1966), pp. 42–45—witnesses as validating an action.
[64] This narrower type of interpretation is to be found in older studies, e.g. G. A. Cooke, The Book of Ezekiel (ICC, 1936), p. xxxi. Cf. also Y. Kaufmann, op. cit., p. 446.
[65] A comparison may be made here with the acceptance of the parables in the New Testament.

that it demands by its very nature recognition by the nations of the world, the *gōyîm*. Yahweh's name must not be profaned in the sight of the nations.'[66]

Ezekiel does not draw precise consequences from this. His concern is to show the reorganization of Israel because it is through this that the name of Yahweh is to be revealed. But he has set the experiences of Israel in a world context, and the consequences of the exile are therefore to be seen in the whole understanding of the purpose of God. It is thus that we may understand the stress which is laid upon the experience of exile as such. In the negative repudiation of those in Palestine who look to the past and take comfort in the thought that 'Abraham was only one man, yet he got possession of the land; but we are many; the land is surely given us to possess' (33.24), Ezekiel expresses his belief that only through the exile, only through the acceptance of the loss of all that seemed to belong to Israel's life and nature, can the vindication of God's name and nature be achieved. The destruction itself makes it plain that 'I am Yahweh'; the restoration equally proclaims it. The one centre of his thought is 'the making visible of the honour of Yahweh in Israel and beyond Israel in all the world'.[67]

[66] *Op. cit.*, pp. 40f. Cf. G. von Rad, *Theology* II, p. 236.
[67] W. Zimmerli, *ZThK* 48 (1951), p. 261 = *Gottes Offenbarung*, p. 147. Cf. G. von Rad, *Theology* II, pp. 236f.; T. Chary, *op. cit.*, p. 23. On Ezekiel, cf. also S. Herrmann, *op. cit.* (p. 61 n. 49), pp. 241–91, and the article by W. Zimmerli, 'Planungen für den Wiederaufbau nach der Katastrophe von 587', *VT* 18 (1968), pp. 229–55, which draws together much of Zimmerli's thinking about the relation between God's action and the plans for the future set out in Ezek. 40–48.

VIII

PROPHECY OF THE EXILE AND THE
IDEALS OF RESTORATION
(*continued*)

B. DEUTERO-ISAIAH

WHAT IS SOMETIMES termed 'critical orthodoxy' divides the book of Isaiah into three main sections, subdividing 40–66 into Deutero- and Trito-Isaiah, 40–55 and 56–66, though without there being any agreement concerning the unity or otherwise of 56–66. We may recognize that there are parts of Proto-Isaiah which have some close affinities with 40–66, and that the structure of the book is not adequately explained merely by subdividing it.[1] In particular, the division between Proto-Isaiah and Deutero-Isaiah, while most often made at ch. 40, ought perhaps to be made so as to link ch. 35, and perhaps also ch. 34, with Deutero-Isaiah—the 'historical appendix' of 36–39 now interrupting this connection.[2] The subdivision of 40–55 and 56–66 has also been questioned, both by Torrey and Smart,[3] and also because there are indications of a different system of division within the chapters themselves.[3a] But although

[1] Cf. J. H. Eaton, 'The Origin of the Book of Isaiah', *VT* 9 (1959), pp. 138–57, which provides a judicious statement of the nature of the Isaiah tradition, and does justice also to those features of the book which enable very conservative scholars to maintain Isaianic authorship for the whole.

[2] For such views, cf. C. C. Torrey, *The Second Isaiah* (Edinburgh, 1928) and J. D. Smart, *History and Theology in Second Isaiah* (Philadelphia, 1965).

[3] F. Maass, ' "Tritojesaja" ?' in *Das ferne und nahe Wort* (*Festschrift L. Rost*), ed. F. Maass (BZAW 105, 1967), pp. 153–63, offers a review of recent work, both criticizing any tendency to oversimplify the relationship between Isa. 56–66 and what precedes, and pointing to some passages in these chapters which, in his view, do not reveal any valid reasons for denying them to Deutero-Isaiah. N. H. Snaith, *VTS* 14 (1967), pp. 135–264, see esp. pp. 139–46, 177–200, 219–43, offers points of detailed analysis showing interrelationships within ch. 40–66.

[3a] Cf. B. O. Banwell, 'A Suggested Analysis of Isaiah xl–lxvi', *ExpT* 76 (1964/5), p. 166, who picks on a feature noted in some of the commentaries, namely that ch.

it is right that the division should be challenged, since there are many points of contact between 40–55 and 56–66 which suggest a close unity of tradition, though not necessarily or even probably of author-ship, it must also be borne in mind that there are differences which are not without their importance,[4] and the uncertainties in discovering appropriate backgrounds for the material in 56–66 are such that it is here particularly easy to fall into the trap of dating the material in order to discover evidence about the period to which it has been assigned.[5] In some respects, the problems in this part of the book of Isaiah are akin to those of Jeremiah and Ezekiel. The former reveals indications of later reshaping of the tradition at many points rather than in a particular and more or less coherent section; the latter has such a coherent section in 40–48, and this may well be of later origin, but it belongs so appropriately with the whole problem of restoration as this is considered by Ezekiel that separation is not really appropriate. Trito-Isaiah is so much less coherent, and may well contain material of such different origin that it appears wisest to adopt a conservative position and treat Deutero-Isaiah as normally recognized here, and subsequently[6] to comment briefly on such parts or aspects of Trito-Isaiah as is appropriate with the recognition that their dating remains uncertain.

The study by J. D. Smart already mentioned, which has brought to the fore again the views of Torrey (already followed up by W. A. L. Elmslie[7] and U. E. Simon),[8] and in addition makes a frontal attack on various other writers, is at many points arbitrary in method and often appears to be wrong in interpretation.[9] While its criticisms of the normally accepted position must be allowed to

---

48 and ch. 57 both end with the same rubric, and 66.24, the closing verse, has a similar form. He further suggests that ch. 40 is an introduction to the three sections thus formed: 41–48; 49–57; 58–66. The suggestion is certainly an interesting one, though there are other possible explanations of what may be a liturgical phrase.

[4] Cf., e.g., K. Elliger, *Die Einheit des Tritojesaja* (BWANT 45, 1928); *idem*, 'Der Prophet Tritojesaja' *ZAW* 49 (1931), pp. 112–41. For other literature, cf. O. Eissfeldt, *Introduction*, pp. 341ff.

[5] Cf. the dangers of this in D. R. Jones, *Isaiah 56–66 and Joel* (TBC, 1964), and *JTS* 14 (1963), pp. 17–22.

[6] Cf. pp. 227ff.

[7] *How Came our Faith* (Cambridge, 1948), p. 191 n.

[8] *A Theology of Salvation* (London, 1953).

[9] Cf. C. R. North's review in *ExpT* 78 (1966/7), pp. 334f., and that of F. Holmgreen in *Interpretation* 21 (1967), pp. 105–10.

raise questions about approach, it provides no satisfying overall explanation of the prophet's activities. This will become apparent in some comments on Haggai and Zechariah in relation to Isaiah 66.[10] A full discussion would demand a detailed verse-by-verse commentary which it is not the intention of this study to provide; but the deficiencies are apparent particularly in relation to the understanding of the relation between history and prophetic activity, and in regard to the place of the Temple in the prophet's thinking.

Smart also raises again the question of the localization of the prophet, and sets him in Palestine on the grounds that there is little real concern with Babylon and little definite evidence to place him there.[11] Certainly his localization is not provable. The balance still seems to be in favour of a Babylonian setting, in view of the tremendous concentration on the release from captivity, on return to the land—which is never very clearly in focus—and the parallels to the Exodus.[12]

The unity of Deutero-Isaiah is again a problem which cannot be satisfactorily resolved; unity of tradition there certainly is, and a growing tendency to treat the whole section as one, rather than artificially separating off such passages as the so-called 'Servant Songs'.[13] The tirade against idols in ch. 44 is perhaps intrusive, but closely connected with the remainder.

Any attempt at dealing with the richness of the thought of these chapters of Deutero-Isaiah immediately comes up against the difficulty of finding an entirely satisfactory method of analysing their contents. It is not that the main themes cannot be readily discerned, in spite of the uncertainties which arise in regard to the detail of text and interpretation. It is that any attempt at producing a logical exposition is frustrated by the complexity of the thought. For the various themes run so closely into one another that at almost every point several themes are present at once, and to quote a particular passage as exemplifying one aspect of the prophet's thought is immediately to discover that, in fact, it exemplifies

---

[10] Cf. p. 156 n. 15.

[11] *Op. cit.*, p. 23. Cf. O. Eissfeldt, *Introduction*, pp. 332f. A. S. Kapelrud, 'Levde Deuterojesaja in Judea', *NorTT* 61 (1960), pp. 23–27, who considers that Deutero-Isaiah saw the return from the viewpoint of Jerusalem. But account must here be taken of that aspect of the Isaiah tradition (in which Deutero-Isaiah stands) which gives prominence to Jerusalem as the focal point of the people's life.

[12] Cf. pp. 128ff.

[13] Cf. pp. 126ff.

various other aspects as well. The whole complex is so interwoven and its richness of thought so abundant that any presentation suffers from being a less than poetic statement of what is here set out with such fervour.[14]

In this brief presentation, which is again limited to what specifically illuminates the exilic situation, it has seemed best to make a division between what we may term the backward and forward looking of the prophet. This corresponds to the consideration in Ezekiel of the understanding of disaster and the prospect of salvation. Here we may distinguish, in spite of obvious interrelationship, between the prophet's understanding of how his people has come to be where it is, and the anticipation which he shows of events in which God is acting and will continue to act to effect his purposes.[15]

I. THE PEOPLE'S PRESENT CONDITION

There is no glossing over in these chapters of the cause of Israel's present state. It is affirmed to be the result of sin and failure, and in this Deutero-Isaiah stands in the tradition of prophecy, closest to Jeremiah and Ezekiel with whose words his own have many points of contact.[16] At the very outset the message of hope is set against this background of failure:

She has completed her compulsory service,
her guilt is paid off.[17]

[14] Cf., for example, the discussion 'Poet or Prophet' in C. R. North, *The Second Isaiah* (Oxford, 1964), pp. 22–28, and also pp. 12–22 on 'Theology of Deutero-Isaiah'; C. Westermann, 'Sprache und Struktur der Prophetie Deuterojesajas', *Forschung am Alten Testament* (ThB 24, 1964), pp. 92–170; J. Muilenburg, *IB* 5 (1956), pp. 386–93.

[15] For a résumé of Deutero-Isaiah's theology, cf. C. Westermann, *Das Buch Jesaja. Kap 40–66* (ATD 19, 1966), pp. 11–25.

[16] Cf., for example, Morna D. Hooker, *Jesus and the Servant* (London, 1959), pp. 25–40, where Dr Hooker traces the close contacts between Isa. 40–55 and Jer. 30–33 and Ezek. 34–37.

[17] *nirṣā*—here rendered 'paid off' (cf. *KBL*, p. 906)—presents the same problem of meaning as in Lev. 26.34, 41, 43 (cf. pp. 89f). If two Hebrew roots *rṣh* are distinguished (as in *KBL*), it is difficult not to feel that the meanings have become in some measure conflated. The sense 'paid off' would then here have the overtone of 'accepted', especially if *ʿāwōn* is recognized as carrying the meaning of both 'guilt' and 'punishment'. The latter indeed provides in some ways a better parallel to *ṣābā*'—'compulsory service'. Cf. on the rendering also C. R. North, *The Second Isaiah*, pp. 32, 70. For this interpretation cf. also below pp. 241f.

> She has received from the hand of Yahweh
> the equivalent for all her sins. [18] (40.2)

The direct association between God's anger and Israel's condition is made clear repeatedly. It is 'Yahweh against whom we have sinned', who deliberately handed Israel over to spoilers and robbers (42.24):

> For a brief moment I forsook you . . .
> In overflowing wrath I hid my face for a moment from you. (54.7f.)

The emphasis on the retaining of control in the hands of God is made in the statement:

> On account of your iniquities you were sold,
> and on account of your transgressions your mother
> was divorced. (50.1)

This is in the context of the rhetorical questions:

> Where is your mother's bill of divorce,
> with which I divorced her?
> Or to which of my creditors
> have I sold you?

It is not as if God has repudiated his people, or as if he has used it to pay off a bad debt. The whole responsibility rests upon the people themselves for their present condition.

The present situation of the people is thus clearly expressed in terms of the rightness of divine judgement. That the point is not so openly reiterated as in Ezekiel may perhaps be explained as due to the point in time. The prophet may not have felt the same need to elaborate the nature and rightness of divine judgement, for the prolonged years of exile have amply confirmed that it has fallen upon the people.[19] There is evident a concern also to explain the continued apparent lack of divine activity[20] and to counter both the complaints

---

[18] So G. von Rad, *ZAW* 79 (1967), pp. 80–82.

[19] Inevitably our lack of information precludes any precise verdict on this point. For not only must we recognize that the nearly contemporary Deuteronomic historians stress judgement, and suppose that either their interests or their understanding of the needs of the situation made such an emphasis appear necessary; but there may also be unknown factors in the activity of Deutero-Isaiah, or perhaps in the precise method of compilation of his prophecies, which have contributed to the present emphasis. In any case, the matter is only relative, since much in Deutero-Isaiah interprets judgement, and therefore implies a greater concern than immediately appears. On the judgement oracles in Deutero-Isaiah, cf. H.-E. von Waldow, *Der traditionsgeschichtliche Hintergrund der prophetischen Gerichtsreden* (BZAW 85, 1963), pp. 42–53.

[20] K. Galling, *Studien*, p. 53. Cf. this point again in Zech. 1.12. Cf. p. 176.

of those who lack faith and the apostasy of those who are drawn into the worship of other gods.[21] In the Deuteronomic History and the Priestly Work we have seen an element of hesitation, of uncertainty as to the outcome, for now so long has passed without any clear indication of God's purpose; so, too, in Deutero-Isaiah there are many elements which belong, in fact, to the themes of the psalms of lamentation,[22] expressive of, though not actually using, the familiar 'ad-mātay ('how long!'). The lack of faith which imagines that the present condition of his people is hidden from God calls forth a reminder that there is no limit to the power of the Creator (40.27–31). To the unspoken complaint, the answer of God is vividly expressed in the turmoil which now—after long keeping silence—he will bring upon the earth, guiding the blind and putting to shame those who have turned from him and trusted in idols (42.14–17). The people—here named the servant of God—is described as blind and deaf, failing to recognize and understand what it is that God is doing (42.18–20); and the same point, and similar language, follow in yet another passage which, emphasizing the blindness of those who have eyes and the deafness of those who have ears, points to the absoluteness of divine action (43.8ff.).

The interwoven character of the prophet's thought makes it natural that there is an easy passage from this to the statements of idolatry and its folly (e.g. 40.18–20; 41.6f., 46.5–7[23]), and that this in its turn is closely bound up with the stress on the creative and redemptive activity of God. To this point we shall return. Another passage provides a different kind of link. The complaint of Zion:

Yahweh has forsaken me
my Lord has forgotten me (49.14)

[21] Cf. O. Kaiser, Der königliche Knecht: Eine traditionsgeschichtlich-exegetische Studie über die Ebed-Jahwe-Lieder bei Deuterojesaja (FRLANT 70, 1959), p. 127.
[22] Cf. R. Press, 'Der Gottesknecht im Alten Testament', ZAW 67 (1955), pp. 67–99.
[23] 44.9–20 is often regarded as intrusive in Deutero-Isaiah (cf. the summarizing discussion in C. R. North, The Second Isaiah, pp. 139–40): but even if it is not directly from the prophet, it is clear that this homiletic passage may properly be associated with his teaching in the same way that such expansive passages of exposition in Jer. (e.g. 10.1–16, cf. P. R. Ackroyd, JTS 14 [1963], pp. 385–90, and T. W. Overholt, 'The Falsehood of Idolatry: an Interpretation of Jer. X.1–16', JTS 16 [1965], pp. 1–12) and in Ezekiel (e.g. the interpretations of symbols in ch. 4–7) belong in the respective prophetic traditions. The line of demarcation between original prophecy and prophetic exposition, by the prophet himself or by his successors, is to be drawn with hesitation (cf. P. R. Ackroyd, ASTI 1 [1962], pp. 7–23, esp. pp. 20f.).

ushers in an assurance of the enduring faithfulness of God to whom Jerusalem is ever present, engraved on the palms of his hands (49.16). And so we are brought to the theme of redemption again, but with a different emphasis, that upon the rebuilding of the city, the coming restoration of the desolated places.

The faithless people, doubting the reality of God's activity, turning away from him to worship other gods, is given its main reassurance in the whole series of confident statements of divine creation and divine redemption (e.g. 43.14ff.; 44.24f.). The answer to the long-continued distresses and devastations is to be found primarily in those words of hope. But there is another aspect to the understanding of the exile which may fittingly be mentioned first, though here again the link with other parts of the prophet's thought is such as to provide a cross-reference to the part which Israel has in the restoration purpose of God.

The mention—which we have already considered[24]—of the release of Jehoiachin from prison indicates the presence of speculation about the future which is tied to the hopes of the renewed Davidic dynasty. It has its repercussions not only in the circles of the Deuteronomists, but also in the relatively modest statements of post-exilic Davidic hope as found in Haggai and Zechariah,[25] and then, though it does not die, it appears to cease for many years to be a prominent element in political thinking.[26] But it is found also strongly in both the Jeremiah and the Ezekiel material, though it is uncertain how far it should be regarded as original there and how far it is an echo of just the kind of hopes which that release of Jehoiachin may have revived.[27] It finds a modest echo also in Deutero-Isaiah, where reference to the Davidic line is found directly only in the assurance of an everlasting covenant which is described

[24] Cf. above, pp. 79ff.

[25] Cf. Hag. 2.20–23; Zech. 3.8–10; 6.9–15.

[26] For its later reappearance, cf. the discussion in S. Mowinckel, *He that Cometh* (ET, 1956), pp. 286ff. Recognition must also be given to the fact that Davidic oracles appear in a number of prophetic books (cf. Isa. 9.1–6; 11.1–9; 32.1–8; Hos. 3.5.; Amos 9.11f.; Zech. 12.7ff.), and that the dating of these is uncertain; some of them, notably Zech. 12.7ff., are likely to belong to the exilic and post-exilic periods.

[27] Jer. 23.5f.; 30.8f.; 33.14–26; Ezek. 34.23f.; 37.24f. In Ezekiel in particular the absence of Davidic material in 40–48 contrasts sharply with the references to a future Davidic ruler in ch. 34 and 37 (cf. pp. 113f.); but it may be that in this respect there has been some conforming of the blueprint of ch. 40–48 to the actual post-exilic conditions, as appears also to be the case in regard to priestly and cultic regulations (cf. p. 113).

as the 'faithful mercies (*ḥasdē*) of David' (55.3).[28] The allusion is to that tradition of the continued mercy which God showed for the sake of David, a confidence that the covenant established for ever with the royal line could not just peter out with nothing to show.[29] We may perhaps see it as a promise reapplied to the whole people.[30] How far is this indicative of a deeper understanding of the experience of the time?

Jehoiachin, the legitimate and recognized king of Judah, was imprisoned for thirty-six years before his release. Viewed from this angle, the captivity of the people from 597 onwards coincides with the captivity of its king, and we do not need to exaggerate the position of the king to realize the significance of this. The more extravagant theories about Old Testament kingship do not need to be substantiated; there is evidence enough of the special position of the king without it being necessary to prove something more.[31] People and king—as witness the Deuteronomic judgements—belong together; and the captivities of both belong together. The captivity and the release point to an understanding of the exilic period in terms of humiliation and discipline; and again, without it being necessary to work out elaborate theories, it is possible to point to a psalm such as 89 and see in it an expression of what the humiliation of the king and so also of the people can mean.[32]

---

[28] Cf. G. von Rad, *Theology* II, p. 240; O. Eissfeldt, 'The Promises of Grace to David in Isaiah 55.1–5', in *Israel's Prophetic Heritage*, ed. B. W. Anderson and W. Harrelson (1962), pp. 196–207.

[29] II Sam. 7.15: *wᵉḥasdī lōʾ yāsūr mimmennū*, 'my *ḥesed* will not depart from him'. Cf. also Isa. 16.5, which refers to the enduring Davidic throne as: *wᵉhūkan baḥesed kissēʾ*, 'a throne will be established in *ḥesed*'.

[30] Cf. G. von Rad, *loc. cit.*; B. W. Anderson, 'Exodus Typology in Second Isaiah', in *Israel's Prophetic Heritage*, ed. B. W. Anderson and W. Harrelson (1962), pp. 177–95, see p. 191; J. Coppens, 'L'espérance messianique royale à la veille et au lendemain de l'exil', in *Studia Biblica et Semitica T. C. Vriezen dedicata* (Wageningen, 1966), pp. 46–61, see pp. 59f. Cf. also below, pp. 128, 252.

[31] For the evidence, cf., for example, S. Mowinckel, *He that Cometh* (ET, 1956), pp. 155–86, and A. R. Johnson, *Sacral Kingship in Ancient Israel* (Cardiff, 1955, ²1967).

[32] Cf. E. N. B. Burrows, 'The Servant of Jahweh in Isaiah: An Interpretation', in *The Gospel of the Infancy and other Biblical Essays* (London, 1941), pp. 59–80, whose approach is perhaps somewhat too literal to do justice to the poetry of Deutero-Isaiah. Cf. also N. W. Porteous, 'Jerusalem-Zion: The Growth of a Symbol', in *Verbannung und Heimkehr*, ed. A. Kuschke (Tübingen, 1961), pp. 235–52, see p. 245, comparing also Lam. 3; O. Kaiser, *op. cit.*, pp. 132f.; J. Coppens, 'Nieuw Licht over de Ebed-Jahweh-Liederen' in *Pro Regno Pro Sanctuario*, ed. W. J. Kooiman and J. M. van Veen (Nijkerk, 1950), pp. 115–23; A. R. Johnson, *op. cit.* (1955), pp. 22ff. and 97ff. on Ps. 89; and O. Eissfeldt, *op. cit.* (n. 28), on

If at this point we were to enter into a discussion of the interpretation of the 'servant'[33] passages in Deutero-Isaiah it would occupy a
disproportionate space and remain inevitably unfinished and incon-
clusive.[34] But again without accepting the full consequences of the
constructions which have been made—particularly in Scandinavia—
connecting the *'ebed Yahweh* with the king, it does not seem inappropriate to see as one element, and this a very important one,
the recognition that Israel and her king have been humiliated, by
reason of sin and failure, and now with the release of Jehoiachin there
is a ray of light. Bound up with it, for the servant concept as presented here is both royal and prophetic,[35] is the transfer of function
to Moses—a link with D and P—who epitomizes the new people of
a new Exodus and entry.[36] It would appear to be out of these
elements, together with the prophet's own sensitiveness to the nature
of the commission which is his (cf. esp. 49.1–7), that there is developed
the understanding of the exilic situation in terms of its relationship to
the total purpose of God, set within the context of the life of the
nations (52.13–53.12). The exile is at one and the same time a
proper punishment for what Israel has been in the past and an act
of discipline by which the future may be assured. But even more
deeply it is related to the ultimate purposes of God, and, in its

---

the relationship between Ps. 89 and Deutero-Isaiah, and especially Isa. 55.1–5.
Such relatively modest interpretations appear more appropriate than the very
elaborate constructions, built at great length, by G. W. Ahlstrom, *Psalm 89: Eine
Liturgie aus dem Ritual des leidenden Königs* (Lund, 1959).

[33] The use of a capital 'S' for servant in discussion of this material immediately
begs the primary question of whether an identification is to be made, or whether
the use of the form should be considered primarily in relation to its context. A
similar question-begging has affected the discussion of the *mōrē ṣedeq* of Qumran.
(Cf. J. Weingreen, 'The Title Môreh Ṣedek', *JSS* 6 [1961], pp. 162–74.) Cf. also
J. Coppens' conception of 'the ideal *ṣaddiq*', esp. in Isa. 53: 'Le serviteur de Yahvé:
vers la solution d'un énigme', *Sacra Pagina* (Bibliotheca Ephemeridum Theolo-
gicarum Lovaniensum XII, XIII, 1959) I, pp. 434–54. H. M. Orlinsky, 'The So-
called "Servant of the Lord" and "Suffering Servant" in Second Isaiah', in *Studies
on the Second Part of the Book of Isaiah (VTS* 14, 1967), pp. 1–133, argues forcibly
against the technical use of *'ebed*. It is not necessary to accept all his conclusions to
recognize the validity of this point.
[34] For full documentation, cf. C. R. North, *The Suffering Servant in Deutero-
Isaiah* (Oxford, 1948, ²1956); H. H. Rowley, *The Servant of the Lord* (London,
1952), pp. 3–57 (Oxford, ²1965), pp. 3–60; V. de Leeuw, *De Ebed Jahweh-Profetieen*
(Assen, 1956), pp. 5–106, 332–40.
[35] Sheldon H. Blank, *Prophetic Faith in Isaiah* (London, 1958), p. 77.
[36] Cf. G. von Rad, *Theology* II, p. 261; J. R. Porter, *Moses and Monarchy* (Oxford,
1963); H. Ringgren, *Israelite Religion* (ET, London, 1966), pp. 293f.

acceptance of the disaster as such, Israel—that is Israel as God sees it in its true relationship to him—promotes the effecting of God's will.[37] Here again we get the note of acceptance which is to be found in the Deuteronomic History—and indeed also in the Priestly Work and Ezekiel—without which the continued working of God for his people and hence for the whole world is frustrated. But in that acceptance the will of God is made effective.[38]

This aspect of the thought of Deutero-Isaiah has been subject to such a wide variety of interpretations that it is idle to hope for more than partial agreement on any conclusions drawn. But more serious is the point that great damage appears to have been done to the understanding of the message of the prophet in the separating out of four so-called 'Servant Songs' from the remainder of the material, regardless of the fact that the same terminology is used elsewhere in the prophecy and that considerable unreality is introduced into the discussion when attempts are made at finding a thought-sequence within the four single passages. The interwovenness of Deutero-Isaiah's thought makes it most undesirable—unless we are to be so arbitrary as to regard these four passages as so independent as to need to be completely separated from the main discussion[39]—to treat them in isolation. They are rather to be set in the main context of his thought and their interpretation depends upon a full apprehension of his message. Nor does it help the interpretation when there is a failure to recognize the poetic nature of virtually the whole of the material of Deutero-Isaiah and its many affinities with the psalms, so that the detail of the language is not susceptible to that kind of

[37] In this may be discovered the significance of types of interpretation which depict Isa. 40–55 as in some way offering a re-presentation of earlier liturgical forms. (Cf. I. Engnell, 'The 'Ebed Yahweh Songs and the Suffering Messiah in "Deutero-Isaiah" ', *BJRL* 31 [1948], pp. 54–93, see pp. 56f.; H. Ringgren, *op. cit.*, pp. 289ff.). It is hazardous to argue back from these chapters to an unknown but postulated liturgy, but there is truth in the appreciation of the actualization of older forms and the opening up of their meaning. Cf. K. Koch, *EvTh* 26 (1966), pp. 232f., on Isa. 43.22–25 as indicating a development of the idea of atonement effected by God, and similarly pp. 234ff. on Isa. 53.

[38] The point is stressed by M. Noth (*RHPhR* 33 [1953], p. 102, ET, p. 280) in his negative assessment of the hopes raised by Jehoiachin's release: 'Israel had to bear the divine judgement in full, without any human hope of some starting-point for a new future.'

[39] As is done by G. von Rad, *Theology* II, pp. 250ff., in such a way as to make for an unreal interpretation of Deutero-Isaiah. The more integrated view represented here is being increasingly maintained against the separating out of the so-called songs: cf., e.g., L. G. Rignell, *A Study of Isaiah Ch. 40–55* (LUÅ, 52.5, 1956).

literalistic interpretation which takes the statements particularly of ch. 53 as precise descriptions of events.[40]

Jehoiachin, captive and released king, in a real sense representative of his people; the transference to the people in exile,[41] humiliated and, though described as blind and deaf (42.19), nevertheless constituting that people through whom God effects his purposes; the figure of Moses, as representative and as mediator in a new Exodus;[42] Deutero-Isaiah himself, the sensitive prophet with his deep consciousness of his call and his awareness of the tensions[43] which belong to the prophetic calling—these are elements which together constitute the essential approach which the prophet makes to the situation of the time. To a people long exiled, in whom hope is dying (compare Isa. 53 with Ezek. 37), the message is one of acceptance[44] and of the realization, as in the psalms of lamentation, that it is in the moment of apparent failure that God is in reality at work. Israel thus has its place in the wider purpose of God and the future hope is both in the divine redemptive action and in the part which Israel is to play.[45]

2. THE FUTURE HOPE[46]

If the appropriation of the exile is often in terms reminiscent of the psalms of lamentation,[47] the setting out of the hope for the future is in terms of the hymnic praise of psalms which proclaim both the

[40] Cf. G. von Rad, *Theology* II, pp. 257f.

[41] Cf. H. G. May, 'The Righteous Servant in Second Isaiah's Songs', *ZAW* 66 (1954), pp. 236–44, on the link to Jeremiah's 'confessions', as 'laments of the persecuted righteous'. Cf. on this latter aspect of Jeremiah, H. Graf Reventlow, *Liturgie und Prophetisches Ich bei Jeremia* (Gütersloh, 1963), pp. 205ff.

[42] The actual figure of Moses does not appear in Deutero-Isaiah, though it does appear in the closely related passage 63.11ff. But the idea of a new Exodus—most strongly depicted in 51.9–11—makes appropriate a recognition of such an element in the prophet's understanding. Again it is unnecessary to subscribe to the extravagances of such a view as that of E. Sellin (*Mose und seine Bedeutung für die israelitisch-jüdische Religionsgeschichte* (Leipzig, 1922)), who resorts to hazardous emendation and interpretation of Hosea to make of Moses a martyr figure; we may nevertheless recognize that the Mosaic tradition contained an element of vicarious suffering (Ex. 32.32, cf. Rom. 9.3).

[43] Cf. this in Jeremiah and Ezekiel, too.

[44] Cf. also P. A. H. de Boer, *Second-Isaiah's Message* (*OTS* 11, 1956), pp. 116f.

[45] Cf. Millar Burrows, *op. cit.* (p. 98 n. 73), p. 123; E. Voegelin, *Israel and Revelation* (Louisiana, 1956), pp. 491–515.

[46] G. von Rad, *Theology* II, pp. 243ff.

[47] For this, cf. esp. the book of Lamentations itself. Cf. above, pp. 45ff.

kingly rule of Yahweh and the creative act by which that rule is declared,[48] and in forms derived from pronouncements of divine salvation.[49] In the most vivid and central statement of all, the act of redemption is proclaimed in terms which sum up in classic form the relationship between creation and the action of God in history both past and future:

> Awake awake be clothed in strength
>   O arm of Yahweh!
> Awake as in ancient days
>   generations of eternity.
> Is it not you who are cutting Rahab in pieces
>   piercing the dragon?
> Is it not you who are drying up the sea
>   the waters of the great deep?
> Appointing the depths of the sea
>   as a road for the ransomed to pass through?
> So the ransomed of Yahweh shall return
>   they shall come into Zion with a shout of joy.
> Eternal joy shall be on their heads
>   gladness and joy will overtake them
>   sorrow and sighing shall flee. (51.9–11)[50]

The actualization of the events of creation and redemption in the present situation is here made most plain. The series of participial phrases in vv. 9–10 here—often erroneously translated as if they were equivalent to past tenses[51]—expresses, as is so often the case also in the hymns of the psalter, the attributes of the God whose power is invoked. The sense of the contemporaneity of history is here most obvious. What God does here and now is both what he did in creation—the mythology of creation conflict[52] expresses that—and what he did in the bringing of Israel out of Egypt. The future event is

---

[48] Cf. R. Rendtorff, 'Die theologische Stellung des Schöpfungsglaubens bei Deuterojesaja', *ZThK* 51 (1954), pp. 3–13; P. B. Harner, 'Creation faith in Deutero-Isaiah', *VT* 17 (1967), pp. 298–306.

[49] Cf. J. Begrich, 'Das priesterliche Heilsorakel', *ZAW* 52 (1934), pp. 81–92 = *Ges. Stud.* (ThB 21, 1964), pp. 217–31; H.-E. von Waldow, *Anlass und Hintergrund der Verkündigung des Deuterojesaja* (Diss., Bonn, 1953), who stresses the cultic context of the material (cf. esp. pp. 64ff.).

[50] In v. 11 'on their heads' preserves the Hebrew idiom, and this seems preferable to 'crowned with never-fading gladness' (so C. R. North, *The Second Isaiah* [1964], pp. 61, 213), since the Hebrew would seem more probably to imply 'anointing with (oil of) gladness'.

[51] So RSV, C. R. North (*loc. cit.*), etc. One might indeed see in the participles a sense of the imminent future. Cf. R. Rendtorff, *op. cit.*, p. 13.

[52] *yām* and *tᵉhōm* might be rendered as proper names, 'Sea' and 'Deep'.

contained in this, for the return of the exiles to Zion in rejoicing is the counterpart of the ransoming of the enslaved Israel and of the overthrow of the hostile forces of primeval chaos.[53] The whole range of the future hope is here drawn together, and from the point of view of our understanding of Deutero-Isaiah's place in the religious tradition it is of very great significance that the expression of the hope is so bound into the historical and creative concepts of the nature of Yahweh. Deutero-Isaiah stands centrally in the tradition of *Heilsgeschichte*,[54] especially as this is expressed in the Psalter.[55] We may trace from this a series of lines of thought.

With Zimmerli we may recognize that 'The real Exodus event . . . lies in the future'.[56] It is a recurrent theme that the events by which the exiles are to be restored are the reality of what is proclaimed in the Exodus events.[57] So in 43.14–21 the 'new thing' which Yahweh will do is, in fact, a renewal of what he did in the former events.[58] These are now no longer to be remembered, because what

[53] On the whole passage, cf. A. Lauha, *Die Geschichtsmotive in den alttestamentlichen Psalmen* (1945), pp. 15f.; L. Köhler, *Hebrew Man* (ET, 1956), p. 140; G. von Rad, *Theology* II, pp. 240ff.; Millar Burrows, *op. cit.* (p. 98 n. 73), pp. 121ff.; B. W. Anderson, *op. cit.*, pp. 193f.; R. Rendtorff, *op. cit.*, pp. 5f.

[54] Cf. G. von Rad, *Theology* II, p. 253; C. Stuhlmuller, 'The Theology of Creation in Second Isaias', *CBQ* 21 (1959), pp. 429–67.

[55] Cf. the affinities of Deutero-Isaiah with the royal psalms, and the use of the royal style. Cf. M. Haran, 'Cyrus in the Prophetic Glass', *El-haʿayin*, No. 39 (Jerusalem, 1964), pp. 43–54.

[56] 'Ich bin Jahwe' in *Geschichte und Altes Testament (Festschrift A. Alt*, Tübingen, 1953), pp. 179–209, see p. 201 = *Gottes Offenbarung*, pp. 11–40, see p. 33. Cf. J. Kahmann, 'Die Heilszukunft in ihrer Beziehung zur Heilsgeschichte nach Isaias 40–55', *Biblica* 32 (1951), pp. 65–87, 141–72; B. W. Anderson, *op. cit.*, pp. 185ff., esp. p. 188; E. M. Prevallet, 'The Use of the Exodus in Interpreting History', *Concordia Theol. Monthly* 37 (1966), pp. 131–45, see pp. 139ff.; F. M. Cross, 'The Divine Warrior in Israel's Early Cult', in *Biblical Motifs*, ed. A. Altmann (1966), pp. 28ff.

[57] Cf. W. Zimmerli, 'Le nouvel "Exode" dans le message des deux grands prophètes de l'exil', in *Maqqél Shâqédh. Hommage à W. Vischer* (Montpellier, 1960), pp. 216–27, see pp. 220–4 = *Gottes Offenbarung*, pp. 192–204, see pp. 197–201, on the richness of allusion here to the Exodus traditions.

[58] C. R. North, 'The "Former Things" and the "New Things" in Deutero-Isaiah', *StOTPr* (1950), pp. 111–26, sees in this passage such an Exodus reference. I am less sure that he is right in finding in some other passages references to events in the more immediate past. Cf. the comments on this view by B. W. Anderson, *op. cit.*, pp. 187f. Cf. also M. Haran, 'The Literary Structure and Chronological Framework of the Prophecies in Isa. 40–48', *VTS* 9 (1963), pp. 127–55, see pp. 137ff., who sees in *rīʾšōnōt* 'prophecies which have been fulfilled' (p. 137). Also his *Between RIʾSHONÔT (Former Prophecies) and HADASHÔT (New Prophecies)—A Literary-Historical Study in the Group of Prophecies Isaiah XL-XLVIII* (Hebrew) (Jerusalem, 1963).

Yahweh is now doing replaces them. Actualization of the past in worship will no longer be necessary, because the past will have been actualized in life. The anticipation of Jer. 23.7–8 is here taken up: a new confessional statement will proclaim the deliverance from the 'north country'. That such a precise change is not, in fact, observable in confessional statements of the post-exilic period does not affect the validity of the point.[59] For, as is clear in the opening chapters of Zechariah, the deliverance from exile, while not expressing itself in the precise terms of the Jeremiah passage, nevertheless shows the appreciation of the exile which is to be found in the later assessments. The new Israel is the Israel which has gone through this experience, just as the old Israel was the Israel of the Exodus events. The departure from exile—and so the Chronicler will understand it (Ezra 1.5ff.)—will be a re-enactment of the first departure, but this time not as in flight, nor in haste, but with the assurance of God's presence (Isa. 52.11f.).[60]

As is characteristic in Old Testament prophecy, the events foretold are not left in the air, but attached to the realities of the political situation, though not limited by them.[61] It is perhaps idle to speculate here again whether the political events provoked the prophecy or the

[59] So, for example, in Neh. 9, where the Exodus still remains central as again later in Judith 5 (cf. below, p. 239).

[60] Cf. B. W. Anderson, *loc. cit.*

[61] This is the point at which the arguments of C. C. Torrey on these chapters (*The Second Isaiah* [Edinburgh, 1928]; *idem*, 'Isaiah 41', *HTR* 44 (1951), pp. 121–36), adopted also by, e.g., U. E. Simon, *A Theology of Salvation* (1953), esp. pp. 15ff., and by W. A. L. Elmslie, *How Came Our Faith* (1948), p. 191 n. (cf. also J. D. Smart, *op. cit.*, esp. pp. 18f.) appear weakest. To argue that, because Cyrus did not do what the prophet anticipated, the prophecy must be symbolic only and belong to a much later date does not do justice to the way in which prophecy is tied in with history, and is not necessarily seeing it in its true perspective. Cyrus did grant permission to rebuild the Temple (there is no good reason to doubt the Aramaic form of the decree in Ezra 6.3–5). The Chronicler—from a later standpoint—saw that this was the event of fundamental significance. The prophet living in the events, speaks with supreme confidence of the activity of God: his message is no more invalidated by the relatively meagre sequel than is that of other prophets whose words were not exactly fulfilled. In fact, as is suggested in ch. X, XI below, the evaluation of the early restoration period is not necessarily to be set so low. At the same time, the strictures of C. R. North, 'The Interpretation of Deutero-Isaiah', in *Interpretationes ad V.T. pertinentes S. Mowinckeil septuagenario missae*, ed. N. A. Dahl and A. S. Kapelrud (Oslo, 1955), pp. 133–45, are too unsympathetic to the discernment of typological elements in the Deutero-Isaianic material. Cf. also U. E. Simon, 'König Cyrus und die Typologie', *Judaica* 11 (1955), pp. 83–88. As has been noted elsewhere, Torrey's approach, while historically inadequate, is often theologically penetrating.

prophet's insight read the events. The interlinkage between prophecy and event is really more subtle than a simple time sequence.[62] In the rise of Cyrus to power and the prospect of the overthrow of Babylon we may see the particularizing of what other prophets (cf. Isa. 13–14 and Jer. 50–51)[63] deal with in more general terms. That Babylon, once seen as the instrument of divine judgement, must in its turn be subjected to that judgement, is evident in the prophetic utterances. The precise delineation of the judgement which will overtake Babylon remains, however, to a not inconsiderable extent a matter of indifference, just as in earlier prophecy the overthrow of Israel or Judah is depicted as being at the hands of Egypt,[64] or Assyria,[65] or in terms which defy precise identification.[66] For Deutero-Isaiah, the certainty of judgement and so the vindication of God's action is primary; but this is crystallized in the summoning of Cyrus (41.1ff., 25ff.; 44.28; 45.1ff.), who is either named or sufficiently clearly identifiable.[67] To look for precise fulfilment of the utterances concerning Cyrus,[68] or to imagine that the prophet must have been too bitterly disillusioned by the failure of Cyrus to acknowledge that it was Yahweh who really controlled his actions, is to miss the nature

[62] Cf. M. Noth, *History of Israel*, p. 301; J. Begrich, *Studien zu Deuterojesaja* (BWANT 77, 1938 = ThB 20, 1963), esp. ch. 5; E. Jenni, 'Die Rolle des Kyros bei Deuterojesaja', *TZ* 10 (1954), pp. 241–56. Cf. also S. Smith, *Isaiah XL–LV: Literary Criticism and History* (1944); M. Haran's writings noted on p 130 n. 58; and W. B. Stevenson, 'Successive Phases in the Career of the Babylonian Isaiah', BZAW 66 (1936), pp. 89–96.

[63] Cf. pp. 219ff.

[64] Cf. Isa. 7.18; Jer. 2.16; Hos. 11. 5.

[65] Cf. Isa. 7; Amos 5.27; 6.14.

[66] Cf. Jer. 6; Zeph. 1.

[67] The excision of Cyrus's name in 44.28; 45.1 is made by J. D. Smart (*op. cit.*, pp. 23f., 115ff.), in a discussion which seems very literal-minded in its reading of the text. So, too, C. C. Torrey, *op. cit.*, pp. 24f., 35ff.; U. E. Simon, *op. cit.*, pp. 119ff., whose typological approach faces much more seriously the position of Cyrus in the tradition, cf. II Chron. 36.22f. To assert, as, e.g., J. D. Smart does (*op. cit.*, pp. 121f.) that to retain the name of Cyrus makes the mind of the prophet appear confused, is again to fail to reckon with the *ad hoc* nature of much Old Testament prophecy (cf. pp. 55f. on Jer.). Cf. the comments on the Cyrus material in E. Jenni, *Die politischen Voraussagen der Propheten* (ATANT 29, 1956), pp. 100–3.

[68] On the interpretation of the Cyrus references in rabbinic writings, and the application of these to Abraham, cf. F. Mettzer, 'The attitude of "Hazal" (The Rabbis of the Talmud) to Cyrus', *El-ha'ayin* No. 39 (Jerusalem, 1964), pp. 55–61. Also M. Zerkavod, 'Cyrus, King of Persia: Vision and Authority in the Bible', *ibid.*, pp. 69–85, on the hopes and their limited realization. Christian commentary, esp. in the medieval period, often simply read 'Christ' for 'Cyrus'. The Abraham interpretation is revived by C. C. Torrey (see *HTR* 44 (1951), pp. 121–36), and by U. E. Simon, *op. cit.*, pp. 68ff., 120ff.

of the relationship between divine event and human agent.[69] Babylon fell: Cyrus was victor and took over the empire. To ask for a more precise fulfilment is to ask of the prophet something which he does not profess to give. For in the political terms is concealed a conviction of the action of God. The real initiator of all the events is God, and just as the Exodus narratives portray the Pharaoh as the one who is to see the glory of God—though this is a historically dubious statement—so Cyrus, without realizing it, is, in fact, fulfilling the purposes of the God who has called him.[70]

The basis of the prophet's interpretation is by no means a skilful weighing of the political chances. If the implied complaint in 45.9ff. is really an expression of the perplexity of the pious that God should choose a heathen ruler as the instrument of his purpose, then the basis of the reply is clearly that since it is God who controls, being the Creator of all things, it is God who is to decide by what means his purpose of restoration is to be effected.[71] Beyond that there can be no motive. And with this affirmation of the Creator God as the controller of events, there is the justification of what happens on the same basis as is to be found in Ezekiel and the Holiness Code. It is because he is Yahweh, because he is the one who is, because of his Name, that he acts. Zimmerli's examination of the use of the expression 'I am Yahweh', '$^a n\bar{\imath}$ $Yahweh$,'[72] shows its considerable frequency in this prophetic material, whether it stands alone or is expanded with larger expressions of the nature of the God who makes this pronouncement. And to this we may add further the use of a phrase which appears to be closely related: '$^a n\bar{\imath}$ $h\bar{u}$', 'I am he' (cf. 41.4; 43.10; 48.12), or '$\bar{a}n\bar{o}k\bar{\imath}$ $h\bar{u}$' (43.25), a phrase which strongly suggests an attempt at theological explanation of the divine name as being equivalent to the personal pronoun, so that just as Ex. 3.14 provides us with the interpretation '$ehyeh$ (I am), Deutero-Isaiah appears to understand the divine name Yahweh as meaning 'He', i.e. 'The one' or 'He who is'.[73]

---

[69] Cf. the interpretation of $m^e\check{s}\bar{\imath}a\underline{h}$ $yahweh$ as 'Yahweh's plenipotentiary'—i.e. anointing being here understood symbolically—by E. Kutsch, Salbung als Rechtsakt (BZAW 87, 1963), p. 61, comparing also Zerubbabel and Joshua in Zech. 4.14. Cf. E. Jenni, $T\mathcal{Z}$ 10 (1954), pp. 254f.

[70] Cf. K. Galling, Studien, pp. 61ff.

[71] Cf. H. L. Creager, 'The Grace of God in Second Isaiah' in Biblical Studies in Memory of H. C. Alleman, ed. J. M. Myers, etc. (New York, 1960), pp. 123–36.

[72] 'Ich bin Jahwe' in Geschichte und Altes Testament (Festschrift A. Alt, Tübingen, 1953), pp. 179–210 = Gottes Offenbarung, pp. 11–40.

[73] If this is the intention of Deutero-Isaiah, then we may properly ask whether it does not provide a further piece of evidence in favour of the pronunciation of the

The absoluteness of the appeal to God as the sole originator of events makes pointed the obviously deep concern of Deutero-Isaiah with the problem of idolatry. Apart from the prose mocking sermon of 44.9–20,[74] there are repeated references to this. In the context of God's calling of Cyrus, it is made clear that he and he alone can know about it because he has done it himself. In contrast with the worthless idols, God is at work. In contrast with Bel and Nebo carried on the backs of beasts—no carriers of human history, but themselves a weary burden to the beasts upon which they are placed, and going into captivity willy-nilly (46.1f.)—God is in control, the sustainer of all, strong to bear the house of Israel as he has borne it from the beginning and will do so to the end of time. The reiteration of the theme must correspond to a particular need of the prophet's contemporaries. The prolonged exile is undoubtedly one cause, for the temptation to abandon the ancestral faith must have been strong under the pressure of Babylonian supremacy and continued power. It may well be that

---

tetragrammaton as *Yāhū* rather than *Yahweh*, though it seems clear that both Ex. 3.14 and Hos. 1.9 lend weight to the latter.

The discussion of this point is based on a suggestion made to the writer in about 1950 by M. B. Dagut; it is to be found now quite independently in S. Mowinckel, 'The Name of the God of Moses', *HUCA* 32 (1961), pp. 121–33, and further investigated by H. Kosmala, 'The Name of God (YHWH and HU')', *ASTI* 2 (1963), pp. 103–6. (Cf. also E. C. B. MacLaurin, 'The Origin of the Tetragrammaton', *VT* 12 [1962], pp. 439–63, see pp. 454ff.) Deut. 32.39–43, Isa. 52.6 and Ps. 102.28 are noted as further significant passages.

Neither Mowinckel nor Kosmala makes use of the very significant statement in Hos. 1.9 where the MT is frequently emended to produce the normal 'covenant' formula, but which actually states: 'I am to you a Not Ehyeh'—i.e. non-existent (cf. P. R. Ackroyd, 'Hosea', *New Peake's Commentary*, ed. M. Black and H. H. Rowley [Edinburgh, 1962], p. 605). Cf. also the negative cultic formula *lō' hū'* in Jer. 5.12. H. Kosmala also develops the same line of comment on this which the writer ventured to suggest in the original form of these lectures, namely that in this we may find an indication of the understanding of the name of God as expressing 'being'—God is 'he who is'. Both Mowinckel and Kosmala appear to regard this explanation as indicating the original meaning of the divine name, and use the evidence to refute the explanation as a hiph'il form. (For a brief review of the literature, cf. F. M. Cross, Jr., 'Yahweh and the God of the Patriarchs', *HTR* 55 [1962], pp. 225–60, see pp. 250ff.; O. Eissfeldt, *Introduction*, pp. 183 n., 743.)

This latter view appears much less probable than the supposition that in Hosea, E and Deut. 32, as also in Ps. 102 and Deutero-Isaiah, we have a type of explanation which, if not to be described as abstract (cf. F. M. Cross, Jr., *op. cit.*, p. 253 n.), appears to be much nearer to abstract philosophical statement than it has been usual to acknowledge in the Old Testament. This discussion does not, of course, have any direct bearing on the problems of the origin and original meaning of the name.

[74] Cf. p. 123 n. 23.

we should also look in the particular circumstances of the reign of
Nabonidus for that greater pressure which followed in these later
years, a pressure deriving from the religious policy which this able
ruler pursued with such evident vigour.[75]

Deutero-Isaiah's prophecies are much more concerned with the
larger questions of the understanding of the present situation and the
prospect of a new act of deliverance than with the details of the return and restoration itself. But there is sufficient allusion to show that
he, too, like Ezekiel, thought in terms of a new land, and that the
idea of a restored land involves for him the idea of a complete renova-
tion of the natural order. The fertility of the land will be assured, with
a richness of water supply which makes the wilderness blossom
(40.1ff.; 41.17–20, cf. ch. 35; 49.19ff.; 51.1ff.; 55.12f.). It will be a
new people (the tribes reconstituted, cf. 49.6), re-established in a
new covenant relationship with God (cf. 55.3–5; 54.9–10; 42.6;
49.8). Jerusalem will be consoled and rebuilt and the cities of Judah,
so long devastated, will be restored (44.24–28), with Cyrus as the
agent of this rebuilding (45.13). The population will increase in a
city refounded and built with precious stones (54.11–14), a city of
righteousness, freed from all fear.[76] Here the new people will be
found, with a picture of the purity of the new city, and an assurance of
the continued blessing of God upon the people (cf. ch. 52).[77] At every
point, these themes are interwoven with the larger concerns of God's
action, so that the interrelationship between restoration in the physical
sense and restoration of the inner life of the people is never lost.
Though little is said of the mechanism, the enduring righteousness of
the newly established and restored people is affirmed.

As the new people of God, re-established in the land, they are

[75] Cf. above, pp. 36ff. Also H. W. F. Saggs, *The Greatness that was Babylon*
(1962), pp. 145ff. The parallel between this situation and that of the second century makes intelligible also the use of traditions and stories, perhaps containing in
part genuine reminiscence of exilic conditions, in the Book of Daniel which clearly
belongs in the time of Antiochus IV Epiphanes.

[76] Cf. E. J. Tinsley, *The Imitation of God in Christ* (London, 1960), p. 47, on the
theme of 'Gerusalemme consolata' in Deutero- and Trito-Isaiah; N. W. Porteous,
'Jerusalem—Zion; the Growth of a Symbol', in *Verbannung und Heimkehr*, ed. A.
Kurschke (Tübingen, 1961), pp. 235–52, see pp. 246ff. = *Living the Mystery*
(Oxford, 1967), pp. 93–111, pp. 105ff. The Targum specifically identifies Jerusalem
here (cf. K. L. Schmidt, *Eranos-Jahrbuch* 18 (Zurich, 1950), p. 224).

[77] On the inclusion in this of Temple rebuilding, cf. E. Hammershaimb, *Some
Aspects of Old Testament Prophecy* (1966), p. 104; M. Schmidt, *Prophet und Tempel*
(1948), pp. 191f., 217. L. R. Fisher, *JSS* 8 (1963), pp. 39f., on ʿîr (city) = 'temple
quarter'.

properly to be described as 'Jacob my servant' (44.1ff.), knowing themselves to belong to God, so that they will rename themselves accordingly (44.5). The glory and the blessings which belonged to the past are renewed (51.1ff.) and there will be no future shame for the people whom Yahweh has saved (45.17). And this is set in a wider context. Just as in Ezekiel the nations are the witnesses of what has happened,[78] so that the name of Yahweh is glorified, so, too, in Deutero-Isaiah the purpose of Yahweh is made known through Israel. The limit of God's purpose is not reached in the restoration of Israel, but in the extension of his saving power to the ends of the earth (49.6). The nations will see and prostrate themselves because of Yahweh's choice again of Israel; for in this, it is clear, they will see the justice of divine action (49.7). The exaltation of the servant of God brings in the nations as the witnesses in amazement at what God has done (52.13–53.12). A complete reversal of fortune will bring the nations to carry back the children of God's people; those who were captive will be set free, and disaster will come upon the oppressors (49.22–26). And the result will be the acknowledgement of Yahweh as the saviour.[79]

The fortunes of Israel, so deeply experienced by the prophet, are seen to be part of the larger purpose of God. Her restoration will be

[78] Cf. pp. 115ff.

[79] Cf. A Causse, Les dispersés d'Israël (1929), pp. 34–45; idem, Israël et la vision de l'humanité (1924), pp. 38–58. Cf. also W. Zimmerli, 'Der Wahrheitserweis Jahwes nach der Botschaft der beiden Exilspropheten', in Tradition und Situation, ed. E. Würthwein and O. Kaiser (Göttingen, 1963). P. A. H. de Boer, 'Second Isaiah's Message', OTS 11 (1956), pp. 80ff., rightly emphasizes the hymnic source of the many phrases which suggest 'universalist' concepts in Deutero-Isaiah. Rightly, too, he points to the central place of the deliverance of Israel. But he overstates this when he says 'Second Isaiah's only purpose is to proclaim deliverance for the Jewish people' (p. 90). For such a narrow view, reference may also be made to N. H. Snaith, 'The Servant of the Lord in Deutero-Isaiah', StOTPr, pp. 187–200, further developed in his 'Isaiah 40–66. A Study of the Teaching of the Second Isaiah and its Consequences', in Studies on the Second Part of Isaiah (VTS 14, 1967), pp. 135–264, see esp. pp. 154–65 and 244ff. Snaith oversimplifies the contrast between universalism and nationalism, failing to recognize that they may be correlative terms. As witnesses, the nations are involved in the acknowledgement of Yahweh's supremacy, and this, while not involving 'missionary' ideas (and here de Boer and Snaith are rightly critical of much that has been written on these chapters), does implicate the nations (de Boer in effect admits this on pp. 100f.). On this theme, cf. also the balanced statements of R. Martin-Achard, A Light to the Nations (ET, Edinburgh, London, 1962), pp. 8–31.

S. Herrmann, Die prophetischen Heilserwartungen im Alten Testament (BWANT 85, 1965), pp. 291–305, argues for a universalizing of Israel's hopes in the final presentation of the oracles of Deutero-Isaiah.

a recovery of that Zion which is the place of God's dwelling, as central to the life of the world (cf. Isa. 2.1–4 = Micah 4.1–4).[80] To some extent the culmination of this is to be found in the further development of this line of thought in Trito-Isaiah, and certainly we may see the realization of this conception of the centrality of Zion in the prophecy of the early restoration period.[81] Here it is seen still against the background of exile, with as yet no expression of the hopes in the actuality of a restored community.

Our next stage is to see the reality of restoration, and to appreciate against the background of the actual political and economic situation of that time what those who lived in it understood it to mean. For just as we have seen in the theological thinking of the exilic period an appreciation of the meaning of events and attempts at projecting into actuality the conception of what God is and does, so in the period of restoration we find a similar combining of the appreciation of real conditions with an understanding of the meaning which lies within them. In some ways perhaps we may appreciate even more the idealism of the restoration period, for it is an idealism confronted by reality; and as both the oracles of the immediate restoration period and those of the subsequent generation show, the period was one in which a fading of idealism was a natural reaction to disappointed hopes.

[80] A. Causse, *Du groupe ethnique à la communauté religieuse* (1937), pp. 207–10, stresses the eschatological and idealizing elements in Deutero-Isaiah (see esp. p. 209 n. 3). He underestimates the historical attachment of these chapters.
[81] Cf. pp. 155ff., 171ff.

IX

THE RESTORATION AND ITS
INTERPRETATION

A. INTRODUCTORY:

The Historical Problems of the Restoration Period

IN AN ESSAY on 'The Age of Zerubbabel',[1] S. A. Cook, after a discussion of some of the problems of the post-exilic prophetic books, continued: 'It is difficult to believe that the last word has been said on the criticism of Haggai, Zechariah and Malachi . . . and when we consider the variety of traditions and the intricacies of the criticism both of Ezra-Nehemiah and of the prophetical writings, we cannot be surprised that many problems of Old Testament history and religion still elude an acceptable solution.'[2] The chapters which follow represent an attempt at contributing something further to the understanding of the prophetic material, primarily that of Haggai and Zechariah 1–8.[3] But the clarification of the historical problems remains a matter of difficulty and uncertainty.[4] With much less

---

[1] *StO TPr*, pp. 19–36.

[2] *Op. cit.*, p. 31.

[3] For comments on the general theme, cf. R. E. Clements, *God and Temple* (1965), pp. 123ff. In his discussion of the post-exilic development of the idea of the presence of God, Clements rightly stresses the tension between ideal and real, and hence the more insistent eschatological note; but he sees insufficiently the 'realized eschatology' (if this term may be permitted) which enabled not only the prophets of the return but also the Chronicler to see a real embodiment of the divine promises in the actual religious life of the contemporary community.

[4] Cf. the reissue of some of K. Galling's studies in revised form in *Studien zur Geschichte Israels im persischen Zeitalter* (Tübingen, 1964) and his general comments on the problems of interpretation in the preface to these (p.v.) Cf. also the review of the problems by M. W. Leeseberg, 'Ezra and Nehemiah: A Review of the Return and Reform', *Concordia Theological Monthly* 33 (1962), pp. 79–90, a summary of a dissertation; and by F. Michaeli, *Les Livres des Chroniques, d'Esdras et de Néhémie* (Commentaire de l'Ancien Testament 16, Neuchâtel, 1967), pp. 253–6, and the

scepticism today about the value of the materials utilized by the Chronicler, we may be willing to recognize the presence of a great deal of useful evidence in the opening chapters of the book of Ezra. But the endeavour to put into some sort of chronological order what the Chronicler has quite evidently arranged much more according to principles of interpretation brings us immediately up against major problems to which there is quite clearly no simple solution. That the Chronicler could arrange his material on his own principles appears clear. The section Ezra 4. (6)7–23(24) (I Esdras 2.16–30) is certainly out of order, since it belongs to the reign of Artaxerxes I, but it has been placed in the two different contexts in which it is now found because it points to a similar situation of opposition to that which met the temple-builders and so could be held to illustrate the same underlying principles.[5] It is probable that the order of the main Ezra narrative has undergone a similar dislocation.[6] If the Nehemiah material was included by the Chronicler, that too is evidently out of order, and it has in any case introduced a further complication into the assessment of the Ezra narratives.[7] The same point may be made —and here with more certainty because of the existence of a parallel text—in regard to much of the David material which has been arranged by principle rather than by chronology.[8]

The views of the Chronicler are part of the understanding of the exile and restoration.[9] But the material of his work offers us source

discussion, with references to earlier literature, in G. A. Smith, *The Book of the Twelve Prophets* II (1898, 1928), pp. 198–221.

Reference is made in what follows to various authorities. Note may be made also of the following: J. de Fraine, 'La communauté juive au temps des Perses', *Bible et Terre Sainte* 39 (1961), pp. 14–16; P. Auvray, 'Les débuts de la période perse', *Bible et Terre Sainte* 38 (1961), p. 2—both simple, and at some points inevitably simplified, accounts of the period. H. Lignée and G. Bourbillon, 'Le Temple Nouveau', *Évangile* 34 (1959), pp. 5–79 (cf. *IZBG* 7, No. 1582), has not been available to me.

[5] Cf. W. Rudolph, *Esra und Nehemia* (HAT 20, 1949), p. 40; O. Eissfeldt, *Introduction*, p. 551.

[6] The reading of the Law in Neh. 8 ought to precede the events described in Ezra 9–10 (cf. O. Eissfeldt, *Introduction*, p. 548).

[7] This question is not relevant to the present discussion except as an illustration of the method. The suggestion, elaborated in one form by K. Galling, *Die Bücher der Chronik, Esra, Nehemia* (ATD 12, 1954), that the Nehemiah material was preserved separately and added later, offers an attractive way of meeting the chronological problems of the Ezra-Nehemiah narratives. Cf. also S. Mowinckel, *Studien zu dem Buche Ezra-Nehemia* II. *Die Nehemia-Denkschrift* (Oslo, 1964), pp. 29–61.

[8] Cf. II Sam. 24 and I Chron. 21 for example.

[9] Cf. below pp. 236f., 239ff.

material of primary importance in the reconstruction of events. The unravelling of the problems of the evidence must assume some of the conclusions of criticism with regard to the Chronicler's methods and intentions, though we shall subsequently be seeing a little more of his own overall picture.[10]

We need not delay to outline the series of events by which Cyrus overthrew the Neo-Babylonian empire,[11] culminating in the defeat of Nabonidus and the peaceful occupation of Babylon itself. Our concern with the situation begins with the indications of Persian policy which are to be seen in the Cyrus cylinder and reflected in the edict which the Chronicler has included in Aramaic in Ezra 6 and in Hebrew in Ezra 1. Other Persian evidence from the period of Darius confirms the general probability of the statements of this edict.[12] The re-establishment of the Temple at Jerusalem can be understood from the Persian side both as offering a resettlement of an exiled god[13] and

[10] Cf. P. R. Ackroyd, 'History and Theology in the Writings of the Chronicler', *Concordia Theological Monthly* 38 (1967), pp. 501–15.

[11] Cf. the brief sketch in W. Rudolph, *Esra und Nehemia* (HAT 20, 1949), pp. XXVIf. and the discussion in K. Galling, *Studien* (1964), pp. 5ff.

[12] Cf. the discussion of Cyrus' policy in K. Galling, *Studien* (1964), pp. 34ff., and pp. 61–77 for the more detailed discussion of the forms of the edict. Cf. also 'Die Politik der Perser und die Heimkehr aus Babel' in *Proc. XXII Congress of Orientalists, Istanbul, 1951*, II (Leiden, 1957), p. 583, for arguments against the release of Jews by Cyrus, and the view that the real return came at the time of Nidintu-Bel's rebellion, as a result of negotiations between Darius and Zerubbabel; L. Rost, 'Erwägungen zum Kyroserlass', in *Verbannung und Heimkehr*, ed. A. Kuschke (Tübingen, 1961), pp. 301–7; E. Bickermann, 'The Edict of Cyrus in Ezra 1', *JBL* 65 (1946), pp. 249–75. F. I. Andersen, 'Who built the Second Temple?', *ABR* 6 (1958), pp. 1–35, makes some judicious comments on the tendency, marked in older studies, to give credence to the prophetic material in Haggai and Zech. 1–8 and so to dismiss the Chronicler. More recent work, however, has shown a much greater appreciation of the Chronicler—though Andersen is off the mark in describing him simply as a historian (so p. 6), since he is much more evidently a theologian. But Anderson is right in indicating that the reconstruction of historical evidence from prophetic material is hazardous, in fact just as hazardous in this instance as it is when the same procedures are applied to earlier prophetic books.

[13] Compare, in the Cyrus Cylinder, the words:
'. . . the gods whose abode is in the midst of them, I returned to their places and housed them in lasting abodes. I gathered together all their inhabitants and restored (to them) their dwellings' (lines 33–34) (quoted from *DOTT* p. 93; cf. *ANET* pp. 315ff.).
Cf. on this passage the comments of K. Galling, *Studien* (1964), p. 35. L. Rost, in *Verbannung und Heimkehr*, ed. A. Kuschke (Tübingen, 1961), p. 302, stresses Cyrus' reversal of Nebuchadrezzar's actions, so particularly the restoring of the Temple vessels. On the latter cf. K. Galling, *Studien* (1964), pp. 78–88. On the propagandist aspects of Cyrus' historical records, cf. G. G. Cameron, 'Ancient Persia', in *The Idea of History in the Ancient Near East*, ed. R. C. Dentan (New Haven, 1955), pp. 79–97, see pp. 82ff.

also as providing support for Persian rule as successor to the royal
line in Jerusalem of which the Temple was the royal shrine.[14] The
concern of the Persians with this particular area may, however, have
a further basis in wider political concerns. As Cyrus' successor
Cambyses was to show, a clarification of the position vis-à-vis Egypt
could not be long delayed. In the following century the appoint-
ments of both Nehemiah and Ezra can be in part explained against
the background of political insecurity in the west of the empire.[15]
So at this period the appointment of two apparently successive
officials, Sheshbazzar and Zerubbabel, would seem in all probability
to be related to the more general situation.[16]

It is not clear when the Palestinian area came effectively under
Persian control. Nominally, from the moment of Nabonidus' defeat,
the whole empire would belong to his successor. But nominal subjection is not the same as full control. Albright has suggested[17] that
the tremendous destruction of Bethel which he traces to the mid-sixth
century could have been in the course of campaigning by Cyrus in
the west, but he admits that it could equally well be associated with
the Syrian revolt against Nabonidus in 553 BC—and we might perhaps postulate some more local cause for the disaster, since there are
indications (cf. Zech. 8) of general insecurity during the period of the
exile and shortly after. It seems to be more probable that the subjection of the west effectively to Persian rule only became possible
under Cambyses,[18] and that Cyrus, fully occupied with many other

---

[14] Cf. M. Noth, The History of Israel, pp. 307–8. K. Galling, Studien (1964), pp.
35f. By the expression 'royal shrine' is meant a shrine associated with the life and
wellbeing of the kingdom (cf. Amos 7.13), not a private 'royal chapel' (cf. the
comments of R. de Vaux, Ancient Israel [ET, 1961], p. 320 and R. E. Clements,
God and Temple [1965], pp. 67f. and the literature cited by the latter).

[15] Cf. O. Eissfeldt, Introduction, pp. 554f., and particularly H. Cazelles, 'La
mission d'Esdras', VT 4 (1954), pp. 113–40, esp. pp. 139f.; L. Rost, op. cit., p. 303.

[16] Josephus, Ant. XI, 1 offers an elaborated account of Cyrus' actions. Similarly in XI, 2, and XI, 4 he utilizes the Chronicler's narrative, and particularly
the material of I Esdras, at times oversimplifying and at times elaborating, possibly
on the basis of extra material, but possibly imaginatively. His anti-Samaritan
tendencies—an extension of those of the Chronicler—are apparent here. C. G.
Tuland, 'Josephus, Antiquities. Book XI. Correction or Confirmation of Biblical
Post-Exilic Records', Andrews University Seminary Studies 4 (1966), pp. 176–92, is
too simplified a discussion, but carefully draws attention to the values of the
Josephus material.

[17] W. F. Albright, Archaeology and the Religion of Israel (Baltimore, ³1953), pp. 172f.

[18] Cf. K. Galling, Studien (1964), p. 25, commenting on Herodotus' (Hist. III,
34) attributing to Cyrus a plan to attack Egypt which Cambyses carried out in
practice. So too pp. 27ff. and pp. 36ff. where Galling stresses that the references to

problems, was forced to accept a rather half-hearted allegiance on the part of the local officials. The governor in Samaria—appointed by the Babylonians,[19] perhaps even a direct descendant of the earlier Assyrian ruling group—may be presumed to have indicated his acceptance of Persian rule, but whether he actively welcomed it is not known. To send a special official to Jerusalem at this juncture would seem to be wise policy, since the re-ordering of the life of this small but important area—important for eventual communications with and control of Egypt—would help to create a more favourable situation in the west. Against this background, too, the apparent failure of the first mission would be intelligible, for it may well have been as undesirable to the then governor of Samaria that Jerusalem should revive fully as it was a century later to Sanballat, the contemporary of Nehemiah.[20]

It appears most probable that the edict authorizing the rebuilding of the Temple and providing some assurance of financial and other support—as it appears in Ezra 6—has been rewritten by the Chronicler in Ezra 1 to fit in with his conception of the actual nature of the restoration as indicated at the end of II Chronicles 36.[21] The appoint-

---

submission to Cyrus by rulers of the western area (Cyrus Cylinder ll. 28b–30a) may well suggest formal submission, particularly by beduin sheiks ('all the kings of the West Country who dwell in tents'); but no immediate western campaign is indicated. Cf. further pp. 39f. The Phoenician cities only submitted to Cambyses in 526 (cf. Herodotus III, 19).

[19] On the continuance in office of officials appointed by the Babylonians—even in Babylon itself—cf. K. Galling, *Studien* (1964), p. 42. Galling notes further (p. 47) the employment of local officers, observing that Mithredath (Ezra 4.7) may be Persian, whereas Rehum (4.8), Sanballat (Neh. 2.19) and his sons Delaiah and Shelemaiah (Elephantine Pap., cf. *DOTT*, p. 264), appear all to be local personages. Similarly, Nehemiah in Judah was of Jewish origin, whereas Bagoas (Elephantine Pap., cf. *DOTT*, p. 262) was presumably Persian. (Cf. further Galling, *op. cit.*, pp. 149ff.)

[20] Cf. K. Galling, *Studien* (1964), pp. 40, 133.

[21] Cf. R. de Vaux, 'Les décrets de Cyrus et de Darius sur la reconstruction du Temple', *RB* 46 (1937), pp. 29–57 = *Bible et Orient* (Paris, 1967), pp. 83–113; O. Eissfeldt, *Introduction*, p. 556. W. Rudolph, *Esra und Nehemia* (HAT 20, 1949), p. xxvi, suggests that ch. 1 contains a later edict authorizing the return. But the similarity of the texts makes this seem unlikely. Cf. further K. Galling, *Studien* (1964), pp. 40f. and 127ff.; also 'Serubbabel und der Wiederaufbau des Tempels', in *Verbannung und Heimkehr*, ed. A. Kuschke (Tübingen, 1961), pp. 67–96. On the Persian concern with authorizing the restoration of the Temple, cf. J. Liver, 'The Return from Babylon, its time and scope' (Hebr., Engl. Summary) *Eretz-Israel* 5 (1958), pp. 114–19, 90*. Liver sees the return as gradual, and not needing any special authorization. Cf. also I. Ben Zvi, 'Cyrus King of Persia and his Edict to the Exiles', *El ha'ayin* No. 39 (Jerusalem, 1964), pp. 33–39; Y. Kaufmann, *History of the Religion of Israel* (*Toledoth ha-emunah ha-yisra'elith*), Vol. 8 (Tel Aviv, 1956), p. 164, on Cyrus'

ment of Sheshbazzar—whose name and identity both remain uncertain—may be presumed to indicate the choosing of an acceptable personage to carry out the royal instructions. That he is described as 'the prince of Judah' and that the Chronicler does not indicate Davidic descent would seem to be strong arguments against the suggested identification of him with the Davidide Shenazzar (I Chron. 3.18),[22] though such identification can already be traced in I Esdras and in Josephus, as also in the LXX.[23] He is more probably to be regarded as belonging to an upper-class family of the kind indicated in Jer. 26.10 as 'the princes (sārē) of Judah'.[24] The statement in the correspondence with Darius that 'Sheshbazzar laid the foundation of the house of God' (Ezra 5.16)[25] is not confirmed elsewhere, but in view of the general impression of reliability in the Aramaic documentary

granting of permission to build the Temple not the city. (ET of the relevant passage in El haʿayin No. 39 [Jerusalem, 1964], p. 10.) The probability that the Chronicler is responsible for modifications and interpretation in Ezra 1 does not necessarily mean that he introduced totally erroneous information. His stress on returned exiles may be seen to be exaggerated, yet it is clear that the impetus to restore the Temple must have come from exiles who could lay their case before the Persian authorities; the permission to restore must imply some measure of permission to return (cf. E. Hammershaimb, *Some Aspects of Old Testament Prophecy* (1966), p. 100). H. H. Grosheide, 'Twee Edicten van Cyrus ten Gunste van de Joden (Esra 1,2–4 en 6,3–5)' *Gereformeerd Theologisch Tijdschrift* 54 (1954), pp. 1–2 (not available to me), defends both forms of the edict (cf. *IZBG* 3, No. 181).

[22] Cf. W. F. Albright, 'The Date and Personality of the Chronicler', *JBL* 40 (1921), pp. 104–24, see pp. 108f., arguing that both names are to be derived from a Babylonian original *šin-ab-uṣur*. This is accepted, e.g. by D. N. Freedman (see below n. 24) and J. M. Myers, *I Chronicles* (Anchor Bible 12, New York, 1965), p. 18. H. Gese, *Der Verfassungsentwurf des Ezechiel* (BHT 25, 1957), p. 118, cites O. Procksch, 'Fürst und Priester bei Hesekiel', *ZAW* 17 (1940/1), pp. 99–133, to support the view that *nāśī'* must indicate a Davidide. So limited a view of *nāśī'* seems improbable.

[23] Cf. M. Noth, *The History of Israel*, pp. 309f. and 310n.

[24] L. Rost, *op. cit.*, p. 302, associates the title with the Ezekiel tradition (cf. Ezek. 45.7, etc.). He thinks it probable that as Zerubbabel was of the Davidic line, so too Sheshbazzar (whether identifiable with Shenazzar or not) is likely to have been. Cf. also K. Galling, *Studien* (1964), p. 81; D. N. Freedman, *CBQ* 23 (1961), p. 439; J. M. Myers, *Ezra-Nehemiah* (Anchor Bible 14, New York, 1965), p. 9.

[25] On the whole question of what *yāsad* means in this connection, cf. the useful discussion by A. Gelston, 'The Foundations of the Second Temple', *VT* 16 (1966), pp. 232–5. He shows that the word has a much broader sense than 'lay a foundation stone'; it means 'repair, restore, rebuild'. Such a discussion of the more general meaning of *yāsad* had already been undertaken by F. I. Andersen, 'Who built the Second Temple?', *ABR* 6 (1958), pp. 1–35, which is not mentioned by Gelston. Andersen, by an examination of a whole series of occurrences of this root, shows how broad the meaning actually is (pp. 10–22). Cf. also below on Haggai and Zechariah, pp. 158, 172. Cf. also C. G. Tuland, *"Uššayyā'* and *'Uššarnâ: A Clarification of*

material here and also the fact that anyone inventing a narrative would not presumably have left such a statement unconfirmed, it would seem to suggest that he actually began work. The material which the Chronicler had at his disposal, leading to the actual completion of the Temple, made it clear, however, that Zerubbabel was the operative character. Speculation about the failure—as we must suppose it—with which Sheshbazzar met can be only very tentative.[26] But the general political situation just outlined would make it seem not improbable that he met with at least reluctance to assist on the part of the governor in Samaria, and perhaps even with direct hostility. How far Persian authority reached and how much the governor of Samaria could risk are uncertain to us. Sheshbazzar simply disappears from the narrative, and we have no means of determining whether he was recalled, whether he died of old age, or whether he simply remained in Jerusalem unable to take any active part in the development of the Jewish community. Of the three, the first would seem to be most probable, especially if he was appointed for a specific function and so perhaps—like Nehemiah at a later date —for a set term of office.[27]

The first period of the return would thus seem to be marked by a rather ineffective attempt at restoration, frustrated by lack of cooperation in Palestine.[28] If, as we have earlier supposed, there was a relatively substantial community already there—though presumably much smaller both in numbers and in area controlled than before the exile—there is no reason to suppose that more than a small number returned at this time from the exile.[29]

Terms, Date, and Text', *JNES* 17 (1958), pp. 269–75 who claims that the forms indicate a rebuilding 'from the very foundations'. This article does not however investigate the usage of *yāsad*.

[26] Cf. K. Galling, *Studien* (1964), pp. 133f., stressing that it was to no one's interest to suggest that Sheshbazzar's work, authorized by Cyrus, had failed.

[27] Cf. Neh. 2.6. Cf. W. Rudolph, *Esra and Nehemia* (1949), p. XXVI; J. de Fraine, *op. cit.* (p. 138 n. 4). The precise status of Sheshbazzar is not clear. He is described as *peḥā* (Ezra 5.14), but the term appears not necessarily to have the narrow sense 'governor'; 'commissioner' would be better. LXX has 'treasurer over the treasure'—influenced by Ezra 1. Cf. K. Galling, *Studien* (1964), pp. 79, 81, 132f. A. C. Welch's view (*Post-exilic Judaism* [1935], pp. 98ff.) that he was governor of 'Beyond the River' is entirely speculative.

[28] Cf. also J. D. Smart, *History and Theology in Second Isaiah* (1965), pp. 281ff. on Isa. 66, which he interprets as a protest against the projected rebuilding of the Temple. Cf. p. 156 n. 15.

[29] The Chronicler's version of the edict of Ezra 1 is presumably intended to

The second stage in the restoration is marked by the activities of Zerubbabel and Joshua, Haggai and Zechariah.[30] The four names appear together in the two prophetic books. They also appear— though the prophets are not mentioned until Ezra 5—in the historical narrative. In assessing the historical significance of the material of Ezra 3.1–4.5, one obvious difficulty is the lack of any precise chronological datum.[31] The statement in 3.1, 'When the seventh month came', appears now as the immediate sequel to the last recorded event, namely the return of Sheshbazzar recorded in ch. 1, where no other date is given than the first year of Cyrus, without any indication of the time of year. Ezra 3.8 refers to 'the second year of their coming' and may be presumed to be the sequel to 3.1. No further date occurs until we reach what appears to be the linking verses of 4.4–5, 6 and 4.24. Now in view of what we know of the Chronicler's policy elsewhere (cf. Ezra 7 which without any ado passes over 70 or even as much as 120 years, depending on the dating of Ezra),[32] and of the similar characteristic of the style of the Deuteronomic historian (who sometimes links events merely with '$\bar{a}z$, 'then', when in fact some

---

give the impression of a much larger response to the invitation to return: it is clearly also elaborated with motifs which suggest that he saw a parallel to the Exodus (cf. Ex. 12.35f.; cf. also Isa. 51.9ff.). It is, however, clear that no large-scale return is likely to have taken place both from the evidence of subsequent appeals to Jews in Babylonia (cf. Zech. 2.10ff.; Ezra 7–8) and from the indications of the difficulties faced by the community in Jerusalem and its environs at this period and subsequently. Cf. also K. Galling, *Studien* (1964), esp. pp. 61–77.

[30] Cf. O. Eissfeldt, *Introduction*, p. 556, commenting adversely on the views of Torrey and others. Further K. Galling, *Studien* (1964), pp. 41f., where he discusses the political problems which permission to return would have created for Cyrus.

[31] On the order of the names, cf. T. Chary, *op. cit.*, p. 138. Chary argues that the prior mention of Zerubbabel indicates, from the Persian standpoint, the greater importance of the civil governor. The order appears thus in Haggai and also in Ezra 3.8; 4.3, and 5.2; but in Ezra 3.2 the order is reversed and Joshua comes first. 5.2 is in the Aramaic material, and might therefore be claimed to be more ancient and correctly in accord with Haggai, but the indications are that the Chronicler did not follow any consistent policy, and it may be doubted whether Chary is right in reading so much into this piece of evidence. The only other possibility here is that the variation in order in the Hebrew section is to be explained as due to the Chronicler's use of a source which followed the order Zerubbabel-Joshua, and that he himself in his own comments reversed the order. Such a supposition is unnecessary in view of the Chronicler's tendency to adjust his source material.

[32] Cf. K. Galling, *Studien* (1964), p. 76 n. 4. Galling thinks it might even be that the Chronicler—dating the dedication of the Temple in Darius' year 6 (Ezra 6.15) and Ezra in Artaxerxes' year 7 (7.7)—identified the two rulers; certainly he did not see the interval as a long one.

considerable length of time may have elapsed),[33] we cannot assume continuity in the events. So it is not possible to argue from this passage that Zerubbabel was a younger contemporary of Sheshbazzar who took over from him.[34] The interval between ch. 1 and ch. 3 may be the interval of nearly twenty years between the time of Cyrus' first year and that of Darius' second year, when—cf. 5.1 (4.24)—the work was begun under pressure from Haggai and Zechariah. In this case, the Hebrew narrative of 3.1–4.5 and the Aramaic one of 5.1–6.12 are virtually parallel,[35] or at least cover two different aspects of the same period. The first relates the establishment of the altar, and a religious celebration, together with the beginning of the building of the Temple, with a note at the end on the opposition which was met. It is characterized by many of the features of the Chronicler's style of presentation. The second relates the building of the Temple and follows this with different detail about the opposition, with a note of the inquiry to Darius and the confirmation of the right to rebuild taken from Cyrus' original edict. If these are parallels, then the Chronicler has used them to bridge the gap of years between the edict of Cyrus and the time of the actual completion of the Temple, and has tacitly put Zerubbabel's narrative next to that of Sheshbazzar without attempting to define the relationship between them.[36] A further motive seems to have been the delineation of the nature of the opposition, and this is now described not only in the opening of ch. 4 and the opening of ch. 5, but also in the obviously intrusive Artaxerxes section in 4.(6)7–23(24) which, as we have seen, reveals how little concern the Chronicler (or his later amplifiers) felt for problems of chronology as such. The decision depends upon a further intangible factor, the date of Zerubbabel's appointment.[37] The long narrative which appears in I Esdras 3–5.6 concerning the three guardsmen at the court of Darius is now used quite artificially to

---

[33] Cf., e.g., I Kings 11.7; II Kings 16.5 and cf. J. A. Montgomery, 'Archival Data in the Book of Kings', *JBL* 53 (1934), pp. 46–52, see p. 49, and J. A. Montgomery *The Book of Kings*, ed. H. S. Gehman (ICC, 1951), p. 204, suggesting that *'āz* has an archival character and may have been substituted for an original exact date. Cf. J. Gray, *I and II Kings* (OTL, 1964), p. 31.

[34] As is implied in e.g. W. Rudolph, *Esra und Nehemia* (1949), p. XXVI.

[35] O. Eissfeldt, *Introduction*, pp. 543, 551.

[36] Cf. W. Rudolph, *Esra und Nehemia* (1949), p. 29 and O. Eissfeldt, *Introduction*, p. 543.

[37] Cf. P. R. Ackroyd, *JNES* 17 (1958), p. 20; W. Rudolph, *Esra und Nehemia* (1949), p. XXVI.

introduce the appointment of Zerubbabel,[38] and hence it is often thought that the appointment must have been made at the beginning of Darius' reign or immediately after his suppression of Nidintu-Bel (Nebuchadrezzar III).[39] It would not be surprising if Darius did take action quickly to deal with the west by the appointment of Zerubbabel, and perhaps by various other means, if he was already aware of the dangers threatening him. He was to have enough rebellions on his hands without encouraging more, and Zerubbabel could presumably be relied on.[40] But if this is correct, it is very curious that the report sent to Darius (Ezra 5.6–17) does not contain any mention of the appointment which Darius himself had made. There is in fact no mention of Zerubbabel at all after 5.2—a point which has led to some extravagant theories about the fate which he met at the hands of the Persians.[41] Unless we are to suppose that the whole narrative of the report to Darius is misplaced, which seems unnecessarily arbitrary, we must surely assume that Zerubbabel was engaged in the work all through.

The effect of this would seem to be to push the appointment of Zerubbabel back somewhat further, and in that case we could consider him as having come during the time of Cambyses—an appointment parallel with the activities of Cambyses in Palestine and Egypt, designed to consolidate the lines of communication—or even as having come during the later years of Cyrus. Of the two, the former would seem preferable.[42] From the time of Sheshbazzar onwards,

---

[38] Zerubbabel is quite unexpectedly identified with the third guardsman in 4.13. The story is however used by A. T. Olmstead, *History of the Persian Empire* (Chicago, 1948), pp. 136ff., in his reconstruction. Cf. the comments in P. R. Ackroyd, *JNES* 17 (1958), pp. 19–21.

[39] P. R. Ackroyd, *JNES* 17 (1958), p. 14 for dates. Darius was certainly recognized in Babylonia from Dec. 522/early 521 to Sept. 521 and again Dec. 521/Jan. 520. On the political background, cf. also K. Galling, *Studien* (1964), pp. 48ff. and 56ff. On the propagandist language of the Behistun inscription, cf. G. G. Cameron, *op. cit.*, pp. 86ff.; R. T. Hallock, 'The "One Year" of Darius I', *JNES* 19 (1960), pp. 36–39.

[40] Cf. K. Galling, *Studien* (1964), pp. 58f.; E. Hammershaimb, *op. cit.*, p. 101.

[41] Cf. P. R. Ackroyd: 'Two Historical Problems of the Early Persian Period', *JNES* 17 (1958), pp. 13–27, for some comments on such theories. L. Rost, *op. cit.*, p. 302, stresses that Zerubbabel was the last of the Davidic line to be entrusted with political authority. On Darius' policy, cf. also G. G. Cameron, *op. cit.*, p. 92.

[42] For a discussion of the issues involved, cf. P. R. Ackroyd, *JNES* 17 (1958), p. 21, and cf. K. Galling, 'Syrien in der Politik der Achämeniden bis 448 v. Chr.', *Der Alte Orient* 36 (1937), pp. 40ff., where he followed Alt ('Die Rolle Samarias bei der Entstehung des Judentums', in *Festschrift Otto Procksch* [Leipzig, 1934], pp. 5–28, see p. 25 = *Kl. Schr.* 2 [Munich, ³1964], pp. 316–37, see p. 335) and

some rather half-hearted attempts were made at rebuilding, but rather ineffectively (cf. Ezra 5.16); with the coming of Zerubbabel, a setting aright of the altar (3.2f.) and other actions were followed by a genuine beginning. But in due course this work was interrupted by the inquiry which went to Darius in the second year of his reign— in other words at a point during or after the prophetic activity of Haggai and Zechariah as it is now recorded. The authorization then permitted a peaceful completion of the work, as is indicated in 6.13ff.

This allows of various possibilities for the placing of Haggai and Zechariah in relation to Zerubbabel. We may postulate that they came with Zerubbabel at the time of his appointment, or that they came subsequently, at the beginning of the reign of Darius, perhaps stimulated by the political situation in Babylonia (cf. Zech. 2).[43] Preserved in Neh. 12 is a list of priests and Levites who returned with Zerubbabel and Jeshua. This does not mention either Haggai or Zechariah, but does mention Iddo, who appears to be the father of Zechariah (unless there is another man of the same name involved). In a further list, which deals with the period of Joiakim, Jeshua's son and successor (Neh. 12.10), Zechariah is mentioned as being the priest, 'head of the family group' of the Iddo family (Neh. 12.16). From this we might perhaps conclude that Zechariah himself did arrive with Zerubbabel, though it is conceivable that he followed his father some time later; there is no evidence to indicate which is the more probable. For Zechariah there are some indications of Babylonian activity, and it would seem necessary to allow for a period of preaching there too;[44] but again there is no precise indication of the moment of his coming. In many ways the idea of a further return in

---

argued for a connection with Cambyses' Egyptian campaign. Cf. also 'The "Gōlā-List" according to Ezra 2 // Nehemiah 7', *JBL* 70 (1951), pp. 149–58, see pp. 157f.; cf. *Studien*, pp. 89–108. Subsequently, *ZDPV* 69 (1953), pp. 4–64 and 70 (1954), pp. 4–32 = *Studien* (1964), pp. 58ff., he has argued for a later date. Cf. also H. W. Wolff, *Haggai* (BS I, 1951), p. 10, arguing for 525.

[43] K. Galling, *Studien* (1964), pp. 56ff., argues for a return not very long before the conditions indicated in Hag. 1; and with K. Elliger, *Das Buch der zwölf kleinen Propheten* II (ATD 25, ²1951 (⁴1959)), pp. 104f., that Zech. 5.1ff. envisages the social and economic problems of exiles only recently resettled. Cf. further pp. 203ff.

[44] Cf. below pp. 173, 197f. and cf. K. Galling: 'Die Exilswende in der Sicht des Propheten Sacharja', *VT* 2 (1952), pp. 18–36; revised form in *Studien* (1964), pp. 109–26.

the beginning of Darius' reign, resulting in an impulse to prophetic activity in Jerusalem by Haggai and Zechariah, would seem to fit the known facts and provide a reasonable picture.

One further point must be touched on briefly, namely the nature of the opposition to the rebuilding. The narrative of ch. 5.3–5 is clear enough. We do not know precisely who the personages involved are, but the inquiry is an official one and undertaken by the governor of the province 'Beyond the River' and various others. There is no indication of the reason for the inquiry; the implication of 5.5 is that the higher officials were not hostile[45]—perhaps because they trusted the account given them of the authority of Cyrus' edict, perhaps because they were mistrustful of the sources by which information had reached them suggesting that something undesirable was afoot. The inquiry concerning the names of those involved in the rebuilding (Ezra 5.4) may, if we follow K. Galling,[46] lead to the consideration of the list of returned exiles which appears in Ezra 2 and Neh. 7. The detailed discussion of the problems of that double occurrence need not concern us here.[47] Whatever its origin—and Galling's view that it is the list belonging to this government inquiry is a very reasonable one—it pictures the returned exiles as a separate entity. For the Chronicler, it offered support for his view of the restored community[48] as consisting primarily of exiles. The whole narrative in Ezra 5–6 is indicative of a point which elsewhere we find the Chronicler making, namely that under God the Persian authorities were favourably disposed towards the re-establishment of the Jewish community. The line runs from Cyrus (II Chron. 36.22–23, cf. Ezra 1.1ff.), through these officials and Darius, to Artaxerxes (II) in his dealings with Ezra. (A similar emphasis is found in the opening of the Nehemiah narrative.)

The other passage which deals with opposition is 4.1–5.[49] The opponents are here described as the 'adversaries of Judah and

[45] Cf. the emphasis by A. C. Welch, *Post-exilic Judaism* (1935), p. 145.
[46] *Studien* (1964), pp. 89–108.
[47] Cf. O. Eissfeldt, *Introduction* (1965), pp. 550f.; S. Mowinckel, *Studien zu dem Buche Ezra-Nehemia* I. *Die nachchronische Redaktion des Buches. Die Listen* (Oslo, 1964), pp. 62–109.
[48] Cf. below pp. 243f.
[49] Cf. A. T. Olmstead, *History of the Persian Empire* (Chicago, 1948), pp. 136f.; R. J. Coggins, 'The Interpretation of Ezra 4.4', *JTS* 16 (1965), pp. 124–7. K. Koch, 'Haggais unreines Volk', *ZAW* 79 (1967), pp. 52–66, see pp. 64f., regards the opposition here mentioned as the Chronicler's own invention to explain the long delay in rebuilding.

Benjamin' (4.1), and further identified as 'people of the land' ('am hā'āreṣ 4.4).[50]

Their behaviour is not altogether unlike that of the opponents of Nehemiah in that they appear to be engaging in an intrigue designed to cause trouble. The statement that they are worshippers of the same God, and that they are descendants of those brought there by Esarhaddon king of Assyria invites a comparison with the story related in II Kings 17 about the settlers in the cities of Samaria after its conquest by the Assyrians in 722 BC. The Chronicler does not relate this story, but since he not infrequently makes cross-reference to stories he has not included, it is perhaps most reasonable to assume that he is referring to the same situation, but has confused the king of Assyria of the time of Samaria's fall with the later Esarhaddon. If

[50] R. J. Coggins, op. cit., p. 126, argues that the 'am hā'āreṣ here can be regarded as the same group as is associated with nationalistic policy in the pre-exilic period. They resented interference by the Persian authorities in the affairs of Judah, just as their predecessors had resented the interference of Assyria or Egypt. He suggests that Haggai and Zechariah (Hag. 2.4; Zech. 7.5) then encouraged them to assist in the rebuilding of the Temple. (On these passages, cf. also F. I. Andersen, ABR 6 [1958], pp. 1–35; cf. pp. 27–33.) But does this not assume too easily, with E. Würthwein, Der 'Am Ha'arez im Alten Testament (BWANT 17, 1936) and others, that this group is a well-defined entity? (Cf. also the more extreme view of M. Bič, noted in Das Buch Sacharja [Berlin, 1962], pp. 92f., and dealt with fully in his dissertation in Czech [Bethel, das Königliche Heiligtum, 1946] there cited. Bič identifies the 'am hā'āreṣ with the former country priesthood.) It is clear that often the term is used much more broadly, as indeed in the two passages mentioned, Hag. 2.4; Zech. 7.5. Würthwein (pp. 51–57) argues that, when used technically in the later period, the term refers to an alien 'upper stratum'. The problem in any given case is to be sure whether there really is a technical sense present. Cf. the cogent criticism of R. de Vaux, 'Le sens de l'expression "Peuple du Pays" dans l'Ancien Testament et le rôle politique du peuple en Israël', RA 58 (1964), pp. 167–72 (with a good bibliography); E. W. Nicholson, 'The Meaning of the Expression 'am hā'āreṣ in the Old Testament', JSS 10 (1965), pp. 59–66; and J. L. McKenzie, 'The "People of the Land" in the Old Testament', in Akten des XXIV Internationalen Orientalisten—Kongress, München, 1957 (Wiesbaden, 1959), pp. 206–8. Cf. also the much earlier conclusions of E. Klamroth, op. cit., pp. 99–101. McKenzie brings out the important point that the term is applicable to non-Israelite peoples (cf. Gen. 23.7ff.; 42.6; Num. 14.9) and has its equivalent in the Inscription of Yehawmilk. Andersen (loc. cit.) also mentions an article by I. D. Amusin, 'Narod Zemli', Journal of Ancient History, Academy of Sciences, USSR (1955, No. 2), pp. 14–36 who shows 'that its application is variable, depending on the prevailing social structure'. (So Andersen, p. 32 n.) We may note that in regard to this opposition of the 'people of the land', J. D. Smart, History and Theology in Second Isaiah (1965), p. 285, produces the rather strange idea that the Chronicler here has a 'vague recollection' of the opposition of those who shared Second Isaiah's opposition to the Temple rebuilding (cf. Isa. 66), they being 'people who were in the land when the exiles returned'. This, of course, depends on his whole viewpoint on Second Isaiah and on Isa. 66 in particular. Cf. pp. 118ff., 156 n. 15.

this is so, then these 'adversaries' are the ruling groups in Samaria who claim to have accepted the worship of Yahweh but who are recognized by the Jerusalem community as being in fact engaged in intrigue, and no doubt, like Sanballat and his associates in the next century, concerned to prevent the redevelopment of Jerusalem. The Chronicler has given a slight twist to the incident by stressing the repudiation of aliens which is to be so important a theme in the subsequent Ezra narrative.[51] That such opponents should then discourage the people of Judah and make them afraid to build (4.4) is entirely intelligible.[52] That they 'hired counsellors' ($y\bar{o}^{ca}\dot{s}\bar{\imath}m$) to frustrate them still further (4.5) would make a reasonable link to the other opposition narrative in ch. 5, for it would suggest that not only did they attempt intimidation but also reported the matter to higher authority, though it must be admitted that the term 'counsellors' could perhaps as well refer to an activity like that of Ahitophel or Hushai at the court of Absalom,[53] where a man by the skill of his advice seeks to persuade people into a course of action desired by him.

A comparable hint of such opposition is indicated in 3.3, which (in spite of Janssen's suggestion that here a new altar was being substituted for an already existing one)[54] may indicate that those who were attempting to re-establish the cultus properly in Jerusalem recognized the nature of the opposition which they would have to meet, perhaps because they were aware of the failure of the earlier attempt under Sheshbazzar.

A quite different point is referred to when it is stated that at the time of the passover after the dedication of the new Temple it was not only the returned exiles who engaged in the celebration but also 'everyone who had separated himself unto them from the pollution of the peoples of the land' (6.21). This is an example of the Chronicler's marked insistence upon the possibility of those who accept the purification of Jerusalem being members of the

[51] On *yaḥad* = 'closed community' (Ezra 4.3), cf. S. Talmon, *VT* 3 (1953), pp. 133ff.

[52] K. Koch, *op. cit.*, p. 65, asks: 'Is it reasonable to suppose that the returned exiles, in a minority and not very familiar with the situation in the land, should have undertaken such an enterprise in opposition to the provincial authorities?' But, as I have suggested, the whole question of who had real authority in Palestine may not have been at this stage completely clear.

[53] II Sam. 17.5ff. Cf. P. A. H. de Boer, 'The Counsellor', *VTS* 3 (1955), pp. 42–71, esp. p. 44, and W. McKane, *Prophets and Wise Men* (1965), esp. pp. 55ff.

[54] Cf. E. Janssen, *op. cit.*, pp. 94f.

community.[55] It is part of his missionary appeal. At no point is there any reference in these events to the opposition of a religious party later to be equated with the Samaritans, perhaps for the simple reason that whatever different elements may ultimately have made up the Samaritan religious community, the core of it must be regarded as having come from the very centre of the Jewish community with which it shared the Pentateuch[56] and which it rivalled in its religious conservatism. But that issue would take us outside our period.

The uncertainties of the period are thus evident enough and dogmatism about the relationship between the activity of the prophets and the historical events is therefore out of place.[57] What follows is an attempt at expounding the message of the prophets with a view to assessing their significance, and we shall deal first with Haggai, and then with Zechariah[58]—on the ground that the dating of these prophets in the period of restoration is virtually certain, even if there is some evidence of earlier material as well as of later re-application—with a brief mention of some other prophetic material.

[55] Cf. the narratives of the division of the kingdom (II Chron. 11.13–17) and of the reform of Hezekiah (II Chron. 30). This point is confused by K. Galling, *Studien* (1964), p. 59, for although he distinguishes the point that in Ezra 6.16 (Aramaic) the dedication is by returned exiles and notes the subsequent reference to those who had joined them and 'separated themselves' (6.21 Hebrew), he fails to bring out clearly that the Chronicler's statement envisages an 'open' community in a very real sense. The lack of sharp division between returned exiles and local population is clear in Haggai and Zechariah (cf. below). The Aramaic source of Ezra 5.1–6.18 is itself already a construction and not a straight historical record.

[56] L. Rost, *op. cit.* p. 303, draws attention to the 'political' aspect of this. The recognition by Persian authority of the acceptance of the law as the basis of membership of the Jewish community, as indicated in the commission of Ezra (Ezra 7.25f.), suggests that the Samaritans too found in the law a basis on which their political status could rest.

[57] Cf. P. R. Ackroyd, *JNES* 17 (1958), pp. 13–27 and *JJS* 2 (1951), pp. 163–76; 3 (1952), pp. 1–13. C. G. Tuland in *JNES* 17 (1958), pp. 269–75, attempts a very close definition of the chronology: it depends too much on a precision in interpretation which is hardly attainable. Cf. also his discussion of Josephus' material in 'Josephus, *Antiquities*. Book XI. Correction or Confirmation of Biblical Post-exilic Records', *Andrews University Seminary Studies* 4 (1966), pp. 176–92.

[58] The very important study by W. A. M. Beuken, *Haggai-Sacharja* 1–8 (Studia Semitica Neerlandica 10, Assen, 1967) appeared too late to make its full contribution to the discussion which follows, though some references have been included. In particular, the author recognizes that these prophetic collections reached their final form in circles akin to those of the Chronicler, and represent a particular view of the restoration period. Dr Beuken's study thus investigates in much more detail a line of thought put forward also in my own earlier studies and followed here. Beuken, pp. 216–29 on Haggai and pp. 230–330 on Zechariah, presents his understanding of the prophets in their original context.

X

THE RESTORATION AND ITS
INTERPRETATION
(*continued*)

B. HAGGAI

THE CHRONICLER, in II Chron. 36 and Ezra 1–6, thinking in terms of a sabbath rest for the land during the exile, now complete, could only suppose, rightly or wrongly from the historical point of view, that the restoration followed ideally upon the end of the exile at the fall of Babylon. Return and restoration and the new period begin there. From his longer perspective he sees this as the fulfilment of the seventy-year prophecy of Jeremiah,[1] and the time lapse between the first return and the dedication of the Temple—a time lapse which is not precisely chronologically indicated—is explained by the frustrations which were introduced by human agency, 'the adversaries of Judah and Benjamin'.[2] The same point in time— seventy years after the destruction—is indicated by Zech. 1.12 and 7.5, and it would seem that Zechariah is conscious that the new age ought to have dawned already but has been delayed—by what agency we are not directly told—so that an appeal is made to God to take action rather than to allow this desolation to be perpetuated. The same sense of urgency is to be found in Haggai. In 2.6 the somewhat cryptic phrase appears ʿōd ʾaḥat mᵉʿaṭ hīʾ[3]—literally 'yet one, and it is

[1] Cf. P. R. Ackroyd, 'Two Historical Problems of the Early Persian Period. B. The "Seventy Year" Period', *JNES* 17 (1958), pp. 23–27, and below p. 240 n. 27 for further literature.
[2] Ezra 4.1.
[3] Cf. Ps. 37.10, which also employs the phrase wᵉʿōd mᵉʿaṭ to express the speedy end of the wicked. The LXX render καὶ ἔτι ὀλίγον. Cf. also Isa. 10.25; Jer. 51.33. In Hag. 2.6 the LXX have ἔτι ἅπαξ = ʿōd ʾaḥat with no equivalent for mᵉʿaṭ hīʾ. It would seem possible that the MT represents a conflation of two alternative renderings: ʿōd mᵉʿaṭ and ʿōd ʾaḥat. Cf. T. H. Robinson and F. Horst, *Die zwölf kleinen Propheten*

only a little one'—which in this context presumably must mean that the events are anticipated as taking place in the immediate future. Such a sense of urgency is characteristic of the prophets. The reality of divine action for them imposes a certain kind of interpretation upon events and situations. It can allow for no delay in recognizing what God is doing, and no delay in making the appropriate response to it. Those elements in the situation which suggest disillusionment, hopes disappointed and expectations postponed, must be understood in the context of a divine action which even now is making itself felt. The dawn of the new age must not then be hindered by any human failure. The assurance that God is at work must evoke response from his people.

The new age as it is understood by Haggai and Zechariah is marked by the expectation of divine presence and blessing. The divine presence, as we might expect from earlier thought both before and during the exile, expresses itself in the Temple as the chosen place of divine self-revelation.[4] The divine blessing issues in a new people with a new life and organization. The correlative term is the fitness of the people to receive, their acceptability. So it is convenient to consider the oracular material of both Haggai and Zechariah under three main points: the Temple, the new community and the new age, the people's response. It is also proper to keep the two prophets separate, even if this involves some repetition, since it by no means follows from their contemporaneity that they thought in identical terms.[5] The fact that they stand together in the Chronicler's tradition (Ezra 5–6), and the probability that the two collections of prophecy have been compiled within one circle of tradition,[6] make it readily

---

(HAT 14, [2]1954), p. 206; Horst omits $m^{e\varsigma}at\ h\bar{\imath}$' and compares F. Delitzsch, *Die Lese- und Schreibfehler im AT* (Berlin, Leipzig, 1920), § 153.

[4] Cf. R. E. Clements, *God and Temple* (1965), and 'Temple and Land', *TGUOS* 19 (1963), pp. 16–28.

[5] Cf. the discussion by G. Sauer, 'Serubbabel in der Sicht Haggais und Sacharjas', in *Das ferne und nahe Wort*, ed. F. Maass (1967), pp. 199–207, where he stresses the differences between them in relation to the figure of Zerubbabel. For Haggai, the emphasis lies on Davidic promise (so esp. 2.20–23); for Zechariah, he is the builder of the Temple. To Sauer, Haggai is a prophet who stands close to the royal line; Zechariah, however, is much more closely bound up with cult and priesthood. The discussion is interesting, but oversimplified and attempts too close a categorization of the prophets' activities.

[6] Cf. P. R. Ackroyd, *JJS* 3 (1952), pp. 151–6; K. Elliger, *Das Buch der zwölf kleinen Propheten* II (ATD 25, [2]1951, [4]1959), p. 94; M. Bič, *Das Buch Sacharja* (Berlin, 1962), p. 9; W. A. M. Beuken, *op. cit.*, esp. pp. 10–20, 331–6.

understandable that they have come to be so closely associated as to allow the interpretation of the one to influence that of the other. Close as they are, we must nevertheless see what each has to say.

I. THE TEMPLE[7]

A substantial part of the prophecies of Haggai turns upon the idea of the Temple. The Temple is 'desolate' (*ḥārēb*) and this is related by the prophet to the condition of the land. This people says:

> It is not the time to come (in)
> (Not) the time for the House of Yahweh to be built. (1.2)[8]

This quotation of the people's words provides the occasion for answering comments and injunctions by the prophet. In the verses which follow there is a series of short sayings, related to the same general topic—the condition of the people and their land, the condition of the Temple and the need for rebuilding.

> Is it the right time for you
> to live in your panelled houses
> while this House is desolate? (v.4)

The contrast is drawn between the richness and adornment[9] of the houses of presumably some of the population and the condition, not altogether clear, of the Temple. Only in this passage and in the

---

[7] Cf. M. Schmidt, *Prophet und Tempel* (1948), pp. 192–7.

[8] The text here may be corrupt. Possibly the phrase '*et-bō*' 'time to come in' is an erroneous duplicate of the following letters '*et-bēt* or the correct reading is: *lō* '*attā bā*' (cf. LXX, Syr., Vg.; so many commentators, including F. Horst, *op. cit.*, p. 204, and D. W. Thomas, *IB* 6 [1956], p. 1041). Yet the use of the root *bō*', 'come in', with reference to religious ceremonial (cf. e.g. Ps. 95.6) and the evidence of an almost poetic rhythm in the oracles of Haggai suggest that the excision of the phrase may destroy the full effect of the comment: 'It is neither a time for religious celebration, nor a time for rebuilding.' On the poetic structure, cf. G. Fohrer, *Einleitung*, p. 504.

[9] Taking *sᵉpūnîm* to mean 'panelled' rather than 'roofed' (D. W. Thomas, *IB* 6 [1956], p. 1041). Cf. also J. Gray, *I and II Kings* (1964), p. 152 note m (where *gēbîm* (*bis*) must be read for *gēbōt*) and p. 157. Gray renders *gēbîm* here as 'coffers', i.e. recessed panelling. On p. 157 he says 'The ceiling, *mispān*, may also have served as roofing', Cf. also pp. 167 on I Kings 7.3 and 169 on 7.7. The stress in the passage in Haggai would appear to be on ornamentation, elaboration of the private houses, rather then merely on the idea of their having roofs.

related verse 1.9 is the word *ḥārēb* applied explicitly to the Temple.[10] In Jer. 33.10–13 we have a similar passage in which it is applied to 'this place', *māqōm*. The indications are that *māqōm* frequently has a technical meaning and this suggests that the primary reference in this passage too is to the Temple.[11] A similar situation is to be found in Jer. 7.[12] In both these passages the central idea of the Temple and its condition is extended in the interpretative material to relate the position there to the position in the land. We appear to have an idea which we have already seen in the Priestly Work and in Ezekiel also in some measure: the whole land is the holy place, the centrality of the Temple signifies that it is not simply in the one narrow locality, but also in the whole land which is his, that God actually dwells in the midst of his people. Desolation, while here in the context of rebuilding it obviously refers to a physical condition—ruins, or at least such a condition as necessitates the fetching of timber from the hills around the city for the restoration of the building (v.8)—yet at the same time carries an overtone of impurity, defilement. The 'perpetual desolations' (*maššu'ōt neṣaḥ*)[13] of Ps. 74.3 are not simply to be interpreted literally, but as expressive of disaster in whatever form it has come, or even as expressive of ritual defilement which makes worship impossible.[14]

So here in the Haggai context, the failure to rebuild is much more than a matter of reconstruction of a building.[15] It is the reordering of a

10 On *ḥārēb*, cf. F. I. Andersen, 'Who built the Second Temple?', *ABR* 6 (1958), pp. 1–35, see pp. 22–27, who suggests, appropriately, that while the state of the building is included in the term, desolation in a more general sense, desertion by its worshippers, may be regarded as part of the meaning here.

11 For *māqōm* = shrine cf. L. E. Browne, 'A Jewish Sanctuary in Babylonia', *JTS* 17 (1916), pp. 400–1, on Ezra 8.17 (but cf. also R. de Vaux, *Ancient Israel* [ET, 1961], p. 339, and cf. p. 291); for biblical passages where *māqōm* = shrine see *KBL* p. 560a. Ps. 96.6 has *miqdāšō*; the parallel text in I Chron. 16.27 has *mᵉqōmō*. In any given passage, there may well be some doubt whether the reference is to the shrine alone or to the whole 'place': cf. below on Hag. 2.9. Cf. S. Talmon, 'Synonymous Readings in the Textual Traditions of the Old Testament', *Script. Hier.* 8 (1961), pp. 335–83, see p. 359. Cf. *TWNT* 8/4 (1966), pp. 194–99 for a review of the whole question of usage and meaning. A comparison may further be made with the usage of *'îr*—'city', but also 'sanctuary'; cf. L. R. Fisher, 'The Temple Quarter', *JSS* 8 (1963), pp. 34–41.

12 Cf. esp. v. 6f. *māqōm* here appears to be virtually equivalent to *bait* in v. 10. In v. 12 *māqōm* clearly denotes the sanctuary of Shiloh and this strongly confirms the meaning 'shrine' for vv. 6–7.

13 Or better 'complete desolation'. Cf. D. W. Thomas, 'The Use of *neṣaḥ* as a Superlative in Hebrew', *JSS* 1 (1956), pp. 106–9.

14 Cf. F. Willesen, 'The Cultic Situation of Psalm 74', *VT* 2 (1952), pp. 289–306.

15 J. D. Smart, *History and Theology in Second Isaiah* (1965), pp. 284f., sees Haggai and Zechariah as representing the viewpoint condemned in Isa. 66. But, quite

Temple so that it is a fit place for worship.[16] Rebuilding is therefore linked to the condition of the people for the service of God.

In two further sayings,[17] the effect of this central defilement is made clear:

Consider your condition
  You sow much—you bring in little.[18]
    You eat but not to satisfaction.
    You drink but not so as to be merry with drink.
    You clothe yourselves but not so as to be warm.
    The wage-earner earns but only into a bag with holes. (1.5–6)

Therefore on your account
  The heavens hold back their dew[19]
  and the earth holds back its produce.
  I will summon drought upon the land and upon the
  mountains, upon corn and wine and oil, upon what
  the ground produces, upon man, and beast and upon
  all the products of their hands. (1.10–11)

The intimate relationship between the presence and the blessing of God, and between his absence and the disasters which take place, is drawn out.[20] The offering of gifts in such a situation, when the Temple is unfit for divine habitation, inevitably produces disaster:

apart from the problems of interpreting that passage (cf. pp. 229f.) there is here a failure to understand the real nature of Haggai's message. Smart writes: 'In the name of God, Haggai promises the members of the community a better time if only they will rebuild the Temple!' (p. 284); and he makes a similar comment on Zechariah. But this misses the real nature of the Temple as it is understood in these prophetic writings. A much more realistic view is taken by G. Buccellati (*Bibbia e Oriente* 2 [1960], pp. 199–209, see esp. p. 209); his tracing in Lamentations of an ardent Yahwist group in Jerusalem after the destruction (cf. above p. 21 n. 20 for a comment on this) and of collaborators in Palestine with returned exiles in the rebuilding of the Temple—and he deliberately refrains from drawing a direct line between the two—gives an imaginative but entirely reasonable comment on the complexity and richness of the religious situation.

[16] Cf. T. Chary, *op. cit.*, p. 127.
[17] K. Koch, 'Haggais unreines Volk', *ZAW* 79 (1967), pp. 52–66, in a form-critical analysis treats 1.2–7; 2.1–7; 2.11–19 as larger units. Cf. n. 23 below.
[18] Cf. Deut. 28.38.
[19] Reading *ṭallām* or *ṭāl* for *miṭṭāl*. The error appears to be due to dittography after *šāmaim*.
[20] Cf. R. T. Siebeneck, 'The Messianism of Aggeus and Proto-Zacharias', *CBQ* 19 (1957), pp. 312–28, see p. 323 on the Temple as a reminder of blessings and a prelude to a glorious future. Siebeneck expresses this in terms which are, however, too futuristic.

You turn towards plenty
and there—it is little:
You bring it into (my) House[21]
and I shall despise it:
And why?—oracle of Yahweh of hosts—
because of my house which is desolate
while you are concerned each of you for his own house.[22] (1.9)

The same point is brought out in 2.10–14, to which we shall turn later, and again in 2.15–19, now apparently placed so as to provide a contrast with the preceding words of judgement,[23] whereas the passage belongs closely in content with the general situation of 1.2–11.

Now then, consider the position from this day onwards.
Before stone was put on stone in the temple of Yahweh,
how did you fare?[24]
A man would come[25] to a heap containing twenty measures,
and it would be only ten.
He would come[25] to the winevat to draw out fifty from the trough,[26]
and there would be only twenty.
I struck you with blight and with mildew,
and all the works of your hands with hail.
But you were not with me—oracle of Yahweh.[27]
Consider the position from this day onwards.
From the day of the restoring of the temple of [28] Yahweh
(i.e. the twenty-fourth day of the
ninth month), consider:
Is the seed still in the granary? Do the vine and the
figtree and the pomegranate and the olive still[29] not bear?
From this day on I will bless.

[21] Cf. F. Peter, 'Haggai 1.9', *TZ* 2 (1951), pp. 150f.
[22] Literally 'run . . . to his own house'. Cf. *KBL* p. 882ᵇ. *bait* here might equally be rendered 'household' and perhaps paraphrased as 'affairs'.
[23] On the order of the material cf. P. R. Ackroyd, *JJS* 2 (1951), pp. 163–76; 3 (1952), pp. 1–13, and 'Haggai' in *New Peake's Commentary* (1962), p. 643. But cf. also K. Koch, *op. cit.*, who argues for unity of structure in 2.11–19. The formalized structure of the whole book may, however, point to the deliberate creation of these larger units.
[24] Reading *ma-hᵉyītem* for *mihᵉyōtām*, cf. BH³.
[25] Or reading *bō'* (inf. abs.) = 'you would come'.
[26] Reading *mippūrā* for *pūrā* (haplography after *hᵃmiššīm*).
[27] The phraseology here suggests the presence either of a gloss from Amos (cf. P. R. Ackroyd, *JJS* 7 [1956], pp. 163–7), or of a deliberate use of a passage of well-known prophetic material by way of comment (cf. also Zech. 6.15). In recognizing the presence of glosses in the book of Haggai, it is not, however, necessary to engage in the extravagant dehydration of the book which is attempted by F. S. North, 'Critical Analysis of the Book of Haggai', *ZAW* 68 (1956), pp. 25–46.
[28] Cf. A. Gelston, *VT* 16 (1966), pp. 232–5.
[29] Reading *ʿōd* for *ʿad*.

It is reasonable to see this as a further reflection upon the people's response (described in a prose narrative in 1.12–14). The teaching of 1.10–11 is now clarified. The disasters which were there indicated as divine judgement because of the condition of the Temple, are here recorded again. The disappointment at bad harvests, the continued shortages of produce, were the result of the Temple situation. Those experiences, the prophet reminds his hearers, were the result of divine judgement, and the intention was that the people should learn from them. Just as in the time of Amos, as the allusion to his words in 2.17 shows, the people have been repeatedly warned by natural disasters and ought therefore to have realized the meaning of the situation, even if they had failed to understand it in relation to his saving acts in the past (cf. Amos 2). But they refused to hear, and refused to return to Yahweh. Now the situation will change, though it is evident that the change is not yet apparent to the people. The meaning of 2.19a is not clear in detail. It may mean: 'Are you still as short of supplies as you were, still finding that there is nothing to indicate that the situation has changed? You are wrong, for already God is blessing, though as yet it cannot be seen.' Or it might mean: 'You are no longer waiting to sow the seed; it is planted and growing now. The fruit trees are no longer barren, but bearing or promising to bear. So the blessing is already apparent.' On the whole the former sense seems preferable,[30] for it indicates the uncertainty in the minds of the people, and the not unnatural anxiety of the prophet to make clear the relationship between Temple and divine blessing. To make the point even clearer, 2.18 again ties the matter to the day of the re-establishing of the Temple, to which a date has been added to make it even more precise. Here too we seem to have a glossator at work, who, anxious to show the precision of divine blessing, makes the correlation between action and response one that can be tied to particular moments, just as in the historical books and still more in the Chronicler, the exactness of correspondence between prophecy and event, between divine will and occurrence, is emphasized. To those involved in a situation, the correspondence is a matter of faith, linked to past experiences. To those who subsequently interpret its meaning, the correspondences can be given a greater degree of precision.[31]

The relationship between the rebuilding of the Temple and the

---

[30] Cf. T. Chary, op. cit., p. 130 n., for a comment, and cf. the discussion in L. E. Browne, Early Judaism (1920), pp. 56ff. and in the commentaries.

[31] T. Chary, op. cit., pp. 130f. P. R. Ackroyd, JJS 7 (1956), pp. 163–7.

establishing of God in his central place in the people's life, for blessing and well-being, is brought out in various phrases in Haggai.

> Go up into the mountains and bring in timber and rebuild the house. Then I will accept it and I will let myself be honoured,[32] says Yahweh.
>
> (1.8)

The 'acceptance' is the technical term for the recognition by God that the sacrificial offerings are as they should be. It sets the seal of divine favour upon the Temple.[33] So too 'I will let myself be honoured' means 'I will accept the worship which tends to my honour.' Without a properly built temple, that is a ritually correct place for the worship of God, such worship is impossible. This is not because God is thought of as being limited to the Temple, but because this is what he has chosen. The linkage of thought to that of Deuteronomy —and also to Ezekiel, to Deutero-Isaiah and to the Priestly Writers— is clear. The God who is lord of heaven and earth, who cannot be contained in a building,[34] nevertheless condescends to reveal himself and to localize his presence in order that blessing may flow out. The Temple is the correlative of the presence of God; its condition only in the sense that this is what God chooses. On that assumption, the demand for rebuilding, for the removal of the barrier of desolation, of impurity, is a recognition of the nature of God, for whom acceptability on the part of his worshippers is essential. The emphasis is not thereby placed upon human endeavour, but upon the recognizable danger of treading unwarily into the presence of holiness.[35]

The same emphasis is found in a context of encouragement to rebuild in 2.3–5, where the distressing contrast between present conditions and the memories of a golden past have brought discouragement and uncertainty about the assurance of blessing.

[32] *we'ekkābedā:* 'I will be honoured' does not bring out the reflexive sense of the niph'al. 'I will honour myself' is too restrictive. The permissive meaning 'I will let myself be honoured' appears most appropriate to the context.

[33] G. von Rad, *Theology* II, pp. 281f.

[34] Cf. I Kings 8.27. Cf. also M. Haran, *IEJ* 9 (1959), pp. 91f.

[35] The words of Amos, 'Prepare to meet your God, O Israel' (4.12) are in the context of Israel's refusal to heed the warnings of disaster; they are a summons to her to be the people of God, because otherwise the meeting will be their destruction. 'To walk circumspectly (so D. Winton Thomas, *JJS* 1 [1948/9], pp. 182–6) with your God' (Micah 6.8) indicates that the relationship with God is one which cannot be lightly undertaken. To 'walk with God' has been the mark of specially distinguished individuals (e.g. Enoch, Noah), and is associated with the divine blessing of the Davidic kingship (cf. e.g. I Kings 2.3; II Kings 20.3). It cannot be possible without due regard for the forms which are the God-given mechanism of relationship.

Now be strong . . . and work,
For I am with you—oracle of Yahweh of hosts
And my spirit stands among you.
Do not fear. (2.4–5)

The assurance is underlined by the glossator, who has drawn his readers' attention to the relationship between this promise and that which attended the experience of the crossing of the sea and the establishment of relationship between God and his people:

The word which I established with you when you came out of Egypt.[36]
(2.5a)

When Israel stood still by the sea, she discovered the reality of the presence of God. It is an echoing of words to be found again in the Chronicler's sermons,[37] for it is proper for man to stand still and discover the presence of God.

In Haggai this is linked with the bringing in to the Temple of the tribute of all nations, and so with an enlargement of the perspective. A shaking of the world will presage this bringing of honour to God:

I will shake all nations,
And the tribute[38] of all nations shall come in,
And I will fill this house with glory—says Yahweh of hosts.
Mine is the silver and mine the gold—oracle of Yahweh of hosts.
The glory of this latter house shall be greater than the glory
of the former—says Yahweh of hosts.
In this place (shrine)[39] I will bestow full life—
oracle of Yahweh of hosts. (2.7–9)

The consequences of the presence of God are made clear. The centrality of the Temple as his dwelling is absolute, for all nations bring as tribute their 'precious things'.[40] In reality all this wealth belongs

[36] Cf. P. R. Ackroyd, *JJS* 7 (1956), pp. 163–7.
[37] E.g. II Chron. 20.15–17. Cf. G. von Rad, 'Die levitische Predigt in den Büchern der Chronik', *Festschr. O. Procksch* (Leipzig, 1934), pp. 113–24 = *Ges. Stud.* (Munich, 1958), pp. 248–61, ET, 'The Levitical Sermon in I and II Chronicles', in *The Problem of the Hexateuch and other Essays* (London, 1966), pp. 267–80.
[38] *ḥemdat.* The singular form may perhaps carry a collective meaning (LXX τὰ ἐκλεκτὰ), though the alternative pointing as plural *ḥᵃmūdōt* is preferable in view of the plural verb.
[39] On this use of *māqōm* cf. above p. 156 n. 11. Here is another passage in which the extension of meaning from 'Temple' to 'land' is apparent.
[40] K. L. Schmidt, 'Jerusalem als Urbild und Abbild', *Eranos-Jahrbuch* 18 (Zurich, 1950), pp. 207–48, compares Isa. 60–62 and Ezek. 40ff., noting that, as also in these passages and in Zechariah, there is to be a cosmic upheaval the survivors of which will glorify Jerusalem.

already to him, but now he claims it as his own, and so it can be used as it properly should for the glorification of his dwelling. His presence will make possible that fulness of life, *šālōm*, prosperity in the full sense of the word, which flows out from him.[41]

2. THE NEW COMMUNITY AND THE NEW AGE

The new age as it is understood by Haggai is centred upon the Temple because that is the place in which God chooses to dwell and to reveal his blessing. Certain consequences follow from this, some of which have already been made apparent in the preceding discussion. They concern the nature of the community in whose life this becomes reality, and the related matter of the kind of response and condition which are necessary correlatives of their being that community.

The framework and narrative material in Haggai uses the word 'remnant' for the people (1.12, 14; 2.2). In the actual words of the prophet, however, the community is referred to as 'this people'[42] (1.2, and also 2.14 if we accept the most natural interpretation of the passage by which the reference is to the same community).[43] It is also described as 'all the people of the land' (2.4, where emendation to 'remnant' as proposed by some commentators is entirely unwarranted),[44] and presumably, whatever technical meanings this latter phrase may have had,[45] it here appears as an equivalent to 'the people'.[46]

This difference of usage suggests that we cannot ascribe the term 'remnant' directly to the prophet but to the compiler. This compiler stands, however, very closely in the tradition of the prophet and has simply made explicit what in Haggai is implicit. In so far as the people, by rebuilding the Temple, open the way for the giving of divine blessing, and themselves become the new people of God on whom that blessing falls, they are in a real sense the 'remnant', the

[41] G. von Rad, *Theology* II, pp. 281f. M. Schmidt, *Prophet und Tempel* (1948), p. 197. T. Chary, *op. cit.*, p. 132. Cf. also W. A. M. Beuken, *op. cit.*, pp. 27–49.

[42] Cf. E. Janssen, *op. cit.*, p. 119 n. Cf. also, on the usage in Haggai, F. I. Andersen, *ABR* 6 (1958), pp. 27ff.

[43] Cf. also below p. 167 and n. 71.

[44] Cf. BH³.

[45] Cf. references on p. 150 n. 50.

[46] So e.g. G. Buccellati, *Bibbia e Oriente* 2 (1960), p. 207; and against E. Janssen, *op cit.*, p. 119 n. 3, who sees in this phrase and in *hāʿām hazze* (1.2) 'a contrast to a particular section of the people'.

divinely chosen survivors of disaster, the purified community in which the promises of the past are made real. We shall see that this way of thinking is more explicitly brought out by Zechariah,[47] and it is natural to think that the application of the term 'remnant' in Haggai is in part influenced by the kind of thought which is represented by his contemporary.

Haggai is, however, aware of the nature of the new community. In his appeal to them to rebuild there is the recognition of what they are supposed to be. Their failure to recognize the present as the moment appropriate for rebuilding has resulted in various disasters, judgements upon them. But it has not invalidated their position as the people on whom the responsibility falls. Similarly, those of them who look back to the past and are therefore conscious of belonging with their forefathers can be encouraged to see that past not in terms of a golden period to which the present cannot possibly measure up, but in terms of divine action and promise which will be expressed in the realities of the present.[48] It is on them, the generation of the founding of the Temple, that divine blessing falls.[49] It is over them, as the executive of God's will, that Zerubbabel will stand.

In the last passage of the book, 2.21–23, a message is directed to Zerubbabel which runs in some respects parallel to the message concerning the glorification of the Temple in 2.6–9. The same shaking of the earth, here combined with the overthrow of the royal authorities of the earth, ushers in the establishment of a new situation. The events are not necessarily to be thought of in military terms, but rather in terms of the subordination to the divine will of those powers which set themselves up as authorities in their own right.[50] The occasion of the rebellions against Darius may well provide the background to the prophecy, but not its cause. The conventional military terminology is to be found also in Psalm 46, in which the primary emphasis is upon divine action rather than human events.[51] It is

[47] Cf. below pp. 175ff.
[48] So especially in 2.3–5, 6–9. Cf. also M. Schmidt, op. cit., pp. 195f., for an emphasis on the significance of the action of God in the contemporary situation.
[49] Cf. also the significant verses Zech. 8.9–10 (cf. below pp. 175, 213f.).
[50] Cf. the use of such imagery in the Psalms, e.g. Ps. 2, and in Ezek. 38–39; Zech. 14.1ff. On connections of this language with the 'holy war', cf. G. von Rad, Der heilige Krieg im alten Israel (1951), pp. 65f.
[51] The same use of military terminology is often to be found in later apocalyptic writings, and in most detail in the War Scroll of Qumran. It has, of course, found its place elsewhere in religious imagery, in the New Testament and in later Christian hymnody and allegory.

'on that day', which in the earlier prophets is the mark of the moment of divine action; we have seen how 'that day' has been related to the disastrous fall of Jerusalem and the kingdom, as expressive of the dark side of Yahweh's theophany.[52]

Zerubbabel is dignified by two titles. On the one hand he is 'my servant', which is probably intended as a designation of royal authority.[53] On the other hand, he is the signet ring, which is both a mark of honour and distinction, and more significantly, an indication of representative function. The possession of the signet makes possible action on behalf of another. Ben Sira expands this, no doubt rightly, as the 'signet on the right hand'.[54] More particularly, here again, there is a royal reference, to be found in Jer. 22.24.[55] The new community has as its leader and head one who acts as a royal representative of God.[56]

This raises questions concerning the nature of Haggai's 'messianic' aspirations, questions which are in part of a political nature.[57] The sometimes far-fetched suggestions as to what became of Zerubbabel and of his co-conspirators[58] nevertheless touch on an issue of importance. How far are these claims for Zerubbabel consonant with political subservience to Persia?[59] How likely is it that the Persians

[52] Cf. pp. 48f.

[53] Compare its use in reference to a number of outstanding Old Testament personalities, and notably David (e.g. II Sam. 3.18) and the Davidic line (Ezek. 34.23f.; 37.24). See W. Zimmerli and J. Jeremias, *The Servant of God* (SBT 20, 1957), pp. 20f.; (rev. ed. 1965), pp. 22f. = *TWNT* 5 (1954), pp. 662f.; R. Press, 'Der Gottesknecht im Alten Testament', *ZAW* 67 (1955), pp. 67–99.

[54] Ecclus. 49.11.

[55] Cf. also Gen. 41.42; Esther 3.10.

[56] Cf. R. T. Siebeneck, *op. cit.* pp. 316ff., on the development here of the Davidic promise. K. Koch, *op. cit.*, argues for Haggai's hope of a Davidide, but with a high priest beside him. This is, however, much less clear than in Zechariah.

[57] Cf. O. Eissfeldt, *Geschichtliches und Übergeschichtliches im Alten Testament* (*ThStKr* 109/2, 1947), pp. 16f., who claims that the prophets together with Zerubbabel and Joshua believed that they could create a real state, independent and powerful. The evidence does not clearly point to this conclusion.

[58] Cf. references in P. R. Ackroyd, *JNES* 17 (1958), pp. 13–22.

[59] Here again we meet with the important point that the same action may be quite differently viewed: Persian policy has its own standards of judgement; the Jewish community—or some members of it—may properly attempt a theological interpretation in line with its own tradition. Within the biblical material—and from outside evidence—we may not infrequently detect this (cf. B. S. Childs, *Isaiah and the Assyrian Crisis* [1967]). To speak, however, of a secret significance of the return for the Jewish community (as Y. Kaufmann does, *History of the Religion of Israel* [Hebr.] Vol. 8 [Tel Aviv, 1956], pp. 161–3), is perhaps to recognize insufficiently the problems of relationship between various types of interpretation. (ET of the relevant passage in *El ha'ayin* No. 39 [Jerusalem, 1964], pp. 11f.)

would admit of such activities as might follow? The opening chapters of Ezra suggest that suspicions about the activities of the Jews in this period were entertained by some of the surrounding groups. Such suspicions may well have been in part engendered by self-interest, but it is clear that the position of a subject governor and subject people was always delicate.[60]

There are three points which strongly suggest that our interpretation of the passage must be primarily non-political—though that term is too restrictive. Zerubbabel was appointed by the Persians, who can hardly have been ignorant of his Davidic descent and indeed presumably chose him for this reason. He was to effect some measure of re-establishment of the community centred on Jerusalem, and for this to be possible, the descendant of the Davidic line would obviously have considerable advantages over any other personage. If risk there was, it was a calculated risk.[61] Furthermore, the record of Ezra indicates that when investigation took place, Darius was willing to confirm the action of his predecessor Cyrus—this being part of his own establishment of himself as legitimate, but no doubt representing his policy of conciliation indicated also in his favourable treatment of other sacred places.[62] It was Jerusalem as royal centre, now part of the Persian empire, whose ruler could be said in some sense to inherit the blessings of David, which Persia was willing to re-establish. In the third place, there is no indication of any interruption of the rebuilding of the Temple subsequently. The work went on peacefully and happily, with the final establishment of its life and worship. We detect no trace of change of policy, nor of violent action against the Jews such as might be anticipated if Zerubbabel's claims were looked at askance.[63]

The conclusion which we must draw from this is that whatever precise future situation was envisaged, the immediate claim which

[60] Cf. G. von Rad, *Theology* II, pp. 283ff. The accusations as recorded in Ezra 5 make no mention of Zerubbabel by name. K. Koch, *op. cit.* p. 65, argues for a hope of a renewed national kingdom, with a forward look to world rule.

[61] Cf. K. Baltzer, 'Das Ende des Staates Juda und die Messias-Frage', in *Studien zur Theologie der alttestamentlichen Überlieferungen*, ed. R. Rendtorff and K. Koch (Neukirchen, 1961), pp. 33–43: see p. 38 on the repudiation by Haggai (2.23) of Jeremiah's oracle on Jehoiachin (Jer. 22.30). Baltzer also notes that the appending of Jer. 52 to the book 'gives the impression of being a deliberate correction'. Cf. also T. Chary, *op. cit.*, pp. 134f.; L. Rost, 'Erwägungen zum Kyroserlass', in *Verbannung und Heimkehr*, ed. A. Kuschke (1961), pp. 301–7, see p. 302. Subsequently Rost comments, however, that no other Davidide was appointed governor after Zerubbabel.

[62] Cf. above p. 140.

[63] Cf. also D. N. Freedman, 'The Chronicler's Purpose', *CBQ* 23 (1961), pp. 436–42, see p. 441.

Haggai is making is that of the sovereignty of God and of his control over all the world. In this, the Temple at Jerusalem is central; alongside it, the establishment of Zerubbabel represents the choice of the agent by whom God effects his rule.[64] The real actor in this is God himself. When Baltzer speaks of 'Haggai's legitimation of Zerubbabel' as descendant of Jehoiachin in answer to the negative oracle of Jer. 22.24ff.,[65] it does not follow that the passage should be given a narrow political interpretation. The real point is the reversal of previous judgement, and hence the reality of the arrival of the new age.[66]

3. THE PEOPLE'S RESPONSE

The condition of the community which is summoned to the task of rebuilding the Temple, and is promised in the Zerubbabel oracle a leadership which will truly express the mind of God in his people, and indeed beyond his people to the world, is also indicated in 2.11–14. In this passage the two other points of Haggai's message are drawn together, and the nature of the people's condition and response is his concern. The difficulties of interpretation of this passage are well known, and to some extent have been dictated by a too close adherence to the chronological order of Haggai's prophecies as indicated by the present form of the Massoretic text.[67] The encouragement and blessing of 2.1–9 appear to be strangely followed by a warning and condemnation in the succeeding verses, and so it has been thought by some that the reference cannot be to the same community as was entrusted with the rebuilding.[68] If the message is taken for what it

[64] Cf. also S. Mowinckel, *He that Cometh* (ET, 1956), pp. 119ff. W. A. M. Beuken, *op. cit.*, pp. 49–64, offers an illuminating statement of the position of the leaders in relation to the rebuilding. See also pp. 78–83 on 2.20–23.

[65] K. Baltzer, *loc. cit.* (see n. 61).

[66] On the relation of the final age to historical experience, cf. E. Jenni, *Die politischen Voraussagen der Propheten* (ATANT 29, 1956), pp. 103f.

[67] Cf. P. R. Ackroyd, *JJS* 2 (1951), pp. 163–76; 3 (1952), pp. 1–13: cf. esp. pp. 171–3. Also A. C. Welch, *Post-exilic Judaism* (1935), p. 162 n. Cf. W. A. M. Beuken, *op. cit.*, pp. 21–26, for a critical discussion of the problem.

[68] Cf. J. W. Rothstein, *Juden und Samaritaner* (BWAT 3, 1908), pp. 5–41, who originally proposed this view, and, among those who have accepted it, L. E. Browne, *Early Judaism* (Cambridge, 1920), pp. 55f., 61f.; D. W. Thomas, 'Haggai', *IB* 6 (1956), p. 1046. Cf. G. von Rad, *Theology* II, p. 283 n., on the restriction to Israel, and also M. Schmidt, *op. cit.*, p. 269 (n. 547). K. Koch, *op. cit.* (p. 157 n. 17), has produced a clear exposition of the inadequacy of Rothstein's interpretation. On this section cf. also the useful article by H. G. May, *VT* 18 (1968), pp. 190–97, and W. A. M. Beuken, *op. cit.*, pp. 64–77.

says without too close an adherence to the dating, this difficulty no longer arises. But even if the dating is accepted, there is still no good reason why such a comment as this should not be made concerning the nature of the people involved in the undertaking. The prophetic books are full of the contrast which is involved in the actual nature of the people of God. It is at one and the same moment a people called by God, obedient to him, fulfilling his purposes, and also a people which does not respond, shows itself to be disobedient, fails to be the people of God as it ought to be.[69]

So here the address may appropriately be to the same called community, responding, as the narrative of 1.12–14 shows, to the summons to rebuild. The occasion for the oracle is a priestly *tōrā*,[70] a fact that is in itself of interest as suggesting a mechanism of prophetic activity which is not elsewhere clearly indicated.

Ask a directive (*tōrā*) of the priests.
If a man carries holy flesh in the skirt of his garment, and with his garment he touches bread or cooked food or wine or oil or any other kind of food, will any of these become holy? The priests replied: No. Then Haggai said: If he touches an unclean body with any of these, will it become unclean? The priests replied: It will become unclean. Then Haggai explained:
So is this people, so is this nation[71] before me;—oracle of Yahweh—
And so is everything which they do,
And what they offer there is unclean. (2.11–14).

[69] This same ambivalence has been observed above in relation to the 'Servant' concept as used by Deutero-Isaiah (cf. pp. 126ff.). Cf. Janssen, *op. cit.*, p. 51: 'The mention of the people in Hag. 2.14 cannot be separated from 1.2.' Janssen relates this idea to a division within the people between faithful and unfaithful, and compares Isa. 56.9–57.13. The idea of a faithful remnant is sometimes thought to resolve this ambivalence. And in one sense it is possible for it to do so. But in fact, as later teaching about the nature of the church clearly demonstrates, even such a faithful remnant, identifiable in theory as the true people of God, remains a human organism and is similarly subject to the strictures which are provoked by its failure to be what it is called to be. Here lies the weakness of any doctrine of the gathered church which does not at the same time emphasize that the chosen people of God is always a people under judgement.

[70] Cf. J. Begrich, 'Die priesterliche Tora', *BZAW* 66 (1936), pp. 63–88, see pp. 79f. = *Ges. Stud.* (ThB 21, 1964), pp. 232–60, see pp. 249ff.

[71] ʿam (as in 1.2) is here used in parallel with gōy. The expression appears to be poetic or semi-poetic. S. Talmon, 'Synonymous Readings in the Textual Traditions of the Old Testament', *Script. Hier.* 8 (1961), p. 343, suggests that the text here contains two alternative readings, phrases which are exact equivalents, resulting in a doublet in the text. There is no justification for seeing ʿam as Jews and gōy as non-Jews (so E. Hammershaimb, *Some Aspects of Old Testament Prophecy* [1966], p. 106); nor any derogatory meaning in the two phrases (cf. K. Koch, *op. cit.*, pp. 61f., for a clear statement on this last point).

In offering an interpretation of this passage, we must be careful not to be too literal-minded in making the application from the directive of the priests to the situation of the people. There is a general relationship between the two, but not necessarily a specific application of each phrase of the directive to the situation envisaged. Two interrelated lines of interpretation seem possible. The emphasis in Haggai's own message to the people concentrates on the uncleanness of the people's offerings in the shrine. If their offerings are unclean—that is, unacceptable—then so is their whole life and condition. The point then lies in the prophet's pointing out to the people that unacceptability in the presence of God means that they are unfit to be the people of God.[72] The corollary to this must be that acceptability demands a whole change of outlook. If we try to make this line of thought more specific, we have to recognize that we cannot precisely tie down the prophet's meaning. In the opening chapter, the meaning of his words is that the people's condition is directly related to their failure to rebuild the Temple; in other words, the failure to respond in proper worship, which demands the Temple in its right order, is reflected in the lack of blessing on their whole life. So we may believe that here, rather more narrowly, Haggai is emphasizing the need for adequate worship because of the effect on their total condition of a failure in this.[73] In this point, Haggai is developing a kind of thought often to be found in earlier prophecy and seen also in the Psalms, that the worship which is offered is unacceptable because, as Isaiah so vividly puts it, 'your hands are full of blood'.[74]

Such a stress links closely with the second line of interpretation.

[72] T. Chary, op. cit., pp. 136f., lays stress on the impurity of worship offered during the exilic period, and compares the similar concerns of Isa. 57.3–10; 65.3–7. On unacceptability, cf. E. Würthwein, 'Kultpolemik oder Kultbescheid?' (cf. p. 5 n. 11).

[73] E. Hammershaimb, op. cit., p. 106, with a reference back to S. Mowinckel, sees here a reference to sacrifice on a mean temporary altar. A similar interpretation is offered by A. C. Welch (Post-exilic Judaism [1935], pp. 167ff.). He sees 2.11–14 as referring to the unacceptability of the altar used during the exilic period by the joint group of southerners and northerners which he discovers in Neh. 10 (cf. pp. 67–86 of his study for this). Such a view is without any clear foundation. When Welch supports it here by supposing that ‘am and gōy indicate a community consisting of two such groups, separately described, this shows a lack of appreciation of Hebrew poetic language.

[74] Isa. 1.15. Cf. Pss. 15, 24; Isa. 33.14ff.; Ezek. 18.5ff.; etc. For a similar interpretation cf. H. Frey, Das Buch der Kirche in der Weltwende (BAT 24, ⁴1957), pp. 28ff.

This would take up rather more exactly the words of the directive by suggesting that the references to 'holy flesh' or to an 'unclean body' are really seen by the prophet to be references to the Temple itself. The contagion of uncleanness then implies that so long as the Temple is not adequately put in order the whole condition of the people will be unclean; what is wrong at the centre of their life will show itself in total unacceptability. But it is possible now to emphasize the obverse of this, and here we seem to go rather further in understanding the passage. The 'holy', if it means the Temple, is shown to be quite properly at the centre of their life, but it is made plain that the presence of that holy Temple does not of itself guarantee the condition of the people. In other words, God's presence and blessing, which have been assured so vividly in 2.6–9, do not automatically guarantee that the people are in a fit condition to worship. The people who are called to be the community of the new age can nevertheless frustrate that new age by their own condition. There is no automatic efficacy in the Temple, no guarantee that by virtue of its existence it ensures salvation. The effectiveness of it and of its worship is determined by the condition of those who worship, that is, whether or not they are in a fit condition to receive the blessings of God.

This line of interpretation does not demand a literal application of the second question to the priests, and it makes good sense of the prophetic utterance, not by demanding exact correspondence but by seeing it as a declaration to the people. Haggai says to them: 'You respond, you rebuild the Temple, you see that it is all in order; but how can you expect to receive God's blessing when you yourselves are unclean?' What this uncleanness means is shown by such passages as Psalm 15 or Psalm 24, and at an early date a gloss was added to this passage which brings out this interpretation:

> Because of their taking of bribes, they shall suffer on account of their evil deeds, 'and you hated those who reprove (or him who reproves) in the gates'. (Cf. Amos 5.10)

We have no means of determining when the gloss was added, except that various points indicate that it was added to the Hebrew text and translated into Greek, so that at least it goes back to a period earlier than the LXX.[75] We cannot be sure that the interpretation it offers is the right one, but it is nevertheless worthy of respect. It is the earliest exegesis of the passage available to us, and it indicates that

[75] Cf. P. R. Ackroyd, *JJS* 7 (1956), pp. 163–7, and references to the literature.

the uncleanness of the people is precisely that kind of moral failure which so often in the prophets and in the psalms is shown to be potent in making worship unacceptable, the people no longer fit to be called the people of God. To those who believe (as did some of the contemporaries of Jeremiah)[76] that the very existence of the Temple guarantees blessing, the prophet is saying quite plainly that there is no such automatic effect. The blessings of God can only be appropriated by a people which is really fit to be the people of God, and in so far as the community of Haggai's time is failing to be just that, it is frustrating the intention of God towards it.[77]

In this so brief collection of prophetic sayings, built together into a unified whole, we have a picture of a restored community, centred on the Temple and needing to know itself as the people of God. It is a people which needs to be purified if it is to appropriate the divine blessings which its position entails, and this position is no narrow or provincial one, for at its centre is the Temple which is where God reveals himself, a centre therefore both to the life of the world and to the total action of God.[78]

[76] Cf. Jer. 7.4. Compare also Isa. 66.1ff.

[77] It is a common misunderstanding of Haggai to see a decisive difference here from what are often called the 'older prophets of doom' in that the future is linked to Temple and cult. (So, for example, E. Hammershaimb, *Some Aspects of Old Testament Prophecy* [1966], p. 105.) However this last passage in 2.10–14 is interpreted, it is still doubtful if we should say, as Hammershaimb does, that 'all ethical considerations are lacking', for this is to make an artificial division, and to overstress one aspect of prophetic, and indeed of Hebrew, religious thinking. The problem is one of relationship to God. We may compare R. C. Dentan's comment on the book of Malachi, a comment equally relevant to Haggai and Zechariah: '. . . disrespect towards the cult is not important for its own sake, but because it is a symbol of general indifference toward God' (*IB* 6 [1956], p. 1119).

[78] Cf. T. Chary, *op. cit.*, p 138.; G. von Rad, *Theology* II, p. 282. It is appropriate to add a word of reference to the essay by F. Hesse, 'Haggai' in *Verbannung und Heimkehr*, ed. A. Kuschke (Tübingen, 1961), pp. 109–34, an essay primarily concerned with problems of method in Old Testament interpretation in the Christian church and directed more especially at H. W. Wolff, *Haggai* (BS 1, 1951). While we may agree with his strictures on a type of interpretation which either looks uncritically at the material or apologizes for it, it appears unsatisfactory to engage in so simple a delineation as to suggest that Haggai stands in the line leading to Judaism, defining that in effect as the opposition to Jesus. 'Haggai is in no way a forerunner of Jesus Christ, he is on the contrary one of the fathers of Judaism' (p. 129). It is such oversimplifications which lead to wrong understanding of the whole post-exilic period (cf. above in ch. I), and do much less than justice to the complexity of religious thought in New Testament times. Cf. also the emphasis in K. Koch, *op. cit.*, esp. p. 66, who stresses the links between Haggai and earlier thought and denies any element of Judaism to him.

XI

THE RESTORATION AND ITS INTERPRETATION

(continued)

C. ZECHARIAH 1-8

THE THREE THEMES which were traced in the exegesis of Haggai may be seen again in the prophecies of Zechariah, viz.: the Temple, the new community and the new age, the people's response. It must be stressed that the division is here too intended only as a rough guide, not as a definition of the prophet's activity in a narrowly constricted scheme.

1. THE TEMPLE[1]

Although references to the rebuilding of the Temple occupy only a small part of the prophecies of Zechariah, the points which are made are of importance. In 4.6b–10a we have a prophetic fragment which now stands in the middle of an elaborate vision and interpretation dealing with the centrality of God in the people's life and the place of the two leaders, Zerubbabel and Joshua. The fragment itself consists of various short sayings, all turning on the assurance that the Temple will be successfully rebuilt.

This is Yahweh's word to Zerubbabel:
Not by might, not by power, but by my spirit,
  says Yahweh of hosts.

---

[1] Cf. T. Chary, op. cit., pp. 139ff.; M. Schmidt, Prophet und Tempel (1948), pp. 198–213, whose discussion of the Zechariah material centres in the Temple, but includes much more of a rather generalized nature on the meaning of the prophet's activity. For a note on J. D. Smart's interpretation of the prophecies of Haggai and Zechariah in relation to the Temple, cf. above p. 156 n. 15. For a different approach to ch. 4, cf. W. A. M. Beuken, op. cit., pp. 258–74.

Who are you, O great mountain? Before Zerubbabel
be a plain.
And he shall bring out the headstone with shouts of
'How beautiful it is!'[2]

The hands of Zerubbabel began this House
and his hands shall complete it.[3]
(Then you[4] will know that Yahweh of hosts sent me to you)

For who has despised the day of small things?
They shall rejoice to see the chosen stone in
the hand of Zerubbabel. (4.6b–10a)[5]

The setting of this group of sayings in the context of the lampstand

[2] K. Galling, *Studien*, p. 138, translates 'Glück zu' = good luck, Godspeed.

[3] Cf. A. Gelston, *VT* 16 (1966), pp. 232–5.

[4] The Hebrew has the masculine singular verb *yāda'tā*, which Galling, *Studien*,
p. 144, sees as referring to the 'remnant'. While the context suggests that a plural
verb would be more appropriate, the whole phrase is so clearly parenthetic that it
may be regarded rather as a comment (cf. 2.15 where the MT has *yāda'at*, the
feminine singular form, and 2.13 and 6.15 which have the plural form *y*e*da'tem*)
than as integrally related to its context. Its purpose appears to be to stress the
reality of the prophet's commission, and in this it takes its place alongside indications in Haggai (cf. 1.13) as also in Ezekiel (cf. e.g. 2.5), of the need for such confirmation. Such phrases correspond to the call narratives of earlier prophets which
may also be viewed as authenticating the prophet's word. Cf. also J. Bright, 'The
Prophetic Reminiscence', in *Biblical Essays* (*Proc. of Die Ou-Testamentiese Werkgemeenskap in Suid-Afrika*, 9, 1966, Potchefstroom, 1967), pp. 11–30.

[5] The text of this passage contains a number of peculiarities which make its
exact translation difficult. *har haggādōl* (4.7) may be simply an error due to haplography for *hāhār haggādōl*. *'et-hā'eben habbedīl* (4.10) is also odd. Should it be *habbādūl*
—'set apart' or *hammabdīl*—'which sets apart'? The point is not vital to the discussion, since it appears clear that some special stone is meant, and without precise
knowledge of the stage in the building intended we cannot know what is implied.
It is also possible that the text originally referred back to *'et-hā'eben hārō'šā* 'the headstone' in 4.7—again its precise nature is not clear, but its place as marking a climax
is indicated by the text—and that the word *habbedīl* is due to a miswriting of some
of the neighbouring consonants—*bydzrbbl*. For 'headstone' (? chief stone) the LXX
suggest the alternative of 'stone of possession' τὸν λίθον τῆς κληρονομίας = Heb. *y*e*rūšā*;
so cf. H. Frey, *Das Buch der Kirche in der Weltwende* (BAT 24, ⁴1957), p. 73, but this
probably represents an interpretative rendering, cf. K. Galling, *Studien*, p. 143 (who
cites for this view H. Junker, *Die zwölf kleinen Propheten* II [HSAT VIII 3.2, 1938],
p. 137).

Cf. also T. Chary, *op. cit.*, pp. 140f., who rearranges the verses in the order 8–10a +
6b–7 and suggests a comparison with Ezra 3 and I Esd. 6.18 for the subsequent
development of Zerubbabel's place in the tradition. The rearrangement offers
little help: it is simpler to recognize the combining here of separate elements.

K. Galling, *Studien*, pp. 138f., prefers in v. 7b to follow the LXX first person
form: 'I shall bring out . . .' as *lectio difficilior*, i.e. God himself will expose the
buried foundations of the Temple so that rebuilding can begin. On pp. 144f. he
interprets the second stone as linked to Joshua the priest and to his institution by
Zerubbabel. This does not appear to be provable.

vision—a vision which may well envisage the completed and restored Temple—suggests that here, as elsewhere in the prophecies of Zechariah, we have the gathering of earlier prophetic oracles designed in part to reinforce the prophet's claim to authority.[6] The completion of the Temple is here made the occasion by which men may know that Zechariah has been divinely sent. In other words, for Zechariah, as for Haggai, the rebuilding of the Temple is related to a new situation.

The sayings of this passage emphasize two points concerning the rebuilding of the Temple. (1) There is the reassurance that what is to be accomplished is to be in the power of the spirit of God.[7] This effectively removes all obstacles (v. 7—not perhaps to be interpreted too literally).[8] It offers encouragement to those who are depressed by their contrasting of the rebuilding with the past (cf. Hag. 2.3–5). It pledges the full restoration, made effective by the presence of God.[9] The situation indicated in Ezra 5–6 may also be part of what is implied. (2) On the other hand the actual completion is promised, and with this is associated the idea of the joy which the occasion provides. The promise of the completing of the work (v. 9) is here linked with two moments, the precise significance of which is not quite clear, because of our uncertainty about the references. But v. 7 would appear to be a reference to the climax of the rebuilding, the placing of the headstone. Verse 10 is less clear, because the phrase here

[6] Cf. K. Galling: 'Die Exilswende in der Sicht des Propheten Sacharja', *VT* 2 (1952), pp. 18–36, see pp. 26ff.; *Studien*, pp. 109–26, see pp. 117f., and further 'Zerubbabal und der Hohepriester beim Wiederaufbau des Tempels in Jerusalem', *ib.* pp. 127–48, see pp. 137ff., 144; L. G. Rignell, *Die Nachtgesichte des Sacharja* (Lund, 1950), p. 152.

[7] Cf. G. von Rad, *Theology* II, p. 285; *Der heilige Krieg im alten Israel* (ATANT 20, 1951), p. 66. Cf. K. Galling, *Studien*, pp. 141f., for the dynamic 'wind' of God, cf. next note; M. Schmidt, *op. cit.*, pp. 201f.

[8] The identifying of the 'mountain' may easily lead to extravagances of interpretation: so, for example, a hostile political power, cf. Jer. 51.24ff. (cf. the Targum and E. Sellin, *ZAW* 59 [1942/3], p. 70); L. Rost, 'Bemerkungen zu Sacharja 4' *ZAW* 63 (1951), pp. 216–21, has no doubt that the reference is to Persian power (p. 220); political obstruction (G. Adam Smith, *The Book of the Twelve Prophets* II [1898, 1928], p. 299); the heap of rubble in the Temple site (E. Sellin, *Das Zwölfprophetenbuch* (KAT 13, 1922), p. 503); the opposition of the 'Samaritan' authorities (K. Elliger, ATD 25, p. 118); a list of difficulties and the temptation to direct military action, cf. H. Frey, *op. cit.*, pp. 74f. For other comments cf. L. Rignell, *op. cit.*, pp. 155f., who himself sees here a reference to the world powers, now impotent. K. Galling, *Studien*, p. 140, compares Isa. 40.4, and considers that it can only refer to an actual mountain of rubble to be miraculously removed. T. Chary, *op. cit.*, p. 142, also compares Isa. 40.4.

[9] Cf. S. Mowinckel, *He that Cometh* (ET, 1956), p. 137.

tentatively translated 'chosen stone' is by no means certain in meaning. This rendering is an attempt to bring out the idea of *separation*, *dividing*, which appears to belong to the word *habbᵉdîl*,[10] but it is possible that in fact the term is a technical building term, and it is conceivable that the reference is to the same stone as in v. 17, marking the climax of the work, and that the two sayings are to that extent duplicates.

The other passage which deals with the rebuilding of the Temple is 6.9–15, which also appears to consist of various sayings, woven now into a particular incident, the performance of a significant enacted prophecy. In two sayings, in vv. 12 and 13, the promise that the rebuilding will be accomplished is again made, as in ch. 4. The first saying runs:

> Behold the man—Branch is his name.
> Where he is, there is flourishing.
> And he shall build the Temple of Yahweh. (v. 12)

> And *he* shall build the Temple of Yahweh
>   and *he* shall put on splendour
> And he shall sit to rule upon his throne
>   and there shall be a priest upon his throne
> And agreement shall subsist between the two. (v. 13)

The full interpretation of v. 13 belongs to a later part of our discussion.[11] For the moment we simply note two sayings which make the same point, though the first is linked to the assurance that the 'Branch' is the mediator of life and well-being, and so his function as builder of the Temple is intelligible.[12] The second starts from this point—the verbal linkage is no doubt a reason for the two standing together—and goes on to explain the consequences for the community. Together with these two sayings there is another in v. 15 which introduces a new point of significance:

The final line, not here quoted, of v. 15 must be considered later

> Those who are distant shall come in to build
>   the Temple of Yahweh
> (Then you [plural] will know that Yahweh of hosts
>   has sent me to you).

---

[10] Cf. T. Chary, *op. cit.*, p. 141. Cf. also p. 172 n. 5.

[11] Cf. below pp. 194ff.

[12] The saying appears to depend upon the interpretation of the name Zerubbabel —zēr-bābili—'offspring, or shoot, of Babylon', cf. J. J. Stamm, *Die akkadische Namengebung* (Leipzig, 1939), pp. 269f.; S. Mowinckel, *He that Cometh* (ET, 1956), pp. 160f.

(see p. 205); it bears a resemblance to other passages in Zechariah and also to Hag. 2.14. Again we note, as in ch. 4, that the rebuilding of the Temple is linked to the authenticity of the prophet's message. The rebuilding is also linked to the gathering of those who are far distant. Its placing serves to elaborate the prophetic symbol which involves men who have returned from the exile (vv. 10–11).

The interconnection between the rebuilding of the Temple and the establishment of the new age[13] is brought out in 1.16, and also in 8.9ff. I have elsewhere suggested that although this latter passage clearly contains original prophetic material, it is to be regarded rather as a general comment on the significance of the prophetic message—both of Haggai and Zechariah—than as necessarily part of the oracular material.[14] Quotations from the oracular material are made the occasion for a general reflection about the continued significance of the message. This interconnection is also implied in other sections, where the place of the 'Branch' is indicated, or where the restoration of Jerusalem—of which, as we may see in the opening of ch. 8, the Temple is the centre—is promised as the indication of the beginnings of that change of fortune which was to follow on the fulfilment of the seventy-year prophecy.

2. THE NEW COMMUNITY AND THE NEW AGE[15]

The idea of the new age, a complete change of fortune over against present conditions, is brought out in the opening chapters of Zechariah. The first vision, in 1.8ff. appears to concentrate on the point that this coming of the new age is not to be confused with the political events which are taking place.[16] The messengers are horse-

---

[13] Cf. L. Rost, ZAW 63 (1951), p. 221.

[14] Cf. JJS 3 (1952), pp. 151–6; W. A. M. Beuken, op. cit., pp. 156–73.

[15] Particular emphasis is given to these themes in the interpretation and comments of M. Bič, Das Buch Sacharja (1962), pp. 13–107; Die Nachtgesichte des Sacharja (BS 42, Neukirchen, 1964).

[16] The political background to this in the upheavals at the beginning of the reign of Darius I is discussed in K. Galling, Studien (1964), pp. 48ff.; cf. also P. R. Ackroyd, JNES 17 (1958), pp. 13ff. M. Bič, Das Buch Sacharja (1962), p. 22, stresses the presence here of mythological elements, the transformation of the hostile deep into a place for myrtle trees, linked, in his view, with the New Year celebration (cf. Neh. 8.15). If such elements are to be detected, they should perhaps be viewed rather as metaphors surviving from older thought; but the line between metaphor and live belief is rarely to be drawn with certainty. On this vision, cf. W. A. M. Beuken, op. cit., pp. 239–44.

men, and in this feature of the vision there may be a reminiscence of the Persian post-system. But it would seem more probable that the more fundamental element in the formation of this vision is the conception of the heavenly court with the attendant 'sons of God' (*benē* *'elōhīm*) as in Job 1 and 2. The two portrayals are not identical; here all the messengers 'patrol' (*hithallēk*) the world, whereas in Job it is only the Satan who is specifically indicated as doing so and nothing is said of the duties of the others. In both there appears to be a reminiscence of the summoning to report of subordinate divine beings—originally the lesser deities of the pantheon (cf. Ps. 82 and Deut. 32.8 reading *'ēl* (cf. LXX) for *yisrā'ēl*)—to whom supervisory duties have been assigned (cf. also Dan. 10.13, 20f.). They have brought the message that the world is now restored to quiet:

> We have patrolled the world, and see, the
> whole world is dwelling in quietness.

> Then the angel of Yahweh replied: O Yahweh of hosts, how long will
> you not show pity to Jerusalem and the cities of Judah against which
> you have shown anger now for seventy years? (1.11–12)

To this complaint at the apparent delay in divine action, the answer comes in a direct word of Yahweh to the angel, and the directness reveals the stress which is laid upon this, the really significant moment of the vision and its interpretation.

> Then Yahweh answered the angel who was talking with me with
> words of good omen, words of consolation.

> So the angel who was talking with me said:
> Proclaim: Thus says Yahweh of hosts,
>   I am jealous for Jerusalem and for Zion with great jealousy.
>   With great wrath I am wrathful against the nations which sit
>   quietly.
>   For I was wrathful only a little, but they multiplied[17] calamity.
>   (vv. 13–15)

The wrath of God against the nations is also the theme of the second vision, and a parallel may be seen between the presentation of the first and the second.

---

[17] *'zr* II = to be copious (Arab *ghazura*), cf. I. Eitan, *A Contribution to Hebrew Lexicography* (New York, 1924), pp. 8f.—proposing hiph'īl *hēm he'ezīrū l'rā'ā*—identical consonants with MT, and treating *l'* as indicating an accusative. This seems better than either the conventional 'help on' or G. R. Driver's suggestion of *zāre'ū*—sow, plot (evil), in *JTS* 41 (1940), p. 173, which is hardly strong enough in meaning.

The first vision and its interpretation are followed immediately by a further proclamation, possibly a fragment of prophecy from another date which is here made into a comment on the declaration of Yahweh's consoling purpose and his attitude to the nations.

> Therefore thus says Yahweh:
> I have returned to Jerusalem in mercy;
> my house shall be built in it
> —oracle of Yahweh of hosts—
> and a measuring line shall be stretched out over Jerusalem. (v. 16)

It is Yahweh's return which makes possible the restoration of his Temple. In this, Zechariah appears to make a point rather different from that of Haggai.[18] But in fact the two approaches are obverse and reverse of the same coin. Haggai's stress lies upon the need for rebuilding, because only thus can the willingness of Yahweh to bless be appropriated by the community. Zechariah's stress lies upon the reality of God's intentions, which find their correlative in the rebuilding which is made possible by his will. Neither prophet loses sight of the underlying truth that the rebuilding of the Temple, even if it seems to be undertaken as a result of human effort, is in fact brought about by the working of the spirit of God.[19] Whether we see this in Zechariah's 'Not by might, not by force, but by my spirit' (Zech. 4.6) or in Haggai's exhortations to the community not to be afraid when confronted with the task (Hag. 2.4–5), we may recognize that the impetus comes from God through the prophets. This same emphasis is laid by the Chronicler in Ezra 5 and 6.

The rebuilding of the Temple and city in 1.16 is followed by a parallel statement in the next verse.

> Again proclaim:
> Thus says Yahweh of hosts:
> My cities shall again overflow with plenty.[20]
> Yahweh will again comfort Zion;
> He will again choose Jerusalem. (1.17)

The restoration of Jerusalem will carry with it a blessing for the

---

[18] Cf. above pp. 155ff.

[19] We may trace stages in the development of this thinking. In I Kings 6.7 the stress is on the absence of workmen's activity on the Temple site. In Ezekiel 40ff., the rebuilding is implicitly the work of God and his divine agents (cf. 40.2ff.; 43.10ff.). Ps. 127.1 makes the same point in theological form.

[20] For a discussion of the interpretation of this phrase, cf. Rignell, *op. cit.*, pp. 53ff.; Rignell prefers a rendering: 'While my cities are still deprived of plenty . . .' which equally emphasizes the expected divine intervention.

whole land, and although the Temple is not here mentioned, it is clear (cf. ch. 8) that it is the centrality of the Temple which makes Jerusalem meaningful.[21] The whole city is in fact sanctified by the very possession of the Temple within it. Holy Temple, holy city, holy land—the ambiguous use of the term 'place' allows of all three possibilities[22]—are all in fact extensions of the central blessing which comes from the shrine which God chooses as his dwelling.

The second vision (2.1–4) is presented in a parallel structure. The vision itself parallels the idea of Yahweh's wrath against the nations in 1.15. To that general statement it adds the more specific and yet at the same time more universal judgement upon the 'four nations'. To identify, popular as this exegetical activity may often have been, as for example in Daniel and in the interpreters of Daniel,[23] is not here of significance. For the 'four nations', like the 'four chariots' of 6.1ff., where the linkage with the winds of heaven is actually made, more probably signify the totality of the hostile nations of the world.[24] There is an anticipation in this of the message of salvation to all nations in 8.20–23. Ideas which are to be found in the royal psalms and in Deutero-Isaiah of the sovereignty of Yahweh over all nations are here brought into relationship with the immediate political situation, but without being limited to it. Those that oppress—and the commentary in 2.10ff. elaborates and makes more precise by referring to Babylon—are all to be subdued, terrified, awed by the power of Yahweh which operates against them.

This vision is then linked with the third, which follows without intervening comment. The reason for this would seem to be that there is here, as in ch. 1, a parallel drawn between that 'external' action which affects the nations and the 'internal' action towards Jerusalem for which it also paves the way. There is great vividness and emphasis in the promise to Jerusalem:

Then I looked up and there was a man carrying a measuring cord in his hand. So I said: Where are you going? He said to me: To measure Jerusalem to see what is its breadth and length.

But look now: the angel who was talking with me was coming out, and another angel was coming out to meet him. And he said to him: Run and tell this young man: Jerusalem is to be an open city because of the

21 Cf. R. E. Clements, *God and Temple* (1965), pp. 124f.
22 Cf. above p. 156 n. 11.
23 Cf. Dan. 2.36–43; 7. On this point, cf. Rignell, *op. cit.*, pp. 61f.
24 So too M. Bič, *Das Buch Sacharja* (1962), p. 27.

number of its inhabitants, both men and cattle. And I will be to it—
oracle of Yahweh—a wall of fire all around, and I will be in its midst
to give glory. (2.5–9)

The subduing of the nations now forms a fitting preliminary to this,
although not presumably originally directly related to it. There
appears to be no question here of polemic against an attempt to rebuild the walls of Jerusalem,[25] but simply a message of the nature of
the new city, which will spread abroad in the land, protected by the
presence of God himself, who being in the city—in the Temple
which is his dwelling—gives glory to it, that is, he makes of it a place
in which the glory of his presence is known.[26]

As in ch. 6, the promise to Jerusalem and of rebuilding is then
linked with a summons to the people who are still scattered to join
with the community at home, and the promises to Jerusalem are
enriched by the prospect of a total new life.

> Ho there, ho there, flee from the north country[27]
> —oracle of Yahweh.
> For like[28] the four winds of heaven I have caused
>   you to take wing[29]—oracle of Yahweh.
> Ho there, O Zion, escape, you who are dwelling
>   in the realm of Babylon.[30] (vv. 10–11)

It is significant that the sense of belonging to the community even

---

[25] On this point, cf. the discussion in T. H. Robinson and F. Horst, *Die zwölf
kleinen Propheten* (HAT 14, [2]1954), p. 225, though Horst implies a contrast between
Zechariah's 'exclusively religious' judgement and Zerubbabel's political concerns
(cf. 4.6b) which cannot be clearly found in the texts. For a more political interpretation cf. P. Haupt, 'The Visions of Zechariah', *JBL* 32 (1913), pp. 107–22, see pp.
109f.; D. Winton Thomas, *IB* 6 (1956), p. 1064. Cf. also W. A. M. Beuken, *op. cit.*,
pp. 244–8.

[26] Cf. Ezek. 40–48 (cf. above pp. 111f.).

[27] On 'flight' cf. K. Galling, *Studien* (1964), p. 55, and R. Bach, *Die Aufforderungen
zur Flucht und zum Kampf im alttestamentlichen Prophetenspruch* (WMANT 9, 1962),
pp. 19f., who aligns the text with the form which he detects in similar utterances
in Jeremiah.

[28] So MT. LXX suggests *mē'arba'* = 'from the four winds'.

[29] Cf. G. R. Driver, *JTS* 32 (1931), p. 252, adducing a meaning 'spread out'
for *prs*. Cf. Rignell, *op. cit.*, p. 80 for a similar rendering.

[30] The MT has *yōšebet bat-bābel*. The word *bat*, 'daughter', may be due to a
dittograph of the last two consonants of *yōšebet*. But whether we read the longer
or shorter text, the phrase has essentially the same meaning; similar phrases appear
in Jer. 46.19 and 48.18 denoting 'the local population', cf. *KBL* p. 159 and
compare also the use of the phrase *bat-ṣiyyōn* in 2.14. On the phrase *bat-ṣiyyōn* and
others like it as appositional genitives, cf. W. F. Stinespring, 'No daughter of Zion:
A Study of the Appositional Genitive in Hebrew Grammar', *Encounter* 26 (1965),
pp. 133–41.

while in exile in Babylon is expressed so strongly that the exiles can be described as 'Zion who dwells in Babylon'. This suggests the same sense of the incompleteness of the re-establishment and of the rebuilding which is envisaged by the summons to those who are afar off to come and assist in the rebuilding (6.15).

> For thus says Yahweh of hosts:
> (It is he whose glory commissioned me *or*
> By a way of glory he commissioned me to the nations
>   which were plundering you)[31]
> He who touches you touches the apple of my eye.
>
> See I am about to threaten them with my hand;
>   they shall be plunder to their subjects
> (You will know that Yahweh of hosts has sent me). (2.12–13)

A twofold refrain here emphasizes (cf. 6.15, etc.) that the prophet is acting in the divine commission (cf. Hag. 1.12ff.)—the obscurity of the text of the first of these statements unfortunately leaves it somewhat in doubt as to what is its precise intention, though the general sense is clear. The protection of the exiles and the subordination of the hostile power—here perhaps directly with reference to the situation in Babylon in the beginning of Darius I's reign—are demonstrable, presumably because at the moment at which the words were given their present context, either by the prophet or by some other, the fulfilment of them in Darius' favourable policy and the rebuilding of the Temple allowed the confirmation of the prophet's position to be recognized.

> Raise the shout of joy and rejoice, inhabitants of Zion (Maiden Zion)
> For I am about to come and dwell in your midst—oracle of Yahweh.
>   (2.14)

[31] This notoriously problematic passage cannot be satisfactorily explained. Vriezen's ingenious suggestion (*OTS* 5 [1948], pp. 88f.) that *'aḥar kābōd* means 'This phrase should stand after the word *kābōd*' i.e. at 2.9, is quite unprovable. The purely conjectural *'ªšer kᵉbōdō* 'whose glory sent me' is not easy to explain on textual grounds. The suggestion *'ōraḥ kābōd* is perhaps the most ingenious (cf. BH³ 'num legendum'), and a comparison is immediately suggested with Ps. 73.24 where a similar proposal has been made (cf. D. Winton Thomas, *The Text of the Revised Psalter* [London, 1963], p. 30). Unfortunately, such a double occurrence of the same textual error does not increase confidence in the correctness of the proposal. Yet an allusion to the 'way of glory' would be very appropriate here. It is by a 'way of glory', a great processional route that the exiles are to return (cf. Isa. 35.8; 40.3). Cf. S. Mowinckel, *The Psalms in Israel's Worship* I (ET, Oxford, 1962), pp. 170f. The explanation of *'aḥar* = with (cf. *KBL* p. 32; R. B. Y. Scott, *JTS* 50 (1949), pp. 178f., who includes this passage) is attractive. The Ugaritic parallel adduced by M. Dahood, *Biblica* 43 (1962), pp. 363f. is possible but not certain, *'aḥar* in the passages compared has more the sense of 'in company with', which is not quite suitable with *kābōd*.

The welcoming of Yahweh with the cultic shout appropriate to his coming shows that in the description of the new age which has now come into being the ideas of the theophany found so frequently in the Psalms are given a historical and suprahistorical context. Immediately, the recognition of the entry of God into his possession is extended with the realization that this will involve not only his own people but the nations which recognize what he is because of what he has done:

> Many nations will be joined to Yahweh in that day.
> And they will become as a people for me.[32]
> and I will dwell[33] in your midst
> (Then you will know that Yahweh of hosts has sent me to you). (2.15)

The 'you' and 'your' here are feminine singular, and since the immediate context of v. 14 suggests that this means 'the maiden of Zion', we have a picture of the people, gathered around Yahweh in Zion, forming the centre of a great concourse of nations who have come to acknowledge him.

> So Yahweh will take into possession Judah as his property
> upon the holy ground,
> and he will again choose Jerusalem. (2.16)

The implication is that with Yahweh himself being present in his Temple in Zion, the whole land—the actual ground itself—becomes holy. The shrine is, as it were, no longer large enough; the whole land in which it is set partakes of its holiness, not because holiness is contagious (cf. Hag. 2.10ff.) but because Yahweh is there.[34]

> Silence, all mankind, before Yahweh,
> For he arouses himself from his holy dwelling (2.17).

The final words of the section contain a cultic refrain.[35] The presence of God is real; the realization of this, made now or imposed upon all the world, must bring a sense of awe at what he is.

[32] Cf. also K. L. Schmidt, op. cit. (p. 161 n. 40) p. 226, on this verse (wrongly quoted as 2.1) and on 1.12f., 16 and 8.3.

[33] LXX suggests wešākenū—'and they shall dwell'. Either reading seems equally appropriate.

[34] Again here we may trace stages in the idea. Cf. I Kings 8.64, where the centre of the court is consecrated because the altar is too small, and Zech. 14.20–21, where the vessels throughout the land must be holy. Cf. below pp. 249f.

[35] Cf. Hab. 2.20; Zeph. 1.7. On the whole passage, cf. W. A. M. Beuken, op. cit., pp. 317–30.

A similar pattern is presented in ch. 6. Here the vision of the four chariots ushers in a symbolic action which, as we have seen,[36] is linked closely with the rebuilding of the Temple. The vision itself is not clear at every point. In particular, the functions of the chariots are obscured by the complexity of the text in vv. 6–7 and by the ambiguity of the wording in v. 8.

> The one with black horses is going out to the north-land and the white ones went out after[37] them; and the dappled ones went out to the south-land.

> The steeds went out intending to go to patrol in the earth. And he said: Go and patrol the earth.
> So they patrolled the earth.

> Then he made me proclaim, and spoke to me thus:
> See, these that are going out to the north-land have caused my spirit to rest upon the north-land. (vv. 6–8)

It is not certain whether both black and white horses are intended to be described as going to the north-land. Possibly the text is in error and it is only the black which go there, while the white go to the west.[38] It is tempting also to complete the sequence and add a reference to the fourth chariot. The same kind of uncertainty affects the translation of v. 8, where it is clear that the climax has been reached. The general picture of the patrolling of the earth presents the sovereignty of God over all nations. But the particular point of concern is the message which is given with emphasis concerning the chariot and horses (black and white, or black) which go to the north-land, i.e. Babylon.[39] Does the 'cause to rest' mean literally 'cause it to rest, to settle', or does it mean 'give it peace, satisfaction'? The latter, appropriate to the black colour of the horses, if it is proper to

[36] Cf. pp. 174f. On this vision, cf. W. A. M. Beuken, *op. cit.*, pp. 249–52.
[37] Or 'with them', cf. R. B. Y. Scott (*op. cit.*, p. 180 n. 31).
[38] Accepting the commonly favoured emendation of *'el-'aḥᵃrēhem* to *'el-'aḥᵃrē hayyām* 'towards the sea'.
[39] It is difficult to follow N. H. Snaith, *VTS* 14 (1967), pp. 247f., when he argues that 'north' = 'Israel, the Palestinian Jews' and that 'south' = 'the Judaeans, the "Babylonians", the returned exiles'. His argument depends on his whole view of the nature of the division within the community, which he traces also in the analysis of other passages in Zech. 1–8. His contention that in Zechariah, Zerubbabel and Joshua do not appear together (though he admits, p. 247 n., that there has been editorial work to alter this), leads him to suppose an earlier state of contention, followed by a *rapprochement* reflected in their appearance together in Haggai. This seems to do considerable violence to the texts and to make for a very unnatural interpretation.

lay stress on this, would indicate judgement for Babylon. God's anger is appeased by bringing disaster there, and this would then pave the way for the returned exiles and the performing of the symbol in vv. 9–15. The alternative would mean that the spirit of God is brought upon the exiles themselves, and so they are inspired to return.[40] A clear and intelligible link with the following verses is here too supplied, so that no argument can be derived from the question of the interrelationship of the two passages. If both black and white horses go to the north, as the Massoretic text now implies, it is possible that the ambiguity of the verbal form in v. 8 is deliberate, and that both judgement and promise are intended.[41] Perhaps so great a subtlety is not due to the prophet but to the later copyists who could then be considered responsible for the present text with its suggestion that both are implied.

The linkage with vv. 9–15 is nevertheless clear, and parallels to either interpretation can be found elsewhere, as for example in 2.1–4 with 2.5ff., or in 1.10–17. The pattern resembles that of the first two chapters in that the idea of rebuilding, in 6.9–15 more explicitly tied to the re-ordering of the community's life, is built on to a section dealing with the preparations for it. In the rather different emphases of ch. 3 and 4, the same kind of thought is also to be found.

The material of these two chapters is much richer, and although there are clear linkages to the thought of the new age and its ordering, both sections provide further information about the nature of the new age and about the mechanism by which it is established, as well as introducing an element which is different, namely the cleansing and acceptance of the community.

The interpretation of 3.1–7 has been the subject of much discussion.[41a] But it appears clear that the real emphasis is laid in v. 2:

> Then he showed me Joshua the high priest standing before the angel of Yahweh, and the Satan was standing on his right hand side to make the accusation against him.
> But Yahweh said to the Satan:
> May Yahweh rebuke you, O Satan,
> May Yahweh who chooses Jerusalem rebuke you.
> Is not this a brand rescued from the burning? (3.1–2)

[40] Cf. T. Chary, op. cit., p. 143, suggesting a link with 6.15 and interpreting: 'They will cause Yahweh's spirit to rest' i.e. so as to stimulate the rebuilding of the Temple.
[41] Cf. M. Bič, Das Buch Sacharja (1962), p. 77.
[41a] On the whole chapter, cf. W. A. M. Beuken, op. cit., pp. 282–303.

Again at this point (cf. 1.13), it is God himself who intervenes in the vision, to make clear that the accusation brought against Joshua is not to be sustained. Since we are not told the nature of the accusation, we cannot arrive at any precise conclusion about the situation. But the words of God in v. 2 help to point in the right direction. Here the rebuking of the Satan—in other words the indication that his accusation, justified or not, is not to be allowed in the court—is made specifically by 'Yahweh who chooses Jerusalem'. The expressive phrase is pointless unless it contains the main emphasis of the vision. It is the God who, as indicated in ch. 1–2, has declared his intention of restoring his city and taking up his place there again. So here it is clear that the accusation against Joshua is not to be interpreted in personal terms, but as one directed against him as representative of the whole community.[42] The following phrase points in the same direction. The 'fire' (*'ēš*) here clearly refers to the disaster of the exile, and a comparison of the parallel in Amos 4.11,[43] together with other passages in which the word '*serēpā*' is used,[44] also points to a sense of total desolation rather than of ordinary fire. The deliverance of Joshua is not a personal matter; it is the rescue of the community of the restoration which has taken place and is here declared even more clearly.

The events of the vision confirm this further.

> Now Joshua was clothed in filthy garments and was standing before the angel. So he (God, or the angel) addressed those who were standing before him:

[42] For other types of interpretation, cf. the commentaries and cf. also L. G. Rignell, *op. cit.*, p. 107, for a brief summary, as well as an outline of mythological types of interpretation, particularly by comparison with the Adapa myth. J. D. Smart, *History and Theology in Second Isaiah* (1965), p. 285, retains a personal interpretation. He points to Ezra 10.18 for a tradition that the sons of Joshua had married foreign women. He fails, however, to note that 10.18–22 contains a number of persons from various priestly families, all accused of the same sin. To interpret Zech. 3 narrowly in relation to this is surely wrong, and to say further 'The likelihood is that in the period before 621 BC Joshua had engaged in some syncretistic practices that are condemned by Second Isaiah' (*ib.*) is unwarranted speculation. A. C. Welch, *Post-exilic Judaism* (1935), pp. 172–84, also offers a speculative interpretation, linked with his general understanding of the exilic age, portraying Joshua here as unacceptable to the priestly order which had kept the religious life alive after 587.

[43] The Amos passage has different wording for what may be a proverbial phrase. Amos 4.11: '*ūd muṣṣāl misserēpā*; Zech. 3.2: '*ūd muṣṣāl mē'ēš*. Cf. S. Talmon, 'Synonymous readings in the Old Testament', *Script. Hier.* 8 (1961), pp. 335–83; see pp. 359–62 for examples of other phrases in which synonymous nouns are used interchangeably.

[44] E.g. Lev. 10.6; Num. 19.6, 17; Isa. 9.4; 64.10; Jer. 51.25.

Remove from him his filthy garments.
To him he said:
See, I have removed from you your guilt, and I will clothe you in clean garments.
Then I said:
Let them put a clean turban upon his head.
So they put a clean turban upon his head and clothed him in (clean) garments. (3.3–5) [45]

It is not really relevant to the discussion of the meaning of the passage to determine whether or not there is here a normal ritual being interpreted—to which analogies have been found, rather remotely in the Adapa myth. [46] The changing of garments—from filthy, i.e. mourning garments, appropriate to a moment of desolation, to clean garments, suggestive in the use of *maḥªlāṣōt* in v. 4 of festive raiment, appropriate to high-priestly vestments which, as Haran has shown [47] bear so great a weight of significance—is a natural symbol, obviously closely related to ritual practice. The acceptability of priest, and hence of people, before God is bound up with the proper clothing which expresses the worship which is to be offered. [48] Special emphasis is then laid upon the turban. It is, of course, not difficult to suppose that the first person verbal form at the beginning of v. 5 is an error for the third person form. Its omission in the LXX is hardly useful evidence, since the omission could readily have been made either because the MT wording seemed a little awkward or because the third person form was repetitive. As the MT stands, the first person form is striking. [49] It suddenly introduces a new element into the vision, the personal intervention of the prophet himself in its events. Just as elsewhere emphasis is laid by the intervention of God, [50]

[45] The last phrase of v. 5 is omitted by LXX and hence by some commentators. It may be better to treat it as the opening of v. 6. Cf. below p. 186.

[46] Cf. above n. 42.

[47] M. Haran, 'The Complex of Ritual Acts performed inside the Tabernacle', *Script. Hier.* 8 (1961), pp. 272–302, see pp. 279–85.

[48] R. de Vaux, *Ancient Israel* (ET, 1961), p. 399. Cf. M. Bič, *Das Buch Sacharja*, pp. 46f., who suggests a penitential ritual, in which in effect the post-exilic high priest is taking over the function of the pre-exilic king. His stress is equally therefore on the representative function of Joshua here.

[49] Cf. L. G. Rignell, *op. cit.*, pp. 116f. Cf. 2.6 where there is a first person intervention. Rignell's argument here is weakened by the recognition that he is in fact all through his discussion working on the assumption that the MT will be proved to be correct in every detail, which is an absurd position to hold. In any given case, it is difficult to determine whether he has really found a good explanation of the present form of the text or has been over-influenced by his conservative outlook. His caution in accepting emendations is, of course, welcome.

[50] Cf. 3.2; 1.13.

so here the emphasis appears to be made by the change to the first person. If the text is correct, then the placing of the turban is obviously a moment of special significance.

This is borne out by the subsequent passage in vv. 8–10, where there is mention of a stone linked to the idea of the removal of sin and guilt. The description of the high-priestly turban in Ex. 28.36ff. shows its connection with guilt and sanctification. It is actually the gold engraved plate which is fastened to the turban upon the forehead of the high priest which is linked with this. But clearly we may associate this in a derivative fashion with the turban too. This, as Haran states, is 'not so much to awaken divine remembrance as to evoke divine *grace*'.[51]

To this vision there is linked a series of further oracular utterances concerning the high priest, his functions and his relationship to the figure of the Branch. It is appropriate to treat these as separate units, linked to the same general line of thought, but not providing precise comment upon it. In fact if we accept the first person form in v. 5, there need be no surprise that this vision has no interpretation as such (the same is true of the visions in ch. 5). Here instead of the prophet putting questions to the accompanying angelic being, we find him intervening with his own comment, just as in 2.6 he intervenes to ask what the man with the measuring line is doing. This may suggest that the symbolism was obvious enough. The changing of the garments, the declaration of forgiveness, clearly applicable to the whole community, evokes simply the culminating demand for the turban without which the ritual cannot be performed.

The oracles which follow are partly more personal to the functions of the high priest, and partly related to the wider issues of the new age which is undoubtedly to be linked to this cleansing symbol. First there is a message to the high priest, proclaiming the nature and conditions of his functioning:

> Now the angel of Yahweh was standing there, and the angel of Yahweh adjured Joshua thus:
> Thus says Yahweh of hosts:
> If you will walk in my ways and will keep my ritual; then you will yourself govern my house and guard my courts.[52]
> And I will grant you right of access among those who are standing here. (3.5b–7)

[51] M. Haran, *Script. Hier.* 8 (1961), p. 285.
[52] Plural, cf. T. Chary, *op. cit.*, p. 148 n., who suggests that this form, rare in the pre-exilic period, points to the influence of Ezekiel's ideas of establishing purity by the enforcing of restrictive barriers.

Interpretation is complicated by the uncertainty as to where in v. 7 a division should be made between protasis and apodosis in the conditional sentence. It is possible—and exegetically justified—to regard the first four clauses as all conditional and so to render the lines: 'If you will walk in my ways and will keep my ritual and will yourself govern my house and guard my courts, then . . .'. This lays stress upon the variety of activities of the high priest, together with the broadening of the conditions upon which access is granted to the heavenly court. The alternative is perhaps to be preferred. The third clause begins very emphatically with w*gam-'attā tādīn, and although this can be taken to continue 'im, it may better be thought to introduce a firm promise.[53] Obedience and faithfulness in the performance of the ritual are tied to the establishment of the high priest as ruler of the temple.[54] This is a firm statement, perhaps designed in the spirit of Ezekiel to obviate any intervention of the secular power in the management of the temple affairs. This would be important in view of what appears elsewhere about the double leadership of the community.[55] But a further emphasis is laid. The high priest is granted access to the heavenly court. It is an emphasis which is paralleled in the various descriptions of the functions of the high priest, acting as intercessor on behalf of the people in P. It also introduces an important correlation between the heavenly court in which the acquittal of Joshua has taken place and the courts of the Temple which is the dwelling place of God by his own choice.[56] Furthermore, we have a link with that conception which is found in the earlier prophets of the revealing of the divine will to them not simply in terms of vision or auditory experience but by direct entry into the heavenly council, the sōd of Yahweh.[57] Ps. 99.6 shows us (Moses and) Aaron as pre-eminent among the priests and Samuel as pre-eminent among the intercessors[58] (possibly with prophetic function specially in mind), but continues by showing that Moses, Aaron and Samuel are all known as intercessors, who hear the word of God

[53] Difference of interpretation is to be found already in the versions, cf. L. G. Rignell, op. cit., pp. 122f.
[54] Cf. Ezek. 45 and P in Ex. 28.29f.; Num. 27.18ff.
[55] Cf. pp. 188ff. on 3.8 and on ch. 4 and 6.
[56] Cf. R. E. Clements, God and Temple (1965), esp. ch. 1.
[57] Cf. Jer. 23.22; Amos 3.7. Also I Kings 22 and Isa. 6 for a general description of such entry into the heavenly court.
[58] So translating b*kōh°nāw and b*qōr'ē š*mō as beth essentiae—i.e. expressing priority. Cf. A. R. Johnson, Sacral Kingship (Cardiff, 1955), p. 62 n. 4; (²1967), p. 71 n. 2.

when they call upon him. That separation of the functions of priest and prophet which is convenient for purposes of description is in fact never a complete separation. The historical development shows a close interweaving of the two types of function which are associated with the two figures, and reveals in particular that the greater emphasis on the priest which marks the post-exilic period does not so much imply the dying out of prophecy as its closer integration into the established order. Since it is of the essence of established orders to become stiff and arid, it is not surprising that at a later stage new 'prophetic' movements emerged to criticize in some measure but also to mediate a new and living spirit of religious faith.

The second oracular addition to the vision of ch. 3 is in v. 8:

> Hear now, Joshua the high priest, you and your associates who stand before you:
> These are men of portent.

A similar expression to this is used in Isa. 8.18, where the prophet and his 'children' are described as signs and portents. The interpretation of this passage is relevant to that of Zechariah. Two possible lines of understanding are available for the Isaiah saying, depending upon whether the term $y^e l\bar{a}d\bar{i}m$ is taken to mean 'children' in the literal sense or 'disciples'. If 'children', then the prophet and the two children[59] mentioned in ch. 7 and 8, Shear-jashub and Maher-shalal-hash-baz, are signs of what is to come. The only certain point here is that the second child clearly refers to disaster, and we may therefore not unreasonably suppose that the first also indicated this originally. The remnant must be in some measure the sequel to disaster, in negative rather than in positive terms. If 'disciples' are meant, then we have a closer analogy to the Zechariah passage, though the message still includes disaster. As in the previous verses there is an allusion to the preservation of the prophetic message—presumably so that when the events to which it refers take place its relevance can be understood (cf. 8.1ff. and 30.8)[60]—so the disciples

---

[59] Conceivably we may add the third child Immanuel of 7.14 if the view is accepted that this too is the prophet's child. (Cf. e.g. N. K. Gottwald, 'Immanuel as the Prophet's Son', *VT* 8 [1958], pp. 36–47.) A full discussion of this question as of the other problems of interpretation of ch. 7 and 8 of Isaiah would be out of place here.

[60] Cf. D. R. Jones, 'The Traditio of the Oracles of Isaiah of Jerusalem', *ZAW* 67 (1955), pp. 226–46, see pp. 230–7; P. R. Ackroyd, *ASTI* 1 (1962), pp. 7–23, esp. pp. 14ff.

and their master are guarantees of the future, and we may perhaps rightly see here an allusion to something more than disaster, namely the sequel to it in terms of promise.

The Zechariah saying runs parallel to this. The existence of the priestly order is a divine sign of the favour which God is about to show to his people. Nowack,[61] inserting 4.6b–10a between vv. 7 and 8 here, suggests that Joshua and his colleagues are signs of the Temple building. But it is unnecessary to make such a transposition. The existence of the priesthood is clearly linked to the existence and restoration of the Temple. The placing of the passage alongside the vision and the oracle of vv. 6–7 makes the same general point. The divine favour is not to be so narrowly limited; it refers—as we shall see in vv. 8b and 9–10—to the whole restoration of people and land, linked to the introduction of a figure who represents that favour.

Rignell suggests that the priests are witnesses of the prophet's earlier words.[62] They can testify to what he said concerning the Branch, for when the saying was uttered, Zerubbabel was not yet active. There is analogy here to the Isaiah passage. Yet one may wonder whether this is quite the full meaning of the use of the word *mōpēt*, 'portent'. Joshua and his associates are not simply there to bear witness; they are themselves, by their very presence, signs of something which is to take place. We learn what that is from two sayings which follow:

I am about to bring in my servant Branch. (8b)

See the stone which I have set before Joshua: upon the stone are seven facets.[63] See I am cutting its engraving—oracle of Yahweh of hosts— and I will remove the guilt of that land in a single day (*or* upon a certain day). (9)

On this a final comment is made:

On that day—oracle of Yahweh of hosts—each man will invite his companion to come under the vine and the fig tree. (10)

The first two sayings—whether they should be separated or not hardly affects their interpretation—point to the twofold leadership

---

[61] W. Nowack, *Die kleinen Propheten übersetzt und erklärt* (Göttingen, [3]1922), p. 342.

[62] *Op. cit.*, p. 126.

[63] A. E. Rüthy, ' "Sieben Augen auf einem Stein" ', *TZ* 13 (1959), pp. 523–9, suggests *ᵃwōnīm*—guilt, sevenfoldness indicating completeness; but this appears to be merely ingenious.

of the community which is so clearly described in ch. 4 and 6. The presence of Joshua and his associates foreshadows the appointment of this royal figure—for the term servant here is clearly technical and the use of the word *ṣemaḥ*, Branch,[64] also indicates royal dignity. The identification with Zerubbabel is not here made, but is clear from the collocation of 6.12f. and 4.6*b*–10*a*. We may appropriately parallel this with the oracle in Hag. 2.20–23, and suggest that here again, with different terminology, the nature of Zerubbabel's real purpose is being made clear to him. The appointment of Zerubbabel to a position of authority by the Persian government may be seen in a twofold manner. On the one hand, the Persians commissioned him to undertake certain responsibilities. On the other hand, the restoration of the Jewish community, which is one of those responsibilities, clearly means something different to the community itself from what it means to the Persians. To the Persians it is a matter of restoring of order, conciliation of a subject people, establishment of a useful outpost on the route to Egypt. But to the community itself it is properly seen as the fulfilment of divine promise, and, no doubt with many differing shades of interpretation, as the means by which the purpose of God not only for his own people but also for the world is being brought about.[65] That larger context is very evident in the Zechariah oracles, particularly in ch. 8.

The first saying in 3.8*b* is immediately followed by the second which points to the place of the high priest Joshua, and in its rather obscure allusion to the stone with seven facets shows his function as being linked with the removal of guilt. The many and varied interpretations of the stone do not need to be discussed here,[66] since the point of significance is clearly the removal of guilt, and this suggests

[64] Cf. Jer. 23.5; 33.15—both royal passages with reference to the future, and paralleled by the alternative term *ḥōṭer* in Isa. 11.1. How much stress should be laid on the difference in the word used? S. Talmon's discussion of synonyms in *Script. Hier.* 8 (1961), pp. 335–83, illustrates from parallel passages that synonyms could be substituted. The passages cited here are not strictly parallel, but they are sufficiently related for it to be reasonable to suppose that no difference of meaning is implied. As in Amos 4.11 and Zech. 3.2 (cf. p. 184), a proverbial expression may underlie the present form of the material. Cf. also S. Mowinckel, *He that Cometh* (ET, 1956), pp. 19f., 160f.

[65] Cf. S. Mowinckel, *He that Cometh* (ET, 1956), pp. 119ff. We may compare the appointment of Nehemiah and that of Ezra. For the Persians these were no doubt sound political moves. To the Jewish community the hand of God was clearly at work. Cf. H. Cazelles, 'La mission d'Esdras', *VT* 4 (1954), pp. 113–40, esp. the summary on pp. 139f. (Cf. above pp. 164f.)

[66] For a summary cf. L. G. Rignell, *op. cit.*, pp. 130ff.

—as does the relationship of the stone to the high priest—that there is here an allusion to the stone in the high-priestly turban (Ex. 28.36–38). The engraving on this stone—*Holy to Yahweh*, or simply *To Yahweh*—is there linked with cleansing from guilt; and elsewhere, in Lev. 4.6, 17; 16.14ff., the number seven appears in a similar context.[67]

The two prophecies together are commented upon in v. 10. The outcome, so this suggests, of the appearance of the Branch and the setting of the stone of atonement before Joshua is the establishment of the new age. The technical 'on that day' points to this, and so too the reference to vine and fig tree which, in I Kings 5.5 and Micah 4.4, are the signs of the blessedness of an age, in the one case that of Solomon, in the other case of the future,[68] in which all men live both in peace and prosperity, in what appears to be the worship of a perpetual autumnal festival. The new age is to be one of perpetual worship of the God who has established it.[69]

The immediate sequel to these sayings in ch. 4 has, as we have already seen, been complicated by the precision of reference to the rebuilding of the Temple in the inserted verses 6b–10a. The main part of ch. 4, the vision and its interpretation, concentrates upon certain aspects of the new age, expressed in terms of divine presence and all-seeing power and in terms of the mediation of the blessing of God through his agents.[70]

Then the angel who was talking with me wakened me again as a man who awakes from his sleep. He said to me:
    What can you see?
and I said:

    I looked, and there was a lampstand all of gold, and its bowl[71] on top of it.

[67] Cf. M. Haran, 'The Complex of Ritual Acts inside the Tabernacle', *Script. Hier.* 8 (1961), pp. 272–302, see pp. 284f. on the symbol as evoking divine grace. Cf. T. Chary, *op. cit.*, pp. 149f.

[68] Cf. also John 1.48, 50, where the use of fig tree may suggest that Nathanael is in some way conceived as representing Israel's eager awaiting of the new age.

[69] Cf. the rabbinic extension of this (refs. in *Str. Bill.* 2, p. 371) to indicate that the study of the law—itself the central worshipping activity of Jewish life—should be 'under the vine and under the fig tree'.

[70] Cf. L. Rost, 'Bemerkungen zu Sacharja 4', *ZAW* 63 (1951), pp. 216–21, see p. 219.

[71] *gullāh*—if correct, this must be understood as *gōl* with possessive suffix. *gōl* is then a masculine form of *gullā* which appears in v. 3. Alternatively, read *gullā* here—'and a bowl on top of it'—or read *gullātā*—'its bowl' (fem.).

And its seven lamps on it, seven spouts to each of the lamps on top of it.[72]

And two olive trees beside it, one to the right of the bowl and one to its left.

Then I answered the angel who was speaking with me:
What are these, sir?

The angel who was talking with me replied thus:
Do you not know what these are?

I said: No, sir.

Then he addressed me thus:[73]
Seven are these, the eyes of Yahweh.
It is they that range over all the earth.

Then I answered:
What are these two olive trees on the right of the lampstand and on its left?

(Then I continued to ask and said to him:
What are these two olive shoots which are at the side of the two gold pipes; they pour [golden] oil from them?)

He said to me:
Do you not know what they are?

I said: No, sir.

He said:
They are the two sons of oil[74] who stand beside the Lord of all the earth (4.1–6a, 10b–14).

It seems simplest to assume that there are two elements in the vision and its interpretation, subsequently elaborated by the addition of a third which cuts across the original meaning. The basic elements in the vision are the lampstand with its sevenfold lamps and the two olive trees standing one on each side. Verse 12 introduces a new element, obscure in detail because of the uncertainty as to how the words are to be understood, but apparently suggesting a different function for the olive trees from that which is indicated in the main vision.

Verse 10b provides the first interpretative statement. This, possibly incomplete, phrase points to the lampstand as the symbol of the divine presence. The sevenfold lampstand (probably to be pictured as a complex lamp, with seven spouts or even with seven times seven spouts), represents the eyes of Yahweh which rove

[72] The detail here is complex, but unless there is some duplication in the text, we may suppose a lamp of a kind possible in vision even if hardly so in real life.
[73] Verses 6b–10a are omitted here.
[74] M. Bič, *Das Buch Sacharja* p. 57, stresses that *yiṣhār* means 'new oil' and suggests that this idea of 'newness' was significant to the prophet. Cf. P. A. H. de Boer in *Words and Meanings*, ed. P. R. Ackroyd and B. Lindars (1968), p. 36.

throughout the world. Nothing is hidden from them. The presence of Yahweh in the shrine—for it is reasonable to assume that the basis of the vision here is a familiar object in the Temple—means that from this central place he is able to watch over all the world and its affairs.[75] The picture draws together the function of the messengers of God in the first vision (1.8ff.) and the assurance of the presence of God in the third (2.5ff.). With this symbol is combined that of the two olive trees, indicated in v. 14 as being two figures, and it cannot be doubted that the figures of Zerubbabel and Joshua are here intended. Their function is not precisely noted, but, as in the last verses of ch. 3, they are evidently connected with the establishment of the new age, with oil as a symbol of blessing.[76] In the latter part of ch. 6 a further indication is provided of how they are to rule, jointly and with harmony between them. Emphasis is laid on both these points in ch. 4 by the repeated question and answer between the prophet and the angel before the interpretation is given.

The additional interpretative element in v. 12[77] introduces apparently a picture of some kind of connection between the leaders, represented as olive trees, or here as olive shoots, and the lamp which they supply with oil. There is here a shift which does not accord satisfactorily with the original meaning of the vision. It can hardly be proper to suggest that the leaders supply God himself. On the other hand, the function of leaders, both secular and religious, in the mediating of divine life and blessing to the community is entirely proper, and it may be that the meaning of v. 12 is intended to be an elaboration of the leaders' function in relation to the people, rather than the mediating of life to the lamp which symbolizes the presence of God. It is a natural extension. The symbol of the olive tree suggests the blessing which comes from its fruit and the connection of olive oil with anointing suggests the mediating of divine power and blessing. The obvious interpretation of v. 12 is that it refers to the supplying of the lamp, but perhaps it is really intended to make a more general

---

[75] H.-J. Kraus, *Worship in Israel* (ET, 1966), p. 233, makes the suggestion that the candlestick—perhaps a sacred object from the pre-exilic Temple—had been installed in the shrine as a symbol of the divine presence and also of continuity with the Solomonic Temple. But he stresses that such suggestions are no more than supposition.

[76] Cf. R. de Vaux, *Ancient Israel* (1961), p. 399. E. Kutsch, *Salbung als Rechtsakt* (BZAW 87, 1963), p. 61, sees in 4.14 a recognition that Zerubbabel and Joshua are acknowledged as 'anointed', even though the ritual cannot have been carried out 'rite' for the former in view of his position as Persian royal commissioner.

[77] Cf. T. Chary, *op. cit.*, p. 153.

comment on the mediating of blessing, since in fact the text does not precisely state that the oil flows into the bowl of the lamp.

The function of the leaders is again in ch. 6 related to the declaration of God's purpose. Here, somewhat as in ch. 3, a number of oracles are gathered, together with a symbolic action which is concerned with leadership and its relation to the new age; and these all follow upon the vision of 6.1–8, which has already been briefly considered,[78] in which the action of God towards the nations and towards his people in exile in Babylon is again set out. We must now look in more detail at that part of 6.9–15 which has not yet been considered.

The symbolic action is unfortunately not completely clear, because of considerable textual difficulties in the verses concerned, and the result is that interpretation is inevitably tentative.

> Then the word of Yahweh came to me:
> Something is to be taken[79] from the captivity, namely from Heldai and Tobiah and Yedaiah. Then you yourself are to enter on that day, you are to enter[80] the house of Josiah the son of Zephaniah into which they came from Babylon. Then you are to take silver and gold and make crowns and place (them) on the head of Joshua the son of Jehozadak, the high priest.
> You are to say to him:
> Thus says Yahweh of hosts;
> Behold the man   Branch is his name
> Where he is there is flourishing
> And he shall build the Temple of Yahweh.
>
> · · ·
>
> The crown shall be to Helem[81] and Tobiah and Yedaiah and Josiah

78 Cf. pp. 182f.

79 The infinitive absolute may stand for the imperative 'Take . . .' but there is no object. The translation here is an attempt to suggest a verbal noun idea—'There is to be a taking'.

80 The text appears to be overloaded, but such repetitiveness is found elsewhere in Haggai and Zechariah, e.g., Hag. 1.2.

81 The appearance of Ḥēlem here for Ḥeldai in v. 10 is very strange. The Syriac assimilates the two; the LXX with τοῖς ὑπομένουσιν appears to have used a word from the root ḥld though this is not certain. (Cf. D. Winton Thomas, 'Some observations on the Hebrew Root ḥdl', VTS 4 [1957], pp. 8–16, see pp. 14f.)

L. G. Rignell, op. cit., p. 235, argues that since Heldai = mole, it is a sort of nickname and Helem appears as his correct name. It would be tempting to suggest, in line with G. R. Driver's discussion of abbreviation (Textus 1 [1960], pp. 112–31; 4 [1964], pp. 76–94) that the second occurrence was abbreviated (? to ḥl) and wrongly expanded; but this would argue for a peculiar state of mind in the scribe who did it. The text has the further peculiarity that Josiah is not actually named (the text reads ûlᵉḥēn ben-ṣᵉpaniā = and to Hen [favour] son of Zephaniah)

the son of Zephaniah as a memorial (and as a sign of favour)[82] in the temple of Yahweh. (6.9–12, 14)

Verses 12–13 have already been considered in relation to the rebuilding of the Temple, though another point concerning their content must be raised in a moment. The remaining material here clearly envisages a twofold symbol, with the possibility that the second stage, in v. 14, is a further elaboration of the original idea, comparable to the further elaboration in ch. 4.

The opening words of v. 10 are awkward and the text does not appear to be correct.[83] What is clear is that the exiles are involved, and presumably the reference in v. 10b to 'they came from Babylon' is to the same personalities as are mentioned in 10a. It has been suggested that Josiah was a goldsmith, but in v. 14 he appears alongside the others in such a way as to suggest rather that he was one of the leading members of the community. If we knew something about any of the persons referred to, it might be that we could understand more fully what is at issue. As so often, the Old Testament provides us with only a tantalizing glimpse of who and what they were.

Returning exiles from whom silver and gold can be obtained is reminiscent of those passages in Ezra which point to contributions made by exiles to the restoration of the Judaean community.[84] Such contributions, whether made by the exiled Jews themselves or by government, fit in well with Persian restoration policy. They also fit in well with the conception of the return as being in some sense a new Exodus, with a new spoiling of the Egyptians (Ex. 12.35–36).[85] So the action here performed is naturally to be linked to the hopes of restoration which follow upon the return to Judah of some of the exiles.

The making of the crown naturally suggests a royal symbol, and what is said in v. 12 about the appearance of the Branch, the identify-

---

and has been supplied in the translation given here (following Syr.). *lehēn* has been taken to belong with *lezikkārōn*. Evidently there is some disorder; and no completely satisfying solution can be found.

[82] Cf. the previous note.

[83] Cf. 79 n.

[84] E.g. Ezra 1.6; 7.15f.

[85] D. Daube, *The Exodus Pattern in the Bible* (London, 1963), pp. 62ff. Pp. 56ff. relate this theme to the release of slaves. He does not adduce the Ezra passages as parallels. G. Gerleman, *Studien zu Esther* (BS 48, 1966), noting the parallels between the Esther and Exodus narratives, points out (p. 25) that Esther 9.10, 15, 16 reveal a deliberate avoidance of this motif in Esther.

ing of this figure with Zerubbabel which appears from the linking of vv. 12 and 13 with 4.6b–10a, and the royal imagery connected with the Branch also in 3.8, make it appear very evident that we have here a declaration similar to that of Hag. 2.21–23. The new age is to be ruled by a royal figure, and the member of the Davidic line appointed by the Persians is appropriately designated.

Because of this it has often been felt desirable to make a change in the text of v. 11. Since v. 12 clearly refers to the Branch, it might be expected that the actual crowning would also apply to him, i.e. to Zerubbabel.[86] The original text would then have been changed as a result of later events, either, if the theory of Persian intervention is accepted, because Zerubbabel fell from favour, and so the prophetic oracles had to be worked over, or as a result of still later developments in the place of the high-priesthood. The first of these theories appears without adequate foundation, as has been suggested above;[87] nor does it appear clear why if editing were carried out to avoid any reference to Zerubbabel this was not done sufficiently consistently to remove his name from 4.6b–10a and also from the book of Haggai where equally plain claims are made on his behalf. If the Persian secret service were thought to be likely to investigate Jewish nationalistic aspirations by reading their prophetic books—a supposition which does not appear to be so very probable—then we must suppose that the editing would have been consistent. The second theory has more to commend it, for the changing fortunes in the government of the Jewish community might well at a later stage suggest that the real emphasis should be laid upon the position and authority of the high priest.[88] But even this cuts across not a little of what is elsewhere said in the prophecies about the dual nature of the authority, which appears in v. 13 and also noticeably in ch. 4. A second alternative is to suggest that originally both names were present in v. 11 and that subsequently, deliberately or accidentally, that of Zerubbabel was dropped. Deliberate omission could follow from one or other of the causes just mentioned, more probably again from the second. Accidental omission would be in some ways easier to understand, since elsewhere in the prophetic material—and

[86] Cf. O. Eissfeldt, *Geschichtliches und Übergeschichtliches im Alten Testament* (ThStKr 109/2, 1947), pp. 16f. on the political aspects of this.

[87] Cf. above pp. 163ff.

[88] Later development of the theme may be seen in the Testament of the Twelve Patriarchs, e.g., Test. Judah 24.1–3 (cf. R. H. Charles' comment in *Apocrypha and Pseudepigrapha* II [Oxford, 1913], p. 323); Test. Levi 18.

obviously in Haggai—both leaders are repeatedly referred to together. But explaining difficulties by postulating accidental omission is never very satisfactory. The plural 'crowns' would also be intelligible on this assumption, though the singular *'ēlāw* 'to him' of v. 12 would have to be explained as a later accommodation of the text.

Are these expedients really necessary? Rignell has argued that they are not. His arguments in favour of the MT are not always persuasive, as has already been remarked.[89] In this case, he has suggested that the actual crowning is itself a symbolic action, and appropriately compares 3.8f., where Joshua and his associates are, as we have seen,[90] men of a portent, and related precisely to this same figure of the Branch as we have here.

Is it not possible to suggest—as has been adumbrated earlier[91]— that the symbolic action takes place at a moment when Zerubbabel has not yet arrived in Jerusalem, but news of his appointment by the Persians has been brought—by the persons referred to in v. 10?—and both here and in ch. 3 the stress is laid upon the relation between the priest(s) and the coming Branch. The building of the Temple which is here indicated as the primary responsibility of the Branch may be then regarded as being the main reason for the sending of Zerubbabel, to complete the task which had not been completed some years earlier under the earlier commissioner Sheshbazzar.

Alternatively, if we assume that the Zechariah and Iddo referred to in Neh. 12.4 and 16 must be the prophet and his father (Berechiah in Zech. 1.1 may be an erroneous insertion), and so conclude that it is likely that Zechariah travelled with Zerubbabel and could not therefore have pronounced an oracle or performed a symbolic action in Jerusalem before Zerubbabel's arrival, we may ask whether in fact this symbol was performed in Babylon at the time of Zerubbabel's appointment, as an act of faith and hope in the new commissioner. The view then that 3.8–10 represent earlier words called to mind because of their significance for the assurance now given to Joshua and so to the community in 3.1–5 would seem to be the right one. We must then, not unreasonably, assume that 6.14—to which we must turn in a moment—represents a later element, and that the last words of 6.10 'who came from Babylon' is a later addition made in the light of the events, at a time when the words of the earlier period were being grouped together or re-expounded by the prophet himself. In view of other indications of Zechariah's activity in Babylon, such a possibility may reasonably be entertained, though it must also be recognized that the lists of Neh. 12 do not necessarily refer to the same persons. Zechariah in 12.16 is described as being the head of the priestly house of Iddo in the days of Joiakim. In 12.10f. Joiakim is described as the son of Jeshua, and the father of Eliashib. The latter appears in the Nehemiah narrative (13.4, 28 etc.) as a grandfather whose grandson is already married in c. 432 BC. Chronologically there are no particular difficulties here, since Joshua could have remained high priest till about 500 and his successors, allowed a period of 30 years each, bring the line down to 430. Zechariah, if comparatively young in 520, could have succeeded his father as head of the household around the turn of the century.[92]

The original direction of the symbol appears to be towards that rebuilding of the Temple which, as in Haggai, marks the essential beginning of the new age. In v. 13a a further point is added, and while it may well be that this saying has been placed here because of the linkage of wording between its opening and the end of v. 12, it nevertheless appropriately elaborates the conception of the leadership of the community which is indicated in 3.9–10 and ch. 4:

> And *he* shall build the Temple of Yahweh
>   And *he* shall put on splendour
> And he shall sit to rule upon his throne
>   And there shall be a priest upon his throne
> And agreement shall subsist between the two.

The italics are intended to indicate the very great stress which is laid in the Hebrew upon these words. The reference in the last line to the peaceful co-operation of the two leaders in the rule of the community suggests the possibility that the first two lines are to be translated as indicating first Zerubbabel—whose function is to build the Temple—and then Joshua—whose function is to 'put on splendour', which may be taken to mean 'take up his office, his splendid office', i.e. to officiate as priest in the Temple which is now being restored.[93] Each sits upon his own throne, and together they

---

[92] This is another argument in favour of rejecting the view that Zechariah and the others were involved in anti-Persian conspiracy. Cf. above p. 165.

[93] K. Baltzer, 'Das Ende des Staates Juda und die Messias Frage', in *Studien*

carry out the rule of the community. To look for political under-currents here is inappropriate. The expression of confidence in harmonious co-operation is not to be taken as a criticism of existing disharmony but as an indication of the way in which, to this prophet,[94] the two aspects of the community's life are to be adjusted in the persons of the two leaders.[95]

The point made in these verses is thus very close indeed to that of 3.8–10. The high priest Joshua is here symbolically crowned in token of the coming of the Branch, just as there the company of priests is a sign of this same figure. This passage elaborates the functions of the Branch, both in the direction of the building of the Temple (cf. 4.6b–10a) and in the direction of rule (cf. Hag. 2.21–23 and Zech. 4—in the main vision and possibly also in 6b–10a). The priest himself takes up his office within the newly restored and encouraged community; in 3.9 he is seen to perform a mediating function (as also in ch. 4); divine grace and forgiveness are declared through him. These different aspects of the people's life are closely woven together in the harmony which exists between them, and not only between them but mediated from them to the community. For the phrase 'counsel of peace' ^{c}ṣat šālōm (6.13) must be interpreted not merely with reference to the interrelationship—though that is evidently its primary intention. It must also be understood to mean—as ^{c}ēṣā does elsewhere—a functioning which promotes well-being, a counsel, undertaken by divinely inspired persons whose purpose and nature are to bring into effect the divine intention.[96] The counsel of well-being between them is an earnest of the blessing which will flow through them. Here, as in 4.12, they are seen to be mediators of divine power.

---

zur Theologie der alttestamentlichen Überlieferungen, ed. R. Rendtorff and K. Koch (Neukirchen, 1961), pp. 41f., lays stress on the legitimation of priesthood and kingship. Though he does not cite this passage, he shows by his mention of both Zerubbabel (p. 41) and Joshua (p. 42 n. 51) that he is concerned with these same problems.

[94] Cf. T. Chary, op. cit., p. 153, who sees the evolution of Ezekiel's hopes expressed in the practical situation of the post-exilic period.

[95] The meaning of the comments on this passage by N. H. Snaith, VTS 14 (1967), pp. 245ff., is not very clear. He appears to offer a translation similar to that proposed here, but no clear conclusions are drawn. The footnote to p. 246 to the effect that 'The "them" has been inserted by the English translators. There is no objective pronoun in the Hebrew text' appears to be wrongly placed and is also unintelligible. It can surely only refer to the rendering of 6.13,'where the Hebrew has šᵉnēhem, correctly translated as 'them both'.

[96] Cf. P. A. H. de Boer, 'The Counsellor', VTS 3 (1955), pp. 42–71.

A further direction is given in 6.14. The verse is textually difficult, and it seems clear that some modification of MT must be accepted.[97] Clearly we have here a new use to which the crowns are put. After the placing on the head of Joshua, and so the guarantee of the blessing which is to come, the crowns are to be placed in the Temple of Yahweh. If the original setting of the symbolic action was Babylon, then we may suppose that it is somewhat later that this was undertaken, perhaps because now the main event—the appointment and arrival of Zerubbabel—had taken place, and yet there remained a hesitation, as we have seen elsewhere in these prophets, because the hoped for day, the new age, had not yet arrived (cf. Hag. 2.15–19). So the crowns which were the symbol of the building of the Temple —we cannot necessarily conclude from v. 14 that the Temple had now been built, though this seems most natural—are placed there so that they may be as a memorial—which we might best paraphrase rather oversimply as a reminder to God of his promised blessing[98]— and as a sign of favour (or perhaps to invite favour). The complete fulfilment of the promise is to come; just as the priesthood is a token of that coming age, indicated in 3.10, so here the blessing waits on the renewal of divine action and favour.[98a].

ᔐ

3. THE PEOPLE'S RESPONSE

Hesitation might well be taken as the mark of much of the remaining material of Zech. 1–8. It is a hesitation already echoed in the interpretation of the first vision, where it is the angel who asks: How long?[99] But it is more fully developed in the context of obedience and response.

The vision of Joshua as representative of the people cleansed by divine command has often been thought to indicate forgiveness and cleansing for the whole community. The point is indeed brought out in 3.9 in comment upon the vision. But the primary intention of that vision is a larger one, set against the background of the exilic desolation from which no restoration is possible so long as it appears that accusation is levelled against the people. We saw that the Satan is

97 Cf. above p. 194 n. 81.
98 On this idea, cf. B. S. Childs, *Memory and Tradition in Israel* (1962).
98a On 6.9–15, cf. W. A. M. Beuken, *op. cit.*, pp. 275–82, and pp. 303–17 on the place of Joshua.
99 Zech. 1.12.

rebuked, and it was suggested that this is not because the accusation is unwarranted—as if the people were being accused in Joshua of some sin which they have not committed—but because God himself chooses Jerusalem again and rescues his people.[100] There is a link here with the *sola gratia* thought of Ezekiel, where God is described as acting for his name's sake.[101] It is, of course, not possible to be sure what function the Satan here performs. The analogy of the opening chapters of Job—not perhaps too far removed from this in date—would suggest that the Satan is conceived as a full member of the heavenly court, and not yet, as he subsequently was, identified with the 'day-star fallen from heaven', the Lucifer-type figure of Isa. 14.12 or with the comparable figure of Ezek. 28.2–10. He appears to be kin rather to those angelic beings of the vision of Micaiah (I Kings 22.19–22) who debate among themselves under the aegis of God as to how the king of Israel is to be destroyed, and whose action is undertaken at the divine command, not on their own initiative. So the accusation against the community in Zech. 3 would seem to be the rightful displeasure which has shown itself in the disaster of exile. But God has turned himself again in favour towards his people. The deserved disaster has come upon them; their restoration is unexpected in that they are under divine displeasure, but it follows from what he is.

The new age comes because of this. But Zechariah has more to say about it, and it is here that the element of hesitation enters in. What is the correlation between divine action and human response? How can the appropriation of the divine blessing be made possible? It is characteristic of Old Testament thinking not to attempt a precise definition. The absoluteness of divine action and the fulness of human responsibility are placed side by side with no exact mechanism indicated by which the two are reconciled. In Zechariah, as also in the exilic prophets (and the same point we have seen briefly indicated in Haggai),[102] emphasis is laid upon the need for the community to be fit for the new age. Purification of its social and religious life is essential, a necessary preliminary to the appropriation of God's blessing.

The oracles and visions of Zechariah are now presented in such a way that this point stands at the outset in the opening words of the book.[102a] The experience of the past is noted, how the message of

---

[100] Cf. pp. 183f.
[101] Cf. p. 105.
[102] Cf. pp. 106ff.
[102a] W. A. M. Beuken, *op. cit.*, pp. 84–115, describes 1.2–6a as a 'levitical sermon'.

earlier prophets to the forefathers of the present generation produced
no response and so disaster overtook them. The words of the prophets
were fulfilled in the events of the exile:

> . . . Yahweh had had great wrath against your fathers. So you shall
> say to them: Thus says Yahweh of hosts: Return to me—oracle of Yahweh
> of hosts—and I will return to you[103]—says Yahweh of hosts. Do not be
> like your fathers to whom the former prophets preached saying: Thus
> says Yahweh of hosts: Turn now from your evil ways and your evil
> deeds. But they would not listen or heed me—oracle of Yahweh of hosts.
>   Now your fathers—where are they? Do the prophets live for ever?
> But as for my words and my statutes which I entrusted to my servants
> the prophets, did they not overtake your fathers?[104] (1.2–6a)

The point of vv. 5–6a is that the example which has been seen in the
exile is a matter of past history. The fathers of the present generation,
to whom these things happened, are now dead. So too are the
prophets who spoke the words of judgement. But what is evident is
that the word of God, proclaimed by the prophets, was effective in
bringing about the judgement which was prophesied. The prophetic
word—a point of importance in understanding the organic nature of
the tradition—does not depend upon the life of the prophet himself;
it continues to be effective.[105] What happened to the fathers is not
just a matter of past history, but a witness to present reality. Let the
generation to whom these warnings are addressed realize that this
applies to themselves.

1.6b is then best understood, not as a continuing comment on the
fathers of the present generation, but as a note of the response of this
generation to the prophet's warning. 'Be unlike your fathers', he said
to them:

> Then they[106] said in repentance: As Yahweh of hosts planned to treat
> us according to our ways and according to our deeds, so he has acted
> towards us.

Thus the people acknowledge the justice of God's action toward
them, and the stage is set for the revealing of the mercy and goodness
of God which is to bring about the restoration of the community.

103 Or 'that I may return to you'. The translation of the verb $we^{\prime}\bar{a}\check{s}\hat{u}b$ as a simple
future is more natural, though the alternative rendering stresses more sharply the
close correlation between human response and divine action.

104 So MT $^{\prime a}b\bar{o}t\bar{e}kem$, rather than accepting the commonly preferred emendation
$^{\prime}etkem$ 'you'. See the discussion of 1.6b below. Cf. W. A. M. Beuken, op. cit., pp. 86ff.,
103ff.

105 Cf. P. R. Ackroyd, ASTI i (1962), pp. 7–23, esp. pp. 15f.

106 I.e. the prophet's contemporaries now addressed.

The complaint at delay in 1.12 is not made by the people but by the angel of Yahweh, who thus acts as the mediator of the direct word from God in 1.13 by which reassurance is given. At the same time the comment in 1.6*b* serves to point to the generation of the return as an ideal generation—so depicted also in the work of the Chronicler —who in spite of hardships succeeded in rebuilding the Temple and in realizing in themselves the promises of the past.[107]

The sixth and seventh visions in ch. 5 are both concerned with the purification of the community, first from evils which are purged out by means of a divine oath in the face of which they cannot stand, and second from idolatry represented as a female figure contained within a large jar.

> Then I again raised my eyes and looked, and there was a scroll which flew. He said to me: What can you see? I said: I can see a scroll which flies. (Its length was twenty cubits and its breadth ten cubits.) He said to me: This is the oath which goes out over all the land. (5.1–3*a*)

The explanation is given in terms of the effects of this oath on those who swear falsely and those who steal.[108]

> For
> Everyone who steals from now on is purged out
> And everyone who swears (falsely) from now on is purged out (according to it).[109]
> I have sent it out—oracle of Yahweh of hosts—and it shall come to the house of the thief and to the house of the one who swears falsely by me, and it shall settle in the middle of his house and bring it to destruction, both timber and stones. (5.3*b*–4)

The choice of 'land' rather than 'earth' for the rendering of v. 3

[107] An alternative interpretation which makes a similar point is given if we treat 1.6*b* as a description of the reactions of the fathers to the disaster of the exile. When disaster fell—though not before (cf. 1.4)—the generation of the exile recognized that what had been done was right. They made their act of repentance, and accepted the rightness of God's action (cf. the same thought in the Deuteronomic History, p. 78). So they serve as a warning and an encouragement to the later generation of Zechariah's contemporaries. Those he addresses are not to be like their forefathers, but are to hear the word of God now; if they fail, that word of God will nevertheless be effective. Even their fathers who refused to hear were forced in the end to recognize what folly had been theirs.

[108] Cf. E. Janssen, *op. cit.*, p. 52, who adopts the oversimplified identification of the offenders as thieves who took over land belonging to the exiles in 587, and as false swearers who are adherents of Canaanite cults.

[109] The phrase *mizze kāmōhā* is very odd. *mizze* appears to mean 'from this point' —i.e. in future; *kāmōhā*—? according to it, i.e. according to the wording of the oath. But this is not very clear; nor do any of the proposed emendations carry complete conviction.

depends upon a consideration of the next vision as well, for the indication that purification is of the Jewish community suggests that the stress should be laid here upon the preparing of the land to be the holy land by the removal from it of all that otherwise hinders the fulfilment of God's purposes. So in this vision the declared oath (not curse) of God is shown to be effective; it is a writ which has the effect of distinguishing between innocent and guilty. The innocent have nothing to fear from it, but to the guilty it becomes a curse and destroys.[110]

The seventh vision is of the 'woman in the ephah' and introduces a more elaborate picture:

> Then the angel who was talking with me came out and said to me: Raise your eyes and see what this is that is coming out.
>
> Then I said: What is it?
>
> He said: This is an ephah[111] which is coming out.
>
> And he said: This is their iniquity[112] in all the land.
>
> Then there was a round lid of lead being lifted up and there was a woman sitting alone in the middle of the ephah.
>
> He said: This is idolatry.
>
> And she was thrust down[113] into the ephah, and the lead cover was placed on its mouth.
>
> Then I raised my eyes and looked, and there were two women coming out with the wind in their wings. They had wings like storks' wings, and they lifted up the ephah into the air.
>
> Then I said to the angel who was talking with me: Where are they taking the ephah?
>
> He said to me: To build for it a temple in the land of Shinar: it will be set up,[114] and it will be placed[115] there upon its pedestal. (5.5–11)

[110] The ordeal may be compared, cf. Num. 5.11–31. Cf. also Hos. 14.10. M. Bič, *Das Buch Sacharja* (1962), pp. 66f., may well be right in seeing in this vision a stress on religious failure, as appears likely in 5.5–11. He compares Acts 5.1ff. for an example of the sin of withholding from God what belongs to him (theft) and of falsehood in relation to God.

[111] Heb. 'the ephah'—i.e. the one in question.

[112] MT has ʿēnām, LXX ἡ ἀδικία αὐτῶν, i.e. ʿᵃwōnām, adopted here. MT might be rendered 'their appearance, resemblance'. L. G. Rignell, *op. cit.* pp. 190f., translates 'what they see', supposing that the -ām ending is not a suffix but a form expressing totality. M. Bič, *op. cit.* p. 69, similarly renders: 'Das ist ihr Aussehen (= so sieht es mit ihnen aus) . . .', considering that it refers back to those mentioned in the previous vision. He finds support for this in the literal rendering of Vg: *haec est oculus eorum*, and sees LXX as offering a not inappropriate interpretation. But the rendering seems rather forced.

[113] Literally 'one thrust her down'.

[114] wᵉhūkan. LXX καὶ ἑτοιμάσαι suggests an active form, possibly wᵉhēkīnū. MT is awkward since the subject of wᵉhūkan is not clear. Is it *bait*, temple (cf. RSV)?

[115] wᵉhunnīḥā possibly a *forma mixta* (GK 78c; cf. L. G. Rignell, *op. cit.*, p. 195) combining wᵉhunniaḥ and wᵉhinnīḥuhā. LXX καὶ θήσουσιν αὐτὸ suggests wᵉhinnīḥuhā.

The operative moments in this vision concern the female figure in the jar: $(h\bar{a})ri\check{s}^c\bar{a}$—wickedness. She is thrust down and contained in the jar by the cover, and subsequently the same figure is set up on a pedestal in a shrine in Babylon. These two points justify the view that $ri\check{s}^c\bar{a}$ is here used in the technical sense of idolatry.[116] The first point suggests a motif to which many later legends allude, namely that of an evil spirit contained within a jar attempting to get out when the jar is opened. The second point suggests scornful reference to the religion of Babylon. What in the holy land ranks as idolatrous is taken there as an object of worship. So by divine action (cf. 3.9) the community is purged of social evils and religious apostasy, and by this process is fittingly prepared for the promises which follow in ch. 6 and for the new age to which those promises are directed.

The whole vision series ends with a brief note of warning:

So it shall be if you will really pay heed to Yahweh your God. . . (6.15b)

The series opened (1.1–6) with a warning from the past, exhorting the present generation to be more responsive than their fathers. It closes with this brief allusive phrase. These things—the rebuilding of the Temple and the attendant presence of God in blessing in a new-built Jerusalem, and in a holy and purified land—will take place if the people shows its responsiveness, if it is fit to appropriate them. The phrase is probably to be regarded as incomplete, and the reference appears to be intended to such a passage as Deut. 28.1, which continues: 'to see that you do all his commandments which I (Moses) lay upon you today, then Yahweh your God will make you supreme over all the nations of the land'. The promise of a new entry into the land, suggested by the Deuteronomic History[117] and the Priestly Work,[118] is here brought out in relation to the obedience of the people. His action towards them may be appropriated by them and become for them blessing and life.

The closely-knit structure of the vision series makes it natural that it should be treated as a unit, and that we should see that it is thus

---

[116] Cf. LXX ἡ ἀνομία, Vg. *impietas*. The Targum interprets of unrighteous trade dealings. The rabbinic view that idolatry ceased with the exile (cf. *Str. Bill.* 3, 111, cf. W. A. L. Elmslie, 'Prophetic influences in the Sixth Century BC', in *Essays and Studies presented to S. A. Cook*, ed. D. W. Thomas [London, 1950], pp. 15–24) may be connected with this last interpretation. There is however ample evidence of idolatrous practices after the exile: cf. Isa. 65.2ff.; 66.17; Mal. 2.11; Ezra 9. Cf. J. D. Smart, *History and Theology in Second Isaiah* (1965), pp. 28f.

[117] Cf. p. 82.

[118] Cf. pp. 96ff.

rounded off with an echo at the end of the point with which it began. But the series is followed by two further chapters which contain a rich selection of material, a little narrative, a good deal of moralizing exhortation like the passages just mentioned in 1.1–6 and 6.15*b*, and a series of sayings, some closely related to the preceding material and others introducing new elements in the picture of the new age. The whole emphasis of these two chapters appears to be on the hesitation, the possible delay, the sureness of the promise which is nevertheless laid under the condition of men's response; for without that response the will of God will not be imposed and the new age will be prevented by men themselves. It is as if the prophet, beginning with the question about fasting which finds its real answer in the assurance that all mournful feasts are turned to joy, realizes that this hope is delayed. If, as seems very probable, the prophet continued to live long after these events of the time of the rebuilding, on into the period which is illuminated for us by the book of Malachi (and by the conditions presupposed in the Nehemiah narrative), then the delay in the promise may well have occasioned such utterances. The Temple has been rebuilt—so we must assume from a number of references in ch. 7 and 8—the assurance of the day of promise is still there. But men must beware lest they are themselves preventing its coming. Only to a holy people, fit for the worship of God, can the promises become real.

The chapters thus contain a mingling of promise and encouragement on the one hand with warning and exhortation on the other. The interweaving is well illustrated by the opening of ch. 7, where an incident is briefly related to which the reply comes only in 8.18f.[119] In the text as it now stands, the reply is separated from the question first by a more general reflection about the question raised, and second by a whole series of warnings and oracles connected with it.

Then Bethel-sharezer the Rab-mag[120] of the king and his men[121] sent

---

[119] So e.g. O. Eissfeldt, *Introduction*, pp. 430f. The suggestion (cf. O. Procksch in BH[3]) that 7.4–8.17 should stand after 8.23 fails to take account of the relationship between this section and the narrative. Cf. F. S. North, 'Aaron's Rise in Prestige', *ZAW* 66 (1954), pp. 191–9, see p. 193. For a different view cf. W. A. M. Beuken, *op. cit.*, pp. 138–56.

[120] Cf. D. Winton Thomas, *IB* 6 (1956), p. 1082.

[121] For this rendering, cf. e.g. O. Eissfeldt, *Introduction*, p. 430, and P. R. Ackroyd, 'Zechariah', in *New Peake's Commentary* (1962), p. 650. Cf. also the survey of renderings in M. Bič, *Das Buch Sacharja* (1962), pp. 87f., supporting this view in the main. F. S. North, *op. cit.*, p. 192, translates '. . . Sharezer and Regemmelech sent to

to seek the favour of Yahweh with this message to the priests who belonged to the temple of Yahweh and to the prophets: Am I to weep in the fifth month, separating myself as I have done now for many years? (7.2-3)

So the word of Yahweh of hosts came to me: Thus says Yahweh of hosts: The fast of the fourth month and the fast of the fifth and the fast of the seventh and the fast of the tenth[122] are to be for the house

---

Bethel . . .' (cf. LXX εἰς βαι θήλ). He then has to argue (see p. 195) that the whole text was glossed to avoid such a suggestion. (Cf. his similar elaborate reshaping of the Haggai text, *ZAW* 68 [1956], pp. 25–46.) Bethel with its Aaronite priesthood had taken the lead, and the Zadokite priesthood had, at this stage, to identify itself as Aaronite in order to restore its prestige. This is building a great deal on a dubious reconstruction of the text. It would appear more probable that the versions reveal the problems of interpretation already then experienced, and are attempts at making sense of a difficult passage.

[122] The appearance in 8.19 of references to four fasts suggests that the reply itself has been subsequently elaborated to cover more than the object of the original inquiry. T. Chary, *op. cit.*, p. 145, argues that since the question was posed in the ninth month (7.1), we are to suppose that, during the rebuilding, each of the fasts in turn was observed but with hesitation as to the appropriateness of doing so: then at length, before the tenth month, a directive was sought. Quite apart from the more general problems of the dates in Zechariah, similar to the problems in Haggai (cf. F. Horst's comment in *Die zwölf kleinen Propheten* [HAT 14, ²1954], p. 239 and P. R. Ackroyd, *JJS* 2 [1951], pp. 163–76; 3 [1952], pp. 1–13), such a view takes no account of the absence in 7.3 of any reference to fasts other than that in the fifth month. An elaboration is already present in 7.5, referring to the fifth and seventh months.

What these fasts were and what they commemorated, is not necessarily as certain as many commentators assume. The fast of the fifth month appears to be a celebration of the destruction of the Temple in 587 (cf. II Kings 25.8ff.). That of the fourth month is said to mark the capture of the city (cf. II Kings 25.3ff.; Jer. 39.2); that of the seventh month, the assassination of Gedaliah (cf. II Kings 25.25; Jer. 41.1ff.; cf. also K. Baltzer, *op. cit.*, p. 37, who comments on the light this fact sheds on the potentialities of Gedaliah's appointment); that of the tenth month the inception of the siege of Jerusalem (cf. II Kings 25.1; Jer. 39.1). All the fasts are thus interpreted with precise reference to events of the period (cf. R. de Vaux, *Ancient Israel* [ET, 1961], pp. 387, 468 for a general comment). Yet while a fifth month fast may well be properly so explained, it would seem not impossible that the seventh month fast is really the Day of Atonement; and the possibility cannot be ruled out that the fasts in the fourth and tenth months represent other practices which are in the new age to be replaced by rejoicing. (T. Chary, *op. cit.*, p. 146, argues that if the prophet had known of the Day of Atonement, he would have mentioned it; he thinks there might be a relationship between the development of the Day and the abandonment of these fasts. More probably the strict ordering of the Day of Atonement represents a precise defining of already existing and ancient practice.) The addition of the seventh month in 7.5 would mark the first stage in elaboration: condemnation of wrong practice is extended to cover the great fast of the year. Gedaliah's death in fact coincided closely with the time of general fasting, as we may deduce from the fact that pilgrims were on their journey to Jerusalem

of Judah for rejoicing and gladness, and as joyful festivals. Love those things which make for a full and faithful life.[123] (8.18–19)

The main justification for this collocation of passages lies in the lack of continuity between 7.2–3 and 7.4ff.,[124] where there is a clear relationship of thought, but the point is different. The answer to the inquiry is not given; instead a message is addressed to the whole community. The matter is complicated by the difficulty of the text of vv. 2–3, for it would appear that at a comparatively early stage the personal name Bethel-sharezer was understood to consist of two parts, the first being the name of the place Bethel, and the second being the name of the person concerned.[125] This interpretation may have been occasioned by the later hostility to the Samaritans, since the place of Bethel as an important shrine of the old northern kingdom may have been thought to symbolize the dissident group which had broken away, as indeed in the narratives of both Kings and Chronicles there are points at which an identification, containing no doubt an element of truth, is made between the later Samaritan community and the old northern kingdom, particularly in its later condition after the fall of Samaria.[126] The verses following could then be understood to be a condemnation of the worship of the schismatic group. But this cannot belong to the period of Zechariah, since it is clear from the Nehemiah and Ezra narratives that a Samaritan schism had not yet taken place. Condemnation of undesirable religious practices—as for example in 5.5–11—is directed against the population in general. While it is not unreasonable to suppose that such undesirable practices may have been more prevalent among those who had remained in Palestine than among those who had begun the movement back from exile (the returned exiles being more probably the religiously enthusiastic, as indeed the several stages of the return all seem to lead to religious and social reform), yet no sharp distinction appears in Haggai and

---

(Jer. 41). Perhaps his assassins chose a moment when he would be off-guard. We may note also the celebrating of a fast in the ninth month in Jer. 36.9, but this is probably a special occasion.

[123] The extremely terse Hebrew *hā'emet wehaššālōm 'ehābū* needs more than this tentative expanded translation to explain it. The two nouns together express that full life of the people in loyal allegiance to their God which is the mark of their proper state.

[124] Cf. T. Chary, *op. cit.*, p. 144, and references on p. 146 n. 1.

[125] But for the more conventional interpretation cf. T. Chary, *op. cit.*, p. 145. Returned exiles are listed at Bethel and Ai in Ezra 2.28.

[126] Cf. II Kings 17 and p. 236 n. 12.

Zechariah. The Chronicler sees such a division, but not in such precise terms as to exclude from the blessings of the restoration those who have separated themselves from the abominations of the land (Ezra 6.21). The present arrangement stresses the dangers of religious observance, the risk that external practice comes to be regarded as the essence of religion. The same point is made in Trito-Isaiah.[127]

The question—directed to priests and prophets at the Jerusalem Temple—presumably about the time of the completion of the rebuilding or after—comes from a personage who, if the textual emendation of Regemmelek to Rab-mag Hammelek is correct, is to be thought of as a high royal official, no doubt a Jew (and conceivably a successor to Zerubbabel). It shows the expectancy of a community for whom the promises of the prophet are real. The Temple is rebuilt; the dawn of the new age is here. How far do the older observances need to continue? Is there in the question something of the hesitation which arises from a consideration of the actual conditions? Is the new age apparently delayed still further? The prophet's answer, now probably expanded but clearly substituting joyful festivals for fasts, makes it clear that the new age has come. But again the message concludes with a note which contains implicit warning: 'Love those things which make for a full and faithful life.' The new age marks no ending of the demand for a right community; indeed the demand is all the more insistent. Only such a right community can truly appropriate the new age as it comes.

The intrusion into this of the other material of ch. 7 and 8 does not fundamentally conflict but amplifies the warning and encouraging notes.

Now the word of Yahweh of hosts came to me:
  Say to all the people of the land and to the priests:
    When you fasted and mourned in the fifth month and in the seventh—now for seventy years—did you really fast to me?
    And when you ate and drank, was it not you yourselves who were eating and you yourselves who were drinking?
    Are not these the words which Yahweh proclaimed by means of the former prophets when Jerusalem was living in security and her cities around her and the Negeb and the Shephelah inhabited? (7.4–7)

(Then the word of Yahweh came to Zechariah:
  Thus says Yahweh of hosts:
    Judge with true justice.

[127] Cf. Isa. 56.1–2; 58.1–7.

Behave loyally and mercifully one toward another.
Do not oppress the widow or the orphan,
the sojourner or the poor.
Let none of you plan evil in his mind against another.) (7.8–10)

But they refused to hear and turned their backs on me in rebellion and blocked their ears so as not to hear. They made their hearts hard as flint so as not to hear the law and the commands which Yahweh of hosts sent by his spirit by means of the former prophets. So there was great anger from Yahweh of hosts.
It came about that as he called but they would not listen,
'So they will call and I will not listen
(says Yahweh of hosts)
And I will drive them away to all the nations which they do not know.'
And the land was desolate behind them, with no one to go to and fro. Thus they made the land of delight into a desolation. (7.11–14)

The structure is again complicated by the inclusion of a separate but related saying in 7.8–10, for clearly the sequel of 7.7 is found in 7.11. The intrusive passage simply emphasizes the main point which underlies the section. The refusal of men to hear the command of God, their refusal to be an acceptable people, has resulted in disaster. So now the message is given again by Zechariah that obedience must exist if blessing is to come and not again be lost.[128]

The main passage—like 1.1–6—points to the experience of the past as a warning to the present. The wrong observance of religious practice, a fasting or a feasting which are directed not to the honour of God but to self-gratification, bring about disaster. This can be appreciated from the warnings of earlier prophecy. No precise account is given of those warnings, but simply that the message was directed towards showing the people that they were dishonouring God. The commands of God mediated to them by the prophets were disregarded. Their refusal to hear God, when he called to them, was followed by the refusal of God to hear their appeals. The point made is the one which comes out clearly in pre-exilic prophecy; the division between God and man is made by man's failure, and the withdrawal of God[129] is the inevitable result of the unacceptability of the people.

---

[128] It has been argued that such passages as this are later insertions (so E. Hammershaimb, *op. cit.*, p. 107). But the relationship of such material to the Zechariah tradition still needs to be taken into account, and its relation also to other passages in these chapters will point to the understanding of obedience and disobedience. W. A. M. Beuken, *op. cit.*, pp. 118–38, discusses this passage as a 'levitical sermon'.

[129] Cf. Hos. 5.6. Cf. also Isa. 59.1f.

Vividly the passage includes what appears to be a direct quotation of the words of God; in the middle of v. 13 the tense and person change.[130] The judgement of God, 'They will call and I will not listen . . . and I will drive them away to all the nations which they do not know', stands out sharply, though the context makes it clear that the reference is to the events of the exile which have already taken place. But by this vivid and unexpected change of tense, the permanence of the divine word is emphasized. What was then true, is so still. It can still appropriately be said that God will do these things if the generation of the prophet fails to make response. The promise of the new age can even now be frustrated by human sin.

7.8–10 underlines this by laying the emphasis on those aspects of obedience which are so commonly stressed in the pre-exilic prophets as marks of the people of God. Placed here side by side with the condemnation of a religious observance which is 'to yourselves' not 'to God', they make clear the relationship between ritual practice and ethical behaviour. That there is no abandonment of the former is clear from the transformation of fasts into joyful festivals.[131] The religious observance is impossible for those who have contravened the demands of God. Those who would stand in the shrine must declare themselves free of the guilt which prevents acceptability.[132]

The various oracles of ch. 8 continue the general trend of thought. With reiteration of phrases to be found in the vision series, the point is repeatedly made that the new age is here because it is God's intention that it should be. Lack of faith on the part of the community, failure to realize the possibilities and the consequences of disobedience, may delay or hinder. Into this is put an exhortation, couched in phrases which belong to the two prophets Haggai and Zechariah, and directed, it would seem, primarily to a later generation, but indicating the appreciation that the faith of the age of restoration was one to be emulated—a point which has also been taken up in the Chronicler, to whom this was one of the great moments of the history.[133]

[130] Many of the commentators assimilate the verbs. This can be done readily in v. 14 by reading a *waw* consecutive construction, but involves rather more radical changes in v. 13.

[131] T. Chary, *op. cit.*, p. 146, strangely finds in Zechariah a resistance to ritualism. This derives from seeing the stress in pre-exilic prophecy as a moral one. Zechariah is described as preserving 'a spark of the great moral preaching of earlier prophets'.

[132] Cf. Pss. 15; 24; Job 31; Ezek. 18.5–13, etc. Cf. E. Würthwein, 'Kultpolemik oder Kultbescheid?' (cf. p. 5 n. 11).

[133] Cf. P. R. Ackroyd, *JJS* 3 (1952), pp. 154–6; W. A. M. Beuken, *op. cit.*, pp. 156–83.

I am jealous for Zion, greatly jealous
With great wrath I am jealous for her. (8.2)

The concern which God feels for his own sacred city, expresses itself
in his intention to restore her place:

I have returned to Zion
   and I shall dwell within Jerusalem
Then Jerusalem will be called the city of fidelity
   and the mountain of Yahweh of hosts, the holy mount. (8.3)

The fact that God has again taken up his place in his holy city[134]
results—as for Ezekiel[135]—in the renaming of the city by a name
which expresses its new nature. The holiness of the divine presence
and the fidelity of the restored city make possible a vision of the
security and blessedness of the new age:

Again there shall dwell old men and old women in the
   open places of Jerusalem,
Each one with staff in hand by reason of great age.
The open places of the city will be full of boys and girls
   playing in the open places. (8.4–5)

The new age is marked by that fulfilment of promise to men which
restores the ancient blessedness of longevity.[136] So too the prosperity
and security are such that the place is filled with children, and its
future is thus assured both by the new generation growing up and by
the recognition that the city is protected by the divine presence
against all danger.

These words of blessing and assurance are then aptly set against a
word of hesitation which prompts the further promise that what God
decrees is sure. Here the undertone of lack of faith is present; men
doubt the reality of the promise. We may reasonably suggest that
such a message as this could express (as does Hag. 2.3–5) the situation at the time of the rebuilding. But it could equally express the
continuing need for faith and hope when with a rebuilt Temple the
new age in the fulness of the prophet's picture still does not come.
This is first in terms of a reassurance of divine power:

---

[134] Cf. for this also L. R. Fisher, *JSS* 8 (1963), p. 40: 'city' = 'shrine' (*'îr*).
[135] Cf. Ezek. 48.35; also Isa. 1.26. On this theme, cf. N. W. Porteous, 'Jerusalem-Zion: The Growth of a Symbol', in *Verbannung und Heimkehr*, ed. A. Kuschke
(Tübingen, 1961), pp. 235–52. On this verse, cf. also K. L. Schmidt (cf. p. 135 n.
76); cf. also p. 112 n. 43, p. 249 n. 61.
[136] Cf. Isa. 65.20.

If it seems too wonderful in the sight of the
    remnant of this people[137]
Is it too wonderful in my sight?
—oracle of Yahweh of hosts. (8.6)

Second it is in terms of an extension of promise with the suggestion—
linking up with the final verse of ch. 6—that just as the rebuilding of
the Temple was to be achieved by the co-operation of those who are
summoned from afar, so too the new age cannot really come without
the complete gathering of the people.

See I am about to rescue my people from the eastern
    country and the western country,
And I will bring them in,
    they will abide within Jerusalem.
They shall be a people for me;
    I will be God to them—
in fidelity and righteousness. (8.7–8)

The echo of the covenant formula,[138] which indicates that the new
age will be marked by the re-establishment of the right relationship
between God and his fully restored people, is followed by a final note
containing a warning. The contrast with the former covenant
relationship is plain. That covenant they broke; it was not kept in
fidelity and righteousness. The new covenant must be so established
that this cannot again take place. The final phrase is better interpreted not as a comment on the fidelity and righteousness of God's
sustaining of the covenant—although this is not in itself inappropriate
—but as an emphatic warning and reminder of how that covenant
relationship is to be permanently preserved. At the same time the
reference to the summoning to Jerusalem of the scattered members
of the community, east and west, Babylonia and Egypt, is an anticipation of a still wider promise with which the whole series of oracles
closes,[139] in which the saving action of God towards his people is
shown to be a saving action directed to all nations, whose hope lies
in the things which God is already doing for his people.

    The verses which follow—8.9–10—introduce a different element,

[137] Omitting 'in those days', accidentally inserted from v. 10, or a margina
note which has crept into the text, designed to emphasize the marvel of divine
protection and blessing in the days of the rebuilding (cf. above p. 211 in the general
comment on ch. 8).
[138] Cf. Hos. 1.9; Jer. 7.23, etc.
[139] 8.20–23.

one which seems to belong rather to general reflection about the post-exilic situation than to the direct utterances of the prophets of that time, though it is clear that the sayings are based upon words of Haggai and Zechariah. The allusions to distress and discouragement are here used to provide an example to the readers of the prophetic material, who are to see in the faith and vision of the restoration period a way for themselves.[140] But this runs on into sayings which stress the reversal of fortune and the nature of the new age in terms of physical well-being and national fortune.

> But now, I am not to the remnant of this people as I was in former days —oracle of Yahweh of hosts.
> For the seed shall prosper,[141] the vine will yield its fruit, the earth will give its produce, the heavens will give their dew, and I will make the remnant of this people inherit all these things. (8.11–12)

The echoes of Haggai are clear, and it is possible that we ought to regard these verses as a continuation of the reminiscing of vv. 9–10. Yet the same essential emphasis belongs to Zechariah,[142] and the assurance of physical well-being is a natural and proper consequence of what has been said in the previous sayings in this chapter about the presence of God in Jerusalem and the blessing and prosperity which are to follow from this. The difficult wording of the opening of v. 12 must presumably bear some such meaning as is here suggested, but we may wonder whether the present, probably corrupt, form of the text is a result of a modification of the wording designed to suggest a blessing on the whole community—it is a community of well-being, prosperity.[143] This is an idea not at all out of harmony with the general context.

The promise is extended by an elaboration of the contrast between present hopes and past experiences.

[140] Cf. P. R. Ackroyd, *JJS* 3 (1952), pp. 154–6.

[141] Reading *kî hazzera' šālōm*. Cf. Horst, *op. cit.*, p. 242; D. Winton Thomas, *IB* 6 (1956), p. 1086, compares Hag. 2.19. LXX δείξω εἰρήνην suggests *'ezre'ā šālōm*. The conjecture *kî zar'āh šālōm*—'its seed' (cf. Procksch, BH³) follows the consonants of the MT but the feminine suffix, referring back presumably to *še'ērīt*, is odd.

[142] Cf. ch. 1–2.

[143] *zera' haššālōm*—(it is) a seed (= 'generation', or 'community' thought of as descendants) of well-being. We may compare the closing words of Isa. 6.13— *zera' qōdeš maṣṣabtāh*—still, in spite of all the arguments to the contrary, best understood as an explanatory gloss pointing to the (post-exilic) community as a holy people, the rescued after a great disaster. Cf. the note by J. F. A. Sawyer, 'The Qumran reading of Isa. 6.13', *ASTI* 3 (1964), pp. 111–13, for a useful comment on this whole question.

So it shall come about that as you were a curse among the nations, O house of Judah and house of Israel,[144] so now I will rescue you and you will become a blessing.
Do not be afraid: let your hands be strengthened. (8.13)

The desolation of the exilic period has naturally given the impression of a total reversal of fortunes for God's people. They have been held up as a warning, as an example of what to hope for one's enemies and not for one's friends and oneself.[145] This new age marks a change, and a recovery of that state in which the name of Israel is invoked as blessing, as in the Abraham story.[146] The final words, again reminiscent of Haggai,[147] may perhaps also be regarded as an injunction to the readers of the message; if originally addressed to the generation of the rebuilding of the temple, they are now a reminder of the faith of that time.

Another assurance follows, again based on experience:

As I intended to bring disaster upon you when your fathers angered me—says Yahweh of hosts—and I did not relent,
So I again intend in these days to treat Jerusalem and the house of Judah kindly.
Have no fear! (8.14–15)

There is an echo of 1.1–6. The certainty of divine judgement which has been experienced vouches for the certainty of divine deliverance which has been promised. But again the note of hesitation; for this promise and its acceptance by the people is conditional.

These are the things you are to do:
Honest speech between yourselves.
In your gates practise a justice which promotes well-being.[148]
Let no one of you plan in his mind evil for another.
Do not love false oaths.
For all these things I turn from—oracle of Yahweh. (8.16–17)

144 'House of Israel' is perhaps intrusive here; but it reveals the application of the message not only to the Judaean community but to the ideal of a reunited people. We may compare the Chronicler's concern with reunion.
145 Cf. Deut. 28.37; I Kings 9.7f.; Jer. 19.8; 25.18; 29.18; Lam. 2.15f.; Micah 6.16; (II Chron. 29.8). The same phrases are elsewhere used with reference to the downfall of other nations.
146 Cf. Gen. 12.3, etc.
147 Hag. 1.12; 2.5. Cf. also Zech. 8.9. On 8.9–13 as a 'levitical sermon' cf. W. A. M. Beuken, op. cit., pp. 156–73.
148 Omitting the second occurrence of '*emet*: cf. 7.9.

The obedience of the people, couched in terms which are reminiscent of earlier prophecy[149] and of the laws, is the necessary prerequisite of the day of salvation. The assured intention of God (vv. 14–15) is undoubted; there is no reason therefore for any anxiety. But it is possible for man to hinder the working out of that purpose. The overtone of judgement is not far off, for this was what God found it necessary to bring upon a previous disobedient generation. The twofold nature of God's word is, as so often in prophetic teaching, brought out in this note of warning; men may so easily miss what is God's good will for them.

Not inappropriately—for the whole long interwoven section from 7.4–8.17 stresses the contingent nature of the age of salvation, while confidently affirming its reality—the answer to the question about fasting is set here next. It is a full and confident statement, but, as we have seen,[150] it too ends with a note of warning. As it is now set, it is clear that while there is a wholehearted note of joyfulness at the anticipation of what God intends to do, there is always in Zechariah the recognition that this action of God depends upon what his word meets when it comes to man. To the responsive community it is life and well-being; to the disobedient it is relentless judgement.[151]

The fulfilment of the true intention of the fasts, issuing in festivals of rejoicing, is enlarged by the taking up again of the motif of universal salvation, made possible through what God has done for his people. The action towards his people is a declaration to the nations of who he is. The realization of that action shows to the nations that God's presence is indeed to be found in the centre of the world, namely in Zion. With echoes of the prophetic oracle duplicated in Isa. 2.1–4(5) and Micah 4.1–5, which perhaps may be held to suggest that there is here a deep-rooted idea of the centrality of Zion, which, like other great religious centres, may come to be thought of as the very navel of the earth,[152] the prophet here indicates in two sayings the response of the nations and the reason for that response.

It shall yet be that peoples will come
    and the inhabitants of great cities.
The inhabitants of one shall go to another saying:
    Let us go now to worship Yahweh

[149] Cf. e.g. Amos 5.10, 12.
[150] Cf. p. 209.
[151] Cf. Hos. 14.10.
[152] Cf. below p. 249 n. 61.

and to seek Yahweh of hosts.
(let me go, yes, me too!)[153]
Great peoples and powerful nations will come
to see Yahweh of hosts in Jerusalem
and to worship Yahweh. (8.20–22)

In those days it shall be that ten men from all the different races will take hold, they will take hold of the skirt of a Jew, saying:
Let us go with you, for we have heard that God is with you. (8.23)

The climax is reached in the realization that the new age of salvation, centred about the promise of God to come again and dwell in the midst of his people in his holy city and mountain in Zion, is meant for the whole world. The acceptance by the nations of the claims of God, as shown in his action towards his own people, offers the real hope for them.

So Zechariah sets out the real basis for hope and assurance. It is God who rescues, who reclaims his own, and through his action to his people declares his purpose and nature to the nations. In the often difficult days of the early post-exilic period, the acceptance of exile and disaster and the confidence in the reality of divine action are here plainly expressed.[154] And with this goes the appeal to that generation to appropriate and not to hinder what God purposes.[155, 156]

[153] D. Winton Thomas: 'The interjection of an enthusiastic member of the prophet's audience' (*IB* 6, p. 1088). Perhaps rather to be understood as the comment of a pious tradent expressing his longing to be there: 'Next year in Jerusalem.'
[154] Cf. M. Bič, *Das Buch Sacharja* (1962), p. 15; *Die Nachtgesichte des Sacharja* (BS 42, 1964), pp. 74f.
[155] It may be stressed that the emphasis is not strictly eschatological (cf. S. Mowinckel, *He that Cometh* [ET, 1956], pp. 121f.), even if we use that term in the sense that G. von Rad does (*Theology* II, p. 288) of the accomplishment in the heavenly world of events anticipated on earth.
[156] Although some references have been made to W. A. M. Beuken's work on Haggai and Zechariah in the preceding pages, its contributions have not been discussed. His fuller examination of the structure of Zech. 1–8, of the relation between vision and word, and of the structure and meaning of the visions themselves deserve careful scrutiny for the many penetrating comments which are made.

XII

EXILE AND RESTORATION: OTHER ASPECTS OF THE THOUGHT OF THE PERIOD

IN THE SURVEYS of the preceding chapters, the major collections of Old Testament material have been utilized to arrive at some understanding of the way in which the exile was experienced and described. For the period of restoration, primary stress has been laid upon Haggai and Zechariah in view of the intimate association between their activity and the revival of the community's life at that time. It may well be that there are in the Old Testament many other passages which reflect the sixth-century situation, but such material is less clearly datable and an element of doubt must inevitably arise. The danger of arguing in a circle is evident. A passage may be assigned to the period on the grounds that it in some measure appears to reflect the conditions of the years of the exile, or that it reveals the situation of those who were endeavouring to restore the community under Persian rule; it may then be used to illuminate the period, and unwarranted assumptions may be made about the evidence it provides.

For this reason, no attempt has been made in this study to select all the material which might be so assigned. In this short chapter, only a few passages are briefly discussed—passages which are probably more or less contemporary with the events, or which appear to shed some light upon contemporary attitudes[1]—and inevitably in some measure also subsequent developments of those attitudes. To that extent, the discussion here overlaps with that of the following chapter, in which an attempt is made to see the more long-term effects of the events and thought of the sixth century BC. The passages

---

[1] Cf. J. Scharbert, *Die Propheten Israels um 600 v. Chr.* (Cologne, 1967), pp. 479–99.

here discussed or mentioned are not fully dealt with, and no attempt has been made to give full documentation or to investigate the very great variety of interpretations which have been offered. For this would not only have demanded much more space than seems appropriate; it would also have produced an imbalance and would suggest a greater stress upon this material than is warranted. For, when all is said and done, it may be that these passages reflect other situations.[2] This exposition may serve simply to show the appearance of similar themes to those already set out.

Our concern will be with oracular and psalm material which appears to be related to the actual experience of exile, and with passages, particularly in Trito-Isaiah and Malachi, which reflect restoration, even if, as is the case with the latter, its date is somewhat later. The situation in the early fifth century may, however, be regarded as sufficiently closely related to the period of the rebuilding of the Temple and the evidently rather unexciting years which followed.

I. PASSAGES REFLECTING THE EXILIC SITUATION

(i) *Oracles of judgement, primarily upon Babylon as conqueror*

Each of the major prophetic books includes a collection of 'oracles on the nations'[3] and such collections on a much smaller scale may

---

[2] No attempt has been made in this study to take account of the now often repeated views of J. Morgenstern, who in a series of articles over the past years has been consistently arguing that quite substantial parts of the writings here discussed really belong to a great upheaval of 485 BC. References to these articles may be found, up to 1965, in O. Eissfeldt, *Introduction* (see index). Morgenstern's is not the first attempt, nor is it likely to be the last, at finding a panacea for the insoluble problems of dating the Old Testament material by associating a good deal of it with an otherwise virtually unattested historical situation. M. Buttenwieser (*The Psalms Chronologically treated, with a new translation* [Cambridge, Mass., 1938]) assigned many of the psalms to the fifth century BC and then wrote the history of that period largely on the basis of the psalms so assigned. Various scholars, including R. H. Kennett ('The Historical Background of the Psalms', in *Old Testament Essays* [Cambridge, 1928], pp. 119–218), have assigned most or all the psalms to the Maccabaean period, partly on the basis of our relatively full knowledge of that period, partly on the basis of arbitrary theory. It has then been possible to illuminate that period by further reference to the details of the psalms. Such a procedure is always easier to detect and criticize in the work of another writer than it is to guard against in one's own. Some elements of prejudgement inevitably affect all one's decisions in the matter of dating and situation.

[3] Isa. 13–23; Jer. 46–51; Ezek. 25–32.

be found elsewhere in the prophetic literature.[4] The structure and purpose of such collections have been much discussed,[5] but this is not the appropriate place to consider either the various theories of their origins or the attempts which have been made at finding for them a situation in the cultus or elsewhere in the life of the community. For our present purpose, it is sufficient to note that pronouncements of doom upon the nations—and in particular upon nations with which Israel was involved in the exilic age—are part of the material available to us for assessing the way in which the sixth-century community—and its successors—looked at its own situation.

Babylon, seen as the instrument of divine judgement on Judah,[6] is in a number of passages itself described as brought under judgement. In Jer. 51.59–64 a setting is depicted for such a pronouncement in the performance of a symbolic action to be undertaken by envoys in Babylon in the fourth year of Zedekiah. The denunciation of Babylon —and reference is here clearly intended to the two preceding chapters, 50–51, which are on this theme, so that these verses provide a kind of colophon to these chapters—is written in a book (sēper), to be sunk in the Euphrates as a symbol of the perpetual downfall of Babylon.

Chapters 46–51 of the book of Jeremiah contain a number of oracles on different lands, and particularly a series concerned with the judgement on those lands at the hand of Babylon itself. Thus Egypt is dealt with in 46 (and with this might be compared the symbolic action described in 43.8–13 which pronounces a comparable doom); 47–49 deal with other countries closely linked with Judah geographically—Philistia, Moab, Ammon, Edom, Damascus, Kedar and Hazor (and with this a comparison might be made with the indication of judgement on neighbouring lands in the narrative and oracular material of Jer. 27.1–11). It is evident that there is in the Jeremiah tradition a place for the kind of pronouncements upon other lands that we find also at an earlier stage developed particularly

---

[4] Cf. Amos 1.3–2.3; Obadiah; Zeph. 2. Cf. also Nahum, which is different in being concentrated on one nation, Assyria, and Habakkuk, which is more problematic in view of the difficulties of interpreting the material and deciding whether it refers to other nations or to Israel.

[5] Cf. N. K. Gottwald, *All the Kingdoms of the Earth* (New York, 1964), and bibliography, pp. 395–418.

[6] Cf. above p. 43 and note also in Isa. 23.13 the application to Babylon of a pronouncement concerning the judgement on Tyre, originally to have been carried out by the Assyrians as divine instrument.

in Amos and Isaiah. No doubt some of these oracles are as closely associated with the prophet as are the comparable sayings in the earlier two prophets, though allowance must always be made for subsequent reapplication and actualization of such words. Indeed here there are specific problems because of the links between some of the sayings and other prophetic material,[7] so that literary problems are present, even if we allow for a considerable use of stereotyped phraseology in a form which clearly has a long history behind its appearance in our prophetic books.

Judgement on these various lands is in part indicated to be at the hands of Babylon; thus 49.28–33 makes this link specifically, as do several phrases in ch. 46 dealing with Egypt. Other passages have no such obvious historical link, and it is doubtful if they contain clear enough allusions to associate them with this period apart from their attribution to the Jeremiah collection and their placing in association with passages which do contain more precise chronological allusions. The final verses of ch. 49 (vv. 34–39) introduce a saying on Elam which appears very little related to the context in which it stands.

The comparable collection in Isa. 13–23 also contains early elements; the indication of reapplication may be detected in ch. 13–14 (where ch. 14 [see v. 25] might originally have been in reality a pronouncement against Assyria, now subordinated to the Babylonian reference provided by ch. 13 and the opening verses of ch. 14) and also in 23.13, as already noted. In addition, it contains an oracle against Babylon in 21.1–10, about which more must be said subsequently. Like Jer. 25 (which in its LXX form includes the foreign nations oracles of MT 46–51), Isa. 13–23 culminates in its present form in a broader, more 'apocalyptic' series of utterances in ch. 24–27.[8] Ezek. 25–32 in many ways seems to belong more closely to the situation in which it is traditionally set and dated.[9] It expresses the broader context of the act of judgement in which Judah is involved, particularly in so far as Judah's neighbours are involved in the same disaster as herself.[10]

---

[7] Cf. the relation between Obadiah and parts of Jer. 49, and that between Jer. 49.27 and Amos 1.4.

[8] The term 'apocalyptic' is used here for convenience and without any pre-judgement of whether such passages as these are in reality to be described in the technical sense as such. The problem of the literary definition of the term 'apocalyptic' urgently needs attention.

[9] Cf. 26.1; 29.1; 30.20; 31.1; 32.1, 17.

[10] Here Ammon (cf. 21.23–26, 33–37), Moab, Edom and Philistia are briefly

The Babylon oracles of Jer. 50–51 raise difficult questions, not least since they are, by the statement of 51.59–64, linked to a moment when, according to another part of the Jeremiah tradition (Jer. 29.7), the well-being of Babylon was being described as integrally related to that of the exiles. It is true that the Jeremiah tradition also contains other hints of anti-Babylonian thought, as in 25.12ff., where an original anti-Judah statement appears to have been transformed into a word of judgement against its oppressors. A similar climax of an 'apocalyptic' kind is found in this chapter, where a brief summary of foreign nation pronouncements in 25.15–26 serves to introduce the more general statement of 25.27–38.

Jer. 50–51, like Isa. 13–14, attests the application of the idea of judgement to the great conquering power. In particular, it may be seen in detail that there has been reassignment of oracular material here, for Jer. 6.22–24, an oracle proclaiming the enemy from the north against Zion, is here used in Jer. 50(9), 41–43, reapplied to Babylon. In the MT presentation, the oracles against Babylon form the climax;[11] similarly, Isa. 13–14 heads a collection of such foreign nation oracles, though in addition Isa. 21 contains an oracle on the downfall of Babylon in another position.

The indications are, in all these cases, that greater prominence has eventually been given to Babylon, and we may properly ask whether this does not reflect rather more than the specific historic circumstances of the exilic period. The absence of the anti-Babylon strand in Ezekiel—as well as the indications of psalmody to be discussed in a moment—suggest that there was relatively limited scope for the violently hostile attitude to Babylon which here takes such prominence, and that, again as we may see in possible interpretations of Isa. 21, only the later years of the exile began to produce the more virulent statements. The elaborate presentation of Jer. 50–51 owes something to the actual historical conditions; but

---

covered (ch. 25); Tyre is dealt with at great length (ch. 26–28), and so too Egypt (ch. 29–32; cf. Jer. 46). Surprisingly Ezekiel contains no prospect of the downfall of Babylon. It has a more 'apocalyptic' conclusion in 32.17–32, which is closely linked with the judgement on Egypt, and ch. 38–39 offer a more general 'apocalyptic' picture.

[11] Cf. the discussion in C. Rietzschel, *Das Problem der Urrolle* (Gütersloh, 1966), pp. 45ff., who argues that this arrangement is earlier than that of the LXX which has been influenced by political circumstances in the Hellenistic age. But, as he rightly recognizes (p. 46), the original order is not preserved in either form, and the placing of the Babylon oracles in the MT is clearly deliberate.

its elaborate structure suggests that it owes more to what we may term the gradual 'idealizing' of the exilic period, so that the consideration of this material belongs rather with what is subsequently said about the significance of the exile in later thinking and the prominence given to Babylon as the enemy *par excellence* of later theological thinking.[12]

If this is so, then we may consider whether Isa. 21, which is not integrated into the main anti-Babylon material, may not provide the basic text, as it were, from which to work in considering these more elaborate passages. K. Galling has associated Isa. 21.1–10 with the period of Nabonidus,[13] suggesting links between this passage and the now available information concerning the last years of Babylonian rule, the prospect of the city's fall being here held out (v. 9) and the oracles in vv. 11–12, 13–15 being relevant to the political situation in the North Arabian area after 545 BC. Hostility to Babylon, as we have already seen, may be in some respects better understood in the later period of the exile, under Nabonidus.[14] With this period too, if we may judge from Isa. 46.1–2, it is appropriate to associate the ridiculing of the Babylonian gods—as in Jer. 50.2–3—though here much older and traditional elements are being elaborated and applied to the concrete situation of the exilic period.[15]

The whole complexes of Isa. 13–14 and of Jer. 50–51 may be seen as elaborate structures containing various elements. The latter in particular[16] contains much that can be paralleled elsewhere. We find themes such as that of the downfall of the tyrant, presented in Isa. 14 in mythological form in the figure of the Day Star (Isa. 14.12ff.); the ridiculing of the gods, already mentioned (Jer. 50.2–3); the raising up of a hostile power (the Medes in Isa. 13.17, and so too Jer. 51.11, 28; cf. Elam and Media in Isa. 21.2); the enemy from the north (Jer. 50.3, 41f.), or one more generally described in other parts of the material (cf. Jer. 50.9f.); the release of captives (Jer. 50.33f.; Isa. 14.2), for both these passages are interspersed with injunctions to

[12] Cf. pp. 243–47.
[13] 'Jesaia xxi im Lichte der neuen Nabonidtexte', in *Tradition und Situation*, ed. E. Würthwein and O. Kaiser (Göttingen, 1963), pp. 49–62. E. Janssen, *op. cit.*, p. 12, also assigns this chapter generally to the exilic situation.
[14] Cf. pp. 36ff.
[15] Such an element is to be found in a number of psalm passages—e.g. Ps. 115.4–8—but also in the Exodus traditions—implicitly in the plague narratives and cf. Ex. 9.15ff.—in the ark narrative of I Sam. 5–6, and in such passages as Jer. 2.13.
[16] Cf. the analysis in O. Eissfeldt, *Introduction*, p. 362.

escape from Babylon (Jer. 50.8, 28), with calls to repentance or the promise of it (Jer. 50.4f.), and promises of restoration and protection (Jer. 50.17–20; Isa. 14.1–3). There can be no doubt that there are elements here of different periods and origins, welded together into larger, perhaps liturgical, forms. The poetry, particularly in the descriptions of the downfall of the enemy, is very powerful; it not only expresses rejoicing at the experience of release from captivity, but clearly represents a measure of reflection upon this, so that the material now transcends the limits of a merely historical situation.

Similar again, and not unconnected with this whole problem of finding precise historical correlations, are the various oracles against Edom—Isa. 34, Ezek. 35, Obadiah, Mal. 1.2–5, in addition to those to be found in the groupings already mentioned. That the exilic situation may have produced a particularly large number of such utterances is possible; the specific situation in which Edom took advantage of the weakened state of Judah—as appears to be implied by Obadiah[17]—may have occasioned this upsurge of bitter feeling. But the hostility to Edom is a much older motif, and insufficient is known about the detail of the relationships for it to be certain that only the exilic age could have produced these passages. And again we may very probably detect here the stylizing of such references, so that Edom becomes very much the 'type' of enemy nation. To argue from such oracles to precise exilic experience is inappropriate; the expression of hostility to Edom, originating in a complex series of historical experiences, belongs to the development of Israel's understanding of the hostile world, that which is opposed to God and his purpose. In this, historic experience had its influence, but was not the sole determinant.

Without any certainty in the dating of so much of this material, we can do little more than state that a development in the exilic age of Israel's understanding of its position in relation to the hostile outside world is probable. This development was not altogether of a negative kind, as the recognition of the place of the nations as witnesses of divine action has shown.[18] But with this more positive appraisal of the purpose of God with his people, there goes the

[17] The parallel passage in Jer. 49 does not include the crucial verses Obad. 11–14 which appear to refer so precisely to the disaster of 587 BC. Cf. O. Eissfeldt, *Introduction*, p. 403; E. Janssen, *op. cit.*, pp. 18f. On Obadiah, cf. G. Fohrer, 'Die Sprüche Obadjas', in *Studia Biblica et Semitica T. C. Vriezen dedicata* (Wageningen, 1966), pp. 81–93.

[18] Cf. on Ezekiel and Deutero-Isaiah, pp. 115ff., 136.

development of a recognition of the hostile world, and of the onslaught and overthrow of the nations, an element detectable in what is probably much earlier psalmody—e.g. Pss. 2 and 46—and which finds its culminating developments in the last battles of apocalyptic imagery.[19]

(ii) *Allusions to the exile in the Psalms*

There is a similarity to these problems of historical relationship in the only unequivocal reference to the Babylonian exile in the Psalter, that to be found in Ps. 137.[20] As has already been noted, and as has been firmly and very rightly maintained by Lauha,[21] it is a mistake to look here for historical references in the simple sense, as if we could discover a precise moment of experience to which the psalm alludes or which can be regarded as the stimulus to its composition. It is rather to be taken as a poetic picture, a general impression of nostalgia, of distress, and of a desire for vengeance.[22] This is Babylon seen not historically but poetically.

Whether we may rightly detect other allusions to the exilic situation in the psalms depends on such uncertainties of interpretation that no very firm statement can be made. Lauha[23] finds expressions of the distress of the exile in Pss. 66.10ff.; 90.15; 106.46; 136.28f.; 148.14, but he admits that these are so generalized that they need not refer to the Babylonian exile at all. D. R. Jones[24] cites the use by Janssen of Pss. 44, 74, 79, 89 and 102;[25] he himself adduces the evidence of Pss. 40, 51, 69 and 102, and, by relating these to passages in Trito-Isaiah, finds confirmation of his thesis that the 'Jerusalem altar was not used for sacrifice after 586 BC until a new altar was built'.[26] But as he rightly admits,[27] other dates have been proposed for these psalms, and the danger of arguing in a circle is very evident

---

[19] The arrangement of foreign nation oracles to lead up to an 'apocalyptic' climax has already been noted. It may be seen also in Obad. 15ff. Pronouncements on the fate of the nations are linked with the 'Day of Yahweh', cf. above pp. 48f., see also O. Eissfeldt, *Introduction*, p. 403, on Obadiah, and G. von Rad, *JSS* 4 (1959), pp. 99ff., on Isa. 13.34 and other passages.

[20] Cf. also pp. 32f.

[21] A. Lauha, *Die Geschichtsmotive in den alttestamentlichen Psalmen* (*AASF* 56, 1945), pp. 123f.

[22] A. Lauha, *loc. cit.*

[23] *Op. cit.*, p. 124.

[24] *JTS* 14 (1963), pp. 24ff.

[25] *Juda in der Exilszeit*, p. 19.

[26] *Op. cit.*, p. 30.

[27] *Op. cit.*, p. 24 n. 1.

here. J. Becker[28] traces comparable references as indicative of what he calls 'eschatological reinterpretation' with reference to the release from the exile and to the settling of Israel's position *vis-à-vis* the foreign nations. He attempts, as other earlier commentators have done, to distinguish the earlier psalm elements from the later, exilic modifications.[29] Thus, in Ps. 102 he distinguishes vv. 2–12 and 24–25*a* as the original individual lament, and vv. 13–23, 25b–29 as referring to the situation of the people in exile and to the return to Zion.[30] He also sees in such psalm material the view that release from the exile is linked to the world of the nations, since in the end the exile itself may be viewed as due to that hostility.[31]

Such attempts are of interest in that they recognize the probability that older psalms have not only continued to be used, but have been understood and in some measure modified in a new situation. Becker's study has been taken as an example because it concentrates a good deal of attention on the exilic period as the point of reinterpretation; but such views may be found in many commentaries on the Psalms. Unfortunately, it is rarely if ever possible to be sure that precise evidence can be detected which makes it obligatory to see the application of the material to one situation of distress rather than another. This is partly because of the substantial use of conventional and stereotyped phrases in the psalms; partly also because particular situations tend to be interpreted in the light of more general understandings of experience and of divine action, understandings which may ultimately be linked to a combining of historical reminiscence and 'mythological' heritage.

(iii) *Passages of lamentation*

Some of the psalms just mentioned—in particular Pss. 44, 74, and 79—might equally well be included here,[32] together with the poems of Lamentations, already briefly discussed. The latter are so generally

[28] *Israel deutet seine Psalmen* (Stuttgarter Bibel-Studien 18, ²1967), pp. 41–68.
[29] An extreme example of this method can be seen in C. A. and E. G. Briggs, *The Book of Psalms*, 2 vols. (ICC, 1906/7).
[30] So too Ps. 69, where an individual lament has been similarly extended, especially in vv. 34ff.; Ps. 22, where vv. 28–32 are designated exilic; Ps. 107, vv. 2–3, 33–43; Ps. 118 which Becker thinks may be due to reinterpretation of elements taken from a thanksgiving liturgy. Similarly also Pss. 66, 85, 59, 9–10, 56, 54, 108, 68. This list is not exhaustive: we might well compare Ps. 14 = 53 which ends in hope of restoration.
[31] Cf. *op. cit.*, p. 42.
[32] Cf. also pp. 45f.

recognized as reflecting the fall of Jerusalem in 587 BC that they have been utilized at an earlier point.[33] The group of psalms, and others like them, contain so little that can be precisely aligned with the exilic situation that we may best see them as the kind of poems which might be supposed to have taken on a new significance in the experiences of this period. Such laments are intelligible in such a context, though not limited to one period, and it may simply be affirmed that, without necessarily postulating some special organization of lamentation ceremonial[34] or, one might more readily suppose, an extension, with a new emphasis, of already existing rituals, the form of the lament would appropriately express the anguish of a community, both in so far as it was sensitive to its being under judgement and in so far as it regarded the disasters as due to a relatively inexplicable withdrawal of divine favour.

The oracles of Trito-Isaiah also include passages of this kind, and it is possible that these belong to a date relatively near to the fall of the city, concerned rather with the problem of the disaster and its acceptance than with the situation of the restoration period to which these chapters are frequently assigned. Thus Isa. 59.1–15a reflects upon the sins which have brought disaster, and the lack of faith which accompanies a consideration of the present condition of the people. It is, however, also possible that here—as a result of the slowness and difficulties in the recovery of life after the exile—we may see indications of the disappointed hopes in the period after the conquests of Cyrus, a reflection of a situation in which the hand of God appears to be 'too short to save', his ear 'too dulled to hear' (59.1). The complaint in Zech. 1 that the disaster of the seventy-year period is still prolonged is answered by the divine assurance of God's purpose to save.[35] Here the answer is the double one of a reminder of the failure on the people's part which cuts them off from God, and a confidence that God will act, to come again as redeemer (59.15b–21).

Similarly, the long psalm of lamentation (for that is what its structure proclaims it to be)[36] in 63.7–64.11 is also undatable with any precision because of the general nature of its allusions. To interpret

---

[33] Cf. pp. 45ff.
[34] So H.-J. Kraus, *Worship in Israel* (ET, Oxford, 1966), p. 226; *id. Klagelieder* (*Threni*) (BK 20, ²1960), pp. 8ff.
[35] Cf. pp. 176f.
[36] So e.g. J. Muilenburg, *IB* 5 (1956), pp. 728f.

particular statements—as for example here the problematic Abraham reference of 63.16—as precise allusions to specific historic conditions[37] is hazardous. We may be justified only in recognizing that while there may here be a historical reference to which we now have no absolutely clear clue, it is much more probable that it is one of the formulae of distress, not perhaps inappropriate to those who feel themselves by reason of their religious sensitivity cut off from the historic community to which they belong. Such a lament could belong close to the events of 587; it could equally be thought to depict the reaction both to that disaster and to the continued disappointments and frustrations of the time in which the Temple is still not restored to its former glory.

2. PASSAGES REFLECTING RESTORATION

Much in the last chapters of the book of Isaiah turns upon the re-establishment of the Temple.[38] The picture of the glorifying of the New Jerusalem in ch. 60 stresses both the appearance of the divine glory, the gathering in of the wealth of the nations,[39] and the centrality to the world's life of the newly-named city. It is to be in truth the city of Yahweh, with walls and gates renamed in expression of the new age which it represents. The rebuilding of Temple and city together mark the presence of the glory of God, a frequent theme in Trito-Isaiah.[40]

Again, the restoration, the returning of the exiles and the redeeming of Zion, are proclaimed by Trito-Isaiah in terms often strongly reminiscent of Deutero-Isaiah. In particular there will be a new land, restored to life because brought back into relation with God (ch. 62), with a new people set in new heavens and earth in which life will no longer be curtailed and vain, but there will be security and the

---

[37] On the Abraham passage, cf. e.g. L. E. Browne, *Early Judaism* (1929), pp. 70–86, who describes the whole passage as 'The Plaint of a Samaritan Prophet'.
[38] Cf. T. Chary, *Les prophètes et le culte* (1955), p. 97.
[39] Cf. Hag. 2.6–9.
[40] Cf. 59.19; 60.1–2, 7, 13; 64.10; 66.11, 18–19. Cf. K. L. Schmidt, *Eranos-Jahrbuch* 18 (1950), p. 224; N. W. Porteous, 'Jerusalem—Zion: The Growth of a Symbol', in *Verbannung und Heimkehr* (1961), p. 248 = *Living the Mystery* (1967), p. 108; E. J. Tinsley, *The Imitation of God in Christ* (1960), p. 47, on the theme of 'Gerusalemme consolata' in Deutero- and Trito-Isaiah; A. Causse, *Du groupe ethnique à la communauté religieuse* (1937), pp. 210ff.; *id.*, *Israël et la vision de l'humanité* (1924) pp. 59–67.

complete re-ordering of the natural world (ch. 65).[41] Into the new community will come foreigners and eunuchs to whom life and the heritage of a name are given within the life of the people. Not only will the 'scattered of Israel' be gathered in, but more even than this (56.1–8); central will be the Temple which is for all peoples (56.7).

Alongside such hopes of restoration we may also tentatively place Ps. 126, a psalm which originally appears to be concerned with restoration in a much more general sense—particularly linked with the harvest (vv. 5–6)—but subsequently probably understood as dealing with national restoration after the exile.[42]

The effecting of restoration, as the oracles of Trito-Isaiah depict it, is clearly related to the present condition of the people, and here the allusions are not easy to understand, as in 56.9–57.13, where condemnation of leaders and accusations of idolatrous practice make it clear that the community is not in a fit condition for the realization of the promises.[43] The emptiness of religious observance (58.1–12, 13f.) shows a wrong attitude towards the nature of the God whose will is to grant deliverance. Similarly it is clear—as in Hag. 2.11–14—that there are those whose understanding of the Temple is as limited as in the time of Jeremiah (66.1–2),[44] with a false notion by which God is limited as if he were not in fact enthroned in heaven and not by any means bound to the Temple, though it is here that his glory appears (64.10 etc.). Indeed set side by side with this is a condemnation

[41] Cf. this theme in Zech. 8 (see pp. 211f.).

[42] For the interpretation of *šūb šebūt*, cf. the discussion and documentation in W. L. Holladay, *The Root Šûbh in the Old Testament* (Leiden, 1958), pp. 110ff. A. Lauha, *op. cit.*, pp. 124f., comments that this psalm too is probably less historical than eschatological—or it could refer to some other occasion.

[43] On the idolatrous practice, cf. D. R. Jones, *JTS* 14 (1963), pp. 18f. The precise allusions, as Jones reminds us, are difficult to interpret. It is, however, not clear whether we really have precise reference to the revival of Canaanite practice, or allusions to wrong thinking described in the conventional terms of idolatry.

[44] Cf. Jer. 7 and 26. Cf. R. E. Clements, *God and Temple* (1965), pp. 84f.; M. Haran, *IEJ* 9 (1959), pp. 91f. J. D. Smart's interpretation (*History and Theology in Second Isaiah* [1965], pp. 281ff.)—which he claims to be the natural one, consistently rejected by the commentators—has been commented on already in relation to Haggai's and Zechariah's understanding of the Temple which Smart does not appreciate (cf. p. 156 n. 15. Cf. also the similar misunderstanding of Haggai and Zechariah in C. Westermann, *Das Buch Jesaja. Kap.* 40–66 [ATD 19, 1966], p. 328). We may further note that Smart is forced to resort to an 'orthodox editor' (p. 282 n. 1), responsible for such passages as 44.28; 56.1–7; 58.13–14, to explain away the warm regard for the Temple elsewhere in the book; though, rather inconsistently, he elsewhere (p. 258) ascribes this love of the Temple to an earlier period—'until it became the stronghold of those who stubbornly refused to hear the word of God' (p. 258).

of sacrificial practice by those who evidently imagine that offerings produce their own automatic effect, and fail to respond to what God demands (66.3–4).[45]

The commonly held view that Trito-Isaiah represents the application of the essentials of Deutero-Isaiah's teaching to the practical needs of the post-exilic community, has much to commend it.[46] The evident pastoral concern of the prophet (cf. 61.1ff.), the injunctions and warnings, the recognition side by side of the dangers and the promises, suggests a link with both Ezekiel and the Deuteronomic school.[47] There is both confidence in the reality of the divine action —in spite of continued delays and disappointments—and a recognition of the need for there to be an acceptable people in whom the promises can be realized. Taken alongside Haggai and Zechariah, Trito-Isaiah shows us similar concerns and similar hopes.[48]

The same pastoral and hortatory tone is characteristic of the book of Malachi. Again we have indications of a prophet who is dealing with the practical and theological problems of the post-exilic community. The perspective is somewhat changed. The rebuilding of the Temple is already past, and the assurance of divine presence which goes with it is open to question because of continuing delay. It is in this situation that an unknown prophet makes a renewed affirmation of the reality of the relationship between Yahweh and Israel, on the basis of the election of Jacob ('I have loved Jacob') and the rejection of Esau (1.2–5). While it is conceivable that we should look for some precise historical background to the statements about Edom here, it is probable that no mere historical situation has pro-

[45] This appears to be the most probable interpretation of these verses, though it remains very much open to question, and it is possible that there is allusion to the alien practices actually being carried out. (Cf. the discussion in C. Westermann, *Das Buch Jesaja. Kap. 40–66* [1966], pp. 328f.)

[46] Cf. O. Eissfeldt, *Introduction*, pp. 342f., for references to the discussion of this point. Cf. esp. W. Zimmerli, 'Zur Sprache Tritojesajas', *Schweizerische Theologische Umschau* 20 (1950), pp. 110–22 = *Gottes Offenbarung*, pp. 217–33.

[47] Cf. pp. 82f., 104f.

[48] Similarly here, we may observe the tendency to depreciate the significance of the actual restoration by comparison with the high hopes of the prophet. Cf. A. Causse, *Du groupe ethnique à la communauté religieuse* (1937), p. 213: 'How mediocre and obscure the attempts at realization were to be by the side of the seers' dreams.'

Reference may also be made here to N. H. Snaith, *VTS* 14 (1967), pp. 218–43, where he analyses and comments on Isa. 56–66. But his discovery of precise evidence of a division between Babylonian and Palestinian Jews—the former standing in a line with Nehemiah and Ezra and the latter ultimately withdrawing as the Samaritan schism—leads to some curious analysis of the material into 'pro-Palestinian' and 'pro-Babylonian'.

vided the basis of the prophet's understanding, but that Edom, as in other passages which we have already considered,[49] has become the symbol of the outside and hostile world. By contrast, Israel has the love of God set upon it.

The prophet directs his concern to two attitudes which run contrary to the recognition of this elective love. On the one hand, there is the whole condition of unacceptability which makes the appropriation of divine action impossible. The failure of the priesthood stands central to this, and here we can see the carrying further of the tradition of Ezekiel, P, Haggai and Zechariah. The central shrine, which should be the place for the honouring of God, has become a place in which God is insulted (1.6–2.9). Side by side with this are indications of the repudiation of Yahweh and of the community which is his, by irreligious and idolatrous practice, and by alien intermarriage (2.10–17). On the other hand, the prophet is concerned with the problem of religious scepticism (2.13–17; 3.13–15). Into this is woven again the stress upon a right response in which alone the divine will can be appropriated. But above all, this is the context for the reaffirmation of divine action, in the great act of deliverance which brings judgement upon the unrighteous and hope for the God-fearers. The continuing state of distress is seen as evidence for the continuing failure of the people. The rightness of divine judgement and withdrawal is stressed. The reality of divine action and intervention is made plain. In all these the continuation may be seen of that understanding of disaster and that appropriation of the centrality of divine action which mark the exilic age and which make the real basis for confidence in a period of restoration in which the maintenance of faith had to be against the background of continued frustration and disappointment.[50]

The material to which reference has here been made again points to the appropriation of the experience of exile, and the consequent deepening in the understanding of the relationship between divine action and political fortunes. Once again we may be impressed by the realism of thinkers who do not oversimplify the problems of their time, and whose recognition of human failure and divine promise is held together in soberness and confidence.

[49] Cf. above p. 224.

[50] A similar point might be made in regard to the present structure of Proto-Isaiah, where in such chapters as 4, 11–12, 34–35 the older words of judgement, themselves reapplied to the disaster of 587, have been answered by oracles of promise and restoration, akin in some measure to Deutero-Isaiah.

√

XIII

THE SIGNIFICANCE OF THE EXILE AND RESTORATION[1]

I. DEVELOPMENTS OF THOUGHT

WITH ALL THE HISTORICAL uncertainties which remain for our appreciation of what happened in the sixth century BC in Palestine and Babylonia where members of the Jewish people were concerned, there is no real doubt about the main outlines.[2] The reality of the disasters of 597 and particularly of 587 is amply attested in the biblical records, sufficiently confirmed in such non-biblical records as are available, and abundantly illustrated in the archaeological discoveries in Palestine itself. It is true that some room remains here for the hope that future excavations may be able to be a little more precise in indicating those areas in which destruction was less and continuity more evident, for the Persian period has only recently come to be of any very special interest to the archaeologists, most of whom have tended either to be concerned with the Hellenistic period or to have been anxious to press back through the Persian period to the more exciting ages which lie behind and beneath it. The nature of Hellenistic building programmes too seems often to have resulted in the practical elimination of strata which lie immediately beneath so that the paucity of archaeological evidence is the more notable. In recent years, however, a growing interest is becoming evident in this sixth and fifth century period and we may hope for greater clarity and understanding of the immediate post-exilic period. Nevertheless the indications of disaster, particularly in the southern part of Judah, and the modest indications of revival make it reasonable to see in the biblical records a not inaccurate representation of widespread devastation and slow recovery.

[1] Part of this chapter has appeared in a slightly different form in the *Canadian Journal of Theology* 14 (1968), pp. 3–12.
[2] Cf. ch. II.

The thinking of the period is amply attested in the records; if any-thing, too amply attested. For while the tendency must be resisted of tracing to the period in which one is taking a special interest almost anything which is even remotely connected with it, there is neverthe-less an abundance of Old Testament material which comes together at this point. The older prophetic material which has been dealt with only briefly in this study, shows many signs of having been re-interpreted in the context of the exile. The older narratives and laws were not only gathered to a quite considerable extent, but in the two great compilations of the period—the Priestly Work and the Deuteronomic History—have been given a definitive or almost definitive form, with a consequent shift in interpretation which results from their older material being seen now against the back-ground of the exilic age.[3] Older psalmody—for we do not need now to doubt its much earlier origin—has been reinterpreted so that references to older disasters have come to be seen in the light of this, the latest and most intense.[4] This again is a matter on which this study has hardly touched, if only because the historical interpretation of psalmody, in view of the lack of precise allusions, is always open to the charge of subjectivism, and it is therefore better to get some of the more evidently fixed points in the thought clear first.

But it is not only the heritage of the past which comes into new focus at this period. The events, themselves necessitating rethinking, have provoked the development of new lines of thought, markedly in the great prophets of the time, Ezekiel and Deutero-Isaiah, and, echoing them and the other thought of the period, in their successors in the immediate post-exilic period, Haggai, Zechariah, Trito-Isaiah and Malachi. The richness too of the differing reactions to the events, and of the understanding of the nature of restoration, shows how deep an impression was made upon the community by the period, and how fertile were the minds which interpreted what happened and what they understood to be the outcome of the events.

Much of the immediate reaction to the events of the disaster itself

---

[3] Cf. the comment of H.-J. Stoebe, 'Überlegungen zur Theologie des Alten Testaments', in *Gottes Wort und Gottes Land*, ed. H. Graf Reventlow (Göttingen, 1965), pp. 200–20, who comments on the significance these older works had for enabling Israel not only to overcome this, the most serious attack on the assurance of its faith, but also to be led more deeply into the understanding of that faith (pp. 201f.).

[4] So we may best see historical allusions to disasters in certain psalms, such as 44, 74, 79; others, e.g. 106, 126, in their present form allude to return from exile.

is to be seen in terms of acceptance. The exile is seen as judgement upon the people's life, but more than that it is understood as lying within the purposes of God not simply as judgement but in relation to what he is doing in the life of the world. The response to it must be the response of acceptance, but this involves not merely a repentant attitude, appropriate and necessary though this is, because the disaster is not simply judgement, not simply a condemnation of the past but also a stage within the working out of a larger purpose.[5] To some extent this was already recognized earlier in terms of discipline. The experiences of disaster had been interpreted, for example by Amos,[6] as a means by which God brought—or sought to bring—his people to the recognition of what they were and what they were doing. But more than this, it was to be understood as providing a means by which the nature of God should be revealed, a process by which both the people on whom it was exercised and also the nations as witnesses of the action should come to the acknowledgement of who he is. For if we were to pick any one phrase which is characteristic of this whole period, it would surely be 'to know that I am Yahweh'—the very expression of the name and nature of God.

With this the thought of restoration is linked, for, as we have seen, the essential emphasis is upon the absolute priority of divine action. The effect and acceptance of disaster have brought an understanding of restoration in terms of God's action. The more effectively the disaster is accepted, and the more realistically the condition of men's life is appreciated, the more evident it becomes that only in divine action can there be hope; and that this divine action is entirely self-motivated and is not to be, as it were, undergirded with the self-pity of the people, the conscious or unconscious expression of the belief that in the end God will forgive: 'c'est son métier'. In this, there is very evident acceptance of the message of the pre-exilic prophets, whose concern is with the unacceptability of the people and so the complete wrongness of their approach to God; hence their condemnation of both contemporary social and contemporary religious life. But more still we find a link here with their condemnation of that superficial attitude which takes God for granted, assumes that the very performance of sacrifice is a meritorious matter, builds on the very existence of the Temple as itself the warrant of the divine

---

[5] On this theme, cf. A. Gamper, *Gott als Richter in Mesopotamien und im Alten Testament* (Innsbruck, 1966), esp. Part II, sections 4 and 5.

[6] Cf. Amos 4.6–11.

presence and power. In his condemnation of religious apostasy and idolatry Jeremiah speaks of those who

> have turned their back to me, and not their face. But in the time of their trouble they say,
> 'Arise and save us.' (Jer. 2.27)

and equally of those who, in what is evidently a ritual form, repeat: 'The Temple of Yahweh, the Temple of Yahweh, the Temple of Yahweh' (Jer. 7.4), as if by the very invocation of the Temple they are able to assure for themselves the help of the God whose declared dwelling it is.

As we have seen, there is at times a certain oversimplification of the human situation in the earlier prophets and in the Deuteronomic History. The possibility of a right choice, of real repentance and turning back to God is envisaged—though often in contexts which make it clear that the prophets and historians also recognized that such a repentance was in the event extremely unlikely, or even impossible.[7] With the exile, this need for repentance and reform is set in the context of a new act of God—implicit in the Deuteronomic History where the appeal to respond is set against the Exodus and Conquest events but is clearly directed to the later situation; explicit in the prophecies of Ezekiel and Deutero-Isaiah, and carried on from them into the convictions of the post-exilic prophets. The correlation between this new act of God and the people's condition is only partially developed here, but more fully elaborated in the Priestly Work, where the implicit new act of God is in the context of the divine promise to Abraham which is now to be redeemed, and the response of the community in obedience and purity is recognized to be both a continuous one, expressed in the minutiae of legal codes, and a repeated one, expressed in the stress laid upon purification. This line too is continued in the post-exilic prophets. Their proclamation of the new age stresses the context of the promised new life for the people. Their concern with the people's fitness both elaborates the stress of earlier prophecy, particularly that of Ezekiel, and also, in its emphasis on hesitation, expresses the concern lest the new age should be indefinitely delayed by the unfitness of those for whom it should come,[8] and so the wider purposes of God for the nations also be frustrated. For it is through a renewed and purified Israel that the

---

[7] Cf. Hos. 5.4: 'Their deeds do not permit them to return to their God.'
[8] Cf. Luke 18.8: 'When the Son of man comes, will he find faith on earth?'

nations are to know God and recognize him in his action towards his people.

There is a further sequel to this in the work of the Chronicler, about which a little more must be said in a moment. The close affinities of the Chronicler in his theology[9] with the Deuteronomic movement of thought make it most desirable not to define his thinking—as was often done in older studies[10]—simply in terms of the Priestly School. At the same time, it is clear that his understanding of the nature of the relationship between God and his people is closely allied to that which is found in the Priestly School.[11] He lays no stress at all in the opening part of his work on the Exodus covenant, but rather shows the continuity of divine grace and promise all through. For him the definitive period is, however, in the age of David, and this because that was the period in which the whole organization of Israel's worship was fully undertaken. His claim is for the legitimacy of that worship at Jerusalem which David established. There is a polemical note here which even the Deuteronomists did not need, for the claim has to be established against that of the Samaritans.[12] At the same time, in the series of reform movements and re-establishments of religious life—Hezekiah, Josiah, the rebuilding of the Temple, the work of Ezra (and of Nehemiah if that originally belonged)[13] we are shown the community being purified,

[9] Cf. P. R. Ackroyd, 'History and Theology in the Writings of the Chronicler', *Concordia Theological Monthly* 38 (1967), pp. 501–15, for a fuller development of these themes.

[10] Cf. C. R. North, *The Old Testament Interpretation of History* (London, 1946), pp. 107ff.; E. L. Curtis and A. A. Madsen, *The Books of Chronicles* (ICC, 1910), pp. 8ff.

[11] Cf. also O. Eissfeldt, *Introduction*, p. 539.

[12] In a paper entitled 'The Old Testament and Samaritan Origins' read to the Society for Old Testament Study in London in January 1968 and to be published in Vol. 6 of the *Annual of the Swedish Theological Institute*, R. J. Coggins suggests that the polemic of the Chronicler should not be understood so narrowly, but rather as a claim for Jerusalem legitimacy over against various other lines of thought, of which one could be designated the forerunner of the eventual Samaritan schism. Although the Chronicler's attitude to the north does suggest a reference to Samaritanism, it is certainly right to consider how far later, more rigid descriptions are really appropriate to the period in which he was active. The aims of the Chronicler may certainly be described as polemical, but it may be better to describe them as being in favour of a certain type of interpretation of the ancestral faith rather than as being representative of 'orthodoxy' contrasted with 'schism' or 'heresy'. The variety of thought within Judaism in the Qumran period is indicative of a much richer tradition than would be suggested by such a description as this last.

[13] Cf. K. Galling, *Die Bücher der Chronik, Esra, Nehemia* (ATD 12, 1954), p. 10.

undertaking the response which testifies to the need for purity, purity of race, freedom from contamination with alien influence, so attesting its real nature as the people of God. The worship shows a joyful people responding to the blessings of God.

But to some extent this consideration of the Chronicler is to anticipate the next point, and in the remainder of this concluding chapter we must look at the whole subject of exile and restoration in a somewhat broader perspective.

2. THE 'IDEA' OF EXILE

This study originated in a consideration of the problems of the restoration period from c. 540–500 BC, but inevitably developed into a wider discussion of the various factors in the exilic age which led up to this and without which it is unintelligible. It has become enlarged also in another dimension. The questions raised are not merely those of the sixth century BC, though an attempt has been made to cover the main lines of thought which can be discerned there. To some extent already in the selection of material it has been made clear that it is not necessarily essential to demand a precise determination of the date of every passage for it to be considered relevant. Indeed if such a prerequisite were to be insisted on, the discussion of almost any period of Old Testament history would inevitably become even more nebulous than it now sometimes appears to be. Important and desirable as historical dating is—and nothing which is said here is in any way designed to underestimate it—it may nevertheless be useful to draw together material which, even if not all of one period, reflects outlooks arising from the consideration of a particular situation. The exile was a historic fact, though its precise description in detail is a matter of great difficulty. But as a fact of Israel's historic experience, it inevitably exerted a great influence upon the development of theological thinking. The handling of the exile is not therefore solely a problem of historical reconstruction; it is a matter of attempting to

---

The theory of a later addition of the Nehemiah material considerably eases the major literary and historical problems concerning the relationship between Ezra and Nehemiah, though it does not solve them. Cf. also S. Mowinckel, *Studien zu dem Buche Ezra-Nehemia* I. *Die nachchronische Redaktion des Buches* (Oslo, 1964), and O. Eissfeldt, *Introduction*, p. 544, who maintains that the Nehemiah material was included by the Chronicler himself.

understand an attitude, or more properly a variety of attitudes, taken up towards that historic fact.[14]

In an important passage which occurs twice in Jeremiah (16.14–15; 23.7–8), the substitution of a new *confessio fidei*[15] is indicated:

> So, the days are coming—oracle of Yahweh—when it shall no longer be said:[16]
> As Yahweh lives who brought up the Israelites
>   from the land of Egypt,
> but
> As Yahweh lives who brought up the Israelites[17] from the north-land and from all the lands into which he had driven them.[18] And I will bring them back upon the land which I gave to their forefathers.[19]

A study of confessional statements[20] makes it clear that the oath-formula used here is in essence a summarizing of the account of what Yahweh had done in the great decisive moment of the Exodus. So we may reasonably assume a re-formulating of that confessional statement—as the prophet anticipates—with a substitution of the new words of deliverance for the old. A 'new Exodus' is to be the central element in the faith as now re-experienced. This indeed is, as we have seen, very much the emphasis of Deutero-Isaiah.[21] But when we look at later passages in which the *confessio fidei* is again expressed —in Neh. 9 or in Judith 5—we find that though some reference is certainly made to the later events, there is no substitution of a new act of deliverance for the original one. Reference is made very modestly to the exile and to the change of fortunes which followed it:

> So you gave them into the power of the foreign peoples, but in your great mercy you did not make an end of them nor forsake them, for you are a God merciful and gracious. (Neh. 9.30*b*–31)

[14] Cf. the discussion by N. W. Porteous, 'Jerusalem-Zion: The Growth of a Symbol', in *Verbannung und Heimkehr*, ed. A. Kuschke (Tübingen, 1961), pp. 235–52 = *Living the Mystery* (Oxford, 1967), pp. 93–111, for a similar approach to the relation between a limited historical entity and its theological significance. Cf. also R. de Vaux, *Jerusalem and the Prophets* (Goldensen Lecture, 1965; Cincinnati, 1965); 'Jérusalem et les prophètes', *RB* 73 (1966), pp. 481–509.

[15] Cf. H.-J. Kraus on Ps. 98, *Psalmen II* (BK 15, 1960), pp. 677f.

[16] 16.14 has *yēʾāmēr*; 23.7 the equivalent impersonal form *yōʾmᵉrū*.

[17] 23.8 has 'and who brought in the descendants of the house of Israel'.

[18] 23.8 has 'I had driven them'.

[19] 23.8 has 'And they shall dwell in their own land'.

[20] E.g. in Deut. 26, Josh. 24. Cf. J. Muilenburg: 'The Form and Structure of the Covenantal Formulation', *VT* 9 (1959), pp. 347–65; B. S. Childs, *VTS* 16 (1967), pp. 30–39.

[21] Cf. pp. 129ff.

But when they had departed from the way which he appointed for them, they were utterly defeated in many battles and were led away captive to a foreign country. . . . But now they have returned to their God, and have come back from the places[22] to which they were scattered, and have occupied Jerusalem, where their sanctuary is, and have settled in the hill country, because it was uninhabited. (Judith 5.18f.)

In other words, the assessment of exile and restoration is not made in terms of the Exodus, of a new act of deliverance, but rather in terms of the continuing mercy and grace of God which operates in spite of the fact that justice demanded the destruction of people and land.

There is a recognition here—different from the point made in the passage in Jeremiah—that the exile is not comparable with the period of the Exodus. For at no point in the Exodus narratives is it suggested that the people in Egypt were brought into subjection by reason of their own sinfulness. The *vaticinium ex eventu* of Gen. 15.13f. offers simply a 'factual' statement of the experience of slavery, and whereas a link could have been made between the envy and sin of Joseph's brothers and the subsequent events seen as punishment, instead the link is made between men's evil intentions and God's overruling goodness.[23] The exile could not be viewed in the same way. It is true that estimates of it varied, but in general the concentration is on the punishment, acknowledged to be just, of the people's failure. So restoration, as viewed by those who experienced it and by those who later considered it, is not simply a great act of deliverance viewed against the background of the evil of the nations (though themes connected with this play their part in the pictorial representation of the restoration);[24] it is an act of mercy, a restoration brought about by the willingness of God to have his people again in their own land. It is 'for his name's sake'.

Alongside this kind of development of thought, we may see also that of the Chronicler, who, as we have seen in connection with the actual description of restoration,[25] is deeply conscious of the providential care of God, but who also attempts a more precise description of the exile so as to bring out its inner meaning.[26] The narrative

---

[22] Lit. 'dispersion', Gk. διασπορᾶς.
[23] Cf. Gen. 50.20.
[24] Cf. e.g. Hag. 2.6–9; Zech. 2.1ff.; Ezra 1 for Exodus themes in restoration.
[25] Cf. p. 149.
[26] Cf. the rather unsatisfactory analysis of the Chronicler's viewpoint in E.

of the final disaster to Jerusalem is punctuated by statements of the reasons for it:

Yahweh the God of their fathers sent to them by the agency of his messengers, and kept on sending, because he had pity on his people and his dwelling-place. But they simply kept on mocking the messengers of God and despising his words and scoffing at his prophets until the anger of Yahweh came up against his people till there could be no healing.
(II Chron. 36.15f.)

When the disaster takes place, the comment is made on the exile:

[The king of the Chaldaeans] exiled to Babylon the remnant which survived violent death, and they became slaves to him and his descendants until the rule of the kingdom of Persia. This was to fulfil the word of Yahweh by the mouth of Jeremiah:
    Until the land has paid off its sabbaths. All the days of desolation it kept sabbath, to complete seventy years. (36.20f.)

The Jeremiah allusion is in fact to be found only in the one phrase 'seventy years', made precise as a determination of the exile;[27] this is

---

Janssen, *op. cit.*, pp. 118–21, which suffers from an insufficiently careful consideration of the relevant texts. B. Albrektson, *History and the Gods* (1967), pp. 84f., stresses the 'episodic' nature of the Chronicler's understanding, but this does not sufficiently view the work as a whole.

[27] I.e. v. 21*b*, cf. Jer. 25.11; 29.10. The 'seventy-year' theme has evoked much discussion. For an older review, cf. F. Fraidl, *Die Exegese der siebzig Wochen Daniels in der alten und mittlern Zeit* (Graz, 1883). As a conventional number, 70 is not uncommon (cf. Judg. 9.2; II Kings 10.7; Isa. 23.15; Ps. 90.10), and also in Egypt, cf. H. Kees, *Ägypten* (Munich, 1933), p. 97; J. M. A. Janssen, 'Egypotological Remarks on the Story of Joseph in Egypt', *Ex Oriente Lux* 14 (1955/6), pp. 63–72, see pp. 71f. As a figure for conquest, cf. D. D. Luckenbill, 'The Black Stone of Esarhaddon', *AJSL* 41 (1924/5), pp. 165–73, see pp. 166f.; J. Nougayrol, 'Textes hépatoscopiques d'époque ancienne II', *RA* 40 (1945/6), pp. 56–97, see pp. 64f.; and R. Borger, *Die Inschriften Asarhaddons Königs von Assyrien* (Archiv für Orientforschung, Beiheft 9, Graz, 1956), p. 15. Borger quotes two passages, elaborating Luckenbill's discussion; these speak of a period of seventy years' exile from Babylon interpreted as due to Marduk's anger [Borger renders 'Until the days are fulfilled that the heart of the great lord Marduk should be reconciled with the land with which he has been angered, seventy years are to pass'] and of the transformation of this into an exile of only eleven years (the point being dependent upon the written form of the two numerals: 70 reversed would be read as 11). Cf. also R. Borger, *JNES* 18 (1959), p. 74, tracing the figure appropriately to a conventional life-span. So Ps. 90.10. Cf. also W. Rudolph, *Jeremia* (HAT 12, 1947), p. 157; (³1968), pp. 183ff.; C. F. Whitley, 'The Term Seventy Years Captivity' *VT* 4 (1954), pp. 60–72 and *VT* 7 (1957), pp. 416–18; A. Orr, *VT* 6 (1956), pp. 304–6; E. Vogt, *Biblica* 38 (1957), p. 236; P. R. Ackroyd, 'Two Old Testament Historical Problems of the Early Persian Period. B. The "Seventy Year" Period', *JNES* 17 (1958), pp. 23–27; C. Rietzschel, *Das Problem der Urrolle* (Gütersloh,

accompanied by another quotation which is not from Jeremiah.[28]
'Until the land has paid off its sabbaths' is evidently an allusion to
the closing passage of the 'Holiness Code':

> . . . and I brought them into the land of their enemies. If then their
> uncircumcised heart is humbled and they then pay off their iniquity,
> then I will remember my covenant with Jacob and my covenant with
> Isaac; even my covenant with Abraham I will remember, and the
> land I will remember. The land will be abandoned by them and it will
> pay off its sabbaths in its desolation without them and they will pay off
> their iniquity . . . (Lev. 26.41–43)[29]

The interpretation of the exile by the Chronicler thus depends upon
a passage in which the exile is regarded as related to the disobedience
of the people, but is also given a more precise meaning in relation to
the sabbath. Here we must recognize two possible interpretations of
the root $r\bar{a}\d{s}\bar{a}$, here rendered 'pay off'. The first occurrence of the word
in the Leviticus passage—as in certain other Old Testament contexts
—clearly means 'pay off' in relation to the people's sin; so too the
third occurrence. It could also have this meaning in its second occurrence in relation to the sabbaths. In some way, not clearly specified,
the period of the exile means a paying off or counting off of sabbaths
(or sabbatical years) which have not been properly observed and are
therefore now to be substituted in an enforced observance. The

---

1966), p. 37; E. Testa, 'Le 70 settimane di Daniele', *Studii Biblici Franciscani Liber
Annuus 9* (1958/9), pp. 5–36; Fr. Vattioni, '*T* settant' anni della cattività', *RivBibl* 7
(1959), pp. 181f. (not available to me); G. R. Driver, 'Sacred Numbers and Round
Figures', in *Promise and Fulfilment*, ed. F. F. Bruce (Edinburgh, 1963), pp. 62–90, on
the Daniel passage.

The discussion by G. Larsson, 'When did the Babylonian Captivity Begin?',
JTS 18 (1967), pp. 417–23, attempts to prove the exactness of the seventy-year
statements, and finds a seventy-lunar-year period from the 'surrender and removal
to Babylon' of Jehoiakim in 605 BC to the arrival in Palestine of the first Jewish
contingent after the liberation by Cyrus. His discussion rests heavily on K.
Stenring, *The Enclosed Garden* (Stockholm, 1966), which is a very odd attempt at
discovering patterns in Old Testament chronology. It also depends upon what is
described as a reasonable assumption that Jehoiakim was included in Nebuchadrezzar's triumphal progress in 605 and that he was subsequently reinstated. The
evidence adduced is not conclusive, that of Dan. 1.1–4 and of Berossus being of
doubtful authenticity, though no doubt revealing ideas current by the third
century BC, but in any case not at any point suggesting that Jehoiakim himself
went to Babylon. The whole argument seems to represent a clutching at straws to
prove the absolute correctness of biblical chronology, which is at best a dubious
procedure.

[28] Cf. W. Rudolph, *Chronikbücher* (HAT 21, 1955), p. 337.
[29] Cf. ch. VI. Cf. also in Lev. 26.34.

emphasis is on punishment and atonement; through the exile the sins of the past are dealt with, as also in Isa. 40.2 where the same root is used. But an alternative interpretation may be obtained by treating the root *rāṣā* here as meaning 'to enjoy'[30] and more particularly 'to be acceptable' (to God).[31] In this case the Leviticus passage plays upon the two roots;[32] the people are *paying off* their sin, and while they do so the land in its desolated state is *enjoying* its sabbaths, and hence is being made acceptable to God. It is a period of enforced fallowness, comparable with the sabbath years of the law.[33] The fact that the Chronicler quotes only the one phrase from the Leviticus context suggests that this was the interpretation in his mind. The exile is not viewed by him simply in terms of punishment —though this is evident enough in the context—but also in terms of the recuperation needed for the new life of the post-exilic period.

Such a link with the seven-year law (and also with the Jubilee laws of Lev. 25.8ff.) is also presupposed by the later use of the same idea in Daniel 9. Here the interpretation of the seventy-year period, having been taken literally in some measure by both Zechariah and the Chronicler, is linked with the weeks of years which mark the sabbath periods of years, and the whole period from the fall of Jerusalem to the restoration under Judas Maccabaeus becomes a period of sabbaths. It is in effect an exile lasting 490 years, and with this we reach an understanding of exile and restoration which takes us well beyond the consideration of the sixth century. Here the exile is no longer an historic event to be dated in one period; it is much nearer to being a condition from which only the final age will bring release.[34] Though bound to the historical reality of an exile which actually took place in the sixth century, the experience of exile *as such* has become the symbol of a period, viewed in terms of punishment but also in terms of promise:

[30] So RSV.

[31] Cf. R. Rendtorff, *TLZ* 81 (1956), cols. 340f.

[32] The phrase 'plays upon the two roots' is to put in more precise form what the author himself would presumably have seen in a rather different way. The distinguishing of two Hebrew roots here is the result of modern philological study (cf. *KBL* p. 906). To the ancient author, the word would simply appear to have alternative meanings, and he seems to be expressing himself so as to suggest both. (Cf. the comment of J. Barr, *ExpT* 75 [1963–4], p. 242 and the fuller discussion by J. F. A. Sawyer, 'Root-meanings in Hebrew', *JSS* 12 [1967], pp. 37–50; also P. R. Ackroyd, 'Meanings and Exegesis', in *Words and Meanings*, ed. P. R. Ackroyd and B. Lindars [Cambridge, 1968], pp. 1–12.)

[33] Cf. Lev. 25.1ff.

[34] Cf. J. Becker, *op. cit.*, p. 42.

Seventy weeks are decreed upon your people and your holy city until rebellion is restrained[35] and sin is sealed up[36] and iniquity is atoned and eternal righteousness is brought in and vision and prophet are sealed off and a most holy one[37] is anointed. (Dan. 9.24)

The understanding of the exile is clearly enlarged far beyond the temporal considerations of seventy years and the precise period covered by Babylonian captivity in the stricter sense. The desecration of the Temple by Antiochus Epiphanes is here regarded as a continuation of that desecration which belongs to the exilic age. A true limit to the exile is now being set.

It is in this that we may see the truth of that type of interpretation of the post-exilic age[38] which points out that the exile came to be seen as of paramount importance, a great divide between the earlier and later stages, but one which it was necessary to traverse if the new age was to be reached. Only those who had gone through the exile —whether actually or spiritually—could be thought of as belonging. The rebuilt Temple was dedicated by returned exiles and those who, forsaking the abominations of the land, joined themselves to them.[39] The Chronicler shows too that in the times of apostasy in the past, at the division of the kingdom, in the reigns of Hezekiah and Josiah, there could be held out the possibility that the faithful who thus separated themselves could rejoin the community.[40] It is an appeal for a gathered community, recognizing that the experience of the exile, the experience of judgement, can be appropriated either by

[35] So MT, though for *kl'* we could easily read *klh* and render 'to bring to an end rebellion'.
[36] So K*ethīb*: *laḥtōm*. Q*erē*: *lᵉhātēm* i.e. 'sin is brought to an end'.
[37] The interpretation of *qōdeš qᵒdāšīm* here is very difficult. N. W. Porteous, *Daniel* (OTL, 1965), p. 140, argues firmly for the interpretation 'holy place' = the sacred shrine itself and affirms that 'In spite of I Chron. 23.13, where the form may conceivably refer to Aaron, there is no justification for the Early Church's view that there is here a reference to the Messiah . . .' The Chronicles passage may be rendered: 'Aaron was set apart so that he might consecrate the most sacred things, himself and his descendants in perpetuity.' But the interpretation of the Daniel passage does not depend on this uncertain analogy. It must be determined by the context. The stages covered by the seventy-week period are defined in Dan. 9.25ff. After seven weeks, there is to be an anointed leader (*nāgīd māšiaḥ*)—Zerubbabel or perhaps more probably Joshua; after sixty-two further weeks 'an anointed one is to be cut off'. The third stage in the final week leads up to the destruction of the destroyer, and 'the most holy' who is anointed would seem most naturally to be an anointed person, the agent of destruction.
[38] Cf. C. C. Torrey's writings, as listed on p. 21 n. 21.
[39] Ezra 6.21.
[40] Cf. II Chron. 30 and 34.6f., 33.

virtue of having gone through it (and proof of this may be furnished by means of genealogies, real or fictitious),[41]—and so the impetus again and again is shown as coming from returned exiles (the 'remnant' of II Chron. 36.20)—or by accepting its significance by the abandonment of what belongs to it, namely uncleanness, pollution of the land.[42] In this the Chronicler is properly elaborating that aspect of prophetic teaching which stressed the absolute necessity of exile;[43] that God's dealings with his people in the future must depend upon a repudiation and destruction of which the exile was the expression. Again with a link to the understanding of the exile by its contemporaries—in Lamentations, in the annotation and re-interpretation of pre-exilic prophecy, in the reinterpretation of the psalms—the experience of exile is as the experience of the Day of Yahweh. It is inevitable and must therefore be accepted; it is judgement and promise, and so the one is impossible without the other.

Such a deepened understanding of the exile as experience and not merely as historic fact may perhaps be traced in two other Old Testament works whose major concerns lie in other directions. The possibility that the book of Jonah contains an elaborate allegory of the exile—Jonah equals the people, the fish equals Babylon[44]—

[41] That the genealogies in the Chronicler enshrine much valuable ancient material is clear: it has been frequently demonstrated in recent studies (cf. references in J. M. Myers, *I and II Chronicles* 2 vols. [Anchor Bible 12/13, New York, 1965]. But the use to which such material was put is indicated by the reference in Ezra 2.59ff. to priests who could not prove true descent. In such a situation, proof of community status depends upon one's ability to prove a satisfactory lineage. Cf. W. F. Stinespring, 'Eschatology in Chronicles', *JBL* 80 (1961), pp. 209–19, see p. 210; R. North, 'The Theology of the Chronicler', *JBL* 82 (1963), pp. 369–81, see p. 371. Also the comment of L. Gry, *Le Muséon* 36 (1923), pp. 20f., on the importance for Jews of the exilic period and after of 'affirming themselves as legitimate members of the people which at the time had disappeared or was resurgent, and hence to set up genealogical laws which would link each of them with the tribe or clan of a known ancestor'. For a similar idea, cf. Isa. 4.1; Zech. 8.20–23.

[42] Compare also the view that Josh. 24 represents an appropriation of the Exodus events as religious history by those who had not experienced it. Cf. G. von Rad, *Theology* I, pp. 16f.

[43] Cf. Jer. 24, Ezek. 33. The Chronicler appears to be utilizing passages such as these which emphasize that hope lies in the exile alone (a view not consistently stated by Jeremiah at any rate, as we may see from his acceptance of Gedaliah's leadership). The Chronicler presents here the interpretation of the expiatory function of the exile in a supposedly historical description by projecting back as history what he believed (and theologically surely rightly) had to happen to his people.

[44] Cf. A. D. Martin, *The Prophet Jonah. The Book and the Sign* (London, 1926). Cf. also G. A. Smith, *The Book of the Twelve Prophets* II (1898), pp. 502ff., for further comment and references.

appears in some respects to do violence to the directness with which the message of the book is given. Yet it is difficult to avoid the impression that the experience of the Jewish people in the exile was in part responsible for that particular representation of their true place in the purpose of God which this little book sets out. Popular tales of men swallowed by great fish and miraculously delivered would seem to be an insufficient ground for including this rather odd piece of mechanism in the story. An allusion to the reality of such an experience in terms of Babylonian exile[45] would lend point to the recalling of the people to their true mission through an experience of utter forsaking and degradation. If this is so, then the appreciation of the people's function in relation to the world of the nations typified in Nineveh, has arisen in part out of this particular moment of its history.

Similarly, such a national and historical interpretation has been given to the book of Job.[46] An exaggerated presentation of such a

[45] It may be observed that the psalm in Jonah 2 utilizes the kind of language which suggests the same application of mythological pictures as is found, for example, in Isa. 51.9ff. Cf. A. R. Johnson, 'Jonah II 3–10: A Study in Cultic Phantasy', *StOTPr* (1950), pp. 82–102. If its allusions are to this kind of historicizing of mythological language, then we may claim that it was the author of Jonah, if he included the psalm, or the scribe who added it later, who made the application of the story to the historic experience of exile. On the theology of this section, cf. G. M. Landes, 'The Kerygma of the Book of Jonah; The Contextual Interpretation of the Jonah Psalm', *Interpretation* (1967), pp. 3–31.

[46] Cf. H. H. Rowley, 'The Book of Job and its meaning', *BJRL* 41 (1958/9), pp. 167–207, see p. 200 n. = *From Moses to Qumran* (London, 1963), pp. 141–83, see p. 176 n.; M. H. Pope, *The Book of Job* (Anchor Bible 15, New York, 1965), p. XXIX, for reference to this view. S. Terrien, *Job* (Commentaire de l'Ancien Testament 13, Neuchâtel, 1963), pp. 23 n. 4, refers to E. E. Kellett, ' "Job": An Allegory.' *ExpT* 51 (1939/40), pp. 250f., who regards the author as 'representing the Deuteronomic school of thought, of which Jeremiah is the chief exemplar' and as looking for a glorious return, indicated in the restoration of Job; and to M. Susman, *Das Buch Hiob und das Schicksal des jüdischen Volkes* (Zurich, 1946; ²1948), which is primarily an analysis of the subsequent experience of the Jewish people. Cf. also D. Gonzalo Maeso, 'Sentido nacional en el libro de Job' *Estudios Bíblicos* 9 (1950), pp. 67–81; J. Bright, *History*, p. 329 n., cites an unpublished paper by G. E. Mendenhall as suggesting that 'the awful problem posed by the fall of the nation was to the fore in the author's mind'. Terrien himself finds direct allusion to the events of the exile in 12.16–25 (see p. 113): see too E. Dhorme, *Le Livre de Job* (Paris, ²1926), p. cxxxiii (ET, London, 1967, pp. clxvif.). T. Henshaw, *The Writings: The Third Division of the Old Testament Canon* (London, 1963), p. 168, also finds allusions to the catastrophes (of 722 and 587) in 3.18ff.; 7.1; 12.6f.; 24.12. Terrien ('Job', *IB* 3 [1954], p. 897) also sees some indications of the theological significance of the exilic background which he believes the book has. See also the arguments for exilic dating in N. H. Tur-Sinai (H. Torczyner), *The Book of Job* (Jerusalem, 1957), pp. xxxviff.

view would seem to produce an unbalanced understanding of the poignant nature of Job's experience. Yet it may be wondered whether such a presentation of a personal dilemma is likely to have taken place in Hebrew circles—whatever might be the origin of the folk-tale of Job—without some cross-reference to the national experience. Some scholars have argued for an exilic date for the book, partly on the basis of interrelationships between the book of Job and the Servant passages in Deutero-Isaiah.[47] Such literary cross-references are rarely satisfactory as evidence of dating, and it would seem more likely that the somewhat later dating in the fifth or fourth centuries is correct, partly on the grounds that more direct allusion to the exilic situation might have been expected in a sixth-century author, whereas to a later writer this experience is expressed rather in a more general understanding of the national fortunes. The stress upon the innocence and integrity of Job is not really a counter-argument, since this is so clearly an element in the folk-tale. The disproportionateness of sin to punishment is, however, a theme of the exilic and post-exilic period, notably in Zech. 1–2, and also in Deutero-Isaiah.[48] To a later writer the experience of disaster is no longer to be explained simply in terms of sin and retribution, but in the larger terms of the whole purpose of God, and one element in the shaping of the writer's think-ing may well be the consciousness that the acceptance of disaster in a way which does no dishonour to God, but results in a deepened appreciation of the relationship between man and God, is one of the things which his people could have learnt and in some measure had learnt from the historic experience.[49]

A further example of such reference back may be found in the rather obscure verses in Zech. 8 in which the compiler appears to be pointing to the age of restoration as an example of faith for his con-temporaries.

47 Cf. S. Terrien, 'Quelques remarques sur les affinités de Job avec le Deutéro-Esaïe', *VTS* 15 (1967), pp. 295–310, and his commentaries cited in the previous footnote.
48 E.g. Isa. 40.2.
49 A. Bentzen, 'Remarks on the Canonisation of the Song of Songs', in *Studia Orientalia Ioanni Pedersen . . . dicata* (Copenhagen, 1953), pp. 41–47, suggests that the linkage of the poems with the season of spring and early summer was sub-sequently rationalized in the light of prophetic teaching, and hence the book was understood in the light of the 'new Exodus' of the exile (p. 46). This suggestion, if acceptable, would point to yet another influence of the exilic experience in the understanding of Old Testament material.

Let your hands be strong, you who in these days are hearing these words from the mouth of the prophets who were at the time of the founding of the house of Yahweh of hosts, the temple to be built. (8.9)[50]

In this verse, and in the verses which follow, which appear to contain prophetic utterances of Zechariah (and perhaps also of Haggai) re-applied,[51] the experience of coming out of exile and rebuilding the Temple and the life of the community is held up as an example of faith to a later generation. If, as seems probable, that later generation is close to that of the Chronicler, then a relationship may be suggested between this appeal to make real, in a now contemporary situation, the promises and blessings of God to the original returned exiles, and the Chronicler's stress upon the exile as the passage through which the community must go if it is to come into the inheritance which God has for it in the final age.

The later echoes of this kind of thinking are to be found—as has already been suggested—in the reinterpretation of the exilic period and the restoration in Daniel and in other apocalyptic works. We may also wonder how far it is also an element in New Testament thinking, for while it is clear that Exodus terminology is often dominant, e.g. in the concept of redemption, the theme of captivity to sin suggests other overtones too. Certainly Babylon becomes the symbol for the hostile world eventually to be overthrown by God in the final age[52] and Babylonian captivity becomes the symbol for the bondage from which release is to be found.[53] These are indications of the way in which the terminology of exile and restoration has entered into later thinking.[54]

3. THE 'IDEA' OF RESTORATION

The three themes which we have used to draw together the thought of the period of restoration—all themes which link back into the

[50] The last clause may be a gloss (cf. Hag. 1.2). But it may be better to treat the whole verse and the following one as a series of glossing allusions.
[51] Cf. P. R. Ackroyd, *JJS* 3 (1952), pp. 151–6. Cf. above pp. 213f.
[52] Cf. Rev. 16.12ff., 19; 18.2ff.
[53] Cf. Rev. 18.4ff., and compare the use of the term 'Babylonish Captivity' in the mediaeval period. We may also compare such a symbol as develops in connection with Herod as equivalent to the devil: *TWNT* 5, 420; ET, *Wrath* (London, 1964), p. 77.
[54] Cf. U. E. Simon, *A Theology of Salvation* (London, 1953), pp. 68–97, on Isa. 41–42.

thought of the exile itself—provide a convenient basis for the further discussion. Again, however, it is clear that they are to be taken simply as guides and not as restrictive descriptions of the totality of post-exilic thought.

(i) *The Temple*

It is sometimes suggested or implied that at the fall of Jerusalem the point had been reached when, under the influence of the personal and spiritualized religious conceptions of Jeremiah, it would be possible to see an end of the institutional religion of the pre-exilic period.[55] Not infrequently such statements are followed by a tracing of the evolution of new institutions during the exilic period—sabbath, synagogue, circumcision—as substitutes for the older practices. And more important, the point is then made that after this high degree of spiritualization, typified further in Deutero-Isaiah, there is a sad decline into the bricks-and-mortar Temple mentality of post-exilic Judaism. Quite apart from the utter inadequacy of such a judgement upon Jeremiah, which is so unreal as to miss the deeper significance of his strictures upon contemporary religious practice, it is clear—and I hope that this point has already been sufficiently emphasized—that in fact the post-exilic period represents a natural development from the thought of the exilic age in the direction of a right understanding of the nature of the presence of God of which the Temple is the most potent symbol.[56] It is not that the Temple as such is a guarantee—any more than Jeremiah would permit it to be—but that it is the outward sign of that manifestation of divine presence and power which is the essential for any kind of reorganization or establishment of life. Enough has been said by way of stress upon the centrality of God to make it clear that there is here no necessarily narrow or pedestrian thinking, but a legitimate attempt—in the terms most readily available—to solve that most persistent dilemma of man's religious experience, namely the gulf between God and man himself. The Temple is the symbol of that presence which God chooses to give. It is as improper to concentrate our whole attention upon the recurrent tendency of man to see the symbol as the reality

---

[55] This is an idea often maintained, recently, for example, in N. K. Gottwald, *All the Kingdoms of the Earth* (New York, 1964), p. 267. Contrast H. Graf Reventlow, *Liturgie und prophetisches Ich bei Jeremia* (Gütersloh, 1963).

[56] Cf. R. E. Clements, *God and Temple* (1965), esp. pp. 135–40; R. de Vaux, *Ancient Israel* (ET, 1961), pp. 325ff.

—for which the earlier period provides so many examples—as it is to judge the contemporaries of the pre-exilic prophets solely in terms of the latter's condemnations or the Pharisees in the time of Jesus solely in terms of his most virulent criticisms. The essential basis of the thought about the Temple is that of the mediation of divine life and power at the will of the deity himself. From this, various lines develop.

We may see the development in the post-exilic period of that deepened love of the Temple, that adherence to Zion which is expressed so richly in the Psalter; older Zion psalms[57] provide material to which this could be attached and come to be the vehicle not only of public worship but also of intense private devotion.[58] It is the focus of much of the religious life of those who either outside Palestine or in its remoter areas could hardly hope to visit the Temple itself except extremely rarely, if at all.[59] The picture which the Chronicler provides of joyous worship; the evident ardour and love for the Temple, even if often tinged with superstition, which are reflected in the opposition to both Jesus and Stephen—these are indications of how deeply rooted this affection became. If it came to be wrongly superstitious, we must nevertheless attest the fact that the final destruction of the Temple in AD 70 did not mark that disastrous end to Judaism which it must have marked had there been nothing but superstitious veneration. Judaism survived that disaster without losing the essential value of the Temple as focus.[60]

Further, we may see how the thought of the exilic age, and after, concerning the extension of the principle of the divine dwelling of the Temple to the idea of a holy city, a holy land, was an indication both of the limitations of a too narrowly based conception, and also of the richness of the idea. The centrality of Zion not only for the life of Judaism but also for the life of the world made it logical to think in terms of a holy land,[61] as for example in the last chapter of the book

[57] For a different view, cf. G. Wanke, *Die Zionstheologie der Korachiten in ihrem traditionsgeschichtlichen Zusammenhang* (BZAW 97, 1966), who, while finding much older motifs in the Korah psalms, regards their formulation as being post-exilic (cf. his summarizing argument on pp. 106–9).

[58] Cf. J. Becker, *op. cit.*, pp. 31f., 70ff.

[59] Cf. L. Rost, 'Erwägungen zum Kyroserlass', in *Verbannung und Heimkehr*, ed. A. Kuschke (Tübingen, 1961), pp. 303f.

[60] Cf. B. Gärtner, *The Temple and the Community in Qumran and the New Testament* (Cambridge, 1965), pp. 17f., and H. Wenschkewitz, *Die Spiritualisierung der Kultbegriffe* (*Angelos*-Beiheft 4, Leipzig, 1932), pp. 22f.

[61] The use of the term *māqōm* for the sanctuary (cf. above p. 156 n. 11) makes such broader interpretation readily available (cf. e.g. p. 161 on Hag. 2.9). On the

of Zechariah, where the multitude of worshippers necessitates the sanctifying of all the vessels in Jerusalem and Judah to serve the needs of those who come.[62] This is for the survivors of the nations who, having gone against Jerusalem in a final onslaught,[63] now come to worship annually at the feast of booths. The place which is occupied in the conceptions of the final age by pictures of a new and heavenly Jerusalem[64] is another aspect of this development.

In the New Testament, these lines of thought are elaborated in the understanding of Jesus himself as the Temple, as that place in which God chooses to manifest himself and in which therefore his power and presence are made known and operative. The Christian community

---

theology of Zion, cf. G. von Rad, *Theology* II, pp. 166–79, 292–7, and B. S. Childs, *Isaiah and the Assyrian Crisis* (1967). Jerusalem comes to be thought of as centre of the world; cf. the indications of mythological ideas connected with this. So N. W. Porteous, 'Jerusalem-Zion: The Growth of a Symbol', in *Verbannung und Heimkehr*, ed. A. Kuschke (Tübingen, 1961), pp. 235–52, see p. 242 = *Living the Mystery* (1967), pp. 93–111, see pp. 100f., with references to other literature; J. Schreiner, *Sion-Jerusalem: Jahwes Königssitz. Theologie der Heiligen Stadt im AT* (StANT 7, 1963), esp. Pt. III; R. E. Clements, *God and Temple* (1965), p. 62, and references; S. Mowinckel, *He that Cometh* (ET, 1956), p. 148; A. Causse, 'Le mythe de la nouvelle Jérusalém du Deutéro-Esaïe à la IIIᵉ Sibylle', *RHPhR* 18 (1938), pp. 377–414, with analysis of relevant passages, particularly from the Psalms; cf. also his *Israël et la vision de l'humanité* (1924), pp. 15–18; and *Du groupe ethnique à la communauté religieuse* (1937), pp. 209ff.; K. L. Schmidt, 'Jerusalem als 'Urbild und Abbild', *Eranos-Jahrbuch* 18 (Zurich, 1950), pp. 207–48—primarily concerned with Christian and Rabbinic developments, linked to their Old Testament roots in Isa. 54.10–13; 60–62; Hag. 2.1–9; Zech. 1.12f., 16; 2.15 (Schmidt erroneously has 2.1); 8.3; and in Deutero-Zechariah he cites 14.10. Although these passages are concerned with the earthly Jerusalem, they nevertheless point to the concept of a heavenly city. For a critical comment, cf. R. de Vaux, *Ancient Israel* (ET, 1961), p. 328; and B. Dinaburg, 'Zion and Jerusalem: their role in the historic consciousness of Israel' [Hebr.], *Zion* 16 (1951), pp. 1–17, 1–11 (cf. *IZBG* 4, No. 1309).

[62] Zech. 14.20–21. Cf. W. Eichrodt, *Theology of the Old Testament* I (ET, 1961), p. 107. On the general theme, cf. also M. Weinfeld, 'Universalism and Particularism in the Period of Exile and Restoration' (Hebrew with English summary), *Tarbiz* 33 (1963/4), pp. 229–42, I–II.

[63] J. A. Soggin, 'Der prophetische Gedanke über den heiligen Krieg, als Gericht gegen Israel', *VT* 10 (1960), pp. 79–83; see p. 81 for a comment on the final onslaught by the nations. This provides another example of an 'idea' as distinct from an 'actuality'.

[64] Cf. Jer. 3.14–18, and the development from Ezek. 40–48 to Rev. 21. Cf. also H. Wenschkewitz, *op. cit.*, pp. 45–49: 'Das himmlische Heiligtum', and the comment of H. Cunliffe-Jones, *The Book of Jeremiah* (TBC, 1960), p. 62, on this passage to the effect that the New Testament sees the answer to the meaning of the presence of God not in a restored Jerusalem but in Christ (John 4.20–26). See also below on the Temple and the person of Christ.

did not thereby abandon Temple ideology, but concentrated it in the understanding of a person in whom the glory of God was revealed, and who could be said to tabernacle among men[65] in the same way that God had chosen to reveal himself in the shrine. The destruction of the Temple is linked with the death of Jesus; the restoring of it is effected in his resurrection. Neither Gerizim nor Jerusalem offers finality, but worship will be in him.[66] From this, extension is made to the understanding of the Christian community as itself the Temple[67] of which Christ is the chief corner stone.[68] By further extension, this applies to each member of that community whose body is itself a Temple of God.[69]

(ii) *The new community and the new age*

The expectation, so amply expressed in the prophetic writings of the exilic and restoration periods, that a new age was about to dawn, linked both with political happenings and still more with the willingness of God to come again to his people, is an aspect of thought which finds large-scale development in the subsequent centuries. There is so great a richness of thought on this subject that any summary does less than justice to the hopes which were expressed not only in new works—and particularly in the later years of the post-exilic period in apocalyptic writings both canonical and extra-canonical—but also in the reinterpretation of older works, and notably of particular passages of psalmody and prophecy.[70] Much of this is very familiar because of the recognition of its importance to the understanding of the New Testament, and recently because of the expression of this kind of thinking in the Qumran documents. I propose to comment only very briefly on three points connected with it.

The first has appeared already sufficiently clearly to need only a sentence or two. It is the recognition that the new age is of cosmic significance, and involves not simply the final establishment of God's promises to Israel, but a complete renewal of the life of the world.

[65] John 1.14.
[66] John 4.21. Cf. also Rev. 21.22. Cf. R. de Vaux, *Ancient Israel* (ET, 1961), p. 330; B. Gärtner, *op. cit.*, see pp. 99ff.
[67] I Cor. 3.16f. Cf. on this E. Lohmeyer, *Lord of the Temple* (ET, London, 1961), pp. 67ff.; H. Wenschkewitz, *op. cit.*, pp. 96ff.
[68] Eph. 2.20f.; I Peter 2.4–8.
[69] I Cor. 6.19. Cf. J. A. T. Robinson, *The Body* (SBT 5, 1952), pp. 76, 64f.; B. Gärtner, *op. cit.*, pp. 49ff.
[70] Cf. e.g. D. S. Russell, *The Method and Message of Jewish Apocalyptic* (1964), ch. X, XI.

This is expressed in terms of a reversal of the present untoward condition of nature.[71] This statement of reversal is to be seen also against the background of thought which is to be found in the older material in the opening chapters of Genesis;[72] this is now, in the final form of the Priestly work (the Tetrateuch), given a new context and a new significance in relation to the later creation material of Gen. 1 with its reiterated emphasis on the goodness of God's creation, and is further expressed in the repeated failures and promises which follow on the initial failure of man and its consequences in the life of the natural world.[73] In the ultimate reordering, the centrality of Israel is a centrality of promise, and expresses to the nations the purpose of God towards all men. The narrowness of particularism and the breadth of universalism are held together in the understanding that what God does for his people—of his own choosing—is significant for all the nations and it is to be so recognized by them.

The second point concerns the place of the Davidic line in relation to this new age. We have seen how this is expressed in various of the prophetic writings—Ezekiel, Deutero-Isaiah, Haggai, Zechariah, as well as in elaborations of earlier prophetic material where older royal oracles have probably been given a wider connotation.[74] The emphasis in this material varies. It is hardly present as a real hope for the future in the Deuteronomic History, though the adumbration of a future Davidic line is there; in the Priestly Work it has found no place except in so far as the royal house is replaced by the priesthood.[75] But subsequently in the Chronicler a compromise line of development is found, in which the concentration of attention on what David achieved means that while Davidic monarchy no longer exists, and virtually no hope remains for its restoration, the essential of what Davidic monarchy stood for is achieved in the life of the purified post-exilic community in its Temple and Worship. The Davidic hope has there been refined, and again we may see here how the Chronicler directs attention to theological rather than to historical realities.[76]

Alongside this there are other lines of thought, culminating in the

[71] Cf. Isa. 55.12f.; 65.25; 11.6–9, and also Rom. 8.19–22. Cf. A. De Guglielmo, 'The Fertility of the Land in the Messianic Prophecies', CBQ 19 (1957), pp. 306–11.
[72] Gen. 2–3.
[73] In Gen. 6.1–4, 5–7; 11.1–9.
[74] Cf. pp. 6of., 114, 124f.
[75] Cf. R. de Vaux, Ancient Israel (ET, 1961), p. 400.
[76] Cf. P. R. Ackroyd (op. cit., p. 236 n. 9), pp. 512ff.

more purely political Davidic-type hopes of later nationalistic groups.[77] The modifications in this thinking would appear to be linked on the one hand to the actual political conditions—so the modification of Ezekiel's projected organization can be traced in the dual-type leadership envisaged in Haggai and Zechariah, and subsequently further modification resulted from the increasingly prominent position of the high priest,[78] representing a link back to the Priestly Work. On the other hand, the idealistic conceptions of the exilic age, themselves linked back into older ideals still, are at work to give rise to other less obviously politically connected thought. The linkage between the new age and a central figure who both embodies divine rule and is himself the guarantee of its reality is an idea of considerable importance for later Messianic thought.

The third point concerns the deferment and actuality of a new age. It is evident from what we know of the history of the post-exilic period that the new age anticipated by both the exilic and the restoration thinkers did not materialize. To that extent there is always therefore an element of deferment, and the same point may be noted in the thinking of New Testament times concerning the *parousia*. But to picture the development of eschatological thought solely in terms of deferred ideals would be erroneous. It seems probable that we should understand the concept of an ideal Davidic ruler—a Messiah in the technical sense—as arising not simply out of the failure of the pre-exilic Davidic monarchy, but out of the embodiment in it of the reality of what it was intended or believed to be; for what likelihood is there that an institution adjudged to have been an utter failure will provide the picture of an ideal future?[79] So too the projection into the future of the hopes of a new age is not simply a matter of dissatisfaction with the present, disillusionment as a result of the deferment of hope. It is a recognition rather of the fulness of what is already tasted as reality. The prophets of the restoration period were both idealists and realists; as such they were able to see in the realities of a not very encouraging situation the earnest of what they believed to be present, namely a new age with the glory of God at the very centre

[77] Cf. S. Mowinckel, *He that Cometh* (ET, 1956), pp. 155ff.
[78] Cf. E. Bevan, *Jerusalem under the High Priests* (London, 1912), pp. 5f. Also H. Gese, *Der Verfassungsentwurf des Ezechiel* (BHT 25, 1957), p. 119.
[79] Cf. S. Mowinckel, *op. cit.*, pp. 96ff., 125ff., and A. R. Johnson, *Sacral Kingship* (1955), pp. 133f. ([2]1967), pp. 143f. Also A. H. J. Gunneweg, *VT* 10 (1960), pp. 340f.

of the community's life. To us the age of the Chronicler, in the after-math of Ezra's reform and with the Samaritan schism an ugly reality and a serious challenge,[80] may well seem somewhat of a disappoint-ment in view of the high hopes which were evident in the work of Ezra. But to the Chronicler, whose sense of the realities was equally acute, this was the age of the fulfilment of promise. The reality of the embodiment of the rule of God in history which the New Testament proclaims is not a denial of that earlier sense of its reality, but a deepening and enlarging of its meaning. Nor does the fact that the new age has still not fully come alter the reality of Christian con-fidence that it is possible to live here and now in the context of that new age.

(iii) *The people's response*[81]

The problem for the exilic thinkers, in the light of failure, was to find a means by which the future people should really embody the divine will. Having laid their stress upon the priority of divine action, and the reality of the new age in which the new life would be lived, they concerned themselves much with this question of mechanism. The development of thought connected with this problem is again very broad; it may be briefly analysed along three main lines. In the first place there is the response of piety, which we have already linked with the idea of the Temple.[82] The maintenance of worship, the development of the synagogue,[83] the marked emphasis on prayer which becomes increasingly clear in the later post-exilic years,[84] all indicate a deep concern with the inner life of both individual and community to ensure the rightness of condition in which the blessings of God can be appropriately received. In the second place, the evolu-tion of law—already a dominant element in earlier thinking, but

---

[80] Cf. above p. 236 n. 12.

[81] Cf. O. Eissfeldt, *Geschichtliches und Übergeschichtliches im Alten Testament* (*ThStKr* 109/2, 1947), p. 16: 'The various programmatic sketches, which came into being in the exile after Judah's collapse in 586 BC, are all borne up by this ideal [i.e. the reuniting of the concepts of 'people' and 'church']. For the new people which, it is confidently hoped, will flourish again after the exile, they set out their dwelling place and constitution, law and cultus.' Eissfeldt stresses the relevance of this also for the revival in the time of Haggai, Zechariah, Joshua and Zerubbabel, as again for that of Nehemiah and Ezra.

[82] Cf. pp. 32ff. Also H. H. Rowley, *Worship in Ancient Israel* (1967), p. 245.

[83] Cf. above p. 249 for the reasons for this being only briefly examined in this study. Clearly, in a discussion of the post-exilic developments, it is in place.

[84] Cf. e.g. *HDB* one-vol. ed. (rev. 1963), pp. 788f.

coming to occupy an increasingly important place in the later period[85] and especially in the post-biblical writings[86]—is marked by a concern both for the purity of the people's life[87]—so especially in the mass of ritual law—and also for the covering of every aspect of life—and so by an inevitable development of casuistry.[88] But it is at heart a right casuistry, for though like all legal developments in religion it readily comes to be thought of in terms which deny the reality of the divine prerogative and suggest the possibility of coming to terms with God,[89] it nevertheless expresses the recognition that there is no part of life which is outside the concern of God, and that the completely fit community is one in which all life is brought under control. The New Testament criticisms of the wrong understanding of law must never conceal the fact that the Christian movement found itself deeply indebted to that sense of divine control which belonged to the Jewish community in which the early Church came into being and from which it only gradually separated itself, and that the Church found it immediately essential, with a renewed understanding of the place which law occupies in the religious life, to evolve its own ethical teaching on the basis of the older law and of the fundamental principles which its founder had stressed. In the third place, the increasing importance of wisdom material in the post-exilic period is itself a witness to this same concern with the fitness of the community.[90] If we are right in understanding wisdom as part of that mechanism by which life is to be rightly ordered,[91] so that the counsel of the wise can appropriately stand alongside the *tōrā* of the priest and the word

[85] Cf. L. Rost, *op. cit.*, p. 303, who notes that the Samaritans too came under the same aegis of the law, as indicating membership of the community.

[86] For this development in relation to psalmody, cf. B. de Pinto, 'The Torah and the Psalms', *JBL* 86 (1967), pp. 154–74, who comments: 'A spirituality of the Torah has been inserted into the framework of the psalter as a whole, and is one of the foremost guidelines of interpretation of the book . . .' (p. 174).

[87] Cf. P. Seidensticker, 'Die Gemeinschaftsform der religiösen Gruppen des Spätjudentums und der Urkirche', *Studii Biblici Franciscani Liber Annuus* 9 (1958/9), pp. 94–138, see pp. 97ff.

[88] Cf. νόμος, *TWNT* 4 (1942), p. 1036; ET, *Law* (London, 1962) pp. 39f. and *TDNT* 4, pp. 1043f. Also E. Würthwein, 'Der Sinn des Gesetzes im Alten Testament', *ZThK* 55 (1958), pp. 255–70, esp. pp. 268ff., and cf. *Die Weisheit Ägyptens und das Alte Testament* (Marburg, 1960); Würthwein traces the relationship between law and wisdom in the later period.

[89] Cf. the warning against oversimplification in W. Zimmerli, 'Das Gesetz im Alten Testament', *TLZ* 85 (1960), cols. 481–98 = *Gottes Offenbarung*, pp. 249–76.

[90] Cf. O. Eissfeldt, *Introduction*, pp. 126f.

[91] G. von Rad, *Theology* I, pp. 418ff., 432ff.; E. Würthwein, *ZThK* 55 (1958), pp. 269f.

of the prophet,[92] then it is clear that the sometimes apparently pedestrian concerns of the wisdom teachers are in fact directed towards that right ordering of life which is part of the necessary response of the community and all its members.[93] The outcome of this may perhaps not inappropriately be seen in the greatly increased influence of wisdom thought in both Old Testament and apocryphal works.[94]

The rounding off of this study with a peroration which draws everything together and leaves a neat impression of orderliness and completeness is beyond my capabilities. But perhaps this is all to the good. My study of the Old Testament—as I tried to show in my inaugural lecture in London[95]—increasingly makes me aware of the richness of its thought and the diversity of its patterns. Its unity lies not in any artificial scheme but in the purposes of God; to set out those purposes in a rigid pattern, an 'economy of salvation', is more convenient than realistic. I have tried to trace some of the patterns of thought which appear to me to be significant, and have tried to avoid the drawing of precise lines where it seems better to indicate similarities and differences. I am conscious that this is only a beginning, but hope that it may have served to draw out something of the wealth of thought and the importance of that great century in which out of the seeming utter failure of Israel's life there were those who had the depth of insight into the nature and purpose of God to enable them to see both the meaning of what they experienced and the outlines of the unfolding purpose of God. It may serve to point to the importance of a deeper appreciation of the later years of the Old Testament as a time not of sad contrast with the brilliance of the prophetic age, but as a time of deep concern with the problems of the meaning and ordering of life.

[92] Jer. 18.18 (cf. Ezek. 7.26 which has 'elders' for 'wise'). On this subject cf. B. Lindars, 'Torah in Deuteronomy', in *Words and Meanings*, ed. P. R. Ackroyd and B. Lindars (1968), pp. 117–36 see pp. 122, 134.

[93] Cf. also W. Richter, *Recht und Ethos. Versuch einer Ortung des weisheitlichen Mahnspruchs* (StANT 15, 1966).

[94] On this last point, cf. H. H. Guthrie, *Wisdom and Canon* (Evanston, 1966), esp. pp. 10–28.

[95] *Continuity. A contribution to the study of the Old Testament religious tradition* (Blackwell, Oxford, 1962).

Israel', *Gesammelte Studien zum Alten Testament* (Munich, ²1960), pp. 346–71; ET by D. R. Ap-Thomas, 'The Jerusalem Catastrophe of 587 BC and its significance for Israel', in *The Laws in the Pentateuch and Other Essays* (Edinburgh, 1966), pp. 260–80

G. VON RAD, *Theologie des Alten Testaments* I, II (Munich, 1957 (²1958); 1960); references mainly to ET by D. M. Stalker, *Old Testament Theology* I, II (London, 1962, 1965). Cf. also *The Message of the Prophets* (London, 1968)

D. WINTON THOMAS, 'The Sixth Century BC: a creative Epoch in the History of Israel', *JSS* 6 (1961), pp. 33–46

R. DE VAUX, *Les Institutions de l'Ancien Testament* I, II (Paris 1958, 1960); references to ET by John McHugh, *Ancient Israel: Its Life and Institutions* (London, 1961)

T. C. VRIEZEN, *Hoofdlijnen der theologie van het Oude Testament* (Wageningen, 1949; latest ed. 1967); references to ET by S. Neuijen, *An Outline of Old Testament Theology* (Oxford, 1958)

C. F. WHITLEY, *The Exilic Age* (London, 1957)
(The approach to the subject in this book differs at many points sharply from the present study.)

W. ZIMMERLI, *Gottes Offenbarung* (ThB 19, 1963). Other important studies by Zimmerli, not included in this collection, are cited in footnotes.

ADDENDA

W. A. M. BEUKEN, *Haggai-Sacharja 1–8* (Studia Semitica Neerlandica 10, Assen, 1967). See above, p. 152 n. 58

J. L. KOOLE, *Haggai* (Commentaar op het Oude Testament, Kampen, 1967). No detailed reference has been possible to this full and valuable commentary, which offers a useful positive evaluation of the theology of Haggai (see esp. pp. 18–22).

SELECT BIBLIOGRAPHY

L. E. BROWNE, *Early Judaism* (Cambridge, 1920)

J. BRIGHT, *A History of Israel* (Philadelphia, 1959; OTL, London, 1960) (This presents a different interpretation of the material from that offered in this study.)

T. CHARY, *Les prophètes et le culte à partir de l'exil* (Tournai, 1955)

R. E. CLEMENTS, *God and Temple. The Idea of the Divine Presence in Ancient Israel* (Oxford, 1965)

S. A. COOK, 'The Age of Zerubbabel', *StOTPr* (1950), pp. 19–36

O. EISSFELDT, *Einleitung in das Alte Testament* (Tübingen, ³1964); references are to ET by P. R. Ackroyd, *The Old Testament: an Introduction* (Oxford, New York, 1965)

W. EICHRODT, *Theologie des Alten Testaments* I (Stuttgart, ⁶1959); II (Stuttgart, ⁵1964); references are to ET by John Baker, *Theology of the Old Testament* (OTL, I, 1961; II, 1967)

G. FOHRER, *Einleitung in das Alte Testament* (10th ed. of E. Sellin, *Einleitung*, Heidelberg, 1965)

K. GALLING, *Studien zur Geschichte Israels im persischen Zeitalter* (Tübingen, 1964). Other important studies by Galling, not included in this collection, are cited in footnotes.

E. JANSSEN, *Juda in der Exilszeit: Ein Beitrag zur Frage der Entstehung des Judentums* (FRLANT 69, 1956)

E. KLAMROTH, *Die jüdischen Exulanten in Babylonien* (BWAT 10, 1912)

A. KUSCHKE, ed., *Verbannung und Heimkehr. Beiträge zur Geschichte und Theologie Israels im 6. und 5. Jahrh. v. Chr. (Festschrift W. Rudolph*, Tübingen 1961)

A. LODS, *Les prophètes d'Israël et les débuts du judaïsme* (Paris, 1935); references to ET by S. H. Hooke, *The Prophets and the Rise of Judaism* (London, 1937)

M. NOTH, *Die Geschichte Israels* (Göttingen, ²1954; ³1956); references to ET revised by P. R. Ackroyd, *The History of Israel* (London, ²1960) 'La catastrophe de Jérusalem en l'an 587 avant Jésus-Christ et sa signification pour Israël', *RHPhR* 33 (1953), pp. 81–110 = 'Die Katastrophe von Jerusalem im Jahre 587 v. Chr. und ihre Bedeutung für

ABBREVIATIONS

AASF	Annales Academiae Scientiarum Fennicae (Helsinki)
ABR	*Australian Biblical Review* (Melbourne)
AJSL	*American Journal of Semitic Languages and Literatures* (Chicago)
Anat. Stud.	*Anatolian Studies* (London)
ANET	J. B. Pritchard, ed., *Ancient Near Eastern Texts relating to the Old Testament* (2nd ed. Princeton, 1955)
Ant.	*Antiquities* (Josephus)
ASTI	*Annual of the Swedish Theological Institute* (Jerusalem, Leiden)
ATANT	Abhandlungen zur Theologie des Alten und Neuen Testaments (Zurich)
ATD	Das Alte Testament Deutsch (Göttingen)
BA	*Biblical Archaeologist* (New Haven)
BASOR	*Bulletin of the American Schools of Oriental Research* (New Haven)
BAT	Die Botschaft des Alten Testaments (Stuttgart)
BDB	F. Brown, S. R. Driver and C. A. Briggs, *Hebrew and English Lexicon of the Old Testament* (Oxford, 1906)
BHT	Beiträge zur historischen Theologie (Tübingen)
BIES	*Bulletin of the Israel Exploration Society* (Jerusalem)
BJRL	*Bulletin of the John Rylands Library* (Manchester)
BK	Biblischer Kommentar (Neukirchen)
BS	Biblische Studien (Neukirchen)
BWA(N)T	Beiträge zur Wissenschaft vom Alten (und Neuen) Testament (Leipzig, Stuttgart)
BZAW	Beihefte zur Zeitschrift für die Alttestamentliche Wissenschaft (Giessen, Berlin)
CBQ	*Catholic Biblical Quarterly* (Washington, D.C.)
DOTT	D. Winton Thomas, ed., *Documents from Old Testament Times* (London, New York, 1958)
Enc. Catt.	*Enciclopedia cattolica* (Rome)
EvTh	*Evangelische Theologie* (Munich)
ExpT	*The Expository Times* (Edinburgh)
FRLANT	Forschungen zur Religion und Literatur des Alten und Neuen Testaments (Göttingen)
Ges. Stud.	*Gesammelte Studien* (*zum Alten Testament*)
GK	Gesenius-Kautzsch, *Hebrew Grammar*, ET by A. E. Cowley (Oxford, ²1910)
HAT	Handbuch zum Alten Testament (Tübingen)
HDB	J. Hastings, ed., *Dictionary of the Bible* (Edinburgh, four-volume

	ed. with supplement, 1898–1904; one-volume edition, revised ed., F. C. Grant and H. H. Rowley, 1963)
Hist.	*Histories* (Herodotus)
HSAT	Die Heilige Schrift des Alten Testaments, ed. F. Feldmann and H. Herkenne (Bonn)
HTR	*Harvard Theological Review* (Cambridge, Mass.)
HUCA	*Hebrew Union College Annual* (Cincinnati)
IB	*Interpreters' Bible* (New York)
ICC	International Critical Commentary (Edinburgh)
IEJ	*Israel Exploration Journal* (Jerusalem)
IrishThQ	*Irish Theological Quarterly* (Maynooth)
IZBG	*Internationale Zeitschriftenschau für Bibelwissenschaft und Grenzgebiete* (Düsseldorf)
JBL	*Journal of Biblical Literature* (Philadelphia)
JEA	*Journal of Egyptian Archaeology* (London)
JJS	*Journal of Jewish Studies* (London)
JNES	*Journal of Near Eastern Studies* (Chicago)
JSS	*Journal of Semitic Studies* (Manchester)
JThC	*Journal for Theology and the Church* (New York)
JTS	*Journal of Theological Studies* (Oxford)
KAT	Kommentar zum Alten Testament (Leipzig, Gütersloh)
KBL	L. Köhler and W. Baumgartner, *Lexicon in Veteris Testamenti Libros* (Leiden, 1953 and later eds.)
Kl. Schr.	*Kleine Schriften*
LUÅ	*Lunds Universitets Årsskrift* (Lund)
NorTT	*Norsk Teologisk Tidsskrift* (Oslo)
Nouv. Rev. Théol.	*Nouvelle Revue Théologique* (Paris)
NTS	*Nieuwe Theologische Studiën* (Groningen, Den Haag)
OTL	Old Testament Library (London, Philadelphia)
OTMS	H. H. Rowley, ed., *The Old Testament and Modern Study* (Oxford, 1951)
OTS	*Oudtestamentische Studiën* (Leiden)
PEQ	*Palestine Exploration Quarterly* (London)
PJB	*Palästinajahrbuch* (Berlin)
PW	Pauly-Wissowa, *Realencyclopädie der classischen Altertumswissenschaft* (Stuttgart)
RA	*Revue d'Assyriologie et d'Archéologie Orientale* (Paris)
RivBibl	*Rivista Biblica* (Rome)
REJ	*Revue des Études Juives* (Paris)
RGG	*Die Religion in Geschichte und Gegenwart* (Tübingen)
RHPhR	*Revue d'Histoire et de Philosophie Religieuses* (Strasbourg, Paris)
RHR	*Revue de l'Histoire des Religions* (Paris)
SBT	Studies in Biblical Theology (London)
Script. Hier.	*Scripta Hierosolymitana* (Jerusalem)
StANT	Studien zum Alten und Neuen Testament (Munich)
StOTPr	H. H. Rowley, ed., *Studies in Old Testament Prophecy presented to T. H. Robinson* (Edinburgh, 1950)

Str. Bill.	H. L. Strack and P. Billerbeck, *Kommentar zum Neuen Testament aus Talmud und Midrasch*, 4 vols. (Munich, 1922–8, ²1956)
TA	Theologische Arbeiten (Berlin)
TBC	Torch Bible Commentary (London)
TDNT	*Theological Dictionary of the New Testament*, ET of TWNT by G. W. Bromiley (Grand Rapids)
TGUOS	*Transactions of the Glasgow University Oriental Society* (Glasgow, Leiden)
ThB	Theologische Bücherei (Munich)
ThR	*Theologische Rundschau* (Tübingen)
ThStKr	Theologische Studien und Kritiken (Berlin)
TLZ	*Theologische Literaturzeitung* (Leipzig, Berlin)
TWNT	*Theologisches Wörterbuch zum Neuen Testament* (Stuttgart)
TZ	*Theologische Zeitschrift* (Basle)
UUÅ	Uppsala Universitets Årsskrift (Uppsala)
VT	*Vetus Testamentum* (Leiden)
VTS	*Supplements to Vetus Testamentum* (Leiden)
WMANT	Wissenschaftliche Monographien zum Alten und Neuen Testament (Neukirchen)
WZHalle	*Wissenschaftliche Zeitschrift der Martin Luther Universität Halle-Wittenberg*
ZA	*Zeitschrift für Assyriologie* (Leipzig, Berlin)
ZAW	*Zeitschrift für die alttestamentliche Wissenschaft* (Giessen, Berlin)
ZDPV	*Zeitschrift des Deutschen Palästina-Vereins* (Wiesbaden)
ZLThK	*Zeitschrift für die gesamte Lutherische Theologie und Kirche* (Leipzig)
ZSTh	*Zeitschrift für Systematische Theologie* (Gütersloh, Berlin)
ZThK	*Zeitschrift für Theologie und Kirche* (Tübingen)
BH³	R. Kittel, ed., *Biblia Hebraica* (Stuttgart, 3rd ed. 1937 and later)
ET	English Translation
LXX	The Septuagint
MT	The Massoretic Text
RSV	Revised Standard Version
RV	Revised Version
Syr.	The Syriac (Peshiṭta) Text
Targ.	Targum
Vg.	Vulgate

INDEX OF SUBJECTS

INDEX OF AUTHORS

INDEX OF BIBLICAL REFERENCES

OLD TESTAMENT

APOCRYPHA and PSEUDEPIGRAPHA

NEW TESTAMENT

OTHER WRITINGS